CAMBRIDGE LATIN AMERICAN STUDIES

65

SOUTH AMERICA AND THE FIRST WORLD WAR

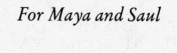

For Maya and Saul

SOUTH AMERICA AND THE FIRST WORLD WAR

THE IMPACT OF THE WAR ON BRAZIL, ARGENTINA, PERU AND CHILE

BILL ALBERT

School of Economic and Social Studies
University of East Anglia

WITH THE ASSISTANCE OF PAUL HENDERSON

School of Economic and Social Studies
University of East Anglia

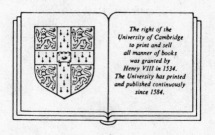

The right of the
University of Cambridge
to print and sell
all manner of books
was granted by
Henry VIII in 1534.
The University has printed
and published continuously
since 1584.

CAMBRIDGE UNIVERSITY PRESS

Cambridge
New York   New Rochelle   Melbourne   Sydney

Published by the Press Syndicate of the University of Cambridge
The Pitt Building, Trumpington Street, Cambridge CB2 1RP
32 East 57th Street, New York, NY 10022, USA
10 Stamford Road, Oakleigh, Melbourne 3166, Australia

First published 1988

Printed in Great Britain at the University Press, Cambridge

British library cataloguing in publication data

Albert. Bill
South America and the First World War:
the impact of the war on Brazil, Argentina,
Peru and Chile. – (Cambridge Latin
American studies; 65).
1. World War. 1914–1918 – Influence and
results   2. Latin America – Economic
conditions
I. Title II. Henderson. Paul
330.98' 0032   HC125

Library of Congress cataloging in publication data

Albert, Bill.
South America and the First World War.
(Cambridge Latin American studies; 65)
Bibliography
Includes index.
1. World War, 1914–1918 – South America.
2. World War, 1914–1918 – Influence. I. Henderson, Paul.
I. Title. II. Series.
D618.A42   1988   330.98' 0033   87–14310

ISBN 0 531 346509

TM

Contents

Tables

Acknowledgments

I was greatly assisted in writing certain sections of this book by being able to draw on material in Paul Henderson's unpublished PhD thesis, "Latin America and the Great War: A study of the effects of the First World War on economic and social conditions in Peru and Chile." Furthermore, besides his detailed comments on the entire manuscript and many other forms of help which he gave, he also wrote the first drafts of the sections on Chile before the war, Chilean trade, and Peruvian and Chilean labor. His contribution was invaluable.

I want also to thank Bill Mathew and Shaun Hargreaves-Heap, for having read the entire manuscript and for their many extremely important suggestions for improvement. Other advice on sections of the work was kindly given by Colin Lewis, Tamás Szmrecsáyni, Donna Guy, Joseph Tulchin, Winston Fritsch, and Charles Jones. I wish especially to thank the staffs of the Public Record Office in London and National Archives in Washington DC for their assistance. Additional research and most of the writing was done during the year I spent at Harvard University. For this I have to thank my wife, who kindly took me along during her tenure as a Visiting Fellow at the Divinity School, and John Womack who arranged for me to become a Visiting Scholar in the History Department. The hospitality shown to me and the facilities generously provided by the Center for the Study of World Religions were greatly appreciated, as was the friendly and efficient treatment I always received at all the Harvard libraries. I owe a particular debt of gratitude to all those working in the Widener and Baker libraries. Finally, I wish to thank the Research Committee of the School of Economic and Social Studies at the University of East Anglia and the Nuffield Foundation for providing financial support for various stages of the project.

BILL ALBERT

Introduction

Peru's Canete valley is about 150 kilometers south of Lima. In the first decade of the century this was about a three or four-day horseback ride or, more usually, and if you had the money, a day or less by coastal steamer. As was the case for most of the country's larger irrigated coastal valleys it was given over to export crops. Here it was cotton, grown on numerous small and medium-sized estates and sugar produced by a single large British-owned *ingenio*. Besides sharecroppers, about 3,000 workers were employed either permanently or on a casual basis on the various estates in the valley. On 10 August 1914, the subprefect called an emergency meeting of local merchants, *hacendados*, and estate administrators in the principal town of San Vicente. A few men sat on chairs, the majority leaned against the walls of the rather small room which was becoming increasingly filled with concern and cigar smoke as the official spelled out the extent of the crisis, of which most of them were already aware. He wanted those who had contacts in the capital to ask them for immediate assistance because there was not enough cash in the valley to pay agricultural workers and estates were having to shut down. There was also a serious food shortage and the likelihood of unrest.[1] The sudden disruption in the life of this valley was evidence that the shock waves of the recently begun European war had reached rural Peru. It had taken less than a week. In the larger cities the impact had been felt even earlier. Before the Germans invaded Belgium on 4 August, banks throughout the continent had shut their doors, factories and workshops had closed, trade had come to a standstill, thousands of workers were laid off and food prices soared. These all happened because the region's life support system had been disconnected. War had severed the many seemingly indestructible strands of finance and trade which bound Latin America so closely to Europe and the world economy.

The crisis which ensued was to show clearly and dramatically how important and deep-seated these external links were.

The war brought chaos to Latin America as well as to most other countries. In its aftermath the world was transformed. When the guns finally fell silent in November 1918, not only was the structure of the international economy altered and the political map of Europe ready to be redrawn, but nineteenth-century bourgeois faith in unlimited progress within a secure framework of positivist rationality also lay in tatters. This faith was shaken not only by the war itself but also, and perhaps more significantly, by the Russian Revolution and the massive and worldwide upsurge in working-class unrest which followed. The powerful influence of these events was felt not only in Europe and North America, but throughout the world. However, while the impact and consequences of war in the metropolitan countries have been the subject of much scholarly attention, regions such as Latin America have been relatively neglected. Partly, this has been due to the fact that the dislocations caused by war, especially in neutral countries, have often been considered as "abnormal", unrepresentative deviations from the long-term trends of socio-political and economic change. According to this view, periods such as the First World War can tell us little about how these processes unfolded in a world at peace. This is not strictly true. For example, because Peru, Chile, Brazil, and Argentina were, to varying degrees, heavily dependent upon foreign capital, imports, shipping and insurance, access to export markets, and in some cases labor, the collapse of the world economy and its subsequent restructuring during the war was an extremely testing experience which created both problems and opportunities for these peripheral countries. This in turn tended to highlight the strengths and weaknesses of the variants of the primary export-based capitalist development which had taken root here. It might be argued that the chaos of war was not representative, but it was the fact that the chaos took quite distinctive forms in the different countries which is so instructive, as it helps to expose the foundations and framework of prewar economic growth. Moreover, in the postwar period the Latin American countries, which had constructed their economies on the apparently firm foundations of the British-dominated international economy, had to come to terms with a new, and in many fundamental respects, weaker, less stable world economic system. Finally, as it had in Europe, the Great War and its immediate aftermath witnessed far-reaching political and social changes in the region, associated in the main with the emergence of a more vocal urban middle class and a more combative working class. In short, studying the impact of the First World War on these four Latin American countries offers insights as to the course of prewar growth as well as the significance of the many changes ushered in by the war.

The principal concern of those studying Latin America during the war period has been whether or not a significant level of import-substitution industrialization was stimulated by the temporary shortage of imported manufactured goods.[2] This interest stems from the assumption that progressive, self-sustained development should be equated with industrial growth and that such growth took place during the war in the more advanced countries of Latin America. Most notably, André Gunder Frank has taken this as support for his thesis that significant economic development can take place only when links between metropolis and satellite are weak or broken.[3] As will be argued, this view is wrong on a number of counts. Industrial growth during the war years was, for the most part, quite modest, and did not depart from its rather narrowly based prewar structure. Secondly, although foreign investment and imports were curtailed, the export trade was greatly strengthened as Allied demand for many of the region's commodities increased. The Allies also imposed an unprecedented degree of control over many aspects of foreign trade, including shipping, purchasing, and the blacklisting of enemy firms resident in Latin America. This meant not a weakening, but a general reinforcement of both a major component of Latin America's external connection as well as the overall grip of primary export capitalism. All this suggests that the central debate over the war period—basically whether strong foreign links had a positive or negative effect on development—has been misconceived and oversimplified. For example, if, as it seems, industry was not particularly buoyant during the war this was more likely to have been due to the limitations imposed by the economic structures created in the decades before the war to support primary export-based growth, and not to partial isolation from the metropolis.

The development of manufacturing industry is an important issue, but it cannot be adequately understood in isolation and was, in any case, only one of the many interesting aspects of the war years. What was of greatest moment was the destruction of the international economy. Although it had suffered numerous and often severe crises, this economy had never totally broken down as it did in August 1914. It was never to regain its prewar coherence. This was due in large measure to the fact that after 1918 the United States became a major international creditor, and Britain was unable to perform the vital equilibrating role which had permitted the expansion and relative stability of the world system before 1914. For a region so externally dependent as Latin America a less secure world system was an extremely serious threat, a threat which was realized dramatically in 1929. Paralleling its enhanced world role, the US also substantially increased its economic interest in the four republics during the war. This change, which was particularly evident in Peru and Chile, marked the beginning of a new form of external domination and was to have far-reaching economic and political effects throughout the region.

Besides the lasting economic impact of the war, the extreme conditions of these years tended to accelerate the development of a number of significant social, political, and cultural movements, many of which had begun to establish themselves before 1914. The cultural trends were extremely diverse, but a common underlying theme was a disenchantment with the accepted system of "rational" European intellectual values and the desire to create a more robust, independent national identity. It is, perhaps, not surprising that both economic and cultural nationalism should flourish at a time when the extent of region's external dependence became so evident and foreign interference so blatant. But the more xenophobic variants of nationalism, especially in Brazil and Argentina, were mainly in response to more domestic issues – the massive upsurge in working-class militancy which came during, and most dramatically, immediately after the war. This was one of the most important developments to come out of the First World War, not only in Latin America, but throughout the world, as economic dislocation and the example of the October Revolution ignited widespread proletarian discontent. In Latin America this posed a direct threat to the virtual total political domination of the landed elites, a domination already under attack before 1914 and also being challenged from the growing urban middle class, particularly badly hit by wartime inflation. The result was a radical shift, except in Brazil, in the political climate, which saw the traditional export elites' authority and control of the state considerably diminished and the beginning of mass politics. All these movements had their separate, complex historical geneses, but in their different ways reflected the nature and contradictions of prewar capitalist development as well as reactions against it.

II

For Latin America the war and immediate postwar years are clearly an important and interesting period to study. There are, however, pitfalls associated with this type of project. In all works which concentrate on an event as cataclysmic as a war there is a strong predisposition to see the major changes which occurred as a direct result of that war. No such claim is made here. In almost every case there were clearly discernible prewar roots for such important wartime changes as the strengthening of most traditional export sectors, the greater economic role of the United States, or the growth of domestic manufacturing industry (where this occurred). What the war did was hasten in hothouse fashion the emergence of these factors. In doing this, and because of the many other strains associated with the war, most noticeably domestic inflation, a number of important prewar socio-political changes such as the rise of economic and cultural nationalism, the increased militancy of the working class, and the political challenge to the export elites were also stimulated and their significance greatly enhanced. The war served as a powerful catalyst.

Another problem which had to be faced, common to any comparative historical study, was the choice of countries and themes. The two choices were closely related. The principal theme explored through most of the chapters is how the region's multifaceted external links helped shape the system of capitalism which took root here and the significance of the similarities observed for understanding the character of Latin American capitalist development. Of course, each country was clearly unique across a wide range of factors, such as population, geography, historical formation, political structure, culture, exports, etc., but they all shared a very substantial degree of external dependence, and because of this and their Iberian heritage many major aspects of their capitalist formation were roughly similar. The central driving force in each economy was the export of primary commodities. Foreign capital, banks, shipping, and merchants were of key importance, and to a greater or lesser degree the ruling elites believed that a European ideal of progress could be attained by their countries adopting the role assigned to them within a seemingly "natural" world division of labor.

In line with the general theme outlined above, Argentina, Brazil, Peru, and Chile were picked for investigation, because although before the war other countries were increasing their economic stake in these republics, in all cases the dominant foreign interests remained British. This gives some degree of symmetry to the character of external involvement as well as making the outbreak of war in these countries that much more traumatic and, therefore, revealing. The author's knowledge and general interest also was a major factor in this particular choice. Finally, it was felt that although it would have been possible to include other countries, such as Uruguay or Colombia, or ones in Central America or the Caribbean, where United States involvement was substantial before 1914, this would have multiplied the external variables, made the study unwieldy, and, in the end, may not have significantly modified the conclusions as to the dynamics of primary export capitalism. Mexico might seem another major omission, but although the war did have an impact here this was marginal when compared to the widespread chaos caused by the Revolution. However, as this work is selective, whether what has been observed was common to all of Latin America must necessarily await the work of other scholars.

Besides choosing the countries and a central unifying theme, the other important decision that had to be made was what sub-topics to explore and how best to handle them. It was decided to limit coverage to four main areas, foreign trade, finance, manufacturing industry, and the labor movement, which although not providing anything like a comprehensive picture of these societies, are of key importance and do allow some useful generalizations to be made about both the nature of Latin America's primary export capitalism and the impact of the war upon it. In order to establish the wider framework for analysis it is important to begin with a general discussion of the development of these four peripheral capitalist countries within the context of the nineteenth-century world economy. This is intended to provide the reader with a brief account of prewar growth and so give the background against which the impact of the war may be more easily understood. The next chapter concentrates on the initial impact of the war. It was during these months that economic and social upheaval was most intense and the similarities of experience among the four countries most marked. Once they began to adjust to the new conditions imposed by the conflict so there was a greater divergence of experience. Because of this it was felt that for the sake of expositional and analytical clarity it was preferable to devote the subsequent chapters to the four issues mentioned above, as well as to deal with each country separately within each chapter. In the final chapter the general state of the region after the war is considered and some of the more interesting economic and social changes which were stimulated by the years of conflict are briefly explored.

1

Before the War

Industrial capitalism was the major revolutionary force in the nineteenth century. It not only transformed the economic, political and social life of much of Europe and the United States, but its influence was also felt throughout the world as over the century it fashioned a multilateral, interdependent world economy to serve its interests. Latin America's role within this system was essentially the same as it had been in the colonial period, to supply raw materials and foodstuffs in exchange for manufactured goods. The decision of the local elites to continue to organize their economies to complement those of Europe, a decision which in general only became clear and strong after some decades of post-independence conflict, was both understandable, and given the prevailing international hierarchy of economic power, realistic. It also admirably suited their own economic interests, which, of course, they equated with the national interest. However, it should not be imagined that there was always agreement or harmony among the various sectors of the elite or between them and foreign capital. There were, for example, varying degrees of intra-elite conflict in all four countries, leading in the most extreme cases to civil war. There were also disputes, often extremely acrimonious ones, between Latin American governments and foreign economic interests. Through all this there was, however, no serious challenge to the basic tenets of development *hacia afuera*. There was simply no other way to accumulate wealth so quickly.

However, it was not a simple desire for financial gain which motivated the elites, it was also that promoting primary exports was the most effective method of achieving and maintaining political stability. As Douglas Friedman has argued,[1] while the world economy clearly made primary export attractive, the manner by which each country was tied to that economy and the impact of that link on economic development must be seen as the result of distinctive historical formation and class struggle. As explained more fully below, without this simple but fundamental perspective it is impossible to explain why countries, such as Sweden, Canada, or Australia, which were also heavily dependent on foreign capital and the export of primary commodities, should have had greater economic success than that achieved by Latin American countries.

The process of external economic subjugation encouraged by the elites was necessarily accompanied and underpinned by the acceptance and promulgation of foreign cultural and intellectual values. In some ways these were as important as the import of capital or technology. They provided a powerful ideological framework of legitimation. For example, positivism in its various forms was widely taken up, and elite spokesmen argued that to incorporate Latin America fully into the international economy was to tread the path to material progress and civilization. Europe and things European were held up as examples to be emulated, while native peoples and cultures were generally denigrated as barbaric. Skidmore writes, "Brazil lay vulnerable, like the rest of Latin America, to racist doctrine from abroad. It could hardly have been otherwise, since these doctrines were a vital part of the North Atlantic civilization so fervently and uncritically admired by most Latin American intellectuals before 1914."[2] These attitudes were to come under increasing attack during and after the war.

But as important as ideas were they could not themselves fashion new societies in South America. In order to meet the demands of the world market for primary commodities major changes were demanded in productive techniques and organization, and ultimately in the relations of production as well. This had been a continuous, albeit gradual, process in many countries up to about the 1880s, but from that time it accelerated as foreign capital and labor poured in, railways and ports were constructed, cities grew and were provided with modern public utilities, and most countries experienced a substantial degree of export-led growth. By 1914 the development which had occurred in the material forces of production was considerable. Almost £2,000,000,000 of foreign capital had been invested, 63,000 miles of railway built, about four million immigrants had settled in Brazil and Argentina alone, and large cities, such as Buenos Aires, São Paulo, Rio de Janeiro and Santiago had become showcases for the solid, self-assured architecture so characteristic of the latter decades of the nineteenth century. Furthermore, exports had increased dramatically, and in all countries industrial sectors were beginning to take shape. With advances in the productive forces there was also an important, although in many cases partial, transformation in the relations of production, and by the First World War a self-conscious urban, and in some regions a rural, working class had begun to make its power felt.

A type of capitalism was, therefore, clearly being established in Latin America, but one which it will be argued was far less progressive and suffered from far more seemingly intractable contradictions than its European progenitor. One reason for this was that the system's foundations were discernibly shaky, built as they were upon the shifting sands of the international economy. This economy generated growth while at the same time fostering chronic instability, which could be especially severe for primary producers. There are a number of aspects to this argument. One of the most important was the fact that many Latin American countries besides having to rely on the ofttimes fickle metropolitan demand for their exports, also became heavily dependent upon constant inflows of capital to service large external debts and maintain balance of payments positions. However, the availability of these funds was largely determined by conditions in the industrialized lender countries, and capital imports tended "...to swell in boom times and dry up in hard times, contributing further to economic instability associated with their frequent dependence on one or a few items of raw material or foodstuffs exports, themselves subject to wide quantity and/or price variation."[3]

These problems did not rule out a successful capitalist transformation, but it can be argued that such a transformation was difficult to achieve partly because of Latin America's position within the world division of labor and the role played by merchant capital in helping to establish and maintain this position. Geoffrey Kay has argued,[4] that capitalism came to Latin America in the form of merchant capital. Although merchant capital promoted commodity production, and, therefore, did stimulate change, because it derived its profits in the sphere of exchange it had no inherent interest, in contrast to industrial capital, in revolutionizing the forces of production, the productive system, or the relations of production.[5] There is much to this argument, although, as will be explained, it seriously underestimates the degree of capitalist transformation which did take place.[6] One possible explanation for this, was that from the last decades of the nineteenth century merchant capital in Latin America was not functioning in its independent form but rather as the agent of industrial capital. Kay writes,

In its independent form where it is separated from the spheres of production and consumption and has no direct responsibility for them, merchant capital trades where it can and what it can without concern or scruple: here slaves, there opium. But industrial capital is directly involved in the process of social reproduction, and so must pay closer attention to its requirements then merchant capital. It is forced to be more *civilized*. And merchant capital in so far as it acts as its agent is forced to adopt a similar code and drop many of its bad habits.

Kay's argument is perceptive, but provides only one part of the explanation of the difficulties in developing a more progressive capitalist system in Latin America. There were other countries similarly dependent under the export of primary commodities and also in receipt of large amounts of foreign capital, but in which successful and substantive development was achieved. It is, of course, impossible even to begin to offer comparisons between the experiences of, for example, Canada, Australia, or Sweden and the countries of Latin America, although one important and possibly key difference lay in the fact that the socio-political systems in the former countries were much more egalitarian and not dominated by the landed export elites as they were in Latin America.[7] This tended to reduce the overall intrusiveness of the foreign connection, and made it easier to achieve a diversified, more domestically oriented economic development. There are many other distinctions which could be drawn, but the main point here is that although the international economy created both opportunities and dangers for peripheral capitalist economies, success or failure depended on the results of the interaction between external forces and local socio-economic and political structures.

While major changes had been wrought in Latin America's socio-economic structure since the beginning of the previous century, capitalist transformation, for all its apparent success, remained flawed at its heart. This was partially due to the fact that merchant capital found its natural allies in the local landed export elites. These elites, although placed in a roughly similar position with regard to capitalist development as had been the European bourgeoisie, whose liberal ideology they fervently espoused, were but a pale reflection of that revolutionary class depicted so vividly in the *Communist Manifesto*. In the first place, the evolution of this class's hegemonic position was distinctive. It came neither in struggle against the landed class as in Britain (in many ways capitalists in Canada or Australia can be seen as products of this struggle) or France nor in the collaboration with this class as in Germany or Japan.[8] For the most part, the Latin American elites *were* the landed class or, at least, a dominant sector of it. Their power derived instead from the coincidence of their economic base in primary exports with the demands of industrial capitalism for these exports. Their interests lay in maintaining and strengthening this relationship. As Cardoso and Faletto argue,[9] "...the system of (external) domination reappears as an 'internal' force, through the social practices of local groups and classes which try to enforce foreign interests, not because they are foreign, but because they may coincide with values and interests that these groups pretend are their own." Among other things, this meant that while substantial economic and social changes were called for so as to facilitate the growth of the export sectors, because this consisted in the main of adapting food and raw material output to external demands the pressure to revolutionize the forces of production was not all that great. The necessary changes involved using relatively rudimentary technical innovations and, therefore, productive structures were changed but slowly. With certain exceptions, they tended to remain characterized by low levels of productivity. This applied both to exports and manufacturing, the latter being confined primarily to basic consumer goods production. Whether because of low labor costs, a strong position in the world market or natural advantage the need to increase the productivity of labor by continually revolutionizing the forces of production—one of the most dynamic elements of capitalism in the metropolitan countries—was not all that strong for primary export production, clearly the leading sector of Latin America's economies.

The foregoing considerations are not intended as a rigid model, but rather a broad framework for beginning to analyze the development of capitalism in Latin America. As the investigation proceeds it will become necessary to modify many aspects of this preliminary schema. Furthermore, it must be stressed once again that however powerful an influence was exerted by the impositions of European merchant capital on the Latin American countries, the result, in terms of the specific character of the political and socio-economic structures which were developed, can only be understood in terms of the interplay of local factors. Marx observed:[10] "To what extent it [commerce] brings about a dissolution of the old mode of production depends on its internal solidarity and internal structure. And whither this process of dissolution will lead, in other words, what new mode of production will replace the old, does not depend on commerce, but on the character of the old mode of production itself." Referring specifically to Latin America, Cardoso and Faletto point out[11] that to explain the diversity of experience in the region it is necessary to investigate the interrelationship between foreign domination and "...the different moments at which sectors of local classes allied or clashed with foreign interests, organized different forms of state, sustained distinct ideologies, or tried to implement various policies or defined alternative strategies to cope with imperialist challenges in diverse moments of history."

Despite the fact that "the character of the old mode of production" as well as its post-independence evolution varied greatly in the four countries under review, there was a remarkable degree of unity with respect to the ubiquity of external factors and also the course, and in many ways, the character of domestic capitalist change. Before discussing the impact of the war, it is, therefore, necessary to offer a brief outline of the nature of each country's economic and socio-political development up to 1914.

Argentina

Describing Argentina in about 1911, James Bryce wrote,[12] "All is modern and new; all belongs to the prosperous present and betokens a still more prosperous future. Argentina is like western North America. The swift and steady increase in its agricultural production, with an increase correspondingly large in means of transportation, is what gives its importance to the country and shews that it will have a great part to play in the world. It is the United States of the Southern Hemisphere." This view was widely shared by contemporary critics who believed it would be just a matter of time before Argentina was counted among the more developed countries of the world. There was a good deal of substance to this belief, even though it was often coloured by the idea that Argentina could simply be equated with Buenos Aires—the "Paris of South America." Compared to the cities of Brazil or the Andean countries, the former with its black and mulatto population and the latter with its many poor Indians, in the modern, thriving Argentine capital "...a general impression emerged of well-dressed, well-nourished Europeans."[13] The prosperity here was based on the massive export of grains and livestock products developed from the combination of foreign capital and immigrant labor supplied to the vast, richly fertile and sparsely populated pampas.

In 1913 Argentine exports were valued at 484,000,000 gold pesos, their highest prewar level.[14] This represented a more than threefold increase from 1900. Expansion had been uneven, but from the mid-1880s the growth of Argentine exports had outstripped that of all other Latin American countries,[15] and before the First World War

Table 1.1 *Argentina's principal exports*
1910–1914

Percentage share	
Wheat	19.4
Maize	17.9
Linseed	10.2
Hides	11.0
Wool	12.9
Frozen Beef	7.6

Source: C.F. Díaz Alejandro, *Essays on the Economic History of the Argentine Republic,* London and New Haven, 1970, p. 18.

exports per capita at $(US)58 were 45% higher than her nearest rival, Chile.[16] She enjoyed favorable trade balances, but the level of imports was also high. In the prewar years much of this was due to the larger quantity of capital and intermediate goods imports, a direct result of increased foreign investment from 1905.[17] Although any estimates of Gross Domestic Product must be treated with caution, Díaz Alejandro calculates that in 1913 per capita GDP in Argentina was 1,030 ($(US) of 1970 purchasing power), more than twice what it had been in 1880 and four times that for Brazil.[18]

The composition of exports had shifted quite markedly from the early years. Whereas in the 1880s wool and hides had accounted for 90% of exports, in the immediate prewar years a much more diversified export base had been established (Table 1.1). Increased European demand, railway extension and the development of refrigerated shipping all contributed to this transformation. The growth of agricultural exports had been the most spectacular, with cultivated acreage increasing by almost ten times between the late 1880s and the First World War.[19] In 1914 there were seven million hectares under wheat alone.

Export production was mainly in local hands. There were some relatively small scale producers, but most of the output came from the owners of large *estancias*. These *estancieros* in the pampean provinces, who generally lived in Buenos Aires and effectively controlled the national government, farmed their land by using immigrant tenant farmers who were moved on after having tamed the soil by raising a few crops of wheat and leaving the land in alfalfa for cattle.[20] This system of ownership and production while generating vast wealth did not lead to widespread rural prosperity. Instead: "The products of the agricultural and pastoral economy flowed toward Europe, and whatever stimulus, commercial or industrial, these products provided was concentrated in the ports which handled and processed the raw materials."[21]

Besides a dependence on overseas markets, of which Britain was the single most important, taking about a quarter of Argentine exports in 1913,[22] the commercialization and processing of exports were dominated by foreign companies. Virtually all grain exports were handled by nine foreign firms, four of which ("the Big Four") accounted for 65% of shipments.[23] Meat-packing was also controlled by foreign firms. In 1913 British and North American companies were responsible for 32.5% and 42.6% respectively of meat exports, the remaining 25% coming from a large Argentine firm.[24] While the specific effects of this overwhelming foreign domination are still debated,[25] it is clear that a very small number of firms were in a position to exert tremendous leverage on the Argentine economy.

One of the main factors underlying Argentina's export success was a massive inflow of foreign capital. The first major boom came in the years from 1884, faltered five years later, and then ended abruptly with the Baring Crisis of 1890. The effects of this collapse were severe, and it was almost 15 years before foreign investors' confidence was significantly regained. In 1900 Argentine's foreign liabilities stood at a little over £200,000,000, and with the next major surge, which began in 1905, the total debt reached about £650,000,000 by 1913.[26] Most of this (between 60–70%)[27] was owed to Britain and was in various infrastructural projects, particularly railways (55.8%) and in government loans (24.6%).[28]

In both absolute and per capita terms Argentina was the largest recipient of foreign capital in Latin America.[29] This afforded many clear advantages to Argentina, including the provision of an extensive transport and public utility infrastructure and the ability to maintain a high level of imports. There were also costs. By 1913 48% of the country's fixed capital assets (excluding land) was owned directly or indirectly by foreigners.[30] More significantly, over 30% of export earnings were needed to service the foreign debt.[31] The country's balance of payments position was, therefore, extremely vulnerable as it came to depend upon continued injections of foreign capital, the supply of which was largely determined by conditions facing the developed countries, particularly Britain.[32]

The railways are often seen as one of the principal benefits derived from foreign investment. They provided the channels to carry exports to the ports and the world market. Railway growth had been most rapid from the mid-1880s to the early 1890s and again from 1905. Between 1900 and 1913 mileage doubled from 10,000 to 20,000.[33] The system was dominated by British companies which by the First World War controlled 70% of the mileage.[34] More importantly, the four largest companies, which had 57% of the track, ran the most profitable and economically vital routes. On the whole the railways admirably served the functions the Argentine elite had envisaged for them. They opened up the pampas, were important in fostering internal peace and national unity and helped to create an impressive export-based prosperity, a prosperity concentrated in the port cities, particularly Buenos Aires, from which the main rail lines radiated.[35] Furthermore, because the system was largely supported by foreign capital, the local elite was freed to invest in more lucrative ventures such as land.[36] In short, the railways were a key element in the country's development, but at the same time they served to strengthen the pattern of growth which made the Argentine economy complementary to and dependent upon the industrialized countries.

Another vital factor for Argentine growth was labor, for in 1860 there were only 1.2 million people in the country's over 1.5 million square miles. It is little wonder that Juan B. Alberdi's 1850s dictum: "To govern is to populate" was taken up by the elite. By 1914 the population of Argentina had reached 7.8 million.[37] This extraordinary rate of growth was fueled by mass immigration, especially heavy from the 1880s onwards. No other Latin American country depended so much on immigrants. In 1914 30% of the country's population and about one half of those in Buenos Aires were foreign-born. The elite encouraged immigration in order to secure a labor force, but, strongly influenced by positivism and European theories of biological determinism, they also felt that Europeans were superior to the native *mestizo* and would, therefore, help establish "civilization" in Argentina.[38] This was another important aspect of foreign domination.

The attitude of the elite toward the immigrants and particularly their impact on Argentine society, had begun to change by the first decade of the century from acceptance to suspicion and hostility, as witnessed by the development of a strongly defined Argentine cultural nationalism. This was partly due to the fact that instead of a docile work force the oligarchy found themselves faced with a growing number of immigrant entrepreneurs, and an increasingly combative urban working class.[39] With respect to the latter, although the roots of organized labor can be traced to the 1850s, the most explosive phase came in the years of anarchist-led strikes from about 1902, which ended with the massive and violently suppressed general strike of 1910.[40] The threat posed to the elite remained, but this defeat left the Buenos Aires working class temporarily demoralized and disorganized, and so it remained until the outbreak of the First World War.[41]

The challenge from the working class was one element which contributed to the seemingly major political changes which occurred just before the war when the dominant landed oligarchy agreed to share power with some elements of the middle class and those from the landed class who had been excluded from government, many of whom, organized in the Unión Cívica Radical, had been in active opposition since the 1890s. This was done by extending the franchise in 1912. However, this "...did little more than open up the political system to the native-born, property-owning middle class groups and to the minority of workers who had also been born in the country.... It was an act of calculated retreat by the ruling elite."[42] It was also an important indication of the tensions created within Argentine society by rapid export-led growth.

By the First World War the growth of grain and livestock exports had created undoubted prosperity in Argentina. "The entire country had changed, not only the rural landscape where the desert had given way to seas of wheat and trees and dwellings, revealing the presence of humans in a formerly empty landscape, but cities where poor, austere structures...were replaced by a style which mirrored the new wealth and strove to repeat the style of the great European metropolises."[43] However it may have looked, this was a prosperity which was both distributed very unevenly and constructed on unsteady foundations. The latter had much to do with the high degree of dependence on world trade, which was vital not only for the sale of the country's products, but which also, through import duties, provided over 50% of government revenue.[44] Large foreign debts, and a reliance on continued inflows of capital were other important features of the country's economic vulnerability. Added to this was the direct control exercised by foreign firms on the economy. Export production was for the most part in Argentine hands, but the transport (both by rail and sea), commercialization, processing and financing was largely dominated by foreign companies. Banking, insurance, and public utilities were other areas where foreign influence was strong. In no other South American economy was the role of foreigners so pervasive. Direct foreign involvement in itself was not necessarily harmful because presumably these firms prospered when the Argentine economy was healthy. But, the problem in terms of long-term materially progressive capitalist transformation was that they did well by maintaining the primary export orientation of the Argentine economy. They were able to do this because it also benefited not only the landed elite, but most other sectors of Argentine society as well. This explains, in part, why although there was vocal criticism of foreign domination, within the country there seems to have been no substantive conflict as to the role of exports before 1930. Struggles centered more on the distribution of the income generated by the export sector.[45] The dependent nature of Argentina's economy was, therefore, largely self-imposed, and must be understood as arising out of the relationship between the interaction of domestic class forces and the pressures exerted and the possibilities offered by the world market.

Brazil

Each of the many travelers to Latin America saw the region with different eyes, and so to maintain a comparative edge James Bryce is called upon once again.[46]

Less here than in Argentina or Uruguay, has one the feeling that the nation is still in the first freshness of youth, eagerly setting itself to explore and furnish its home and to develop resources the possession of which it has just begun to realize....Comparatively few shew themselves sensible of the tremendous problems which the nation has to face, with its scattered centres of population to draw together, its means of communication to extend, its public credit to sustain, its revenues to be scrupulously husbanded and applied to useful purposes, above all, its mass of negro and Indian population to be educated and civilized. Nowhere in the world is there a more urgent need for a wise constructive statesmanship.

Generalizations about a country as vast and diverse as Brazil are always suspect, but Bryce's views, including his racial pessimism, were more or less shared by other contemporary observers. Compared to Argentina, Brazil seemed less dynamic, a hot, tropical country, clearly not "in the first freshness of youth" weighed down as it was by a colonial heritage of plantations and slavery. It had been ruled by the

Emperor Dom Pedro II, until the declaration of the Republic in 1889, and it was only in the previous year that slavery, in decline from about mid-century, was finally abolished. By 1914 a very small proportion of the Brazilian population (10%) lived in cities of over 20,000 people, subsistence agriculture was widespread, and large areas of the country stagnated, suffering either from the decline of a former export, such as sugar in the Northeast or a collapse of a new one, such as rubber in the Amazon. While this meant that for the country as a whole rates of economic growth were not all that dramatic, nonetheless, a form of rapid capitalist transformation, based mainly on the spread of coffee cultivation, had taken place in the central southeastern part of the country around Rio de Janeiro and São Paulo. These cities grew rapidly, colonial architecture was replaced by self-consciously grand European styles and manufacturing industry expanded. As had happened in Argentina, the transformation was propelled by the combination of primary exports, and a massive influx of immigrants and foreign capital.

The value of the country's exports increased by 4.5% per year between 1883 and 1913,[47] with an acceleration in growth from 1897 to the outbreak of war.[48] Imports also grew, but an increasingly healthy balance of trade was maintained until 1913, when the first trade deficit for many years was experienced. Exports were of great importance, but in the years 1911–13 they accounted for only 16% of gross domestic product.[49] In per capita terms Brazilian dependence on imports and exports was much less than either Chile or Argentina. Only Peru could boast a lower figure (Table 1.2). This is indicative of both substantial interregional trade within Brazil and the very large domestic agricultural sector, the latter, which because of its low productivity, may have[50] retarded the pace of economic development. This in turn helps to explain why by the First World War Brazil's per capita GDP (in US$ of 1970 purchasing power) was only 230, less than a quarter of that achieved in Argentina.[51] Nonetheless, because of the massive expansion of coffee production the southeast of the country experienced much more substantial progress than indicated by this countrywide figure.

By the late 1830s coffee had emerged as Brazil's leading export, displacing sugar, which with its archaic production methods was finding it increasingly difficult to compete in the world market. With this change the economic heart of the country shifted from the Northeast to the Central-Southeast, and there it remained. Initially coffee cultivation was concentrated in the Paraíba valley, in the

Table 1.2 *Per capita value of imports, exports
and national debt 1911. Brazil, Argentina,
Chile, Peru and the USA*

	(US dollars)		
	Imports	Exports	National debt
Argentina	48.57	51.45	91.50
Brazil	11.16	14.68	38.60
Chile	37.82	35.83	62.38
Peru	4.58	6.93	5.76
USA	16.39	21.56	10.88

Source: *United States Statistical Abstract for 1911,*
cited in *Anuario estadístico de la República de Chile
1911,* pp. 94–5.

hinterland of Rio de Janeiro. The *fazendeiros* here adopted extractive,
land-extensive techniques and by the 1870s and 1880s, burdened with
debts, soil exhaustion and a depleted number of slaves, the area was in
irreversible decline.[52] It was at about this time that São Paulo assumed
the position of leading coffee producer as the extension of the railway
and the beginnings of large scale immigration helped the rapid spread
of plantings into the western part of the state. Coffee continued to be
grown in Rio as well as the states of Espírito Santo and Minas Gerais,
but the most explosive growth occurred in São Paulo.

Brazil's other major export in the latter part of the nineteenth
century was wild rubber from the Amazon.[53] A great deal of money
was earned in its collection and sale, but the way in which the industry
was organized and the nature of the region itself mitigated against
either improvements in production or the profits made serving as the
basis for any form of diversified economic expansion. When the effects
of competition from Asian plantation rubber began to be felt after 1910
there was little that could be done. It is true that Brazil's economic
health relied increasingly on a single commodity, but other exports
such as sugar, yerva-maté, hides, cotton, cocoa, tobacco, etc. were
important regionally. Although their contribution to the nation's total
foreign earnings may have been relatively small (Table 1.3), their local
importance should not be ignored, particularly as more sugar, meat
products, and raw cotton were sold within the country than sent
abroad.

Table 1.3 *Percentage share of commodities in*
Brazilian exports 1821–1914

	1821–1823	1871–1873	1912–1914
Cotton	25.8%	16.6%	2.9%
Sugar	23.1%	12.3%	0.3%
Coffee	18.7%	50.2%	60.4%
Leather	13.5%	6.4%	4.7%
Tobacco	3.2%	3.2%	2.6%
Cocoa	0.6%	0.8%	2.9%
Rubber	0	5.3%	17.4%
Yerva-maté	0	1.6%	3.3%

Source: Leff, *Underdevelopment*, p. 85

In Brazil, as in Argentina, although there were some large
foreign-owned estates (in 1911 8,000 of São Paulo's 57,000 estates were
under foreign control),[54] the majority of all commodity production
was in local hands. This meant that exports generated substantial
domestic income, and in the southeastern part of the country this led
to a radical economic transformation, including rail building, rapid
urbanization and the growth of manufacturing. Leff observes that,[55]
"...nineteenth-century Brazil was not a classic export economy. The
conditions which in other underdeveloped countries made for large
external leakages and a small spill-over effect from expanding trade on
the domestic economy were much mitigated in Brazil." Nonetheless,
there was an extremely strong direct foreign influence in the Brazilian
economy, particularly in commerce, banking, the provision of social
overhead capital and in government loans.

The coffee trade was dominated by a few large foreign merchant
houses. By the turn of the century about 60% of the coffee sales was
controlled by six or seven companies.[56] German firms alone were
responsible for the same percentage of rubber exports.[57] The foreign
merchant was in an immensely powerful position *vis-á-vis* the planters
or the *aviadores* (middlemen in the rubber trade) because of his
international market contacts, control of credit, and, in the case of
coffee, his increasing interest in processing and warehousing. Not
surprisingly, this aspect of foreign domination was the subject of much
complaint and bitterness. Greenhill writes,[58]

...the coffee trades structure increasingly favoured the foreign merchant, who
forced lower prices on the producer in a depression while protecting himself

by his employment of the world's marketing machinery. Producers, unable to reduce wages and overheads, naturally resented "the fat profits which the merchant seemed to be making." The very fact that disorganized *fazendeiros* depended on a few powerful houses, financed abroad and working in close proximity, inevitably aroused suspicion.

However, the planters were not powerless. In 1906 valorization (taking coffee off the market to force up the price) was first introduced. This clearly benefited the planters, but the scheme only worked because it was also in the interests of the foreign merchants and bankers who gave it their active support.[59]

The other area of major direct foreign intrusion in the Brazilian economy was finance. Foreign banks were particularly active here. In 1913 they controlled 46% of all Brazilian deposits, about 20% more than similar institutions in the other three countries.[60] Brazil also had an extremely large external debt (Table 1.2). The total was £407,600,000, £151,700,000 of which was owed by the government (national, state and municipal).[61] The latter represented the highest ratio of public debt to export earnings in Latin America.[62] Among other difficulties, this made the country's balance of payments position highly vulnerable, and often put the government at the mercy of foreign banks. In the period 1860–1913, besides official borrowing, over £290,000,000 was invested by foreign companies, of which £255,900,000 was outstanding in 1914.[63] As elsewhere, British firms accounted for the largest proportion of this (62%), and over 60% was devoted to basic services such as urban transport, gas and electricity companies, ports, and railways.

The railways were by far the single largest recipients of foreign loans. There was £66,500,000 invested in foreign companies alone.[64] To this must be added the sums borrowed abroad both by local lines and state and federal governments, the latter needing to support both their own railways and interest guarantees given to private companies. It was the increasing burden of the latter obligation combined with a crisis in government finances which forced the steady nationalization of railways from 1900.[65] This was essentially an operation in financial retrenchment. The government did not, therefore, want to assume the responsibility for operating the lines, and most were rented out to private companies. In 1914 only 20% of the railway mileage was state-run, although it owned over 60%. The railways in Brazil were built primarily to facilitate export expansion. Because of this and the physical difficulties of construction a national network was never created. The most comprehensive system of lines was in the

Central-Southeast, reflecting and helping to perpetuate the regional bias of the country's coffee-based development.

The railways not only carried coffee, but also the hundreds of thousands of immigrant workers who came to work on the *fazendas*. Brazil did not suffer from as serious a labor shortage as did Argentina, but it proved easier and cheaper to bring in workers from abroad than to try to force labor out of the subsistence sector and/or recruit workers from the impoverished Northeast or elsewhere in the country.[66] European immigrants were also generally welcome because, in line with Brazil's quite distinct variety of racism, it was believed they would help to "whiten" the population.[67] Unlike the influx into Argentina, a large part of Brazilian immigration was heavily subsidized. A scheme devised by the new federal government in 1892 was suspended three years later, but in the state of São Paulo, where about 50% of new arrivals first landed, an active recruitment program was continued.[68] Here, between 1889 and 1900, 80% of the immigrants received subsidies and a system was established to channel workers directly to the coffee plantations.[69] From the beginnings of mass immigration in the 1880s to the First World War, over 3 million people came to Brazil, mainly Italians (40%), Portuguese (28%), and Spaniards (13%).[70] There are no net figures, but it seems approximately half stayed in the country. According to the 1920 Census, of a total population of over 30 million only 1,565,000 (5.2%) were listed as foreign or naturalized.[71] Their impact on the country was, however, out of all proportion to this relatively small number because they were heavily concentrated in the southeastern coffee-producing states, and in the cities, especially São Paulo. For example, in 1905 56% of the agricultural laborers in rural São Paulo were immigrants,[72] and five years earlier it had been estimated that more than 90% of the state's industrial workers were foreign-born.[73] Immigrants not only made up a large proportion of the growing urban proletariat, but many of the emerging urban capitalists, the most famous example being the industrialist Francisco Matarazzo, were also immigrants.[74]

As had happened in Argentina, in order to increase its wealth and maintain its power the landed elite in São Paulo had to import labor and institute a capitalist transformation of its agricultural system. In doing so it set in motion a process which was to lead to rapid urbanization, industrial growth, and overall the emergence of a much more complex society in which their authority was to come under attack. A somewhat similar phenomenon took place in some neighboring states, especially Rio de Janeiro, but elsewhere in the country relations of production were not radically altered and the balance of class forces remained relatively more stable. From about the turn of the century, most forcefully in the cities of Rio de Janeiro, Santos and São Paulo, the urban proletariat began to organize and assert itself. This was quite clearly not part of the elite's plans for modernization, and the state moved fairly quickly, forcibly suppressing working-class agitation and deporting labor leaders.[75] But, despite the strong reaction, the movement here was far weaker than in Argentina. Pressure from the workers did not, for example, help bring about any major political changes in Brazil. This would have been quite difficult to do in any case, for because of the extreme federalism established under the First Republic, there were literally no national political movements, the states were more or less left to themselves and the central government was controlled by the elites of São Paulo and Minas Gerais. This may, in part, account for the fact that during these years there were no viable political alternatives to elite rule in Brazil similar to that presented by Yrigoyen in Argentina, Alessandri in Chile or Billinghurst and later Leguía in Peru. The absolute political power of the Brazilian landed classes did not begin to be materially threatened and little compromise was necessary until the multiple crises brought by the First World War led to a working-class revolt and greater assertiveness on the part of the urban middle classes.

Bryce and other observers at the time always drew quite sharp distinctions between Brazil and Argentina, and these were, on the whole, well-founded. They were very different countries in terms of their populations, geography, social and political structures, export products, and history. Nonetheless, on the eve of the Great War many underlying similarities could also be seen. From the 1880s both countries had undergone dramatic agrarian-based capitalist transformations, involving extensive railway construction, mass immigration, urbanization, and varying degrees of industrial development. Productive sectors were controlled primarily by nationals, but there was extremely strong foreign domination of overseas transport, commerce, banking and insurance. Government finances were similarly dependent on import duties and continued foreign loans, and economic prosperity rested on the volatile base of primary exports. In Brazil this base was particularly narrow. Finally, elites in Argentina and Brazil fully embraced the Ricardian notion of comparative advantage as well as the European ideal of progress and much of the cultural baggage that came with it. Brazil's external orientation, most importantly the central-southeastern states' primary export capitalism, represented, as did Argentina's, a conscious choice on the part of the country's rulers. While the world economy functioned more or less smoothly and the export sector continued to generate income it was a choice which was widely accepted by all classes, at least in the prosperous coffee-growing states. However, the war was to shatter the many fundamental nineteenth-century economic and cultural assumptions and in so doing prompt a major reaction against what became perceived as Brazil's subservient status.

This reaction was manifested in a rising tide of nationalism.[76] Although it drew on a substantial body of nineteenth-century work by such writers as Manuel Bomfim and Alberto Tôrres,[77] it was, in Skidmore's words, "a New Nationalism," in that it represented, among other things, a major shift in the conception of how the international economy worked and of Brazil's position within it.

Since the 1880s the Brazilian elite had been explicitly committed to the integration of their country into the North Atlantic economy and culture. Brazil would export agricultural products needed by the North Atlantic world while at the same time attracting their immigrants and investment. The occasional nationalist critics were argued down on the grounds that nationalism had become obsolete...the war, however, was a brutal reminder that nationalism was far from obsolete. The conflict within Europe had contradicted the liberal ideology, which in effect prescribed for Brazil a minor role within a world increasingly dominated by Europe.[78]

This new-found nationalist critique extended over more than economic issues. "By destroying so many nineteenth-century illusions," Bello writes,[79] "The war of 1914 stimulated the desire for autonomy in all fields, and made the new generation of Brazilian intellectuals more curious about everything to do with their own country."

Chile

After passing through Bolivia and the "dreary and waterless wastes" of northern Chile, the well-traveled James Bryce arrived in Santiago. There he found a city much to his liking.[80]

Prosperity and confidence are in the air. Great, indeed, is the contrast between the old-fashioned Lima...and this brisk, eager, active, modern city, where crowded electric cars pass along crowded streets and men hurry to their business or their politics even as they do in western Europe or North America. Santiago is a real capital, the heart of a real nation, the place in which all the political energy of the nation is focussed, commercial energy being shared with

Valparaíso. Here there are no loitering negros, nor impassive Indians, for the population is all Chilean.

The "all Chilean" population Bryce saw was in the main *mestizo*, and for a number of Chilean intellectuals, as for their counterparts in Argentina, the *mestizo*, like the black or the Indian, represented an inferior race which stood in the way of "progress." The solution was to encourage immigration, preferably from northern Europe to "whiten" the population. However, unlike Brazil or Argentina, Chile with its over three million inhabitants in 1907, was already fairly densely populated (with respect to arable land).[81] There was, therefore, little demand for agricultural labor, the main spur to foreign recruitment in Brazil and Argentina. Despite various efforts to foster immigration, only about 4% of the population was foreign-born at the 1907 Census. These relatively few immigrants were to play an important role in the country, but this was as professionals and enterpreneurs in the cities, not proletarians as in the two east coast republics.

As there were many among the elite who would have disagreed with Bryce's rosy view of the country's racial character, there were also those who were critical about the way the economy had developed, particularly the extent of direct foreign control.[82] However, the country had experienced rapid economic growth from the end of the nineteenth century. In the two decades from 1890 the value of exports rose by an annual average of 9.3% and 7% respectively, while imports increased by 6.6% and 8.7%.[83] In 1910 the country had an extensive, and largely state-owned, railway network, and, judging by the numbers enrolled in school, it could also boast the most comprehensive educational system in Latin America.[84] Manufacturing industry had made important strides, and Chile also experienced rapid urbanization in these years. By 1907, 22.2% of the population lived in cities of over 20,000.[85] The vast majority were in the Santiago–Valparaíso–Concepción triangle, where commerce, finance, and industry were concentrated. There are no GDP figures comparable to those for Brazil and Argentina, but in 1914 national income per capita (in US$ of 1980 purchasing power) was about 1,000, a substantial achievement.[86]

Despite these signs of success the country's capitalist transformation was uneven and troubled. Much of this was due, as in other Latin American economies, to the fact that growth was led by primary exports. In the first three quarters of the nineteenth century Chile had relied primarily on the export of copper, silver and wheat. But the success of these commodities had been based on natural advantage not on improvements in productivity, and by the 1870s when prices began to fall all three went into decline. The economy was rescued by the War of the Pacific which broke out in 1879. Chile's victory over Peru and Bolivia, left the country in complete control of the vast nitrate deposits of the Atacama Desert. This completely transformed the pattern of export growth and marked the beginning of a new period in the country's economic development.

In 1884 the value of Chile's nitrate exports was 67,000,000 pesos (of 18 pence sterling). By 1913 this had reached 315,000,000 pesos.[87] The strong demand from European agriculture for nitrate as a fertilizer and the fact that Chile possessed a virtual monopoly of its supply led to a degree of dependence on a single commodity unparalleled in other countries. In the period 1910–13 nitrate and its by-product iodine accounted for a staggering 77% of the total value of exports, with copper representing only 8%.[88] At the same time, the British Empire, Germany and the United States took 80% of the country's exports and provided 77% of imports.[89] The success of nitrate production was considerable, and within a short time the entire fabric of the Chilean economy came to rely on the fortunes of this industry. It is true, as Sunkel and Cariola have argued,[90] that the prosperity brought by nitrate exports facilitated the further expansion of capitalism in terms of manufacturing industry, commerce and transport, but there can be little doubt that such a high level of dependence on one product also left the entire economy excessively exposed to outside pressures and severe fluctuations in employment and output. This became apparent with increasing force from 1914.

The economy's external link through nitrate was complemented by a substantial degree of foreign investment. Public indebtedness was considerably less in Chile, than in either Brazil or Argentina, although the government did borrow abroad, mainly in Britain, to finance railway construction and other public works.[91] The most striking difference in Chile was the extent of direct foreign investment in export production. By 1894, 92% of the country's nitrate was being produced by foreign firms, most of which were British.[92] Although by 1921 Chilean capital seems to have recovered and controlled about half the output, according to McQueen,[93] this came about mainly by "...the Chileanization of enterprises and individuals primarily foreign, rather than the development of new enterprises by purely Chilean interests." This meant that a substantial proportion of nitrate profits flowed directly abroad. It is estimated that between 1880 and 1930, 30% of nitrate export earnings were repatriated, representing about 7% of the country's gross domestic product.[94] This process of foreign domination was to gain considerable momentum during the war, as improvements in technology permitted large United States mining companies to begin to exploit Chile's massive deposits of low grade copper ore.

Notwithstanding the problems caused by dependence on nitrates and foreign capital, by the First World War Chile was one of Latin America's most materially advanced countries.[95] An important indication of this was the country's prominent manufacturing sector.[96] Its development can be traced to the period before 1879, but with the stimulus provided by nitrate exports, industrial output grew more rapidly from this time. According to the National Census, by 1913 there were almost 8,000 industrial firms, although many must have been little more than small workshops. They employed about 85,000 workers and Palma estimates that by this time about 16% of the Chilean work force was in manufacture.[97] Yet as impressive as this achievement was, manufacturing industry showed few signs of playing the revolutionary transforming role which it had in the more advanced capitalist countries. The reasons for this must be sought in the nature of Chile's class structure and its relationship to the main engine of economic growth, the nitrate sector.

Essentially, industrial growth did not throw up a national bourgeoisie with the power to transform Chilean society. Manufacturing continued to be seen as secondary to the export of primary commodities, upon which it was in any case dependent. Furthermore, because the income from nitrates was extracted through export duties and distributed by the state, it did little in economic or political terms to disturb the dominant position of the country's traditional landholding elite. Bauer observes that:[98] "The nitrate fields produced a torrent of wealth but paradoxically this went to fortify an elite whose principal value was still landholding." It is not surprising that, despite the critics of foreign control, there was little done to challenge the economy's external orientation or the increasing direct control of foreign capital. This situation not only suited the elite, but in terms of the income generated, it also provided immediate benefits, albeit ones which were grossly unequal, for all classes within Chilean society.

The country's political system was well-suited to perpetuate these conditions. Throughout most of the nineteenth century Chile enjoyed a level of political stability uncommon in Latin America, or indeed anywhere in the world. Except for two short-lived rebellions in 1851 and 1859, and the Civil War of 1891, there was a peaceful and ordered succession of elected regimes. But as was the case in Europe or the United States, a functioning parliamentary system did not indicate a democratic society. In Chile, although dissident political voices were raised and for the most part tolerated, the elite remained in secure control of the apparatus of the state. In many ways parliamentary politics represented little more than bargaining over the distribution of patronage on the part of the oligarchic Liberals and Conservatives who essentially shared the same overall view on how the country should be developed. Moreover, bribery and corruption were rife at election time and in any case only an extremely small number of people participated in the electoral process. In 1915, for example, only 5% of the population actually voted in the presidential election.[99] James Bryce looked on with apparent approval at the ordered way in which Chilean elections were conducted. He wrote:[100] "I saw an election proceeding under it [proportional representation] in Santiago. The result was foreknown because there had been an arrangement between Liberal sections which ensured the victory of the candidates they had agreed upon, so there was little excitement. Everything seemed to work smoothly."

While this election seemed to work smoothly, this was increasingly not the case with respect to Chilean society generally. As elsewhere in Latin America, the elite had fostered primary export capitalist development, only to find its political hegemony threatened by the working class and to some extent by an urban middle class which that development demanded and had created. Although the Chilean state adopted a more or less *laissez-faire* approach to industrial relations, when it appeared that labor might be gaining the upper hand, like states throughout the world, it was quick to act in the interests of capital. What distinguished the actions of the Chilean state was their level of brutality. For example, in 1905 over 300 people were gunned down during food riots in Santiago, and four years later, in what was probably one of the worst massacres of workers ever in Latin America, more than 1000 striking nitrate miners and their families were massacred by troops in Iquique.[101]

By 1914 Chile had achieved substantial material progress. However, it was progress built on a narrow and vulnerable foundation. The outbreak of war was to show just how vulnerable it was. Furthermore, as class conflict increased in the years before the war so the country's seemingly stable political structures began to show signs of cracking under the strains. The events of the war years were to intensify the pressures and lead to major changes in the nature of class relations and Chilean politics.

Peru

In Peru, our traveler found a country markedly different from Brazil, Argentina or Chile. Here it was the past glories of the Inca and Spanish empires which seemed more impressive than any recent developments. [102]

> Lima retains more of an old Spanish air than do the much larger capitals of the southern republics, Argentina, Chile, and Uruguay...there is no growth of industry or commerce. The Limeños are not what a North American would call either "progressive" or "aggressive". The railways and mines of Peru are mostly in the hands of men from the United States, shipping business in the hands of Englishmen and Germans, retail trade in those of Frenchmen, Spaniards, and others from continental Europe...Some day or other Lima will be drawn into the whirlpool of modern progress. But Europe and North America are still far off, and in the meantime the inhabitants, with their pleasant, courteous manners and their enjoyment of the everyday pleasures of life, are willing enough to leave mines and commerce to the foreigner.

Although this was both somewhat inaccurate and too harsh a judgment on local enterpreneurial abilities and attainments, it does reflect the fact that compared to the other countries under review Peru seemed far less dynamic, far less "modern."

Possibly the most striking difference about Peru was the fact that it was essentially an Amerindian country, and that the majority of the population lived in the *sierra*, far away both physically and culturally from the centers of political and economic power on the coast. There are no reliable population figures between 1876 and 1940, but it is estimated[103] that in 1906 there were about 3.6 million people in the entire country, 63% of whom lived in the *sierra*, 12.5% in the jungle and *montaña*, and only 24.5% on the coast. Lima was growing, but in 1908 there were still but 140,884 people in the city. By 1920 a further 83,000 had been added.[104] It was here that most of the country's small number of immigrants were to be found. The two largest groups were the Chinese and the Japanese, both originally brought over as contract labor for the coastal estates.[105] There was also a sizable Italian colony. They and most other foreigners in Peru were either artisans or engaged in various forms of commerce, although some immigrants did find their way into the ranks of the country's elite.

There were increasing direct and indirect economic links between the white and *mestizo* coast and the Amerindian *sierra*, but in many ways the two worlds remained distinct. The Peruvian novelist José María Arguedas wrote of his first visit to Lima from his home in Andahuaylas in 1919,[106] that in the capital *serranos* were viewed as "...strange and unknown, not as citizens and compatriots." But then it was also true that, "In the majority of small Andean villages the significance of the word Peru is unknown." The lack of a common cultural and national identity was found to varying degrees in every country, but it was much stronger in Peru than elsewhere. This had a major impact on the pace and character of the transition to capitalism, as well as reaction against it.

The key to this transition was the growth of exports. The central place of silver in the colonial period had been replaced from about the 1840s by guano and later by nitrates. Times changed once again when by the 1870s the most productive guano deposits had been exhausted, and Peru lost her nitrates to Chile following the War of the Pacific. It was not until the mid-1890s that the country's export sector began a sustained recovery.[107] The value of exports grew very rapidly, increasing by almost 20% per annum between 1895 and 1900, and then showing a fluctuating but considerably slower rate of growth up to the First World War. Despite this, in comparison with the other three countries (Table 1.2) Peru's export development had been relatively modest. Imports also increased, but the trade balance remained positive during the years leading up to the war. What emerged by this time was a far more diversified export mix (Table 1.4) characterized by an extremely wide geographical distribution. From the coastal valleys came sugar and cotton, petroleum was exploited on the far north coast, silver, copper, and wool were produced in the *sierra* and rubber collected in the jungle.

Until recently it was widely held that by the First World War Peru's major export sectors were directly dominated foreign capital; that they were in effect enclaves.[108] However, it is clear that while the country was firmly tied to foreign markets, and that a few large merchant houses such as Duncan Fox, W.R. Grace & Co., Balfour Williamson, Graham Rowe & Co., and Wm & Jn Lockett, did dominate commerce and credit, three of the most important export sectors, sugar, cotton and wool remained largely in local hands.[109] Direct foreign control of exports was, nevertheless, of major importance in Peru, particularly in mining and petroleum, with the major takeovers coming immediately before the war. Although Peruvian capitalists had been active in

Table 1.4 *Percentage share of major*
Peruvian exports 1910–1913

Sugar	17.5%
Cotton	13.8%
Copper	20.5%
Petroleum	6.3%
Rubber	12.3%
Wool	7.7%
Total	78.1%

Source: Peru, *Extracto estadístico del Perú*,
Lima, 1926, p. 62.

developing various mining ventures, from about 1900, US capital, represented principally by the Cerro de Pasco Mining Company, began to buy up and consolidate copper mines. The First World War saw an extension and acceleration in the process of foreign takeover, with Anaconda and the American Smelting and Refining Company also taking part. In petroleum two major British-owned companies (formed about the turn of the century) were bought by Standard Oil of New Jersey in 1913 and 1914, giving the US company (through its Canadian subsidiary, the International Petroleum Company) control over the large Negritos field. Of the other two major oilfields, the one at Lobitos was owned by a British company[110] and the other at Zorritos was run by a Peruvian entrepreneur.

Despite the substantial scale of foreign involvement in the years leading to the First World War, the amount of foreign capital invested in Peru was far less than that in any of the other countries. By 1913–14 British investment was about £ 25,600,000, and that from the United States stood at only £7,300,000.[111] Furthermore, unlike the other republics, the government's foreign debt was extremely small. In 1914 it was only £p1,800,000. Peru's per capita national debt (Table 1.2) was but a fraction of those found elsewhere. This was not a sign of better financial management, but was due mainly to the fact that in 1889, by terms agreed in the Grace Contract, large outstanding debts had been consolidated and the creditors repaid with shares in the Peruvian Corporation, to which most of the country's railroads were given. The signing of this infamous contract was highly significant event in the country's history, for besides a number of other concessions, virtually the entire railway system fell at one swoop under direct foreign control. While the economic impact of this takeover is still debated,[112] it remained a powerful symbol of foreign domination and a rallying point for nationalists.

Although James Bryce painted a picture of recumbent locals leaving "modernization" to North Americans and Europeans, in fact Peruvian capitalists were far from passive. Thorp and Bertram make a strong case that from the mid-1890s to about 1907 there was a significant economic boom characterized by a high degree of diversification based on locally controlled export sectors associated with high returned value which in turn generated substantial demand.[113] This was coupled with relative prices which made manufacturing a profitable option for Peruvian enterpreneurs. These years witnessed an increase in banking, insurance, the opening of a stock exchange, and the beginnings of industrial development, most significantly a local cotton textile industry, which by 1908 was supplying 47% of the local market. The growth was not, however, sustained as relative prices moved against local industry, and leading export sectors were taken over by foreign capital. This capital played a key role in reintegrating the country into the international economy after the War of the Pacific. "In practice, foreign investment came as an inseparable part of the package, and was accepted because another component of the same package was an export-oriented State dominated by the pro-foreign classes of Peruvian society."[114] According to Thorp and Bertram. "...the net impact of foreign capital on Peruvian growth up to 1930 was negative."

It is broadly agreed that during these years, and especially in the period known as "La República Aristocrática" (1895–1919), the country was ruled by an oligarchy made up of various groups linked to the export sectors; mineowners, Lima bankers and those engaged in foreign commerce, and coastal landowners.[115] Of these groups, it was the sugar producers with large estates in the northern coastal valleys who were most prominent. However, the oligarchy was far from united or monolithic.[116] There were major divisions along regional, family, and economic lines and their political grouping, the Partido Civil, was constantly being shaken by internal disputes. Furthermore, although the Partido Civil did control the state, but for the short-lived Billinghurst regime (September 1912-February 1914), it was not always possible for the coastal landowners, the dominant group within this coalition, to push through their favored policies because on many key issues there were irresolvable conflicts of interest within the elite. This lack of political cohesion and purpose was to prove uncomfortable for the Civilistas in the seventeen months from September 1912 and, in terms of their exclusive political dominance, fatal for them in 1919. But, despite their internal divisions, the oligarchy were united in their dedication to export expansion, welcomed foreign investment, and saw modernization coming through closer links with and emulation of Europe and North America.[117] As enthusiastic collaborators with foreign capital they, therefore, profoundly shaped the structure and direction of the Peruvian economy. In this they were very similar to the ruling elites in other countries.

All of this "shaping" was achieved not only despite intra-elite conflict, but perhaps more significantly, in terms of the country's subsequent history, against a rising tide of class conflict. It is curious that it was in Peru, where capitalism was weakest and the urban working class an extremely small proportion of the total population, that one of the most significant labor victories in Latin America should have been recorded in the prewar years. This was the election to the presidency in September 1912 of Guillermo Billinghurst, a populist leader and champion of Lima's workers.[118] Because he was not of the working class, but a dissident member of the bourgeoisie, most Peruvian historians tend to depreciate Billinghurst's importance.[119] This is a mistake. Although his election was partly due to disagreement among the oligarchy, and while he clearly was no revolutionary,[120] the very fact that aggressive action by urban workers and artisans could lead to the election of such a man was remarkable in the Latin American context and testifies to the considerable relative strength of the emerging working class in Peru. The *relative* nature of this strength must, however, be emphasized, for rather than reflecting particularly well-developed organization or wide-spread and advanced working-class consciousness, it can be seen as arising largely from the fragility of the oligarchic state in Peru.

The prewar years had witnessed a dramatic upsurge in working-class militancy in both rural and urban areas, as well as continued unrest among the Indians in various parts of the *sierra*,[121] but in February 1914 the elite was able to reestablish some degree of political control when Billinghurst was overthrown by a military coup. Nonetheless, as events were to show, the oligarchy's hold was not very secure. This did not, however, significantly disrupt the course and direction of the country's economic transformation. On the eve of war in Europe, direct foreign control of Peru's resources was continuing to increase and locally owned export sectors were also growing rapidly, tying the country more firmly to the international economy. Compared to

Chile, few in Peru had raised their voices against the mounting foreign takeover or the brand of modernization which was sweeping through the country.[122] Both were actively encouraged by the elite groups. But as happened in different ways in the other countries, the massive strains that these changes brought within Peruvian society could not in the end be contained within the chronically weak oligarchic state. The crisis of the war years was to lead to a renewed and more extensive wave of working-class unrest, and middle-class disaffection with the oligarchy's vision of Peru. This in turn resulted in important changes in the nature of the state and the manner in which the country's foreign domination was politically mediated both externally and within the country.

Conclusion

It is clear that although the four countries were highly dependent on primary commodity exports and the world market, the course of their economic and social development was characterized by considerable diversity. In Argentina and Brazil the foreign economic presence was felt most strongly in finance, public utilities, railways, and the commercialization of exports. These forms of external control, were operative to varying degrees in Chile and Peru as well, but here foreign capital also assumed a direct and leading role in export production. Among other things, this had important implications for the amount of returned value (the percentage of the value of exports retained in the producing country) and, therefore, local capital accumulation. There were also important differences in the impact on economic and social change which followed from the type of export produced and the productive relations associated with it. For instance, local development was significantly different in the Argentine province of Santa Fé, where wheat was grown by colonists on their own land from the province of Buenos Aires with its short-term tenant farmers. There were also distinctive economic linkages set up by production of coffee in São Paulo, sugar in the Northeast of Brazil, rubber in the Amazon or nitrates extracted from the Chilean desert.

The differences mentioned above were of great importance, and while in no way wishing to play these down, it seems apparent that there was also a substantial element of shared experience, especially from the latter decades of the nineteenth century. Much of this derived from the power and pervasiveness of external forces. For example, the dominance of primary export sectors, the dependence on foreign capital, the strong position of foreign merchants, the influx of immigrants from Europe, the adoption and adaptation of the European ideology of capitalist progress by the elites and the counter-ideologies of Anarchism, Syndicalism and Socialism by the workers were all important in shaping these Latin American societies in the years leading up to the First World War. Furthermore, in order to creative viable political systems and to maintain their hegemony within them, the elites in all these countries sought to foster a type of capitalist transformation based on the export of primary commodities. This led to a number of seemingly contradictory results. The variant of capitalism established was associated with rapid economic growth and a great deal of substantive socio-economic change. At the same time it remained excessively vulnerable to a wide range of exogenous constraints. This was a major, although not the sole factor, which made it weak in terms of its ability to foster more broadly based materially progressive change. The other component in this somewhat defective equation was the nature of the social structures found in Latin America. While there were local exceptions, on the whole these structures, dominated by the landed export elites, made it difficult to exploit primary export growth as a springboard to a more diversified form of capitalist development because, somewhat paradoxically, the elite, as well as the urban middle class and a good part of the working class derived immediate pecuniary benefits from the maintenance of export dependence.

This did not, however, mean that there was either social harmony or that the system was static. The impact of the First World War was to demonstrate this quite clearly. The process of imposing primary export capitalism had set in motion a series of far-reaching social changes, such as urbanization and proletarianization, the mounting pressures from which increasingly could not be easily contained within existing political forms. An important aspect of this conflict was that even at the best of times the distribution of the benefits of economic expansion was grossly unequal. The war years were not the best of times for the workers or the urban middle class. Both suffered from inflation and falling real wages. The crisis of the war and immediate postwar period, therefore, served to bring these social tensions to a head, resulting in a fundamental change in the structure of politics and political dialogue. This was one of the most important outcomes of the period as it marked the end of the absolute political authority of the landed elites.

In terms of economic dependence the war was also significant. The extraordinary demand of the period enhanced the attractiveness of the production of primary exports, increased specialization, and probably contributed to the world problem of oversupply and falling prices which began to affect numerous commodities from 1925. The war also both led to a major shift in the structure of the international economy and marked the onset of increasing US economic power in the region. These changes altered the framework and the nature of Latin America's external dependence. Finally, the conflict delivered a major shock to the region, demonstrating how deep-seated, pervasive, and powerful the various foreign ties were. This helped to stimulate the beginnings of an economic nationalist reaction against what was perceived as Latin America's internationally subservient posture. At no time did this perception seem more valid than during the first few months of the war when economic dislocation was at its most severe. It is the subject of the following chapter.

2

The early impact of the War

As soon as blood began to flow on the battlefields of Europe the war claimed an unseen, but important, victim–the international economy. Its carefully balanced multilateral structure, which had withstood the battering of other wars and innumerable crises, soon lay in complete ruins. The outbreak of war came at a time when the world economy was still suffering from recession, largely brought about by the wars in the Balkans (1912–13), and all Latin American countries seem to have been badly affected by this. But its consequences were to prove rather mild when compared to the calamitous and widely felt impact of the war. In August of 1914 there was virtually a total collapse of the financial and commercial infrastructure which underpinned world trade and upon which Latin America relied so heavily. None of the basic services could be readily found. Shipping and insurance became scarce and expensive, banks shut their doors, capital and credit completely dried up, and sterling bills disappeared. Not surprisingly, the import and export trades were all but suspended. In consequence, government finance, local commerce, the supply of food and fuel, industrial production and employment were all severely disrupted. The war-induced crisis was, of course, felt throughout the highly interdependent world economy, but of the neutral countries it was in the primary product exporters, with many of the levers of economic power directly controlled by foreigners and economies particularly vulnerable to externally generated disequilibrium, that the shock waves extended most rapidly and penetrated most deeply into the interstices of society. The extent of the disruption as well as the Allies' subsequent manipulation of markets, finance, and shipping dramatically illustrated a fundamental weakness in Latin America's primary export capitalism. It also provided a painful, salutary lesson to many Latin Americans as to the costs of allowing foreign capitalists and foreign institutions to play such a major role in their economic life. Economic growth had been bought at the price of economic dependence. At no time was this demonstrated more clearly than in the early months of the war.

I

At the outbreak of war, economic conditions in Latin America were generally unfavorable. The reasons for this can be traced to the growing political unrest in Europe and the war in the Balkans which by late 1912 had started to affect the major financial centers. At the end of that year the Bank Rate was raised in London to protect exchanges and prevent an outflow of gold.[1] This created monetary stringency, made foreign borrowing more difficult, and by generally slowing economic activity adversely affected the price of many primary exports. These conditions continued throughout the following year, and only began to ease early in 1914.

Although all of Latin America suffered because money was tight in Europe, the exact nature of the crisis differed in each country. For Argentina the main difficulty was that the inflows of foreign capital, upon which the balance of payments position depended, were sharply curtailed, new Argentine issues in London falling by 40% between 1912 and 1913.[2] While exports were strong in the first half of 1913, gold began to flow out of the country from March. This led to a sharp restriction of credit and a decline in both bank deposits and the amount of money in circulation. All of this coming after four years of rapid economic expansion and increasing speculative investment touched off a sharp recession in the Argentine economy. The US representative wrote that although conditions in European money markets were being blamed for the crisis, "...there are several factors which have contributed to making it especially severe. Overspeculation in real estate, inflated prices, reckless borrowing, and general extravagance on all sides have helped to make the crisis more acute."[3] The situation was significantly aggravated from the end of 1913 when the wheat harvest failed and total export earnings fell by over 100,000,000 gold pesos (28% between 1913 and 1914). Depression continued until the beginning of the war.

Brazil too was hit by events in Europe, but here it was a combination of excessive government borrowing and a collapse of export prices which touched off the crisis, and brought the export boom, begun in 1909, to an end. In 1913 both rubber and coffee prices fell, the value of exports dropped, and the country experienced its first trade deficit since 1885–6. The government was able to negotiate a large foreign loan in May, but most of this was used to consolidate previous debts and, therefore, gold had to be exported to cover the trade deficit and maintain exchange. This led to a contraction of the money supply and of credit.[4] The US Consul in Rio observed[5] that because of the Balkan War the Brazilian Government was finding it difficult to raise money in Europe or from local banks. As a result few firms were bidding for state contracts and the Government was unable to pay an estimated $ 16,000,000 owed to merchants in Rio alone. Many firms in the city were, therefore, facing bankruptcy, and the problem extended throughout the country. To make matters worse foreign banks were sending their gold stocks and surplus cash to Europe.

The West Coast was also economically troubled in 1913. The immediate prewar years were a time of industrial and commercial depression in Peru.[6] This was partly due to the situation in Europe as well as the falling prices of two of the country's main exports, sugar and rubber. Conditions were made considerably more difficult by, what was for the ruling elite, a threatening upsurge of labor militancy and by the related political unrest which saw the newly elected president, Guillermo Billinghurst being unable to deal with a hostile, uncooperative Congress. This led to financial problems for the government, which were not helped by the coup in February.[7] Rowe comments,[8] "The outbreak of the World War found Peru, therefore, in the most unfavorable economic, financial and governmental situation to withstand the strain which the European conflict involved."

According to Chile's Sociedad de Fomento Fabril[9] by January 1914 commerce and industry were feeling the impact of the economic crisis. Bankruptcies and short-time working were widespread. Of the thirteen British nitrate companies whose 1913 accounts were listed by *The Economist*,[10] all but two showed lower earnings. Generally, however, despite complaints,[11] prices were fairly steady, both the value and quantity of nitrate exports continued to rise, and the country's total export earnings declined only very slightly.[12] While conditions were not buoyant and credit was restricted, the downturn was extremely mild when compared to that in either Argentina or Brazil.[13]

In the year and a half before the war all four countries felt the impact of changing political and economic fortunes in Europe, but because of differing local conditions the specific course of events varied. This variation demonstrates the important influence of domestic factors, but does not gainsay the immense power exercised by the metropolis-dominated world economy over these countries. The events of these years also provide a clear illustration of how the "normal" functioning of the international system could work against the interests of the peripheral economies. An important aspect of this phenomenon is described by Ford, who writes,[14]

It was easy for a creditor country to obtain immediate relief from pressure on its exchanges by contracting its foreign lending, long and short: in a period of stringency it was difficult or even impossible for a debtor country (with a past history of depreciation) to offset gold exports by increasing its borrowing abroad. In short, in 1912–13 Britain gained relief in her balance of payments at the expense of making certain debtor countries (one of whom was Argentina) uncomfortable.

The relatively benign nature of this discomfort was put in proper perspective with the eruption of full-scale war in August, 1914.

II

During the economic downturn of 1913, as in previous crises, there may have been some reduction in their numbers, but foreign ships bringing goods from Europe and the US and carrying away primary products continued to move in and out of Latin American ports. Although the system was disturbed on occasion, it continued to function. The start of the First World War was significantly different. By the first days of August around the continent the always busy docks came to an almost complete standstill. British vessels, which carried most of the cargo, laid up awaiting orders or naval protection, while many German ships were interned or simply trapped in port. Standing on the Muelle de Guerra in Callao, Peru, a German merchant surveyed the great number of his country's steamers resting at anchor and exclaimed, "Fifty years work gone in an hour."[15] *The Economist* reported[16] that there was virtually no shipping along the entire Pacific coast. Conditions were the same on the Atlantic seaboard. The US Consul in Bahia claimed that this port city was hurt relatively more by the suspension of shipping than Rio, Santos, or Buenos Aires because it was not a principal point of departure for sailings, and when ships were scarce they tended to concentrate on the major entrepôts.[17] All of the many smaller ports on both coasts were probably similarly affected.

The number of ships engaged in the Latin American trade fell and freight rates soared. This situation became worse as the war progressed. In Argentina the cost of sending grain from Rosario to Europe rose from $2.28 per ton in January to $14.60 by December of the same year.[18] Coffee, which before the war was carried to the US for about $.40 per bag, cost $1.25 by the end of 1914.[19] In Peru and Chile it was not simply a question of higher charges, but that even if exporters could afford them it was often impossible to find a ship.[20] L.S. Rowe observed that no area of commercial life in Peru had been affected so badly as ocean transport. "It is safe to say that had Peru enjoyed adequate transportation facilities at reasonable rates, since the outbreak of the war, she would have been able to extricate herself from the disastrous depression which has hung as a cloud over the country."[21]

These difficulties were the direct result of the foreign domination of long-distance shipping. All the countries, except Peru, had small coastal fleets, but as before the war British and German firms, which together controlled the vast majority of the trade, had made overseas transport readily available at reasonable cost it was economically sensible to leave the field to them. The disruption caused in the ports by the war demonstrated that all costs were not necessarily reflected in the price charged. "When the foreign shipping tonnage became so decreased that the exportable grains lay rotting and the railways feared demoralization on account of scarcity of fuel and the inability to obtain repair materials, then the Republic [Argentina] realized the disadvantages of complete dependence upon foreign shipping."[22] Such a demonstration was not required by everyone. For example, the Sociedad Nacional de Agricultura in Chile complained that "We have not needed European wars or other such exceptional situations to suffer intensely the consequences of the oppression by foreign shipping companies."[23] Here and in Argentina there were attempts during the war to create an overseas merchant fleet, but very little seems to have been achieved. It would have been an immense task to replace a significant proportion of the tonnage needed to carry goods to and from these countries, and local shipyards were not up to the job in any case.[24] Furthermore, the prosperous export sectors proved to be more attractive for local capital.

III

Until the war, shipping was taken for granted in Latin America and so was the ability both to finance trade and, to a lesser extent, raise long-term loans in Europe. Events showed that none of these was all that secure. The heart of the international financial system was essentially in the City of London, and was based on sterling bills and the gold standard.[25] There were clear signs of financial problems as early as May and by July short and long-term funds were being recalled to London. On 27 July the acceptance of bills in the City ceased and four days later the Stock Exchange shut its doors. On the suspension of acceptances, Hartley Withers comments,[26] "And so here was another handle with which London, when crisis overtook her could give a sudden tug at the economic entrails of all the civilized world. Such was the force of the tug that England put all the rest of the world in a corner."

In Latin America the "tug" from London had immediate and devastating consequences. There were runs on the banks and between 2–4 August, bank "holidays" were declared in Argentina, Peru and Brazil.[27] Chile was not immune to the financial panic, but here the banks did not have to be closed, for unlike the situation in the other countries, Chilean paper currency was inconvertible and the banks were able immediately to draw additional note issue from the Oficina de Emisión. Further help came on 3 August after the government authorized the issuance of interest-bearing treasury bills (*values de tesoreria*).[28] When one to two weeks later the banks reopened, various kinds of moratoria on debt had been declared in all the countries. In Argentina this lasted only for a couple of months, while in Brazil and Peru, where the early effects of the war were more protracted, the moratoria lasted well into the following year. The Chilean moratorium applied only to debts payable in gold and remained in force until September 1915. In all the countries the export of gold was prohibited and in Argentina and Brazil the currency was made inconvertible. In Peru this was not necessary for there was no paper currency. However, because coins quickly disappeared from circulation and the banks were desperate, on 22 August £1,100,000 of *cheques circulares* (essentially bank notes) were issued by the government, another £p1,400,000 being added in October. The Brazilian government increased the country's inconvertible note issue by 250,000 contos ($80,000,000) and although in Argentina no new paper was created, 30,000,000 gold pesos were made available to the Banco de Nación for rediscounting.

Despite the many measures to ease the financial crisis, both exports and internal commerce were massively disrupted as credits and loans became almost impossible to obtain. The foreign banks, so crucial in the financing of trade, seem to have reacted with particular vigor.

When the war broke out British banks were already under pressure from their London offices and began calling in loans, reducing advances to overseas customers and pressing for remittances from their branches.[29] In Bahia, for example, comparing December 1913 with conditions one year later, British banks had reduced their loans and overdrafts by 36% and bill discounting had fallen by two-thirds.[30] The immediate consequences of this were similar in all four countries, although the rate of recovery differed. The US Consul in Pernambuco observed that,[31] "... the banks of this city are only working on current accounts and absolutely refuse to receive or transmit bills of exchange...the amount of business transacted is quite insignificant." His counterpart in Rio submitted a similar report on conditions in that city.[32] Because of the extreme restriction of credit, normal business was also difficult to carry out in Chile.[33] Not only was it difficult to do business, but it quickly became impossible for firms to find enough money to pay wages. Many workers in Lima went without pay, and on the north coast sugar estate of Cayaltí, wages had to be given in fiat money.[34] In Chile, southern agriculturalists and northern mineowners suspended operations because of cash shortages,[35] and the high levels of unemployment reported in Argentina and Brazil undoubtedly owed much to the same general problem. In this way, as in others, the ubiquitous tentacles of the London financial market reached out to affect the lives of workers throughout the world.

The collapse of the international system of credit had the most immediate and dramatic impact on Latin America, but access to long-term loans, upon which Brazil and Argentina were particularly dependent, also became extremely difficult and was to remain so throughout the war. Initially, all countries were adversely effected by the cessation of new inflows of capital for this cut off the major source of gold, put exchanges under pressure, led to the suspension of many construction projects, and created difficulties for governments, all of whom were running budget deficits. Brazil was the worst affected by this, for in the ten years before the war the external debt had more than doubled to £145,251,961,[36] requiring a yearly interest payment of about £15,000,000 (23% of the value of exports).[37] Because the government had such an excessive accumulated deficit (£20,745,890 between 1909 and 1913)[38] in 1914, it depended on foreign loans to meet interest payments as well as its domestic obligations (in 1914 the floating debt was between US$80-$100 million).[39] Immediately before the war negotiations with Rothschilds were in progress over a large funding loan, but these collapsed with the outbreak of hostilities and the insecurity this caused considerably deepened the crisis in Brazil. The requisite loan (£14,500,000) temporarily eased the financial pressure on the government.[40]

The financial chaos brought by the war was a salutary reminder to Latin American elites of the highly conditional, partial nature of the capitalism which they had been busy fostering. Of course, no country tied into the highly interdependent world economy could escape the effects of such a fundamental jolt to the heart of the financial system. Nonetheless, what was clearly demonstrated was that the financial structures created in Latin America during the prewar phase of outward-directed growth were in place to perpetuate that economic orientation. Furthermore, because these structures were both excessively sensitive to external vicissitudes and heavily influenced by institutions whose principal interests (and boards of directors) lay outside Latin America, they were able to do very little to offset the impact of exogenously generated crises and, therefore, could afford little protection to the domestic economy. In fact, if anything, they served to transmit foreign generated shocks throughout the country. It was a graphic example of how limited economic independence really was for these countries.

IV

The war threw the import and export trades into complete disarray (Table 3.1). The paralysis of credit and shipping were major factors in this slump, as were the Allied blockade of the Central Powers and the temporary suspension of the purchase of some commodities with the consequent drop in prices. Such a sudden and precipitous decline in export earnings delivered a massive shock to countries in which the vast majority of economic activity centered on or derived from the export sector. The movement in the terms of trade was mixed, but the capacity to import was reduced in all countries and, with some exceptions, remained low or declined during the war (Table 3.2). The quantum of imports also fell sharply, in Brazil and Argentina considerably more than that of exports. Besides being affected by difficulties of finance and transport, imports were reduced because many manufacturers in Europe turned to war production, and the sale of certain goods was restricted. Furthermore, the US, which was eventually able to replace a sizable proportion of European imports, did not have the financial network or shipping necessary to fill the gap during the early years of the war.[41] It might be thought that a lower import bill would be welcomed because this allowed the countries to maintain positive trade balances in 1914 despite the reduction in export sales. (With the exception of Chile in 1919, all countries registered surpluses throughout the war period, Table 3.1) But this was not the case. These countries' economic well-being was as dependent on imports as it was on exports. It was part of the same peripheral capitalist syndrome. Domestic commerce was badly hit by lack of imported goods to sell, and industries which relied on imported raw materials, semi-finished goods and capital equipment, were also adversely affected. The curtailment of coal supplies was a particularly serious problem, and became apparent as soon as war was declared.[42] Another important result of the fall in imports was the crisis this created for government revenue, for all states relied very heavily for their revenue on customs receipts.

On the four economies, Chile and Brazil, because of their narrow export bases and the nature of their major exports, were the most severely affected in the early months of the war. Coffee was not considered an essential commodity by the Allies, and consequently suffered, especially in terms of shipping allocation, throughout the war. Furthermore, the German and Austrian markets were cut off, and they accounted for over 20% of coffee sales as well as 19% of the country's total exports.[43] Between 1912 and 1913 the New York price had fallen by 24.5%, and because of a large harvest in 1913-14 (3 million bags greater than the previous year)[44] and the effects of war, by 1914 the price was down another 24%. This was somewhat cushioned by the downward movement of exchange, which meant that the export price in Brazil fell by only 15% in 1914.[45] Nonetheless, there was a massive decline in the quantity of coffee exported. Comparing the last five months of 1914 with the same period a year before, coffee shipments had dropped by 38%, and for the year the value of sales (in milréis) fell by 28%.[46] There was no sign of recovery until late in 1915 and when it came improvement was only modest. Most of country's other major exports also did badly in 1914, except for sugar which showed a dramatic increase as output was shifted from local to the more lucrative export market.

Unlike Brazil, Chile's principal export was vital for the war effort, being a major constituent of explosives. Nonetheless, the early part of the war seems to have been worse for nitrate than for coffee. Prices had started to move lower before the war, and from August they collapsed. From 8s per quintal (101.4 lbs) on the Chilean coast in August 1913, nitrate had fallen to 7s3d a year later and by September was 6s.[47] These prices were essentially nominal as there was almost no market for the commodity.[48] The quantity exported dropped from 29 million quintals in the last five months of 1913 to only 9.5 million quintals a year later, while the yearly value of nitrate sales fell by almost a third and by January 1915 only 43 of the country's 170 *oficinas* were working.[49] Financial chaos and the lack of shipping were obvious factors, and conditions were aggravated by the fact that when the war erupted considerable stocks were held abroad. These were estimated at 4.6 million quintals, 1.4 million greater than in the previous year.[50] Before the war about 75% of nitrate was sold for fertilizer and this did not have priority in the first months of the war. Furthermore, three quarters of sales were to Continental Europe, Germany accounting for over 30%, making it Chile's single most important customer.[51] It was not until well into the next year that increased demand from Allied munitions factories and an improvement in shipping led to a revival of the industry. The country's other major export, copper, although not as severely disrupted, was not immune to the impact of the war. The price had fallen during the 1913 recession, and, while there was a short-lived rise at the outbreak of war, large US stocks and a collapse in North American demand soon pushed the price to a record low, recovery coming only after November.[52] The Sociedad Nacional de Minería claimed: "The temporary restriction of credit, together with the paralysis of the European markets, has momentarily brought great harm to copper producers...."[53] However, it was a "momentary" disruption, and with the upward movement of prices both the volume and value of copper exports showed a slight improvement in 1914.[54]

To the north in Peru the early months of the war also brought problems for exports, but they were not as serious as those experienced in Chile. The price of sugar, one of the country's major commodities, almost doubled between July and August, as panic hit the London market.[55] The British government reacted quickly, making large purchases in the East and setting up the Royal Sugar Commisson. Three days after it was established, the Commission, having obtained six months' supply of sugar, closed the British market, and by the end of October prices had fallen from their August high of 21s per cwt to 15s. This was still fairly remunerative when compared to prewar prices, but Peruvian growers could not take full advantage of it as shipping was scarce, and this, plus the understandably slack demand in the important Chilean market, led to sugar being piled up at the docks in October and November. Despite these problems, 1914 was prosperous for the sugar industry. There had been a great deal of investment in this sector before the war and because of this, production and exports were up by about 25% in 1914, and with higher prices foreign earnings were pushed up by 87%. *The West Coast Leader* commented[56] that during the 1914–15 crisis sugar "...had been one of the sheet-anchors that has kept the Peruvian economic position head to the gale.... Peru has long been famous for its mineral deposits, but the best paying mines in Peru today are the sugar-mines (sic) of the Pacific littoral." The other main coastal export, cotton, was badly hit by the war. The disruption of the European textile industries, extraordinary increases of up to 300% in freights on cotton, and the collapse of short-term credit upon which growers relied, combined to depress the industry, which did not begin to recover until 1916.[57] As in Chile, copper production was disrupted only briefly. The large Cerro de Pasco and Morococha mines closed in early August, but were reopened by the 19th, albeit with a reduced work force.[58] Nonetheless, production and exports were slightly down in 1914, and the value of exports fell by 16%. Because of the strong performance of sugar and copper both the quantum and value of Peru's exports exceeded prewar levels by 1915 (Table 3.2), showing a much quicker recovery than either Brazil or Chile. It is important to note, however, that because of continuing government financial problems and political uncertainty it was not until February 1916 that exchange regained its prewar level.

In the early months of the war Argentine trade came to a standstill because of the same problems experienced elsewhere, lack of credit and ships. Exports between July and December 1914 fell from US$183,800,000 (in the last six months of 1913) to $131,100,000, with about half of this being due to the loss of the German market.[59] By October exchange had returned to par, the meat-packing plants were back to work and there were large orders from France and Britain for horses, saddlery, and blankets, but generally trade remained depressed.[60] Although crop prospects seemed good at the beginning of 1915, and the sinking of a German cruiser squadron lifted the threat to shipping, there were still worries that the harvest would suffer because of a lack of credit and high freight charges.[61] These problems seem to have been overcome for the production and export of all major cereal crops were up in 1915 and with wheat price 40–50% higher, the value of agricultural exports rose by 67%. This was largely due to Allied demand, as was the rise in the export of meat and related products.[62]

The pattern of export trade disruption was more or less the same in each country during the first months of the war, but there was considerable variation in the extent and timing of recovery. The latter seems to have rested for the most part on how vital particular commodities were for the Allies, and in the case of agricultural goods, the bountifulness of the harvest. With respect to imports, the experience of each country was reasonably similar, at least in 1914. Brazil's imports fell off considerably more than elsewhere. It was claimed that the country had been overstocked with foreign goods in 1913 and a cutback had begun from the first months of 1914.[63] From August, however, the level plummeted, averaging only about one third of the previous year's. In 1915 there was a further sharp drop in all countries except Argentina, where the quicker recovery of exports meant an improvement in the capacity of import and probably also led to there being somewhat more shipping. In all countries the class of imports worst affected tended to be heavy equipment, construction material, semi-finished goods, raw materials and coal.[64] This continued throughout the war years and proved a serious brake on efforts to increase industrial capacity.

The massive decline in imports had a more immediate effect on government revenues,[65] for in all countries, except Chile, more than 50% of these came from import duties.[66] In the latter, customs receipts made up 35% of the total and another 50% came from the export tax on nitrates.[67] This twofold dependence made Chilean finances particularly vulnerable. Fortunately, even though the state-owned railways were losing money there were no budget deficits in the immediate prewar years.[68] However, the deficits in 1914 and 1915 did cause problems for the government as they had to meet the substantial cost of trying to prop up the nitrate sector. A modest degree of tax reform helped, but it took the recovery of the nitrate trade to lead to any substantive improvement in the government's financial position. Brazil's problems were more severe, mainly because of the extremely large prewar deficits and the inability to service the foreign debt. In 1914 import revenue dropped by over 40% and the federal budget deficit rose to almost £15,000,000, a fourfold increase from 1913.[69] The crippling financial crisis facing the government was not eased until the Rothschilds' funding loan was agreed in October, and this provided only temporary relief. Deficits and financial problems continued throughout the war. Argentina, like Brazil, carrying a huge foreign debt and a string of substantial budget deficits, was also put in an untenable financial position by the fall in customs duties. The usual recourse in such situations had been to European capital markets, but with these virtually closed the government was forced to raise a series of short-term loans in New York and also tap the domestic market, substantially increasing the floating debt.[70] As the war progressed this may have dampened the rate of domestic capital formation, if we accept Tulchin's argument that the government's financing of its overspending internally absorbed a great part of local savings and wartime profit.[71] This question is explored more fully in chapter 4. In Peru customs receipts were almost halved in the last months of 1914 and fell even more in the first six months of the next year.[72] Although not on the scale of Argentina or Brazil, Peru's Treasury was facing difficulties when the war began, and the reduction of revenue created problems which did not begin to abate noticeably until 1916.[73] In all four countries the systems of public finance hinged on the fortunes of trade and when these were bad so the ensuing crisis was given an added push. As with the structure of finance, the manner in which states raised revenue served to exacerbate rather than forestall or ameliorate economic difficulties. However, it also has to be noted that it was the landed elites who organized taxation so as to minimize their own financial burden. It was, along with the overall export orientation, not an externally imposed system but one that grew out of and reflected the interets of that dominant class within Latin America.

V

While much was made at the time, and has been made here, of the agony of trade and finance, as with all capitalist crises, it was the workers and their families who most directly felt real anguish and physcial deprivation when the system floundered. Rowe commented:[74] "The difficulties and hardships encountered by Chilean merchants and manufacturers as a result of the European War sink into insignificance when compared with the widespread suffering and misery the paralyzation of commerce and industry entailed on the working classes." Throughout Latin America the war brought with it mass unemployment as the collapse of imports and exports made the ports and railways idle, and closed down industry, mines and agricultural enterprises. To this was added soaring food prices, especially, but not exclusively, in the urban areas.

Because of dependence on nitrate, the worst conditions seem to have been experienced in Chile. The nitrate districts were the hardest hit for there was virtually no other work that could be done in the waterless desert where all workers as well as food and other supplies had to be brought in from outside. Therefore, once shipping stopped and the *oficinas* began to close there was nothing to be done but abandon the region. By August 13th there were 8,000 unemployed workers in the Iquique area and a week later another 2,000 had been added. Hundreds of workers and their families were sleeping on the docks awaiting government-supplied transport to the south. Although probably unintended, it was a nasty irony that the ship sent was the crusier Esmeralda, whose machine guns had been used to slaughter striking workers during the violent unrest of 1907.[75] The government offered subsidies and loans to nitrate producers to keep their plants open, but this policy met with only limited success, as did their program of public works. By mid-September 14,000 workers and their families had been shipped south. Within three months the total rose to 30,000.[76]

Moving the nitrate miners to the southern provinces may have averted starvation and riots in the north, but once there it was difficult to find work for them. No provision for dealing with unemployment in the nitrate fields was made during prosperous times and when that crisis hit, the government was financially unable to respond adequately.[76] Stickell concludes that, "the worker who produced much of the nation's wealth was sacrificed to the instability of world markets."[77] The exodus from the north also tended to aggravate the difficult conditions facing workers in the south where factory closures had led to layoffs and wage cuts. There was also the problem of sharply rising food prices to contend with. It was said of Santiago in October 1914 that: "It is doubtful whether the volume of poverty is increasing, but it is certain that it is becoming more evident, for not only have soup kitchens and other centers of aid been opened in all the districts, ... but begging has increased considerably and processions of unoccupied laborers are to be seen in the streets."[78] Southern agricultural laborers seem also to have suffered. Although nitrate workers were reluctant to take badly paying jobs in agriculture, it seems that their influx may have pushed down already low wages here.[79] It was not only other workers who had cause to worry about this mass relocation. *The South Pacific Mail* commented,[80] that because the nitrate worker was accustomed to high wages and freedom of movement, "...he is a dangerous element to introduce in large numbers among the working class in the Centre and South of the Republic." These fears were never realized and, in fact, the severe depression of 1914–15 tended to undermine labor organization and lessen strike activity.

Elsewhere the same general conditions of high food prices and unemployment prevailed, although, at least the latter, was not as dramatic as in Chile. In Peru about three quarters of La Libertad's

9,000 sugar workers were laid off as sugar piled up at the docks, and at Cerro de Pasco miners were either dismissed or put on half-time working.[81] Factories closed in Lima and Callao and docks stopped work. By 10 August it was reported that 4,000 were unemployed.[82] When the effects of the war struck Argentina there was already a significant degree of unemployment because of the existing trade depression. In the first days of August conditions deteriorated considerably. In Roserio, by 3 August, 1,000 were out of work and four days later the figure had reached 4,000, mainly stevedores and day laborers employed by grain shippers.[83] Riots were feared here and in the capital where meat and bread prices were up 25% by 5 August and unemployment was increasing rapidly.[84] *The Economist* reported tht wages had been cut by 10% to 20%,[85] and by the the third week in August, with prices continuing to rise, unemployment had reached 30,000.[86] The US representative in Pernambuco, Brazil reported on 15 August that food had trebled in price, 2,400 men had been laid off by the port and the local light and power company and all factories and businesses in the cities were firing workers. About a month later he wrote, "...conditions in general in Pernambuco are daily growing worse. Foodstuffs and other necessities are becoming scarcer. The families of many men formerly employed on the railroads, tramways, port works and factories are suffering from hunger to which cause the increase in the daily number of robberies reported to have been committed in various part of the city may be partially attributed."[87] In Rio, São Paulo, Santos and other major cities similar conditions prevailed.[88]

The response of workers to these extremely harsh conditions was remarkably muted throughout the region. There were few, if any, strikes and even incidents of mass protest were relatively rare. In Santiago there was a large demonstration demanding rent reductions in October, in the following months daily street protests of the unemployed were reported, and serious riots erupted in Valparaíso in December 1914 and the following February.[89] However, the first wartime strike reported in Chile did not occur until July 1915, and it was a modest affair which ended within a week. In Peru there were only two strikes in the last months of 1914, Argentina experienced some minor riots, and little of note seems to have happened in Brazil. This lack of reaction is even more curious in that there had been considerable union organization and militant labor activity before the war in all four countries. The quiescence can be explained by both the immediate prewar experience of labor and the particular kind of crisis set off by

the war. All countries had been suffering from the 1913 recession and
to the extent that this increased unemployment, organized labor was
weakened. The war intensified this problem and so made effective
action even more difficult as it was impossible to mobilize the
unemployed and those in work were no doubt reluctant to risk their
jobs. Furthermore, in some countries the workers' movements had not
recovered from major prewar setbacks. The Argentine workers were
still smarting from their defeat in the violently suppressed general
strike of 1910, and unemployment in 1913 further sapped their
strength. "When World War I began... Buenos Aires' working class
was demoralized, economically and organizationally weakened..."[90]
In São Paulo a major strike in 1912 had been crushed and many labor
leaders deported. With the economic downturn in 1913 and then the
war, union membership throughout Brazil was decimated and Maram
claims that the movement effectively ceased to function.[91] Peruvian
workers had suffered a major political defeat in February 1914, when
President Guillermo Billinghurst, who they had supported in the
previous year's campaign, was overthrown. When the war broke out
they were leaderless, uncertain and cowed by government
repression.[92] In Chile there had been no outstanding setbacks
immediately before the war. In fact, the years 1909 and early 1914 were
a time of successful organizational resurgence.[93] A general strike in
Valparaíso in October and November 1913 had ended with some
workers' gains, although the railway workers, the main protagonists,
failed completely. De Shazo claims, however, that the unions were still
too weak to withstand the widespread unemployment ushered in by
the war.[94] The various labor movements exhibited considerable
diversity in their structure and experience, but none was powerful
enough to stand up to a major depression. As will be seen, it was only
during periods of economic expansion that the workers could begin
with any degree of success to confront capital and the state by which it
was supported.

VI

In the first chapter the diversity of the four Latin American countries'
prewar development was stressed, and it is clear from what has been
presented in this chapter that their experiences during the early months
of the war also differed. However, as important as the differences
were, and were to become from 1915, during this initial period they
were largely swamped by the suddenness and intensity of the external

shock which hit the region. It was the general similarity of the crisis in the four countries which was so remarkable and of relatively greater significance for understanding the workings of the region's brand of capitalism. Rowe's observation about the early effects of the war on Peru can, therefore, be taken, with certain reservations, as being roughly applicable to the other three countries. He wrote,[95]

Peru is a country consuming but a very small percentage of the articles which it produces. Any curtailment of the foreign market, therefore, immediately reacts upon the entire internal situation. It is this complete dependence on the foreign market combined with the fact that all the important national enterprises are dependent on foreign capital, that gave to the European war such a disastrous influence on Peru's foreign trade and upon her domestic financial and commercial conditions.

It is hardly surprising that the war's destruction of the basic mechanisms of the international economy should have had such a dramatic effect. Economic change in Latin America, as in most other parts of the world, was inexorably tied to that economy. In the first months of the war when the powerful, seemingly indestructible strands of credit, capital, trade, and shipping by which the entire system was bound together, were either severed or hopelessly entangled, there was financial panic, commercial and industrial collapse, mass unemployment, falling living standards, and for governments a series of problems which must have seemed unresolvable. There had been externally generated crises before, but the extent and severity of this one was unprecedented, and in the harsh glare cast by the conflagration in Europe the fundamentally weak and vulnerable structures upon which the regions' brand of capitalist development had been based were starkly illuminated. This is not to deny that there had been a substantial degree of materially progressive change and rapid growth stimulated by direct and indirect foreign intervention, material and intellectual, in Latin America during the classic era of imperialism. The difficulty was that these exogenous, "progressive" forces were not temporary catalytic agents. They sunk deep roots both in the economy and within the minds of the elite. To the extent that key economic institutions and sectors were operated by foreigners in the interests and at the dictates of European industrial capital, they represented a formidable barrier to a stronger, more nationally independent, progressive capitalist transformation in Latin America. In November 1914, Paulo Silveira, a Brazilian reporter remarked: "We watch the formidable European struggle, dumbfounded, our existence paralyzed and our activity drugged, complete slaves of Europe."[96] This feeling, which had been expressed by a growing number of Latin American intellectuals before 1914, was to gain increased currency as the war continued and the Allies imposed more and more openly on the region's economic and political sovereignty.

3

The recovery of trade during the War

The nineteenth-century system of international economic relations collapsed in August 1914. It was never rebuilt. In the postwar period Britain was unable to play the pivotal role as free trader and investor which had underpinned the balance and sustained the momentum of the world economy. But when the war erupted the British had to establish some means of maintaining trade, for imports of food and raw material were vital for her survival and that of her allies. A strong, though selective, demand for most Latin American commodities, therefore, soon began to make itself felt. However, the rules of the game were now very different. The free play of the market was significantly circumscribed by state regulation and control. Shipping was strictly regulated either by direct compulsion or the rationing of bunker coal. Centralized buying was somewhat slower to develop, this being in line with the British government's "liberal" reluctance to impose economic controls.[1] At first the British took over only the purchase and distribution of sugar. This was one of the country's two most important food imports, all of which came from abroad, and before the war about 75% of which had come from Germany and Austria–Hungary.[2] It was not until 1916 that wheat and other key imports were brought under formal control, although unofficial bulk purchases through agents had been carried out before this time.[3]

Another important aspect of the change to the system of world trade was the economic war waged by both sides. Germany mounted a U-boat campaign, although this did not become a serious menace to the Allies until 1917. The Allies for their part established an economic blockade against the Central Powers.[4] This went through various stages and was reinforced by the imposition of blacklists prohibiting trade with designated enemy firms in neutral countries. When the United States finally entered the war in 1917 these restrictions were further extended. All this tended to reduce the already small degree of

Table 3.1 *Export and import values 1911–1919*

	Argentina (million gold pesos)		Brazil (million contos)		Chile (million gold 18d pesos)		Peru (million £p)	
	imp.	exp.	imp.	exp.	imp.	exp.	imp.	exp.
1911	405	342	794	1,004	349	339	5.5	7.4
1912	447	502	951	1,120	335	383	5.1	9.4
1913	496	519	1,008	982	330	396	6.1	9.1
1914	322	403	562	756	270	300	4.8	8.8
1915	305	582	583	1,042	153	328	3.1	11.5
1916	366	576	811	1,137	223	514	8.7	16.5
1917	380	550	838	1,192	355	712	13.5	18.6
1918	501	801	989	1,137	436	764	9.7	19.97
1919	656	1,031	1,334	2,179	401	302	12.2	26.9

Sources: Argentina, Dirección General de Estadística de la Nación, *Análisis del comercio exterior argentino en los años 1910 a 1922* (Buenos Aires, 1923), p. 120. *Brasil em números*, p. 84. Chile, *Sinopsis estadística*, p. 64. Peru, *Extracto estadístico 1926*, p. 38.

Table 3.2 *Export and import quantums, terms of trade, capacity to import 1911–1920*

	1911	1912	1913	1914	1915	1916	1917	1918	1919	1920
Argentina (1937 = 100)										
a. Quantum of exports	43	63	65	49	62	54	39	56	66	64
b. Quantum of imports	85.5	89.7	98.2	63.4	52.9	50.7	42.9	38.6	53.5	70.2
c. Export prices	78.4	78.2	78.6	80.8	92.4	104.4	138.7	140.7	153.6	160.5
d. Import prices	69.1	72.7	73.7	74.3	84.3	105.3	129.4	189.1	178.9	194.3
e. Terms of trade (c/d)	113.4	107.6	106.6	108.7	109.6	99.1	107.4	74.4	85.8	82.6
f. Capacity to import (a × e)	48.8	67.8	69.3	53.3	68.0	53.5	41.8	41.7	56.6	52.9
Brazil (1937 = 100)										
a. Quantum of exports	54	57.5	63.9	56.9	79.4	67.6	67	57	74.3	68

Table 3.2 *(contd.)*

	1911	1912	1913	1914	1915	1916	1917	1918	1919	1920
b. Quantum of imports			145.7	75.5	47.2	51.2	43	44	61.2	82.8
c. Export prices			30	26	25	33	34	39	58	50
d. Import prices			13	14	23	30	37	42	41	48
e. Terms of trade (c/d)			231	186	109	110	92	93	141	104
f. Capacity to import (a × e)			148	106	87	74	62	53	105	71
Chile (1937 = 100)										
a. Quantum of exports	56.4	58.3	62	47	51.7	66.7	71.4	71.4	34.8	67.7
b. Quantum of imports	158.2	165.7	165.1	131.5	79.3	110.1	135.3	132.8	104.8	94.2
c. Export prices	215.9	223.9	217.7	216.8	215.5	261.9	339.6	275.3	308.6	395.8
d. Import prices	169.2	155.1	154.4	159	149.4	155.4	194.1	229.4	285.2	356.6
e. Terms of trade (c/d)	127.6	144.4	141	136.4	144.2	168.5	175	120	108.2	111
f. Capacity to import (a × e)	72	84.2	87.4	64.1	74.6	112.4	125	85.7	37.6	75.1
Peru (1900 = 100)										
a. Quantum of exports	238	246	261.3	242.3	300.7	367.2	313.9	307.3	388.3	291.2
b. Quantum of imports										
c. Export prices	80.7	93.7	87.7	100.5	129.4	126.1	167.9	180.8	198.2	349.1
d. Import prices	113.7	119.3	121.1	121.1	124.1	153.1	210.3	253.4	296.1	337.9
e. Terms of trade (c/d)	71	78.6	72.4	83	104.3	82.4	79.8	71.3	66.9	103.3
f. Capacity to import (a × e)	169	193.4	189.2	201.1	313.6	302.6	250.5	219.1	259.8	300.8

Sources: ECLA, *Economic Survey of Latin America,1949* (New York, 1951), pp. 98, 211, 271; Peru: Shane Hunt, *Price and Quantum Estimates of Peruvian Exports,* 1830–1962 (Princeton, 1973), p. 28. (Note: The base year has been altered.) (Price data for Peru provided by Rosemary Thorp from an unpublished working paper.)

economic independence enjoyed by Latin American countries. At the same time, the demand for most exports greatly increased. Among other thing, this led to the Latin American economies being subjected to a greater degree of open and direct external economic coercion than ever before as the Allied governments sought to monopolize supplies, keep down prices, and with an eye to the postwar situation, destroy the substantial base of economic power established by Germany in Latin America before 1914. This process was to demonstrate that while all countries were interdependent, some were clearly more dependent than others.

Despite coercion, export earnings recovered in all countries by 1915 (Table 3.1). The extent of the recovery varied considerably in this year and during the remainder of the war, Chile and Peru doing relatively better than either Brazil or Argentina. Improvement came about for the most part because of higher export prices, not an increased quantum of exports (Table 3.2). The failure to improve output substantially had much to do with the scarcity of shipping, the inability to get needed machinery and raw material imports, and the vagaries of nature. It is also interesting to note that the changing priorities of Allied demand contributed to there being a shift in the composition of exports in each country (Table 3.3). These changes had some temporary impact, but of far greater significance was the fact that because of high prices, export production became increasingly attractive for both local and foreign capital so tending to reinforce the region's existing economic pattern of primary export-based capitalist development. This is turn calls into question Frank's argument that the war brought real isolation or provided the opportunity for a substantive change in economic direction.

The value of imports, which had been slashed in 1914, began to improve from 1916 onwards, except in Brazil where this happened in 1915. The extent of the recovery varied greatly, and can only be explained by a closer examination of each country's experience. In all cases the increase in value was due entirely to higher prices, for nowhere, except possibly in Peru,[5] did the physical amount of imports reach prewar levels before 1920. This was despite the fact that in all countries except Brazil local exchange was at a premium throughout most of the period, which would have tended to lower import prices. Furthermore, although all imports were hit, it was capital goods, fuels, and raw materials which were most critically affected. Efforts to modernize and expand both industry and export production were thereby made more difficult. *The South American Journal*

Table 3.3 *Structure of exports before and during the First World War*

Argentina	
1910–1914	Wheat 19.4% Maize 17.9% Linseed 10.2% Hides 10.2% Wool 12.9% Frozen beef 7.6%
1915–1918	Wheat 12.9% Maize 9.6% Linseed 5.4% Hides 9.0% Wool 12.9% Frozen beef 15.3% Tinned meat 5.9%
Brazil	
1908–1912	Coffee 54.2% Rubber 27.9%
1915–1920	Coffee 47.4% Rubber 8.8% Hides and Skins 7.7% Sugar 4.5%
Chile	
1910–1913	Nitrates and Iodine 86% Copper 8%
1915–1920	Nitrates and Iodine 74.6% Copper 17.3%
Peru	
1910–1913	Sugar 17.5% Cotton 13.8% Copper 20.5% Rubber 12.3% Petroleum 6.3%
1915–1920	Sugar 27.6% Cotton 18.3% Copper 26.3% Petroleum 7.5% Wool 7%

Sources: Argentina: Calculated from E. Tornquist & Co. Ltd., *The Economic Development of the Argentine Republic in the Last Fifty Years,* (Buenos Aires, 1919); Brazil: *O Brasil em números;* Chile: McQueen, *Chilean Public Finance;* Peru: *Extracto estadístico 1926.*

commented[6] that although trade balances in Latin America were extremely healthy, the inability to obtain needed imports was significantly retarding the region's "progress," "... big commercial surpluses are not an unmixed blessing. Real value can only be returned by the intrinsic value of commodities, and only when this is again possible will the solid prosperity of South America be again underway." It was the "success" of exports and the decline in imports which distinguished the external shock delivered by the First World War from that of the 1930s, when both imports and exports experienced a catastrophic collapse. Also, the resulting exceptionally strong balance of trade position tended to offset pressure on the balance of payments created by the ending of the inflow of foreign capital.

Bearing in mind that the figures in Table 3.2 must be treated with some caution (there is no indication of how all except the Peruvian data were constructed), the relationship between the movement in export and import prices shows no clear overall trend. It would seem, however, that there was something of a general decline in the terms of trade in the last years of the war. There was also no discernible trend in the capacity to import, with considerable falls in Brazil and Argentina, but with Chile showing a sharp increase in 1916 and 1917. In Peru there was improvement until 1915, and despite a subsequent decline wartime levels remained significantly higher than before 1914. Nonetheless, where there was a decline in the terms of trade this indicates a transfer of income abroad. The question of who in Latin America bore the burden of this loss can only be understood by looking at the course of the class struggle in each country. Because of their particularly weak position, largely due to high levels of unemployment, workers' real and money wages were forced down in the early war years. Although later wages began to be pushed up, they continued to lag behind price rises. Even in those cases where the terms of trade moved in a favorable direction, because both import and export prices were rising, workers were liable to suffer. They did not have the power to demand a share in their employers' higher export earnings, were forced to pay more for locally produced, and frequently exportable, foodstuffs, and imports were also dearer. These conditions were a major part of the background to the intensification of labor unrest from about 1917.[7]

Another important change which affected all the countries during the war, and was to have the most profound long-term consequences, was the greater role assumed by the United States as a market, a supplier of imports and as an investor. This was achieved to some degree at the expense of the British, but mainly it was German trade that suffered. The US had been steadily extending its economic influence in the southern Latin American republics before the war, and by 1914 was already Peru's major trading partner, as well as Brazil's most important market. Furthermore, US firms controlled a very large part of the Argentine meat-packing industry and virtually dominated petroleum in Peru and copper, both there and in Chile.[8] The war presented an excellent opportunity for the US to improve its position. In his annual message to Congress in December 1914, Woodrow Wilson said it was not only an opportunity but a *duty* for the United

States to move more forcibly into Latin American markets.[9] William Gibbs McAdoo, Secretary of the Treasury, wrote[10] "With the coming of the World War (the) entire structure of commerce (in South America) went to pieces. The South Americans were like the customers of a store that had burned down; they were looking for a place to spend their money. The prospect of attaching a considerable part of their trade to the United States seemed promising." The emergence of the US as the most powerful foreign power in Latin America marked the beginning of a new phase in the external capitalist domination of the region which saw British merchant capital gradually being ousted by the more dynamic US industrial capital. This was to mean greater direct economic control from abroad and a significantly more pervasive political influence in Latin American affairs.

In the following sections the general changes outlined above will be considered in greater detail by looking at the export and import trade of each country during the war years. The main concern is to assess the course of foreign trade during the war and what it reveals about the strengths and weaknesses of prewar capitalist growth, which featured trade as its primary driving force. Secondly, attention will be given to the extent and impact of Allied interference and coercion. Finally, major new directions for trade will be assessed, especially the greater importance of the US as a market, supplier of imports, and direct investor in export production. Once again, it is essential to stress that while there were certain experiences common to all the countries, this was most apparent in the first few months of the conflict. Once the initial chaos created by the outbreak of war had been overcome, differences in the nature of economic and socio-political structures and of external demands and constraints began to reassert themselves.

Argentina

I

Argentina, in the midst of a severe recession in August 1914, was further battered by the impact of the war. Nonetheless, some observers looking at the goods she exported, were optimistic about prospects for recovery. Wheat and meat, the country's two most important products, promised to be vital for the warring countries, and rising prices were expected. Export values did fall sharply in 1914, but by the following year there had been a substantial recovery. 1916 saw a slight decline, although the level of earnings remained near the prewar high and with greatly reduced imports, the balance of trade was very healthy. Export values rose from 1917 and did not fall again until the worldwide postwar collapse of 1920–21. One measure of the apparent strength of the Argentine economy was the movement of exchange. Before the end of 1914 the peso was above par and remained at a premium throughout most of the war.[11] Despite this and both favorable and strong trade and payments balances, which help account for the exchange position, the Argentine economy did not do all that well during the war. The volume of exports did not surpass the 1913 figure until 1919, and then only slightly. Furthermore, the years 1913–17 saw real GDP (at 1950 prices) fall by almost 20%, and although there was improvement during the next two years,[12] in the period 1915–19 GDP averaged only 96% of the previous quinquennium and 75% of the following one.[13] Why, with her commodities in such great demand, and foreign trade averaging about 25% of GDP (1915–24)[14] did Argentina's economy not flourish more during the war?

Writing in June 1918, William Robertson, the US Consul General observed that,[15] "...there has been no serious effort made to increase the cultivation of foodstuffs, the raising of cattle, or the number and variety of its industries. With the enormous advance in the prices for exports, and in spite of the even greater advance in the costs of imports, the people and the government here have been content to leave the present well enough alone, and let the future look after itself." Was he correct? With respect to exports, a look at the quantum figures seems to support his contention. Between the periods 1911–13 and 1915–18 the export quantum fell on average by 7.5%, while prices rose by 52%. At least part of this decline, as well as the even sharper fall in the volume of imports, can be attributed to extreme scarcity and high cost of shipping. The problem for neutrals became increasingly serious as the war progressed and Allied control of shipping was steadily made more comprehensive.[16] For example, in 1913, 6.7 million tons of shipping cleared the port of Buenos Aires. This had been cut to only 2.16 million tons by 1917.[17] All trade was affected by this massive fall in shipping, but some exports were hit harder than others. The decline of agricultural exports was most marked, especially in 1914 and 1917, years of extremely poor harvests (Table 3.4). The export of livestock products was generally more buoyant, with frozen and canned meat doing particularly well because of wartime demands (Table 3.3). To understand these changes it is necessary to look in more detail at the performance of the different export groups.

Table 3.4 *Agricultural production and export of wheat, maize, and linseed 1911–1920*

	1911	1912	1913	1914	1915	1916	1917	1918	1919	1920
Wheat										
Area planted (000 HA)	6,253	6,897	6,918	6,574	6,261	6,645	6,511	7,234	6,870	7,045
Production (000 MT)	3,973	4,523	5,100	2,850	4,604	4,600	2,289	6,391	4,904	5,905
Export (000 MT)	2,286	2,629	2,812	980	2,511	2,294	935	3,228	4,718	5,265
Average Price (BA pesos per 100 kilos)				9.65	12.0	9.8	16.2	11.75	18.5	27.0
Maize										
Area planted (000 HA)	3,215	3,422	3,830	4,152	4,203	4,018	2,630	3,527	3,340	3,312
Production (000 MT)	703	7,515	4,995	6,684	8,260	4,093	1,495	4,335	5,696	6,571
Export (000 MT)	125	4,835	4,807	3,542	4,330	2,873	893	665	2,485	4,474
Average Price (BA pesos per 100 kilo)				5.75	4.75	4.95	9.8	6.5	11.0	8.9
Linseed										
Area Planted (000 HA)	1,504	1,630	1,900	1,834	1,723	1,619	1,298	1,309	1,384	1,766
Production (000 MT)	595	572	1,130	938	1,144	895	102	498	782	1,267
Export (000 MT)	415	515	1,017	842	981	639	141	391	855	1,050
Average Price (BA pesos per 100 Kilos)				14.6	10.7	14.0	21.8	25.6	24.7	—

Sources: Area planted and Production: Díaz Alejandro, *Essays,* pp. 436, 440. Exports and 1914 prices for August: Di Tella and Zymelman, *Las etapas* pp. 281, 301, 300–1. Other prices: Gravil, "Anglo-Argentine," pp. 77–8.

II

In the period 1910–14 Argentina's three main agricultural exports accounted for about 43.5% of foreign earnings. This proportion declined to 27.9% in the next four years. During the war the quantity exported of the three principal commodities either fell or showed no tendency to rise, with wheat sales alone improving strongly from 1918. But it was only in 1914 and 1917, years when drought and locusts led to severe harvest failures, that there was a substantial drop in output. In the latter year the disaster was on an almost Biblical scale. The drought, one of the worst known, lasted from April to December 1916, the winter was extraordinarily severe with repeated frosts and much of what was left of the crops was finished off by swarms of ravenous locusts. If this was not enough, there were also outbreaks of cattle disease, and the sugar crop in Tucumán failed. The provinces of Córdoba, Entre Ríos and Santa Fé were particularly hard hit.[18] Of the three main grain crops, linseed acreage was cut back most markedly. By 1918 the area in flax was but 69% of the 1913 total, while for maize and wheat the figures were 92% and 110% respectively. The main reason for these declines, as well as the fall in maize exports, was that linseed oil was used as a base for paints and maize as animal feed. They were in demand, as witnessed by the rise in prices, but because they were not essential foodstuffs the Allies considered them of only secondary importance. The necessary shipping space was not, therefore, made available and despite high world prices large surpluses became a serious problem in Argentina.[19] The generally rather indifferent export performance of wheat, seems to have been to do with the need to insure domestic supplies in the years of poor harvests, the lack of shipping and Allied intervention in the market. This latter factor, which has been studied in detail by Gravil,[20] deserves close examination as it offers one of the clearest examples of the how direct economic coercion was applied to Latin America during the war.

Until 1917 Allied concern over the Argentine grain market was less over securing needed supplies for themselves than with making sure the Germans did not receive any grain from the River Plate. This fear was well-founded because before the war German merchant houses directly and indirectly controlled about 60% of the country's grain trade, and in 1915 sales of maize to Northern European neutrals had risen suspiciously. It was clear that this was nothing but a roundabout route into Germany.[21] Nonetheless, because there were no pressing shortages and Empire producers were being given preference there was little effective control exercised over Argentine grain exports by the British until the imposition of the blacklist in March 1916. When the blacklist was finally imposed it seems to have had at least as much to do with the long-term purpose of displacing German competition as with the immediate prosecution of the war. For example, on the use of the blacklist a British official noted,[22] "It is further hoped the way may be opened for the extension of British commerce and influence, both now and after the war, through the temporary or complete elimination of enemy competitors." The United States consul in Buenos Aires arrived at a similar conclusion. The British he said were using the blacklist "in a ruthless fashion" in order to dominate South American commerce in the postwar period.[23]

Did this affect cereal prices in Argentina? There was a clear feeling in Argentine that it did, particularly as the trading restrictions hit the German merchant houses responsible for the majority of grain sales. *La Prensa* commented that the blacklist created a monopoly which "... assumes the characteristics of a veritable extortion when combined with the control of shipping."[24] The Argentine government also suspected that it did because the imposition of the blacklist more or less coincided with a substantial fall in grain prices during the first half of 1916. A special committee was set up to investigate. They found, however, that the lower prices were "... perfectly natural phenomena, free from any sinister machinations on the part of the Allies or their enemies, or anyone else trying to bring down the value of Argentine produce."[25] While there was not at this stage a concerted policy aimed at holding down prices, as there was soon to be, the general shortage of cargo space and the Allied policy of giving preference to certain commodities obviously influenced the level of prices.

In mid-1916 efforts were made to arrange an Anglo-Argentine grain deal, but this failed when in October Yrigoyen, who was something of an economic nationalist, came to power and insisted on more favorable terms. While a world surplus of wheat late in this year reduced the pressure on the British to control Argentine supplies, there were fears of renewed shortages, and in October the Royal Commission on Wheat Supplies was formed. This formalized grain and flour purchasing and distribution, which up to this point had been centrally directed but carried out using private companies. Beveridge writes[26] that no other foodstuff was so tightly controlled during the war. Besides centralized buying for the Allies, which offered obvious leverage in the world grain market, shipping came to be more rigorously controlled at about the same time. But the Argentine harvest was a disaster in 1917, output dropped by 50% and despite substantially higher prices, the President, in order to protect local consumption, imposed an embargo on new wheat exports and limited outstanding orders to 40% in March.[27] Permission to export wheat or flour was given from time to time, but the decree was not rescinded until the following February. Gravil suggests that this move was essentially a counter to the extension of Allied control in the market. Although this may have been a factor, the Radicals' concern to maintain the support of the urban middle class and not to exacerbate working-class unrest[28] by allowing the rise in the cost of living to get completely out of hand was probably more important. As a result of this policy, pressure on the Argentine to sell wheat was applied by both the British and US governments. Threats were made not to renew loans, to cut off coal, and restrict shipping.

Fears of a wheat shortage finally pushed the Allies into serious negotiations with Argentina over grain supplies. These began in November 1917, the French and British being the principal parties, with the US taking an important but informal role.[29] The bargaining was tough, and at one point, frustrated by Argentine demands the following note was sent,[30] "If the Argentina government do not accept this proposal, a statement will be issued to the Argentine public describing these negotiations and stating that as a consequence of their failure it will be necessary for the Allies to cut down their purchases of Argentine produce and to divert their tonnage, coal supplies and general trade elsewhere." The effect of this threat is unclear, but agreement was eventually reached and the so-called Loan Convention was signed the following January. It provided for the purchase of 2.5 million tons of cereals during the year and stipulated minimum and maximum prices. The deal was to be financed by an up to 200,000,000 gold peso credit from the Argentine government. This helped to solve simultaneously both the Allies' exchange and grain difficulties. While it is entirely reasonable to conclude, as Gravil does that this was essentially "... an agreement in which an underdeveloped country loaned £40,000,000 to two advanced countries in order to continue selling its grain after Allied policy had eliminated most of its other customers,"[31] it also offered some benefits to the Argentines. For a country dependent on her exports, the peso's rapid appreciation was causing problems, particularly for exporters, whose local currency income was being reduced. Because of this and other reasons by helping to stabilize exchange the agreement, at least from the point of view of exporters, had much to recommend it.[32] Furthermore, by a separate "informal understanding" with the United States, which the Argentines considered an essential part of the arrangement, it was agreed "as far as possible" to supply ships as well as coal "for the actual requirements of the Argentine people."[33] According to the Argentine Minister of Foreign Affairs, in a conversation reported by Frederic Stimson, the US Ambassador, the desire to obtain coal was the main reason for Argentina's interest in the contract.[34] The shortage of coal was one of the most serious problems facing the Argentine economy during the war years.

The course of the negotiations show the immense pressure put on Argentina by the Allied countries, but more damaging coercion was applied subsequently when in order to keep prices at a "reasonable level" neutral buyers in the Argentine market were "persuaded" to make their purchases through the Inter-Allied Wheat Executive.[35] Persuasion also consisted of putting pressure on banks not to finance sales to neutrals, the threat of withholding bunker coal and, at one point, even the censoring of cables was considered.[36] When in June 1918 the Mexicans tried to purchase a large quantity of grain in Rosario, the deal was blocked by the British Ambassador, who told the potential agent he would put every possible obstacle in the way of the sale.[37] Although it is, of course, impossible to judge how far Allied actions held down prices, especially as there was a bumper harvest in 1918, the effective stifling of competition in this market could not have helped but exert downward pressure on prices. Nonetheless, as important as this may have been, it only had any real impact during the last year of the war. Over the entire war period agriculture here was probably more seriously hurt by the two harvest failures, the high price of essential imports, and the chronic shortage of cargo space, although these last two factors can be attributed more or less directly to exigencies of Allied demands.

III

Argentina's other major group of exports, livestock products, did much better during the war, essentially because while there were many sources of cereals which could be tapped, as far as meat was concerned the Allies' options were much more limited. Furthermore, Britain was heavily dependent on meat imports from the River Plate. In the prewar years over 40% of domestic consumption was supplied from abroad, 80% of the beef coming from Argentina and Uruguay.[38] At the same time Britain had been virtually Argentina's only market, in 1913 taking 96.5% of the latter's livestock exports as against only 37.1% of grain.[39] The meat-packing industry was dominated by US firms, which in 1913 accounted for almost 60% of meat exports (British firms 31.3%, Argentine 9.8%). However, as Hanson comments: "The British monopoly of insulated tonnage was one great weapon that could be found to bring the American packers into line." During the war this weapon was used to the full. The Board of Trade moved

Table 3.5 *Exports and prices of Argentine meat 1912–1920*

	(000 metric tons)								
	1912	1913	1914	1915	1916	1917	1918	1919	1920
Frozen beef	317.6	332.1	328.3	351.0	411.6	355.8	567	482	454
Frozen mutton	70.2	45.9	58.7	35.0	51.3	39.8			
Chilled beef	25.3	34.2	40.7	11.7	16.2	39.0	1.0	2.0	51
Canned meat	17.7	12.6	13.1	31.9	44.6	100.8	193.0	126.0	15
Total	430.8	424.8	440.8	429.6	523.7	535.4	761	610	520
Average price Cross-breed cattle BA (pesos m/n)	125	156	174	181	190	173	195	224	
Livestock Export value (million gold pesos)	209.4	200.8	198.7	234.9	295.6	376.0	500.2	548.7	312.6
Percentage of total export	41.7%	38.7%	49.3%	40.3%	51.6%	68.3%	62.5%	53.2%	29.9%

Sources: Smith and Collins, *Argentina*, pp. 42, 88; Hanson, *Argentine Meat*, pp. 200, 204, 212; Di Tella and Zymelman, *Las etapas*, p. 335; Argentina, Dir. Gen. de Estadística de la Nación, *Análisis del comercio exterior argentino en los años 1910 a 1922* (Buenos Aires, 1923, p. 116.)

quickly to regulate prices once the war had begun and in 1915 refrigerated shipping was requisitioned by an Order in Council. Although the intensification of submarine activity in 1917 affected deliveries, by and large the meat trade was not hit by the wartime shortage of shipping as was grain.[40]

It was soon realized in Britain that securing a reliable meat supply for the army was of vital importance, and in late August 1914 a contract was made by the British government (through intermediaries because of Argentine neutrality) for monthly meat deliveries of 15,000 tons. Of this 80% was destined for the army, while 20% could be disposed of by the packers in the civilian market in Britain. Demand was further centralized when in January 1915 the French agreed to buy through the British. The following May, a new contract increased the quantity to 25,000 tons per month, and a year later an agreement, which was to run until ninety days after the war's end, was entered into between the packers and the Board of Trade for 50,000 tons. Gravil argues that through these contracts and the manipulation of packing house shares of the trade the British government purposely discriminated against the one large Argentine firm, Sansinena. Because of this, by the end of the war the position of British packing houses, particularly Vestey Brothers, had greatly improved at the expense of the Argentine company, whose share of exports had been more than halved between 1913 and 1918.[41] However, it was the North American companies, Swift, Armour, Morris, and Wilson which continued to dominate the industry, in the latter year accounting for 57% of meat exports.

Despite British actions, it is clear that the meat-packing firms made extremely high profits during the war. For example, Swift's Argentine operation paid yearly dividends of 12%, 15%, 15% and 37.5% between 1914 and 1917, and similar levels were achieved by other companies.[42] But what of the Argentine cattlemen? Hanson argues that they also profited because of the increased demand, but there are a number of reasons, many given by Hanson himself, for concluding that they did not do as well as might be expected given the heavy demand for beef. Prices did not rise all that much and there was an important shift in demand away from the more carefully bred, quality fat stock needed for chilled meat to leaner, lower grade cattle suitable for freezing. This meant that many breeders who had lavished time and money on improving their herds were not rewarded for their efforts during the war, but had to watch while those raising inferior animals reaped the higher prices. The *invernadores*, who fattened cattle for the chilled meat market, were also particularly badly affected. Joaquín S. de Anchorena, one of the country's wealthiest landowners and president of the Sociedad Rural Argentina, commented that the ones to profit most from the war were, "The *estancieros* of Corrientes, some in Entre Ríos, others in the north of Santa Fé, in general all those that have inferior estates." He further argued that the packers had made such high profits because their contracts were made assuming they were buying the better quality cattle, whereas because canned and frozen meat was demanded they were able to get by using the leaner and relatively cheaper *criollo* animals.[43] As exports of chilled meat became the leading product after 1919, the special character of wartime demand can be seen as having a less than positive impact on the sector's long-term development.

By 1917 many cattlemen were getting angry about the extreme disparity between their profits and those of the packers. In the following year this discontent led to demands that the foreign packing companies be expropriated.[44] Partly in response to this, but also to high domestic meat prices, a commission was established by the Cámara de Diputados in 1919 to investigate the possible operation of a trust in the meat industry as well as other sectors of food production. The limited amount of evidence taken by the commission qualifies its findings, but these suggest that while cattlemen were unhappy there was no formal buying trust in operation among the packers.[45] Nonetheless, as the US Consul perceptively observed, because the Allies had total control of refrigerated shipping, "Thus the Argentine cattle breeder will not be able to secure any extraordinary benefits from the situation caused by the European war."[46]

Gravil is correct in arguing that the scope of foreign economic coercion was unprecedented during the war.[47] But to what extent can the slow growth of output and exports be blamed on Allied interference? There is no way of providing a satisfactory answer to this question because of the many factors which determined prices and the level of output. Without at least some data on costs and profits the task is made even more difficult. It has been argued that for farmers the two major harvest failures were probably of greater overall importance in accounting for their indifferent supply response during the war. The blacklist, controls on shipping, and, latterly, more direct Allied intervention in the market also hurt the farmers, but more research would be needed to establish to what degree and whether this played any part in accounting for lower levels of investment. On the face of it the cattlemen seem to have been more clearly affected by the British monopoly of refrigerated shipping and the early establishment of centralized contract buying. But they were at one remove from the final market, and since the packers made very high profits, if the producers did not do all that well it is, as suggested above, to their relationship with the packing firms that we must look.

What has been argued should not be taken to suggest that the *estancieros* did not make money during the war. For example, Allied demand did push up prices enough to contribute, along with other price rises, to a substantial drop in Argentine meat consumption. Alejandro Bunge, the country's foremost economic statistician, estimated that domestic meat prices rose about 15% between 1913 and 1918, while consumption in Buenos Aires fell from 124 kilos per person to 90 kilos over the same period.[48] In 1919 the local price reached its highest level, 45% up from 1914.[49] Gravil contends that in Argentina "...British policy caused a depression of internal grain prices and an inflation of internal meat prices..."[50]. However, it would seem that for Argentine consumers bread prices, at least up to 1918, were a more serious concern, as they rose by 32%.[51] If, as is usual, the demand for bread was relatively less elastic than that for meat, this might offer a partial explanation of why a seemingly moderate rise in meat prices should lead to such a large fall in consumption.

Table 3.6 *Bank deposits and advances in*
Argentina 1913–1919

	Discounts and advances	Deposits (000,000 paper pesos)
Dec. 1913	1,540.8	1,463.5
1914	1,195.6	1,242.0
1915	1,242.2	1,469.1
1916	1,317.0	1,657.1
1917	1,553.5	2,013.7
1918	1,884.8	2,843.6
1919	2,113.3	3,009.8

Source: E. Tornquist & Cia, *Business Conditions in Argentina*,
Report 147, 31 January 1920, p. 11.

In both the major Argentine export sectors (which together
accounted for about 95% of total earnings) Allied policy was used to
gain control of needed commodities, "moderate" price rises, and, in
the case of grain, to try to break the strong German position in the
trade. For Argentine producers this meant effectively a reduction in
the potential level of profit. Nevertheless, money was made by farmers
and ranchers. Prices of both livestock and agricultural goods rose
(Tables 3.4 and 3.5), and with wages kept down, profits no doubt
increased. There is a very general indication this was the case in that
the volume of bank deposits grew by about 105% during the war,
(Table 3.6) while discounts and advances increased by only 37%.[52]
Tulchin argues, albeit rather tentatively, that these wartime profits
were not invested in productive activity but were instead loaned
through the banks to the government, whose domestic borrowing
increased greatly during the war.[53] However, Hanson maintains that
from 1917–18 there was a rash of speculative investment in livestock
because of high prices and expectations of a greatly expanded postwar
market. Borrowing increased, breeding stock was improved, herds
built up and pastures extended.[54]

In the rural sector generally, investment continued during the war
and was far greater than in other areas of the economy. For example,
between 1915 and 1919 total investment (at 1950 prices) in Argentina
fell (compared to the period 1912–14) by an average of 66%, while for
the rural sector the drop was only 15%.[55] Díaz Alejandro shows that

between 1910–14 and 1915–19 there was a 14% increase in the index (1935–9 = 100) of physical capital stock in the *campo* and that imports of agricultural materials and equipment (at 1950 prices) rose by 60% over roughly the same period.[56] Too much weight should not be given to this data, for in the period 1913–18 total capital imports (in current gold pesos at official values) fell by 85.1%, while imports of agricultural machinery fell by 61.2%.[57] Because these figures were constructed using constant official values, they give a better idea of the change in the physical quantity of imports. Combined with evidence of static or falling crop acreage, the great reduction in the number of imported mowers, reapers, plows, threshing machines, etc. strongly suggest that while ranchers may have begun to invest more heavily from the last year of the war the rate of material development of the productive forces in agriculture was appreciably diminished in this period. Nonetheless, both farming and ranching seem to have been more attractive to investors than other sectors of the economy, presumably because of relatively high profits to be made. One important effect of this was to reinforce the existing pattern of primary export dependence.

What of the wider economic impact of the apparently varying fortunes of the different rural sectors? If, as it seems, livestock producers did relatively better than farmers this would have meant that the major gains went to the relatively smaller group in the countryside, for generally cattle and sheep were raised on fewer large estates, while farming was carried out on small and medium-sized holdings.[58] The effect on employment, and, therefore, on effective demand, would also have been less, fewer workers being employed on ranches. It is interesting to note that although at the beginning of the war it was feared that net migration from Argentina would create a labor shortage during the harvest season this did not happen. For example, in 1916 the US Consul in Rosario reported that workers were "abundant and cheap."[59] And in Buenos Aires it was chronic unemployment which emerged as the major difficulty throughout most of the war.

IV

For a country such as Argentina economic prosperity cannot be assessed simply in terms of the volume or value of exports. The crucial issue is what could be purchased with these exports for, as argued above, Latin American countries were, for various reasons, extremely import-dependent. On this score Argentina did not do very well during the war. Although the movement was uneven, the terms of trade were

Table 3.7 *Argentine imports by category 1913–1920*

| | (000,000 gold pesos (1906 official values)) | | | | | | | |
	1913	1914	1915	1916	1917	1918	1919	1920
Type of goods								
Consumption	166	116	86	106	102	86	104	128
Luxury	32	18	13	16	13	12	15	25
Fuel	43	36	45	25	16	13	25	33
Intermediate	72	37	49	43	36	38	58	65
Capital	109	65	34	27	17	16	30	49
Total	422	272	227	217	184	165	232	300

Source: *Análisis 1910–1922*, pp. 94–5.

Table 3.8 *Argentine capital goods imports by category 1913–1920*

| | (000,000 gold pesos (1906 official values)) | | | | | | | |
	1913	1914	1915	1916	1917	1918	1919	1920
Type of goods								
Railway	31	22	6	6	5	4	8	13
Electricity	9	6	3	3	2	2	3	4
Agriculture	10	4	4	5	2	4	6	7
Building	42	21	15	11	6	5	10	17
General Machinery	8	5	2	2	2	2	3	7
Iron and other metals	9	7	3	.7	.4	.3	.6	2
Total	109	65	33	27	17	16	30	49

Source: *Análisi 1910–1922*, pp. 96–7.

generally adverse and, more significantly, the capacity to import fell (Table 3.2). The real value (adjusted for price changes) of imports did not regain its 1913 level until 1918, but the volume fell steadily until 1919. Table 3.7 gives an excellent picture of the change in the quantity of imports as the prices used are those set officially by the 1906 Tariff. This shows clearly that by far the largest decline was that of capital goods. While by 1918 total imports had fallen to 40% of their 1913 level, for capital goods the figure was 14%. When this is broken down still further (Table 3.8) it can be seen that the two major losers were the railways and construction which suffered the worst percentage falls and also accounted for 70% of the total loss. Rail building was almost entirely dependent on foreign capital and its cessation during the war virtually ended the extension of the system. Between 1914 and 1918 only 762 miles of new track were laid down, an increase of about 3.5%.[60] To the extent that construction was of projects such as ports, drainage, municipal transport, water and power facilities, it too would have been badly hit by the interruption to the inflow of capital from abroad. In Buenos Aires building seems to have fallen considerably judging from the sharp decline in urban land sales, building permits, and mortgages.[61] This may have been due in part to the difficulty of obtaining imports but was probably more a reflection of the economic recession which was so pronounced from 1913 to 1917

While the decline in consumer goods imports created opportunities for local industry the massive decrease in machinery and intermediate goods imports made any effective industrial development extremely difficult.[62] A US report in 1918 claimed that there was a direct link between the scarcity of imports and a lower level of economic activity generally.[63] The import most widely and sorely missed was coal. Argentina had come to rely heavily on relatively cheap imported coal from Britain to operate her railways and ships, and generate gas, light, and power. The country was one of the world's largest coal importers, absorbing about half of all coal sold to Latin America.[64] There were coal deposits in the country, but they were not close to railways and their quality was uncertain. Wood and petroleum were used as substitutes, but both were expensive and the former was only one third as efficient as coal. Although oil production developed reasonably rapidly (60% per year 1913–18), because of the lack of positive government policy and adequate financing for the state oil fields in Comodoro Rivadavia domestic petroleum supplies did not grow fast enough to offset the coal shortage.[65] Despite the fact that the changeover from coal was not always easy to effect, by 1916 wood accounted for 70% of the fuel used by the railways, and two years later it was said that three quarters of the country's entire fuel needs were being met by wood. Towards the end of the war even maize was being burned in locomotives and power stations.[66] But none of this really solved the fuel crisis. Prices remained high, the government did relatively little to encourage the exploitation of coal or oil deposits, and throughout these years the entire country suffered from the effects.

Table 3.9 *Argentina's wartime fuel supply 1913–1919*

	1913	1914	1915	1916	1917	1918	1919
Coal							
Imports (000 metric tons)	4,046	3,242	2,544	1,885	708	822	1,000
Price per ton (gold pesos)	9.3	10.5	15.5	14.0	30	50	40
Oil							
Imports (000 cubic meters)	280	235	460	365	355	185	540
Local production (000 cubic meters)	21	44	82	138	192	215	211
Price per cm (paper pesos)	n.a.*	23.3	21.8	41.8	62.0	82.9	62.4
Wood							
Local production (000 metric tons)	1,205	2,452	1,866	2,765	2,853	n.a.	n.a.
Price per mt (paper pesos)	26.0	25.0	23.5	27.0	31.3	42.5	

Source: Solberg, *Oil and Nationalism*, p. 26. Coal prices from 1914 and 1915 from War Trade Board, 'The Coal situation.'
*Not available.

V

Besides the extreme movements in the volume and value of imports and exports, there was also an important shift during the war in Argentina's markets and sources of supply. Germany, which had been the country's second most important trading partner was completely displaced and with Europe unable to provide the goods demanded the United States became the principal supplier to the Argentine market. This included almost the entire range of imports from coal to automobiles, cotton cloth to cement.[67] The United States also took more of Argentina's exports, but because of the similarity in the two countries' rural output the increase here was relatively modest. Britain, with her strong demand for grain and especially meat, remained the single most important export market. The growth of US economic interest was important. It not only involved increased trade, but the estalishment of banks, increased investment and a growing number of US firms, already so evident in meat-packing, being set up in Argentina. This was the beginning of a new phase of external domination which was to see a change in the main foreign protagonist and, in many respects, the character and consequences of that domination. However, in Argentina this was to be a much more

Table 3.10 *Argentine trade with major trading partners 1913–1920*

				(percentage shares)				
	1913	1914	1915	1916	1917	1918	1919	1920
US								
Imports	14.7	13.4	19.2	29.2	36.3	33.8	35.5	33.2
Exports	4.7	12.3	13.0	20.3	29.3	20.6	18.3	14.8
UK								
Imports	31.1	34.0	35.6	28.2	21.8	25.0	23.5	23.4
Exports	24.9	29.3	24.4	29.4	29.2	38.2	28.5	26.8
Germany								
Imports	16.9	14.8	4.5	.2	.1	—	—	4.8
Exports	12.0	8.8	—	—	—	—	—	2.3
France								
Imports	9.0	8.2	5.6	6.9	5.9	5.2	3.9	5.9
Exports	7.8	5.7	8.1	11.9	13.2	14.1	11.1	6.8
Italy								
Imports	8.3	9.2	9.8	9.8	6.9	3.4	3.3	4.4
Exports	4.1	2.4	9.8	5.0	5.3	5.0	4.0	3.3
Brazil								
Imports	2.2	3.5	4.8	3.6	10.0	9.9	7.2	5.4
Exports	5.0	4.5	3.9	4.5	4.1	4.2	3.6	2.1
Total								
Imports	82.2	83.1	79.5	77.9	81.0	77.3	73.4	77.1
Exports	58.5	63.0	59.2	71.1	81.1	82.1	65.9	56.1

Sources: Smith and Collins, *Argentina,* pp. 98–100, *Análisis,* pp. 123–36.

protracted process than elsewhere in Latin America, for British economic links with the River Plate were stronger and more deep-seated than in any other part of the region.

VI

It is necessary to return now to the question posed at the beginning of this section. Why did the Argentine economy not do better during the war? Direct, strong and persistent Allied intervention, while clearly coercive, explains relatively little of Argentina's seemingly poor economic performance. The only area where Allied policy did have a major influence was on shipping. Scarce and expensive ocean transport created difficulties for both importers and exporters throughout the period. In the case of both wheat and meat exports there were other factors which were more significant, particularly bad harvests and the change in demand for meat which allowed the packers to switch to the use of cheaper cattle. The shortage of many key imports, especially coal, also had a powerful negative influence. What does all this tell us about the nature of the Argentine economy? Does it suggest, as Gravil argues,[68] that rather than Frankian dependency creating underdevelopment "...Argentina appears similar to cases of staple development, economic growth diffused through international trade and investment, which under peacetime conditions could not be so thoroughly manipulated against the republic."? This is to define "development" far too narrowly, to ignore the fact that the economic and political structures created in the process of growth can act as obstacles to broader, more self-sustaining, more integrative capitalist development. Of course Argentina "did better" when foreign capital was flowing in, when imports were available and export markets open, but the price paid for this was to reinforce a dangerously brittle politico-economic system which relied on the fertility of the pampas, and was heavily addicted to continued injections of capital, raw materials, and technology from abroad. When the latter were disrupted during the war the economy had few of its own independent structural resources to fall back upon. Besides the centrality of trade and the dependence of government revenues on import duties, transport, public utilities and important parts of both the commercial and financial sectors were controlled from Europe. It is hardly surprising that the economy could do little more than splutter during the war years. This is not a particularly impressive testament to the efficaciousness of prewar development, but rather an indication of its severe limitations.

Brazil

I

While Argentina's main exports were generally in heavy demand during the war, the two principal commodities produced by Brazil, coffee and rubber, were not. In spite of this, at first glance the latter's aggregate trade figures suggest that compared with Argentina it did not do all that badly during the war years. There was a sharp fall in the value of exports in 1914, but the following year witnessed a substantial

Table 3.11 *Brazilian exports and imports 1911–1919 in contos*

| | £ (000 *contos*) | | | (Million £) | | |
	Exports	Imports	Balance	Exports	Imports	Balance
1911	1,004	794	210	67	53	14
1912	1,120	951	169	75	64	11
1913	982	1,008	− 16	65	67	− 2
1914	756	562	194	47	35	12
1915	1,042	583	459	54	30	24
1916	1,137	811	326	56	40	16
1917	1,192	838	354	63	45	18
1918	1,137	989	148	61	53	8
1919	2,179	1,334	845	130	78	52

Source: Brazil, Ministry of Industry, Agriculture and Commerce, *Economical Notes on Brazil*, 2nd edn Rio, 1916, 4th edn Rio, 1921.

recovery and from then until the boom of 1919, the value of Brazilian exports remained fairly steady showing a slight tendency to rise. Furthermore, there was a balance of trade surplus throughout the period. There were, however, serious problems. Compared to the other countries export prices were extremely sluggish and the export quantum, after a brief resurgence in 1915, fell steadily until 1919. When the trade figures are expressed in pounds sterling the lackluster export performance is made more evident (Table 3.11). During this period the terms of trade were generally unfavorable, and the capacity to import also declined. These difficulties together with the government's need to issue a great quantity of inconvertible paper money during the war to cover revenue shortfalls and to prop up coffee led to the milréis being the only one of the four currencies to remain below par over the entire war period.[69]

Williams maintains, as did many other contemporaries, that despite all these apparent difficulties Brazil experienced something of an economic surge during the war years based on industrial development and the growth of new export sectors.[70] This more or less impressionistic view has been challenged recently by a number of scholars. Although there are no national income figures for Brazil before 1920, Peláez, using monetary data, has argued that during the war the Brazilian economy either regressed or at best stagnated.[71] On the other hand, Haddad's study of industrial production lends support to

Williams' thesis, suggesting that the war years saw significant progress.[72] In order to assess these views, and to understand exactly what happened to the Brazilian economy during the war the first task is to examine the performance of exports.

The health of the Brazilian economy at this time is generally equated with the performance of coffee exports as they accounted for 50% to 60% of foreign earnings in the prewar period. For the country as a whole this is a legitimate measure, but it does not reflect the quite distinct regional nature of Brazilian exports. Coffee was grown mainly in the eastern-central states of São Paulo, Minas Gerais, Rio de Janeiro and Espírito Santo. It is interesting that although the relative importance of coffee declined somewhat during the war (to 47.4% of exports), in the period 1917–20 this region, which contained 46% of the country's population, increased its share of total export earnings from 50% (1910–14) to 64%.[73] The temporary diversification of Brazilian exports during the war only led to a more marked regional concentration of export production in these "coffee states." The reasons for this as well as the performance of other important exports such as cotton, cocoa, meat and hides, sugar, tobacco, rubber, and a host of other goods crucial for prosperity in other parts of Brazil will be considered after detailing the mixed fortunes of coffee.

II

The market for coffee was restricted throughout much of the war mainly because it was not considered of strategic importance by Allied governments. Shipping was not, therefore, made readily available. The coasting trade carried by national ships remained fairly steady, but by 1917 the number of foreign ships calling at Brazilian ports had fallen by 60%, and total overseas tonnage had been even more severely reduced.[74] Not surprisingly, freight charges went up sharply. For example, before the war it cost about 1s1 1d per cwt to ship coffee between Santos and London. By 1916 this had risen to 9s9d.[75] Furthermore, the major German and Austro-Hungarian coffee markets (22% of exports) were cut off by the Allies. German merchants also moved more than 20% of Brazil's coffee, Theodor Wille & Co. being one of the two or three largest exporters. The blacklists made it virtually impossible for them to function, and this undoubtedly created problems for many planters.[76]

Notwithstanding the aforementioned difficulties, up until 1916–17 world consumption was maintained at a reasonably high level[77] as were Brazil's coffee sales, although prices continued to fall

Table 3.12 *Coffee. Brazilian exports and prices and imports 1911–1920*

	A Volume (1000 60 kg bags)	B Value (Cr1$000)	B/A Export price (1$000/bag)	New York price (cents/pound)
1911	11,258	606,529	54	13.41
1912	12,080	698,371	58	14.46
1913	13,268	611,690	46	10.91
1914	11,270	439,715	39	8.28
1915	17,061	620,490	36	7.53
1916	13,039	589,201	45	9.36
1917	10,606	440,258	42	9.27
1918	7,433	352,727	47	9.77
1919	12,963	1,226,463	95	
1920	11,525	860,958	75	

Sources: O Brasil em números, 87–88. Delfim Netto, "Foundations," p. 95.

(Table 3.12). For planters this fall was offset to an important degree by the 20% devaluation of the milréis between 1914 and 1916. In 1915 there was a surge in coffee exports, as Germany temporarily found a way to funnel its imports through Holland and the Scandinavian countries. Brazilian exports to Norway, Sweden and Denmark jumped from 173,000 bags in the months August to December 1913 to 1,795,000 bags over the same period in 1915.[78] The United States bought more coffee, and during the war its purchases increased from a little more than a third to about half of Brazilian sales. The French also took more coffee and even the British imports rose until 1917. It was in this year that coffee began to feel the full impact of the war. The Allied blockade was made more effective from 1916, the circuitous route to the Central Powers being effectively closed. As a direct consequence sales to Scandinavia dropped precipitately from 2,730,059 bags (July–February 1915–16) to only 77,285 bags (July–February 1916–17).[79] In 1917 the German U-boat campaign hit shipping, and between February and July the British prohibited all imports of coffee as well as other "Non-essential" goods such as cocoa, another major Brazilian export.[80] When the US entered the war, coffee was officially made a restricted import. By 1918, sales to the United States had fallen 32%.[81] To make things worse, in 1917, Brazilian exchange began to improve, reducing further the already falling milréis receipts of the growers. The crisis did not lift until the war ended and a combination of severe frost damage to the coffee crop and pent-up demand sent prices skyrocketing.

Because of its dominant share of world production (over 75%) Brazil was not without defenses against adverse changes in the coffee market. The first valorization in 1906, for all its problems, seems to have provided at least a short term solution for excess supply and falling prices.[82] Faced with what seemed a drastic contraction in the market and the prospect of an extremely large harvest (some forecasters predicted a 20 million bag season), planters, especially those in São Paulo, called in 1915 for a new valorization programme to maintain prices. The *Brazilian Review* argued that such a scheme was necessary not only to protect growers, but also to prop up exchange, reduce import costs and avoid the double burden on the government of reduced income and higher foreign payments.[83] The government, needing to provide for its own financial needs, issued 350,000 contos in August 1915, 150,000 of which was earmarked as a loan to the state of São Paulo to buy up surplus coffee. However, by the time all this had been arranged prices began to rise and the money was never used.[84]

Two years later coffee prices were again threatened. As shipping became harder to obtain world consumption fell by almost 25% or over 5 million bags. At the same time the 1917 harvest promised to be large, stocks in Brazil rose, it was feared that there would be a surplus of 4 million sacks, and the value of the milréis increased. Unable to find money abroad to finance valorization the government issued 150,000 contos which was loaned to São Paulo, 110,000 of this was used and 3.1 million sacks were eventually taken off the market.[85] But there seems to have been little urgency on the part of the state to purchase surplus coffee, only 1.48 million bags having been taken by December 1917.[86] Its buying may have moderated price declines, but it did not arrest them completely. Although a very gradual improvement began in November, it was not sustained and from the beginning of 1918 prices once again fell. By March the situation was desperate, stocks in the three major Brazilian ports at 6.8 million bags were more than 4 million greater than in the previous year, prices were extremely low, and it was, claimed: "Today, but for what the São Paulo Government buys – in such small driblets as to be of little assistance to the market – coffee is for all intents and purposes unsaleable!"[87] It was not until June that prices showed any substantial improvement and then at the end of the month the frost hit, destroying about half of trees in São Paulo and severely damaging another 30%. Prices advanced abruptly, but were moderated by the fact that because of the continued shortage of shipping, stocks in Brazil remained extremely high (9.2 million sacks in December 1918 compared with 4.8 million in 1917). It was not until the war ended in November that prices began to climb to high levels. In 1919, despite the damage caused by the frost, many planters did extremely well.

Even though coffee was not a strategic commodity Brazil was still subject to Allied pressure on her export trade. Ostensibly there were two main reasons for this: to deny supplies to the Central Powers and to conserve valuable cargo space. But there were other reasons as well, the most important of which was to cripple Germany's position in Brazil permanently. Shipping was obviously a problem for the British in 1917 and it was claimed that the country already had a four-year supply of coffee.[88] But, in December 1916, the British government asked Rothschilds to suggest to the São Paulo government, who would in turn suggest to the federal government, that a £2–£3,000,000 purchase of coffee would be made if the 43 German ships trapped in Brazilian ports were seized and turned over to the British.[89] This did not work. Brazil complained of the British restrictions, threatened to stop remittance of interest and would not turn over the ships, thirty of which were given to the French at the end of 1917 in return for a £2,000,000 contract for the purchase of coffee and an undertaking to use the ships to carry goods to and from Brazil.[90] Strong objections were also made to the blacklists and the British European blockade.[91] In 1918 the longer term objective of British policy became clear when an interdepartmental committee was set up to look into ways of improving Britain's position in postwar Brazil.[92] The object of the exercise was candidly summed up by one British official who commented, "... what we are after is not so much laying in stocks of this or that commodity for ourselves, but destroying German trade not only for the present but for the future. It is not coffee we are after but the country, Brazil. We want to take it away from Germany."[93] This policy could not help but create immense difficulties for Brazil as German firms occupied important positions in the country's commercial infrastructure, particularly in banking and the import and export trades.[94] By 1918 over 500 "enemy firms" in Brazil had been blacklisted.[95]

What was the impact of Allied restrictions on Brazil's coffee industry during these years? Once again, it is difficult to separate the many factors which determine price variations. In the case of Brazilian coffee the problem is complicated because of government intervention, the exceedingly long time it takes for supply to respond to price change, and the fact that there was a wide variation in yearly output. It seems clear that, whether to further their war aims or their postwar economic plans, as in the case of Argentina, the Allies had little compunction in trying to impose their political will by direct and indirect interference in Brazil's domestic and international economic affairs. For Britain this was a logical extension of its dominant role in the prewar economic relationship with these countries. For the United States it was a foretaste of what was to develop after 1920. However, despite the various pressure and limitations they placed on Brazil's economic sovereignty, it was not until 1917 and 1918 that planters began to feel seriously hard-pressed as a direct result of Allied policy. This seem to be borne out if we look at the profits earned in the coffee sector.

While the general movement in the trade and the extent of wartime restrictions are fairly clear, how did the planters fare during the war? Only a very tentative answer can be offered, based as it is mainly on extrapolating to the entire industry an adjusted profit figure based on the earnings of the second largest producer in the state of São Paulo, the Dumont Coffee Co. Ltd. In 1912 it had almost 4 million coffee trees,[96] and two years later it was reported that the firm cultivated 13,271 acres using 4,963 *colonos* (tenant farmers).[97] The main difference between this company and the many other coffee growers, besides its size and foreign ownership, was that it produced a particularly high quality coffee which was sold by the firm in London.[98] Profits, therefore, tended to be greater than for most ordinary *fazendeiros* who grew an average grade bean and had to work through a separate merchant house. The level of the company's profits (Table 3.13) was considerably lower between 1914 and 1917 (no detailed data were found for subsequent years) than in the immediate prewar years, but this was mainly because the prices in the 1911 and 1912 were so abnormally high. Looked at over the longer term, the profit per hundredweight during the war was not significantly different from what seems to have been the "normal" level. For example, between 1905 and 1910 profits averaged 12s per cwt, while in the years 1914 to 1917 the figure was 11s4d. Although in the latter period costs in Brazil were slightly reduced, both in real terms and because of movements in exchange, freight and insurance charges rose steeply and this rise was not offset by sufficiently higher prices. These

Table 3.13 *Production, costs and profits – Dumont Coffee Co. Ltd* *1901–1917*

Year ended (December)	Production (cwt)	Profits (£)	Cost/cwt (fob Santos)	Cost/cwt	Price/cwt average (cif London)	Profit/cwt
1907	87,965	59,830		32s8d	44s3d	11s7d
1908	119,965	76,356	13s4d	30s5½d	41s5¾d	11s¼d
1909	110,558	54,902	15s3d	33s2¾d	41s8½d	8s5¾d
1910	109,368	119,387	17s2d	36s5¾d	56s10½d	20s5¾d
1911	102,520	167,754	18s3d	38s4¼d	69s3½d	30s11¼d
1912	103,102	154,383	23s	44s	72s6d	28s6d
1913	86,489	53,234		46s2d	56s4d	10s2d
1914	84,413	54,535	22s8d	43s6½d	56s4d	12s9½d
1915	85,533	41,573		41s8½d	50s7d	8s10½d
1916	86,244	77,425	21s2¼d	42s8½d	60s	17s33½d
1917	106,671	41,753	21s2d	27s10d (Santos price)		6s8d

Source: WBR, 30 August 1907, pp. 886–7; 20 July 1909, pp. 738–9; 26 July 1910, pp. 707–8; 8 August 1911, pp. 800–1; 30 July 1912, pp. 887–8; 19 August 1913, pp. 866–9; 3 August 1915, pp. 377–8; 24 August 1915, pp. 420–3; 28 August 1917, pp. 176–8; 22 August 1918, pp. 1012–14.

prices fell in 1915 and again in 1917. In the latter year not only did prices fall and exchange rise, but because of the closure of the British market and a severe shortage of shipping the company was forced to sell all its coffee in Santos instead of disposing of it in Europe. This accounted for considerably lower profits in that year. Overall the company seems to have fared reasonably well, but its shareholders did not. Dumont had paid 15%, 20% and 3% dividend on its ordinary shares between 1911 and 1913, but except for a modest 4% payout in 1916 no dividends were paid during the war.

The only other company data to hand are for another British firm, the Agua Santa Coffee Co. Ltd, which while very much smaller than Dumont, with a production of only about 17,000 cwt per year, earned in 1916 and 1917 average profits of 15s4d per cwt and 5s10d per cwt respectively.[99] Thus, while Dumont's profits were probably higher than the great majority of more modest planters, they do seem to

Table 3.14 *Estimated profits for coffee producers 1909–1917*

	milréis	£
1909	67,405,873	4,217,348
1910	87,581,814	5,867,342
1911	154,231,280	10,262,245
1912	152,159,480	10,143,965
1913	59,788,587	3,974,248
1914	69,552,452	4,247,478
1915	85,979,619	4,461,338
1916	134,141,600	6,680,974
1917	39,360,184	2,083,322

(Calculated by multiplying total coffee exports by the average Dumont profit divided by two.)

reflect the general level of earnings in the industry and suggest that, despite all the difficulties, coffee producers did not do badly during the war until 1917 when they were hit successively by Allied policies and then a year later by the devastating frost. Taking Dumont's profits and halving them (which, given the Agua Santa figures, may be too harsh) to allow for higher cost producers and the fact that most *fazendeiros* had to sell their coffee through merchant houses, a very rough estimate can be made of planters' total earnings during the war (Table 3.14). This represents little more than an informed guess but, for what they are worth, the figures suggest that contrary to some accounts coffee-growers did not do too badly until 1917. In fact, while the extraordinary profit levels of 1911 and 1912 were not repeated, there was a steady improvement in fortunes from the low in 1913. Only at the very end of the war did things begin to go seriously wrong. Therefore, while coffee's grip on the economy was somewhat loosened during the war it was not broken, as reasonable profits and government support continued to encourage new plantings.

III

Rubber did not do as well as coffee during the war, but gathering in the Amazon was already in serious trouble before 1913. Prices had soared and then collapsed disastrously in 1910 (Table 3.15). The decline

Table 3.15 *Brazilian rubber. Production, world production, prices, export values and share of national export earnings 1910–1919*

Year	World Production (Metric tons)	Brazilian Production (Metric tons)	Earnings (contos)	Price per kilo (milréis)	Earnings (000 £)	Price per kilo (shillings)	Share of Exports (%)
1910	71,453	40,800	376,972	9$780	25,254	13s1d	40.1
1911	76,530	37,730	226,395	6$195	15,049	8s3d	22.6
1912	99,564	43,370	241,425	5$709	16,095	6s7d	21,6
1913	108,628	39,560	155,631	4$296	10,345	5s8d	16.0
1914	120,080	36,700	113,334	3$386	6,921	4s2d	15.1
1915	158,722	37,220	135,786	3$861	7,056	4s	13.0
1916	202,100	37,000	152,239	4$834	7,582	4s10d	13.4
1917	256,879	39,370	144,080	4$238	7,622	4s6d	12.1
1918	282,208	30,700	73,727	3$253	3,955	3s6d	6.5
1919	423,495	34,700	105,536	3$174	6,328	3s10d	4.8

Sources: Weinstein, *Rubber*, p. 218; *Economical Notes*, 2nd edn and 4th edn. Exchange rates from Villela and Suzigan, *Government Policy*, p. 352.

continued, with a brief respite in 1915–16, into the 1920s. The main factor accounting for this was the extraordinarily rapid increase in plantation production in Asia (from .3% of world output in 1908 to 60% in 1914 to 90% in 1919) which within a few years destroyed Brazil's and Africa's wild rubber trades, outstripped world demand, and led to a major price fall. There was little Brazilian producers could do in the face of this onslaught. Although they had been aware for some time of the potential threat of plantation rubber, when it finally became a reality it happened so suddenly that the impact was overwhelming, making any effective action impossible. It has been argued that while wild rubber was easily available and prices reasonable there was little pressure for fundamental change from the various sectors of the rubber trade. When combined with a lack of government interest or financial support for expensive plantation development such cultivation was never a viable option.[100] Furthermore, the most powerful sector in the industry, the merchants, would have been made redundant if plantations replaced rubber gathering.[101] The events of the war may have accelerated the industry's demise, but by 1914 it was already well on its way. Writing to *Wilemen's Brazilian Review* in August 1915, a correspondent from Manaus noted,[102] "On the Amazon, as elsewhere, the fittest will survive and sooner or later the Brazilian rubber industry (will?) be a thing of the past. Apart from the nonsense one hears about 'inferior quality,' I should say Brazil does not even now take Eastern competition seriously enough; people here mostly not only ignorant, but with no wish to learn."

During the war Brazil's rubber output was more or less maintained, but lower prices meant a fall in earnings (Table 3.15). There was some short-lived prosperity in 1916 as prices rose and exchange fell,[103] but over the entire period economic conditions continued to deteriorate. From late 1917 prices began to drop markedly and in January of the next year the Federal Government, through the Banco do Brasil, began to buy up stocks in a half-hearted attempt to valorize rubber, a hopeless proposition given Brazil's greatly reduced share of the world market.[104] This did nothing to recoup the situation and 1918 became a nightmare for those in the rubber trade. Most of the problems stemmed from overproduction, but conditions were made worse by United States restrictions on imports introduced in April. By July, stocks of rubber in Belém and Manaus had reached an all-time high of over 10,000 tons.[105] While Allied actions did affect rubber exports, especially the blacklisting of German firms, which had shipped over 60% before 1914,[106] compared to the longer-term malaise which affected the industry, the overall impact of these policies must be considered as a relatively minor factor.

In Belém bankruptcies among merchant houses dealing in rubber (*aviadores*) reached epidemic proportions from 1911 and continued throughout the war years.[107] However, amid all the economic gloom in the state of Pará, there were a few flickers of light. From about 1910 agricultural production had picked up significantly and between 1914 and 1917–18 deliveries of beans, corn, rice, manioc flour, tobacco and cotton from the interior of the state to Belém all increased dramatically.[108] The greater export of these commodities offset, but could not reverse, the decline in export earnings from the state.[109] Amazonas, the second most important rubber-producing state, suffered more from the collapse, having seen no appreciable increase in agricultural production. In other states an increase in the export of goods listed above together with sugar, chilled meat, hides, manganese ore, and cocoa blunted the edge of export declines or led to a degree of export prosperity.

IV

The states which seem to have done particularly well with respect to export earnings were Bahia, Pernambuco, Rio de Janeiro (which includes some exports from Minas Gerais) and Rio Grande do Sul.[110]

In Bahia it was mainly cocoa which provided the basis for wartime prosperity, although the state also exported most of the country's tobacco as well as a number of other commodities such as sugar and manganese, the export of which increased during the war. By late 1914 cocoa and tobacco prices were rising and despite the fact that Germany took 80% of the latter crop, 1915 was extremely prosperous. Other markets were found for the tobacco and there was a record cocoa crop. In the following year there was a setback when Britain temporarily restricted cocoa and tobacco imports, but from 1917 export earnings grew and the region seems to have flourished considerably during the remaining war years.[111]

Sugar was the key to Pernambuco's apparent prosperity. The industry here had been steadily declining for many years,[112] but high wartime prices provoked a short-lived revival. In 1913, admittedly a particularly bad year for exports, of the 142,000 tons of sugar produced[113] only 5,012 tons, worth 919,026 milréis, were shipped from Pernambuco. In the following years production increased steadily, except during the severe drought of 1915–16, and by 1918 exports had reached 75,931 tons and a value of 62,488,190 milréis.[114] However, as was common in many sugar growing regions, when the wartime bubble of high prices burst in 1920 severe crisis ensued. Substantial profits had been made but, being unable to import equipment or institute needed reorganization, when the conflict was over Pernambuco's sugar industry remained by world standards extremely backward.[115] It was, therefore, unable to compete successfully when prices fell in the 1920s and even lost out in the domestic market to the more efficient and better placed growers in Rio and São Paulo.[116] The unusual conditions of the war had simply been a temporary reprieve for a chronically unsound system of production.

Sugar was also an important wartime export in Rio de Janeiro, the value increasing from 31,820 milréis in 1913 to 21,311,642 milréis in 1918 (16% of the total increase). But much of the state's growth in export earnings was from Minas Gerais which shipped its goods via the Central Railway to the port of Rio. The most important of these commodities was manganese which was in great demand for steelmaking in the United States, as former supplies from Russia and India had been cut off. In 1913 only 120,000 tons (2,751,788 milréis) was sold, but exports rose to over 500,000 tons (45,842,000 milréis) in 1918, all but a small proportion coming from Minas Gerais and representing 35% of the increase in Rio's total exports.[117]

Allied demand also stimulated the development of meat-packing in

Brazil, with the same US companies found in Argentina, Swift, Armour and Wilson, as well as the British Vesteys, constructing plants in Rio, São Paulo, Rio Grande do Sul and Minas Gerais. There were also a number of Brazilian firms involved.[118] Total exports of chilled and frozen beef rose from one ton in 1914 to 60,509 tons valued at 60,755,196 milréis by 1918.[119] The plant in Rio Grande do Sul was not in operation before 1918 and, therefore, exports during the war were split more or less evenly between São Paulo and Rio de Janeiro.[120] To the south in Rio Grande do Sul, it was mainly livestock products which accounted for the export boom, but here canned and jerked meat were most important together with hides, tallow and lard. There was also an appreciable increase in agricultural exports such as rice, beans, potatoes, etc. Although much of this went to other Brazilian states, Allied needs were a crucial factor in explaining the nature of export expansion.[121]

The successful export performance of particular Brazilian states demonstrates the danger of trying to judge the economic condition of the entire country by what happened to coffee and rubber. For example, although the problems with state export statistics must be kept in mind, it appears that roughly 60% of the population lived in states where foreign earnings rose appreciably between 1913 and 1918. This is not to argue that the mass of people did well because of this. They clearly did not. It is only to suggest that it is wrong to characterize Brazilian exports as stagnant in these years. Even in Rio and Minas Gerais, where coffee was the principal export, the growth of mining, meat-processing, and sugar offset the decline in coffee. Furthermore, it has been shown that this decline may have been exaggerated, at least with respect to the early part of the war. It was only from 1917 that serious problems arose and by mid-1918 these were rapidly being overcome. The contemporary claim that Brazil experienced prosperity during the war does not, therefore, seem so farfetched. However, as in other countries, it was a prosperity which tended to reinforce the structures of export dependence. These structures were strengthened despite the apparent growth in manufacturing output during the war.

V

The problems experienced by Brazil with imports were very similiar to those which plagued Argentina. But in Brazil, because export prices increased so slowly, the terms of trade and capacity to import deteriorated more dramatically. Peláez argues[122] that the terms of trade fell mainly because of rising import prices and, although this is

Table 3.16 *Quantum indices of Brazilian imports 1910–1919*

	1911	1912	1913	1914	1915	1916	1917	1918	1919
	\multicolumn{9}{c}{(1910–13 = 100)}								

	1911	1912	1913	1914	1915	1916	1917	1918	1919
Class of goods									
Consumer goods	94.7	108.9	106	66.6	45.3	43.6	38.9	38.8	48.6
Durable	90.8	116.3	115.6	80.3	23.0	28.5	38.4	29.9	57.6
Nondurable	96.5	106.3	102.9	61.4	53.7	49.2	39.2	42.3	44.9
Fuels and lubricants	88.7	108.8	120	86.0	75.7	73.0	56.8	41.4	79.6
Raw materials	88.7	94.9	107.2	54.4	48.7	57.2	41.7	47.0	63.8
For manufacture	89.7	113.3	113.2	44.7	24.5	25.9	21.4	17.6	41.3
For other industry	99.4	105.2	103.3	59.4	60.8	72.9	51.9	64.2	74.1
Construction material									
For Metallurgical industry	69.5	107.0	148.4	38.5	10.5	8.5	10.9	6.3	17.6
For other industry	80.5	104.8	135.6	48.9	30.9	35.6	21.6	12.8	40.8
For agriculture	105.5	93.9	104.2	61.1	39.7	30.1	20.8	13.0	18.5
Capital goods	90.9	133	109.2	42.9	16.3	21.1	22.9	21.4	45.7
For industry	106.9	142.9	106.2	44.1	17.5	22.4	22.3	25.7	45.0
For agriculture	89.3	116.8	68.5	23.4	13.2	21.7	18.0	14.8	41.5
Transport equipment	63.3	145.3	142.6	40.0	15.6	23.9	24.5	13.9	47.4
Other	109.2	123.0	94.5	47.0	16.6	19.0	22.8	22.0	45.9
Total	93.8	111.4	109.5	59.7	45.6	48.8	39.5	39.9	58.2

Source: Based on Villela and Suzigan, *Government Policy*, p. 364. *Note.* The figures they give are 1901 = 100. These have been recalculated so as to give a clearer picture of change during the war.

true, when compared to the other three countries it is the indifferent performance of export prices, mainly coffee and rubber, which distinguishes the Brazilian case. Furthermore the import quantum fell to a greater extent here than in either Argentina or Chile, although the 50% drop between 1913 and 1914 may reflect in part the overstocking that is alleged to have occurred during the first year.[123] It was capital goods and raw materials, especially those for manufacture, construction and agriculture which were worst affected (Table 3.16). This and the fall in consumer goods imports had important implications for domestic industrial development. The massive decline in imports also had a dramatic effect on government revenues, receipts from duties falling by an average of 50% in the years 1914–18.[124]

Looking at the changes in the quantity of certain key imports allows a more graphic illustration of the full impact on Brazil of the collapse of imports. For the majority of Brazilians the most immediate concern was food, and the decline in imports, especially of wheat and flour, created real hardship throughout most of the war. Between 1914 and 1916 the price of flour in Rio de Janeiro rose by 42%.[125] Conditions were probably made worse by the export for the first time of such important staples as beans, rice, corn, potatoes and manioc flour. Local production of all except the last had been supplemented by imports before the war.[126] Villela and Suzigan see this as an example of import substitution,[127] suggesting that output increased sufficiently to supply the domestic market and yield a surplus for export. This is impossible to ascertain as there are no agricultural production data for Brazil before 1920. The steep rise in the cost of living suggests that even if national production did increase, the export of many of these goods was made at the expense of the urban consumers. This became a major social issue in Brazil, as it did in all the countries studied, and it raises important questions about the massively complex relationship between primary product export, the exploitation of labor, political power, and class struggle.[128]

The imports of railway materials and equipment fell spectacularly, and this, together with the lack of foreign capital and the financial problems facing the states and the federal government, made any major extension of the railway network impossible. A degree of growth did continue, albeit at a much reduced level. In 1914 there were 26,062 kilometers of line in operation and this had risen to 28,127 by 1919, an increase of about 420 kilometers a year. This represented a substantial drop from the average yearly increase of 1,200 registered between 1907 and 1914.[129] The reduction in rail building cut employment and the difficulty of maintaining existing lines probably made transport less efficient and more expensive. But perhaps the most important factor contributing to this was the shortage of another key import, coal. The quantum index suggests that relative to other imports, fuel did not do too badly, but this was not the case (Table 3.17). By 1916 coal imports were less than half their prewar level, while by the following year the price at 114$200 per ton was over four times what it had been in 1913 (26$000), most of this increase being due to higher freight charges.[130] Because of the cheapness of British coal there had been no systematic

Table 3.17 *Quantity of selected Brazilian imports 1910–1919*

	(1000 metric tons)									
	1910	1911	1912	1913	1914	1915	1916	1917	1918	1919
Foodstuffs and Fodder					920	723	694	695	436	589	682
of which:											
Wheat					438	382	371	424	192	298	312
Flour					170	134	129	118	110	149	216
Railways											
Locomotives	9	13	17	14	5	2	4	4	2	5
Railway Cars & Wagons	15	18	63	69	6	1	.3	.2	.3	6
Axles, wheels etc. for RR	6	7	14	11	8	2	3	4	2	6
Rail, plates & RR parts	172	161	235	262	53	5	9	6	2	15
Fuel											
Coke	9	13	13	17	9	4	3	2	—	5
Coal	1,582	1,736	2,099	2,262	1,540	1,164	1,025	818	638	927
Patent fuel	182	220	207	239	242	109	64	5	12	33
Gasoline	3	7	16	29	9	18	22	18	21	26
Fuel oil					10	35	62	101	51	10	161
Construction											
Cement	264	269	367	465	180	145	170	96	52	198
Steel for Buildings	36	33	51	71	19	5	3	4	2	7

Sources: Brazil, Ministério da Fazenda, Diretoria de Estatística Comercial, *Comércio exterior do Brasil 1910 a 1914*, 2 vols., Rio, 1915; *Comércio exterior do Brasil de Janeiro a Dezembro de 1913 e 1914*, Rio, 1915; *Comércio exterior do Brasil, Janeiro a Dezembro 1915, 1916, 1917, 1918, 1919*, Rio, 1920.

attempts before 1914 to develop the coal deposits in Rio Grande do Sul and Santa Catarina, and the small output from the fields in these states during the war did nothing to offset the massive decline in imported coal. There were no exploitable oil deposits in the country and so, as was the case in Argentina, less efficient wood was the main substitute.[131] Having constructed transport and power generating systems around the assumption of cheap imported coal, both Brazil and Argentina suffered considerably during the war by its absence.

VI

Brazil's trading network was altered by the war (Table 3.18). The United States already provided the country's major export market, but its position was considerably strengthened as it took not only a greater percentage of coffee, but also almost all the manganese, and the largest single share of hides, skins, cocoa, and rubber. Britain lost some ground, but until 1918 more or less maintained its share of Brazilian exports by increasing its purchase of sugar, raw cotton and tinned and frozen meat. The US definitively replaced Britain as Brazil's leading supplier, achieving a dominance which the latter country had not exercised since the nineteenth century. However, on aggregate, the British gave up only a relatively small proportion of the Brazilian market. As in the case of Argentina, most of the gains made by the US were at the expense of the Germans. The significance of this change was that Brazil was brought more fully under the economic domination of the US.[132] This contrasts with the situation in the Argentine where both the British market and capital remained of central importance into the 1930s.

The lack of key imports was a major problem throughout the war and, to the extent that substitutes could not be produced at a reasonable price locally, Brazilian economic development was undoubtedly hampered.[133] However, exports did better than is often supposed, especially before 1917. What lasting impact, if any, did this have on the Brazilian economy? Some sectors were undoubtedly given a boost, but this was in most cases temporary, it drew local capital into new export sectors and thereby simply reinforced the vulnerable structures associated with primary product export. Rather than being an opportunity to modify the country's external orientation, the persistence of Allied demand for certain goods may, therefore, have done little more than strengthen this orientation. Of course, neither the Brazilian elite nor the government were passive spectators, and the latter's support of coffee valorization gave an important boost to continued export specialization.

As was the case in the Argentine, the war was not a period of isolation for the Brazilian economy. The direct and indirect coercive Allied actions were an important part of this. Except for a relatively brief period, the material economic damage resulting from external interference was probably minimal. But, the fact that Britain and latterly the United States felt they had the right to intervene is significant in itself, showing, especially with respect to the cynical nature of blacklisting, that Brazilian economic or political sovereignty was considered of little moment. The country was a prize to be won on

Table 3.18 *Brazil's trade with other countries. Percentage shares 1913–1919*

	1913	1914	1915	1916	1917	1918	1919
Country							
United States							
Imports	15.7	18.2	32.2	39.2	47.1	36.0	48.0
Exports	32.7	41.5	41.8	47.0	46.1	34.6	41.4
Britain							
Imports	24.5	23.9	21.9	20.4	18.0	20.4	16.2
Exports	13.3	14.3	12.1	11.7	12.6	10.1	7.2
Germany							
Imports	17.5	15.5	1.5	—	—		
Exports	14.1	8.8	—	—	—	—	
France							
Imports	9.8	7.6	4.9	5.2	4.0	4.8	3.8
Exports	12.3	9.2	11.4	16.1	14.0	9.0	21.3
Argentina							
Imports	7.4	9.6	15.9	14.1	13.1	19.0	15.3
Exports	4.7	4.7	5.1	6.6	9.2	15.2	4.4

Sources: Redfield, *Brazil*, pp. 86, 93. *Comércio exterior 1915–1919*, pp. 9–10, 12–13.

the battlefield of imperialist rivalry. Whether or not they were effective, the fact that Allied policies were carried out so blatantly and with such scant regard for Brazilian sensibilities angered many people and highlighted the country's subservient position *vis-à-vis* the industrialized countries. This, together with the shock delivered to the economy by the outbreak of the war, led many Brazilians to question with renewed urgency the efficaciousness of what must have seemed the virtually immutable pattern of the country's outwardly directed development. Valla writes,[134] "This was not the first crisis that had affected the type of economy which Brazil had, but the sudden blow of war seemed to define the problem much more clearly for the Brazilian Government." A similar perception of Brazil's precarious economic position within the world was also the basis for a growing nationalist reaction against it.[135]

Chile

I

Chile's narrowly based export trade was devastated by the outbreak of the war. Yet within less than a year Allied demand for nitrates, copper, and various foodstuffs began to stimulate both a revival of trade and of the economy. Although the US Consul General reported[136] that by the end of 1915 higher prices for nitrate and copper and increased production had "... reestablished trade conditions on as normal a basis as could be expected, in view of the disturbed state of the import, export, and financial markets of the world at large." There were still doubts being expressed about the future. For example, at the end of December 1915, *El Diario Illustrado* of Santiago commented[137] that "The situation in the country is difficult. It has recovered or is on the way to recover all its productive force, but it cannot count with safety on the foreign market." This observation, which was to prove prophetic in the postwar period and in the 1930s, was soon swamped by an export boom of unprecedented proportions.

After two years of relatively low export earnings, there was a dramatic improvement in 1916. This was maintained until the catastrophic postwar collapse in 1919. To some extent this prosperity was due to an increase in the volume of exports from the 1914 low, but in the three most prosperous years the export quantum remained almost static. The boom seems, therefore, to have been due mainly to higher prices rather than to a particularly dynamic response on the part of the nitrate producers, responsible for the great majority of export sales (Table 3.19). The copper-mining companies, as well as the farmers and ranchers, showed a somewhat greater ability to improve output, and the former's share of total exports rose substantially in these years.[138] During the war the balance of trade was extremely healthy, and even though the value of imports had surpassed prewar levels by 1918, in that year the trade surplus was almost five times the 1913 figure. Although there are no reliable figures, it appears that the balance of payments was probably also in surplus throughout most of these years.[139] Unlike the other countries, Chile enjoyed both mostly favorable terms of trade and a rising capacity to import. Both came to an end in 1918, probably because of the control exercised by the Allies over nitrate sales and the fixing of the copper price in the United States.[140] The value of the inconvertible peso closely reflected the country's changing trading position, exchange rising from a low of 7.5 pence in January 1915 to 16.8 pence in August 1918.[141] It had fallen to

Table 3.19 *Percentage shares of Chilean exports 1912–1921*

	Nitrate & iodine	Copper	Agricultural goods	Livestock‡ products
1912	76.2%	8.8%	4.2%	4.7%
1913	80.7%	7.8%	4.1%	5.7%
1914	72.7%	10.6%	4.8%	6.8%
1915	74.7%	13.9%	5.5%	8.4%
1916	70.1%	16.9%	3.2%	7.3%
1917	68.0%	18.9%	4.3%	6.6%
1918	69.7%	15.1%	4.3%	7.0%
1919	42.1%	16.3%	13.9%	15.3%
1920	68.8%	12.7%	4.2%	7.9%
1921	66.2%	8.7%	6.7%	7.1%

Source: Sinopsis 1924. Note. ‡Includes frozen and dried mutton.

9.3 pence by the following March, as demand collapsed for the country's two major exports. This demonstrated the extreme volatility to which the Chilean economy was subject due to its reliance on such a narrow export base.

II

In October 1914, the British Minister in Santiago, considering the prospect of high demand for nitrate, observed that,[142] "...the war may yet prove to be a blessing in disguise." So it was, although the "blessing" was but temporary and it took some time before the war-induced crisis was overcome. It was overcome due mainly to the switch in demand for nitrate as a fertilizer, which had accounted for about 80% of prewar sales,[143] to its use in the manufacture of explosives and other chemicals, and to the growth of the US market and, to a lesser extent, the British market. All this more than offset the loss of sales to Germany (Table 3.21). Prices seem to have increased very slowly, however, with substantial rises not coming until 1917. Furthermore, prices in Chile did not move upwards to the same degree as those abroad (Table 3.20). Williams attributes this to the large stockpiles of nitrate in Chile and the difficulty in finding shipping.[144] Not only was shipping hard to come by, but it was also extremely expensive. Immediately before the war it had cost 20 shillings to ship a ton of nitrate to Europe by sail and 10 shillings more by steamship.

Table 3.20 *Nitrate production, workers, export, and prices 1912–1920*

	Oficinas producing	Workers	Production (000 metric tons)	Export (000 metric tons)	Export[a] (000 pesos of 18d)	Price[b] (per quintal in Chile)	Price[b] (per quintal in London)
1912	118	47,800	2,586	2,493	297,713	8s	11s1d
1913	127	53,161	2,772	2,738	310,489	7s10d	11s1d
1914	137	43,979	2,463	1,847	217,025	7s	10s2d
1915	116	45,506	1,755	2,023	225,386	7s4d	12s8d
1916	123	53,470	2,913	2,980	358,614	7s7d	17s9d
1917	129	56,378	3,001	2,776	488,391	11s2d	—
1918	125	56,981	2,859	2,919	532,324	11s9d	—
1919	125	46,245	1,703	804	127,077	9s8d	—
1920	97	nd	2,524	2,746	535,602	13s8d	14s11d

Source: *Sinopsis estadística*, 1918 and 1924.
[a]including iodine [b]to the nearest pence.

Table 3.21 *Nitrate markets, percentage shares 1912–1920*

	GB	Germany	Rest of Europe	US	Other
1912	5.7	37.9	31.6	23.6	1.1
1913	4.9	32.9	43.6	17.4	1.2
1914	13.9	23.0	37.5	23.0	2.6
1915	15.0	0	60.4	22.4	2.2
1916	23.7	0	34.3	40.4	1.6
1917	9.3	0	42.7	46.7	1.3
1918	19.4	0	23.3	57.1	0.2
1919	0.9	0	36.1	60.9	2.1
1920	6.4	5.8	47.1	33.5	7.2

Source: Monteón, *Nitrate Era*, p. 112.

By 1916 the cost had risen to 140 shillings and 160 shillings respectively.[145] Also, coal and fuel oil, essential in the processing of nitrate, more than doubled in price during the war. Monteón argues that notwithstanding all these difficulties the nitrate producers made massive profits during the war. By 1916 dividends were already two to three times greater than in 1915. The prosperity was, however, bought rather dearly, as the inability to obtain this vital commodity stimulated the German production of synthetic nitrate. After the war other countries, aware of the potential insecurity of supply, also began to develop their capacity for nitrate production. Whereas in 1912 only 4.5% of fixed nitrogen was produced artifically, by 1920 this had increased to 43.5%.[146] Although this change would have happened eventually in any case as nitrate deposits became exhausted, the war greatly accelerated the process. The writing was clearly on the wall for Chile's nitrate industry.

Nitrate was of crucial importance to the Allies, and because of this was subject, as were many other Latin American commodity trades, to an unprecedented degree of external interference during the war. Initially this interference was limited to the blockade of trade with Germany and the imposition by the British of blacklisting in February 1916. This proved fatal to the German nitrate interests. After only one year of war, Gibbs & Co. were in a position to do most of the nitrate business formerly undertaken by a number of German merchant houses.[147] At this time Gibbs, who were acting as agents for the British Government, were responsible for 31% of Chile's nitrate exports.[148] Not surprisingly, protests were made against the blacklists. *El Diario Ilustrado* pointed to the damaging effects of the lists on German, Chilean and also British business in Chile, but seems to have been more or less resigned to them as inevitable given the pressures of war.[149] When the US entered the war in 1917 they followed the British policy. The US Government was soon involved in a major conflict with the Chilean authorities over a local court's ruling against the failure of US oil companies to honour agreements with German nitrate firms.[150] The US War Trade Board cut off oil supplies to the nitrate fields (by refusing export licenses), and the Chilean government was soon forced to set aside the court's decision.

The kind of coercion described above was annoying and humiliating for the Chileans, but was probably of minor importance when compared to the controls imposed on nitrate purchasing. The marketing of nitrate had always been in foreign, mainly British, hands, but from the end of 1917 this was strengthened with the creation of the Nitrate of Soda Executive to act as a single Allied buyer. By 1917 the British felt that prices were being pushed up by speculators and the "cutthroat" competition with US buyers.[151] It therefore seemed logical that after the United States' entry into the war the two nations should cooperate rather than compete. The North Americans were certainly in favour of such an arrangement. The US Ambassador in Santiago had been discussing this with his British counterpart in September, when he confided that at that time there was even competition for nitrate between different departments of his own government.[152] The British Consul in Antofagasta also felt that cooperation was both necessary and possible. He wrote,[153] "If this could be arranged it would mean, practically, the control of the nitrate market and would put an end to speculation, and it would furthermore be a very much more satisfactory arrangement for both the nitrate producers and the Allied Governments, including the States..."

In December 1917, the Allied governments agreed to a division of the nitrate market and the following February the Nitrate of Soda Executive was formally established.[154] Herbert Gibbs was appointed Director of Purchases and it was agreed that his firm, already acting for the British Government, would purchase the nitrates required by all the Allied countries except the United States. With respect to the latter, W.R. Grace, Dupont, and Wessel Duval would divide the market in a manner agreed between themselves and the US War Industries Board.[155]

In 1918 the Executive's refusal to pay more than 12 shillings per quintal (in Chile) was greeted with understandable dismay, and the British Ambassador reported there was hostility toward Allied price fixing.[156] Monteón observes,[157] that "...neither the producers nor the government initially believed that they could prevent its [the Executive's] control of the market. Elite opinion accepted this outcome." In any case, "Many of the producers and the company managers were English and thought the Executive would protect their interests." Subsequently, the Executive through manipulating stocks and suspending new purchases from Chile sought to drive down the price and the government, which in May had tried to set up a producers' trust, responded by taking over local stockpiles and entered into negotiation with the British Minister of Munitions, Winston Churchill, who had been appointed by the Allies. The Chileans were able to sell their nitrate stocks, but failed in their attempt at getting a long-term contract. This proved beneficial for the Allies for, when the war ended a few months later, nitrate prices collapsed. This, together with the slack demand for copper, led to a drop of over 60% in the country's export earnings and initiated a crisis which was more severe than that experienced at the outbreak of the war.

Far from providing Chile with a respite from foreign control and external pressures, the war saw a substantial increase in both, as was the case elsewhere in the region. Although this blatant interference was no doubt resented, reaction against it tended to be somewhat muted probably because extremely high profits were made and government revenues from export duties were buoyant.[158] Furthermore, rather than offering Chile a vision of an alternative economic path, by temporarily strengthening the nitrate industry, the war tended to reinforce the existing economic pattern, which essentially combined foreign export dependence with direct foreign control. This pattern was extended during the war by the activities of US capital in copper mining.

III

Chile had been the world's leading copper producer before the 1870s, but once the high grade ore had been depleted the industry had not been able to compete effectively in the world market and went into decline. Its revival began to take place from the first decade of the century, after Daniel C. Jackling, an American engineer, demonstrated that low-grade ore, of which Chile had massive deposits, could be profitably mined.[159] The large-scale financing needed to support such schemes was beyond the capacity of local capitalists. Their difficulties were compounded by the need to find additional funds to improve the transport infrastructure and assure fuel supplies.[160] All this was well within the financial power of the large US companies which began their takeover of the industry in 1904 when the Braden Copper Company bought the large El Teniente mine. Four years later this became part of the Guggenheim empire. In 1912, the Chilean Exploration Company, another Guggenheim enterprise, obtained Chuquicamata, which by 1914 was considered to be the largest copper deposit in the world. Another important mine, Potrerillos, was taken over by a subsidiary of Anaconda in 1913.[161]

Although prices did fall sharply in 1914 (Table 3.22), the outbreak of the war did not have the same devastating effect on the copper industry as it had on nitrate. Many smaller companies were forced temporarily to suspend operations, but the giant US firms continued working and investing in new plant and equipment. At El Teniente production increased and the extensive improvements already underway continued, and the Chile Copper Company stepped up its construction work at its Chuquicamata mine.[162] Throughout the war major improvements continued to be made by both companies, and by

Table 3.22 *Chilean copper. Production, exports, prices 1912–1920*

	Production (metric tons)	Export (metric tons)	Export (gold pesos)	Price* (per ton in London)
1912	41,647	40,897	33,550,041	£73/12/5
1913	42,263	41,323	30,894,556	£68/1/3
1914	44,665	45,227	31,891,726	£59/14/7
1915	52,341	53,587	45,409,745	£73/5/5
1916	71,289	71,904	86,639,941	£112/19/7
1917	102,527	94,987	132,760,069	£123/10/0
1918	106,814	92,534	114,916,315	£113/10/0
1919	79,580	71,002	49,227,171	£89/5/10
1920	98,952	85,165	98,571,905	£98/10/6

Source: *Sinopsis estadística 1924* *Average price of standard bar copper.

1918 it was estimated that $50,000,000 had been invested in Chuquicamata alone.[163] In 1916 development work began on the Potrerillos mine. This promised to be another major deposit and plans were made to build a railway, a hydroelectric plant and port works at Chañaral.[164] It was not until ten years later that production here came on stream.

Commercial production was inaugurated at the Chuquicamata mines in May 1915, by the Chilean President, Barros Luco, who pressed a button in Santiago which symbolically started up the machinery at the port and the new 10,000 tons per day mill.[165] In that year net profits were but $30,468 whereas increased output and very much higher prices resulted in profits of over $4 million in the next year.[166] The opening of Chuquicamata made a major contribution to the increase in the country's total copper exports in that year. By 1918 output in Chile had increased almost 2.5 times and, with prices rising sharply, export earnings went up dramatically. It is probable that the figures for 1917 and 1918 would have been greater but for a move to centralized buying and the price-fixing intervention of the US War Industries Board in September 1917, following the United States' entry into the war.[167] The price was set at 23.5 US cents a pound (in New York), whereas it had reached 31.5 cents in March of the same year. An 11% increase was granted the following July, but this was more than offset by rising freight charges.[168] As 60% of Chilean copper exports went to the United States and the move by the government here reduced the world price, it could hardly have been welcome by Chilean producers. Once again, Allied wartime policy had succeeded in limiting both the price rises and the profits of a major Chilean export sector. In this case, however, the damage was inflicted more on US companies than directly on the Chilean economy, for by 1920 the two largest US firms were responsible for 80% of the country's copper production.

During the war years (1915–20) copper's share of exports had averaged 17.8% more than double its prewar level. However, local capital took almost no part in this expansion, having been easily pushed aside by the massive financial power and technical expertise of the large foreign firms. Even the government showed little interest and during the war no attempts were made either to regulate the industry or to impose export duties similar to those levied on nitrates. The returns to the Chilean economy were, therefore, not very great. As a contemporary observer remarked,[169] "It has been the good fortune of Chile to attract foreign capital to develop her mineral industries and at the same time her misfortune to have the product of her mines enrich the citizens of other countries."

IV

Although the narrow mineral base of Chilean exports has been stressed, a good deal of the country's large agricultural production from the central valleys and livestock products from the far south were also sold abroad. During the war output fluctuated but generally rose and although the export quantum did not increase markedly, except for wool and frozen mutton, higher prices pushed up export values.[170] With the large increase in copper and nitrate earnings, the percentage share of agricultural exports remained reasonably steady, although the relative importance of livestock products did rise (Table 3.19). The agricultural interests felt that the war had presented the greatest opportunity for them since the California Gold Rush.[171] However, the Sociedad Nacional Agraria argued that pressure from the press and the public over high food prices had restricted exports and, therefore, the growth of production. Despite these protestations, it would seem that the authority given in 1914 to the President to restrict food exports[172] was never used, even though there were strong demands for such action. Perhaps the agriculturalists were simply feeling hard done by because they were being blamed for the high cost of living.

V

As in all countries, it was Chile's imports which showed the most dramatic transformation during the war years. The capacity to import did improve in 1916 and 1917, and although there was some recovery in the quantity of imports in 1917 and 1918, they remained substantially below prewar levels. Generally, the pattern of change was the same in Chile as elsewhere. The greatest decline was in capital and intermediate goods and fuel, while consumer goods showed more resilience. For example, in the period 1914–19 capital goods averaged only 61.6% of the 1912–13 figure, while consumer goods stood at 75.9%, the highest of any of the import categories. This was not a particularly advantageous combination for Chilean industry.[173]

As in Brazil and Argentina, and for the same reasons, the shortage of fuel was a major problem for the Chilean economy. However, overall, the latter was not as badly affected because she was the largest South American coal producer and with an annual output of one million tons, was able to supply about 40% of her own needs.[174] But Chile only produced soft coal, and so the sharp reduction in imports, falling from about 1.5 million tons to 400,000 tons between 1913 and 1916 did have a major impact on the economy.[175] Petroleum imports did increase and in the nitrate fields there was an important degree of substitution of oil for coal, however, in the period 1914–19, total fuel imports (coal and petroleum) averaged only 51.3% of their prewar quantity, the most badly hit of all import categories.

Imports may have fallen even more dramatically if it were not for the willingness and ability of the United States to move quickly into the position which the European countries were forced to abandon. Not only was Germany eliminated as a trading partner, but Britain's long-established role as both Chile's main supplier of imports and export market was effectively challenged by US business. This was one of the most significant changes brought about by the conflict, for although Europe regained some of its importance once the war had ended, by this time the centre of foreign domination had clearly shifted. In all likelihood this would have occurred even if there had been no war, because before 1914 US capital, with the active support of the government, was pushing vigorously into South America. But, the First World War made the process that much easier and far more rapid.

As well as capturing a larger proportion of the country's trade, US banks, as they were doing throughout South America, began to be

Table 3.23 *Quantum index of Chilean imports and import structure 1912–1920*

	Capital goods* QI % share	Raw materials QI % share	Fuel QI % share	Consumer goods QI % share	Total
			(1912–1913 = 100)		
1912	102.7(15.4%)	99.6(42.8%)	93.2(12.2%)	93.5(28.8%)	97.2
1913	97.3(13.8%)	100.4(40.8%)	106.8(13.2%)	106.5(31.0%)	102.8
1914	60.1(10.8%)	71.1(36.6%)	97.8(15.3%)	99.2(36.6%)	81.2
1915	33.7(10.0%)	46.3(39.4%)	49.2(12.7%)	61.1(37.3%)	49.1
1916	48.8(10.4%)	75.8(46.2%)	63.7(11.8%)	71.6(31.3%)	68.5
1917	84.3(14.7%)	96.4(48.2%)	46.7 (7.1%)	82.6(29.6%)	83.6
1918	77.5(13.7%)	100.6(51.0%)	34.3 (5.3%)	81.7(29.7%)	82.4
1919	70.5(15.8%)	74.7(48.0%)	19.4 (3.8%)	70.4(32.4%)	65.1
1920	48.7(12.0%)	65.7(46.4%)	27.0 (5.8%)	69.7(35.3%)	59.2

Sources: Import price index calculated with a change in base year from Palma, "External disequilibrium," Appendix 32. Divided into an index of imports calculated from Henry W. Kirsch, *Industrial Development in a Traditional Society. The Conflict of Entrepreneurship and Modernization in Chile*, Gainesville, 1977, p. 163. Percentage shares from *ibid.*, p. 164. * Capital goods includes transport equipment.

Table 3.24 *Regional breakdown of Chilean foreign trade 1913–1920*

	Exports British Empire	USA	Germany	% of total	Imports British Empire	USA	Germany	% of total
1913	38%	21%	21%	80%	35%	17%	25%	77%
1914	38%	16%	26%	80%	31%	21%	6%	58%
1915	37%	43%	—	80%	31%	33%	6%	70%
1916	31%	49%	—	80%	30%	44%	—	74%
1917	21%	59%	—	80%	22%	50%	—	72%
1918	24%	64%	—	88%	24%	46%	—	70%
1919	24%	42%	—	66%	26%	48%	—	74%
1920	24%	44%	10%	75%	31%	31%	5%	67%

Source: Scott, *Report*, p. 95.

established in order to facilitate trade and to promote dollar exchange. A branch of the National City Bank of New York was opened in Santiago in 1916, and there were plans to open branches in Valparaíso,

Concepción, Iquique, Antofagasta, and Valdavia.[176] It was, however, through the direct control of the copper industry that the US was to become such a dominant force in Chilean affairs. This became increasingly apparent in the 1920s, and painfully evident to Chileans after the collapse of the nitrate industry in 1930.

Although both nitrates and copper had many of the attributes of enclaves, with a substantial proportion of the profits flowing directly abroad, in the case of the former, because it was a monopoly supplier to the world market, the state was able to capture a fair proportion of the earnings through the taxation of exports and redistribute them within the domestic economy.[177] While this allowed the country to experience a substantial degree of economic growth in the prewar period, the elite's minimal direct interest in export production tended, among other things, to slow the rate of the country's socio-political transformation. The war substantially reinforced these conditions. There was a degree of Chileanization of nitrate deposits, but this represented little new domestic investment, and the industry's days were numbered in any case because of the development of synthetic production methods. At the same time, the copper mines, destined soon to become the country's new leading export sector were taken over almost completely by US capital. The war did, therefore, serve to work an important change in the prewar pattern of export earnings, but at the same time it strengthened the overall structure of external dependence and direct foreign domination. Although Chile's main export sectors were distinguished from those in Brazil and Argentina by being both extractive and mainly foreign-controlled, it would seem that the war had a roughly similar impact here as it had on the east coast. There was no letup in exogenous pressures, no real opportunity for an internally oriented capitalist transformation.

Peru

I

Peru's export trade was the quickest to recover from the initial disruptions caused by the war. There was but a slight fall in the total export quantum in 1914 and this, together with a favorable movement in the terms of trade, made Peru the only country in which the capacity to import increased in this year. Export earnings continued to grow throughout the war, although at a much reduced rate in 1917 and 1918. The balance of trade remained favorable, but Peru was unique in that the import quantum had surpassed the 1913 level by 1916 (Table 3.30). This was due to an extremely strong export performance and the fact that commercial links with the US seem to have been closer here than in the other countries. Initially, because of political uncertainty and distrust of the emergency issue of paper currency, Peruvian exchange did not reflect the buoyant trade position.[178] It was not until February 1916, following José Pardo's election to the presidency and when government finances seem to have been brought under control that the sol began to appreciate substantially.[179] By July, 1918 it was demanding a 17.5% premium against the pound sterling (Table 4.24). This is indicative of the fact that Peru experienced a massive export bonanza during the war, seemingly the most extensive and longest sustained of the four countries. However, the effects were not, on the whole, particularly beneficial for the country's economic development. Foreign capital's hold on mining and petroleum was strengthened while domestic entrepreneurs, rather than using their windfall gains to diversify, for example, by investing in local industry, put a great deal of their money instead into cotton and sugar. These industries enjoyed inflated wartime profits but were destined to decline dramatically in the interwar period, leaving the most dynamic export sectors in the hands of foreign companies.[180]

II

Sugar had emerged as the principal mainstay of the Peruvian economy after the War of the Pacific and, as the *West Coast Leader* noted, it also served as a "sheet anchor" for the country during the crisis of 1914–15.[181] It remained one of the country's three major exports throughout the war (Table 3.25). This was due to a combination of improvements in the local industry and far-reaching changes in the world market. Up to 1914 beet sugar had accounted for more than 50% of world sugar output, and Britain, the largest free market, had obtained about 90% of its supplies from Austria–Hungary and Germany.[182] The war caused panic in the international market and prices rose to record levels.[183] The British government was quick to act. On 11 September, the Royal Sugar Commission was established, the first of the wartime food control institutions, and large purchases were made from cane producers in the Far East. When they had obtained sufficient sugar the British market was temporarily closed.[184] British manipulation of the market and the shortage of shipping created problems for all sugar exporters, problems which in Peru were compounded by the slack demand in the depressed Chilean market, generally the single most important outlet for Peruvian sugar

Table 3.25 *Percentage distribution of main Peruvian exports 1910–1920*

	1910	1911	1912	1913	1914	1915	1916	1917	1918	1919	1920
Sugar	20	20	15	15	30	26	24	22	21	31	42
Cotton	14	14	11	16	16	11	10	15	19	25	30
Rubber	18	8	14	9	5	5	4	3	3	2	1
Wool	7	5	4	6	6	5	6	9	14	6	2
Petroleum	2	5	8	10	10	10	8	6	7	9	5
Copper	13	22	25	22	19	29	36	34	29	18	12

Source: *Extracto estadístico 1926*, p. 69.

Table 3.26 *Peruvian sugar 1912–1921*

	Hectares in cane	Sugar output (mt)	Sugar exports (mt)	Sugar exports (£p)	Number of workers	Output per worker (tons)	Price of sugar in London (Sh d/cwt)	Main markets (% share)		
								Chile	GB	USA
1912	37,129	187,641	149,189	1,406,673	19,723	9.51	11/0	47.3%	44.7%	5.7%
1913	39,556	179,387	142,902	1,412,665	20,832	8.61	9/6	55.4	35.6	3.2
1914	40,728	223,369	176,671	2,640,952	21,789	10.25	11/7	38.1	37.8	12.9
1915	42,804	257,677	220,258	2,976,605	24,393	10.56	14/4	42.9	21.2	25.9
1916	40,732	271,294	239,010	3,978,779	23,359	11.61	24/3	30.0	8.5	41.7
1917	45,085	248,384	212,040	4,111,463	22,797	10.90	31/6	45.6	15.5	26.6
1918	49,804	283,190	197,986	4,162,595	25,041	11.31	33/0	46.8	27.8	9.2
1919	48,754	282,458	227,123	8,311,321	26,496	10.66	38/5	32.5	30.8	21.3
1920	49,077	307,849	249,963	15,584,888	28,860	10.67	58/0	21.0	21.1	47.6
1921	50,847	263,288	239,356	4,696,385	27,746	9.49	18/3	40.2	37.9	11.4

Sources: Prices, Noel Deerr, *The History of Sugar*, London 1950, p. 531; Peru, Ministerio de Fomento, *Estadística de la industria azucarera en el Perú*, Lima, yearly from 1911.

(Table 3.26). The result was unsold sugar piled up at the docks and, although overall 1914 showed an increase of 24% in volume and 87% in value in exports (Table 3.26), the last months of the year were anxious ones for local producers.[185]

Britain's strict controls and continued problems in finding long distance shipping led to a decline in Peruvian sugar sales in this vital market. Peru was easily able to find alternative markets, but it seems likely that British actions kept world prices below what would have been their free market level. For example, in 1916 Henry Kendall and Sons, a major British merchant house, claimed that, but for government interference, sugar would be selling at 24s per cwt rather than only 19s.[186] Restrictions on the market were further extended when the United States entered the war in April, 1917. They joined the British in setting up the International Sugar Commission.[187] According to Bernhardt it was felt that "... some form of cooperation with the Allies was imperative so that there would be no further competition among them in securing sugar supplies. The soaring prices which must necessarily rule if the law of supply and demand were allowed full play would thus be eliminated."

Not only did the Allies interfere in the market, but Casa Grande, one of Peru's largest sugar estates was blacklisted by the British and later the United States, because its owners, the Gildemeister family, were considered to be German.[188] Not content with blocking sales, the US government tried to force the transfer of the estate to US business interests. However, the Gildemeisters were not willing to sell, and the Peruvian government, needing to keep the *ingenio* in operation, both because it was a major employer and because the export duties on its large output were a vital component of the state's revenue, put the administration of Casa Grande under temporary Peruvian control. As with British blacklisting policy in the Argentine, the United States was trying to cripple German interests in Latin America and help pave the way for a more dominant role here for its capitalists after the war. In January 1918, both the Treasury and the State Department were encouraging New York bankers to get together to take over not only Casa Grande, but also German-owned tramways and power companies in Buenos Aires, Santiago and Valparaíso.[189] It was claimed that "This would be far the best solution of all these questions, since it would give the country [the US] an enormous start in South American commerce."

Despite the various external pressures, the Peruvian sugar industry enjoyed unprecedented prosperity during the war. Although world prices did not reach their full potential, they did rise substantially (Table 3.26), and this was undoubtedly the principal reason for the bonanza. But Peru was also in an excellent position to take advantage of this. Her major market, Chile, was so close that it was not greatly affected by shipping difficulties, and the boom in nitrate sales assured a strong demand for sugar. Also immediately before the war the Panama Canal had opened, halving the distance between Callao and Liverpool and cutting the trip to New York by two thirds.[190] This made it easier for the United States to take a larger proportion of the Peruvian crop, and the importance of the British market diminished. Added to these market advantages was the fact that the extensive investments in factory and milling capacity which had been underway since about 1908 began to come fully on stream in 1914.[191] Because of this, production soared in this year and, apart from the poor harvest of 1917, up to 1920 there was a steady increase in output and exports and a massive rise in earnings (Table 3.26). Over this period the area under cane was expanded, and employment increased as did labor productivity.

All this led to unheard-of profit levels for the *hacendados*. For example, between 1909 and 1914 the Hacienda Chiclín's profits had averaged £p9,029. In the period 1915–20 this had increased more than tenfold to £p97,344 per year.[192] The Hacienda San Nicolás recorded net profits of £p10,728 in 1913–14 and by 1918–19 this had risen to £p73,017.[193] This represented a spectacular increase in the profit per quintal of sugar from .685 soles to 4.86 soles. In the three years 1911 to 1913 the Aspíllagas had earned a total of £p70,285 from their estate of Cayaltí, but, in 1914 alone, earnings were up to £p71,713 and by 1919 had reached £p222,243. It is no wonder that Antero Aspíllaga wrote in 1918,[194] "... as many other sugar producers and industrialists we give thanks to the Germans for the bonanza that has come to us..." It is important to note that the benefits from this "bonanza" were appropriated mainly by the producers, for the workers' real wages apparently fell in these years.[195] This in turn provides an important part of the background to understanding the upsurge in unrest in the coastal valleys during and immediately after the war.

One important result of the prosperity in sugar was a great deal of increased investment in the industry. More land was brought under cane, and in the immediate postwar years, when it once again became possible to import machinery, there was a rush to re-equip the sugar plantations.[196] Also, at least four major estates were bought from foreigners by Peruvians.[197] The outcome for the Peruvian economy was, in the opinion of Thorp and Bertram, detrimental, as local capital rushed into an export sector which was to decline badly in the interwar period.[198]

III

Cotton was Peru's other major coastal export.[199] It was much more seriously affected by the outbreak of war than sugar. Whereas the price of the latter commodity rose immediately, cotton prices actually fell and did not begin to move upwards until mid-1915 (Table 3.27). The US Consul observed that[200] "Of all the Peruvian agricultural industries cotton was most affected by the European war during 1915." Freight rates had doubled by August 1915[201] and had doubled once again by early 1916.[202] Also, the dislocation of the financial system occasioned by the war made it extremely difficult for growers to obtain the short-term credit upon which they relied to finance planting.[203] The Aspíllagas, who besides their sugar enterprise also owned a cotton estate (Palto) in Ica, instructed their cotton-growing tenants to plant food crops and wait for better times. "...when the war ends and industry returns to normality."[204]

Growers did not have to wait this long. From the middle of 1915, Allied demand for Peru's long staple cotton began to increase, especially for the Matafifi variety which was used as a substitute for the now difficult to obtain Egyptian cotton. This was a key component in the manufacture of rubber tires and aircraft fabric.[205] So, despite the continued shipping problems, exports and earnings hit record levels in 1916 and, although the drought of 1917 reduced the harvest, higher prices meant a continued rise in export value in this and subsequent years. In September 1917, Ramón Aspíllaga wrote his brother:[206] "The enthusiasm for the planting of cotton, the prices of this article and that of the land, are greater than they were in 1860, during the War of Succession in the USA."

All this led to a rapid extension of cotton acreage. There are no reliable data before 1917–18, but it appears that there was an increase of between 75% to 100% in land planted in cotton during the war.[207] By 1919–20 there were over 100,000 hectares and 36,000 workers were being employed, although many of these were seasonal laborers hired only for the harvest. It had been possible to extend cotton acreage so rapidly because putting land into cotton was relatively simple and inexpensive as opposed, for example, to the planting of cane. Another important factor was that cotton processing (ginning) is both fairly basic and was generally carried on separately from growing. It was, therefore, quite easy for those with small plots of land to switch to cotton. But it was precisely on these small plots (*chacras*) that much of the coastal valley's food crops were raised. Besides the favorable movement in relative prices (Table 3.27), the commercialization of cotton – its processing, transport, sale, loans to growers – were highly organized by foreign merchant houses. This in itself gave cotton an important advantage over production of food for the local market. Although Thorp and Bertram strongly argue that at this time there was no trade-off between the production of export and food crops,[208] much of their case rests on questionable acreage data, and a wide cross

Table 3.27 *Peruvian cotton. Exports, prices, production, area cultivated, workers 1904–1921*

	Exports mt	Exports £p	Price (Peruvian Smooth d/lb)		Area cultivated (Ha)	Production (mt)	Workers
1910	14,106	1,014,823	8.68	1904–05	20,000	10,000	16,000
1911	15,887	1,028,254	7.63				
1912	19,231	1,042,866	7.48				
1913	23,918	1,424,230	7.77				
1914	22,900	1,405,220	7.12				
1915	21,124	1,260,477	6.61	1915–16	55,635	24,603	20,154
1916	24,226	1,722,805	9.98	1916–17	64,030	27,125	22,366
1917	17,376	2,878,515	18.26	1917–18	77,872	30,187	27,358
1918	21,522	3,760,812	27.65	1918–19	88,863	33,558	32,047
1919	37,710	6,635,782	26.46	1919–20	104,287	38,386	35,877
1920	34,129	11,190,061	34.28	1920–21	108,356	40,352	38,704

Sources: 1904–5, A. Garland, *Reseña industria del Perú*, Lima, 1905, pp. 66–7; Peru, Ministerio de Fomento, *Estadística de la industria algodonera en el Perú*, various years; *Extracto estadístico 1926*, p. 69; Bell, *Cotton*, Table 20.

section of contemporary opinion felt that the attractions of "el oro blanco" was having a detrimental impact on food supply and prices.[209] As early as December 1914 a farmer in the valley of Barranca wrote to the Sociedad Nacional Agraria complaining that because of the profits to be earned, even the smallest plots were being planted in cotton and there was an increasing scarcity of beans, rice, maize and potatoes.[210] In 1917, Ramón Aspíllaga, whose family was actively engaged in extending their cane and cotton lands, observed that around Lima[211] "The high prices of cotton are lessening the lands dedicated to pasture and food crops and are contributing to the dearness of necessities *even milk.*" As high food prices were seen as a major cause of social unrest, the government made a number of efforts during the war to increase food plantings and control the price and/or supply of some basic commodities. These measures met with little apparent success in either moderating price rises or forestalling unrest.

The boom in cotton during the war period greatly increased the size and importance of this industry. It not only produced for export, but also supplied raw material for both the local cotton textile industry and oil processing factories. Even though its expansion, through its pressure on food supplies, contributed to social unrest, it would seem to have been, on balance, a case of successful capitalist response by local entrepreneurs who dominated production. However, Thorp and Bertram contend[212] that although cotton had significant linkage effects and, because of its high returned value, generated considerable demand within the economy, its essentially small scale productive structure was "...not so favourable for the mobilisation of surplus for investment outside the sector. Cotton, in short, was an efficient 'engine' for keeping local demand buoyant, but rising cotton exports could not in themselves lead to a process of economic diversification."

IV

Although the production of both sugar and cotton was controlled by Peruvians, either natives or immigrants, there was still a good deal of foreign involvement. About 25% of sugar production came from foreign-owned estates,[213] and foreign merchant houses dominated the trade in both commodities. In mining the situation was markedly different. Here, as in Chile, by the outbreak of the First World War foreign domination of production, processing, and marketing was virtually complete. In about 1906 the deposit which was to produce about 80% of the world's supply of vanadium (a mineral used to harden steel) was taken over by the American Vanadium Company. About 90% of the country's copper, the single most important mineral export, was produced by two US firms, the Backus and Johnson Company and the Cerro de Pasco Mining Company.[214] The former had been set up in the 1880s by two American engineers who had worked with Henry Meiggs, the man who in the 1860s and 1870s had built railways in Peru and Chile, while the latter firm, incorporated in 1902, was backed by a syndicate led by the US mining magnate James Ben Ali Haggin and included J. P. Morgan, the Vanderbilts and Hearsts, Henry Clay Frick, and Darius Ogden Mills. Both firms consolidated their hold on the industry by a relentless campaign of buying out local miners. By the First World War Cerro, which controlled mines at Cerro de Pasco and Morococha as well as extensive coal deposits and a railway, was responsible for about 75% of Peru's copper exports.[215]

The industry here was affected by the changes in the world market outlined above. At the outbreak of war, production was stopped, and although work had begun again by 19 August, output in the last months of the year was reduced by about 50%.[216] Backus and Johnson closed one of its two blast furnaces, workers were laid off and wages cut. A visitor to Cerro de Pasco at this time observed, "The huge chimneys which reach menacingly into the heavens only occasionally belch their enormous puffs of smoke into space."[217] By the end of the year the noxious smoke was billowing once again from the smelters, as market conditions settled and began to improve. In fact, total exports for the year fell only marginally. With the strong recovery in price from 1915, output in Peru rose rapidly. The quick response to higher prices was possible because both major companies had carried out a program of extensive improvements, many of which were just coming on stream when the war broke out. For example, in 1913 Backus and Johnson finished its converting plant, and a new blast furnace was brought into production in the following year. Both companies also began to use their recently built hydroelectric plants in 1914.[218]

Output rose during the war and as prices increased until 1917, so did export earnings. Price fixing imposed by the US government in 1917 and the subsequent unstable market conditions immediately after the war meant that copper did not enjoy such an extended boom as Peru's agricultural exports. Nonetheless, judging by Cerro's performance,[219] earnings held up well, and although profits fell from the extraordinary levels reached in 1917, they too remained fairly substantial until 1921. The mining companies' sudden prosperity attracted the immediate interest of the government, desperate to increase its revenues because of the massive fall in import duties. Late in 1915 a sliding scale tax was imposed on both agricultural and mineral exports.[220] This was obviously not popular with the mining companies, but with international demand so strong and profits at such high levels they could easily afford to pay.[221] Duties on copper soon accounted for a substantial share of government revenue (Table 3.28).

The war brought windfall profits for the mine owners and also saw further consolidations and US takeovers. Bollinger writes[222] "... it is a remarkable fact that almost every major proven copper deposit in Peru was in United States hands by 1921." Besides the continued buying up of Peruvian mines, in 1916 the Anaconda Company took an option on major copper deposits near Arequipa, which they purchased in 1920. In the north, the American Mining and Smelting Company obtained an option on the Gildemeister's copper mines in Quirvilca. In 1919 Cerro, now reorganized as the Cerro de Pasco Copper Corporation, absorbed Backus and Johnson.[223] The War seems, therefore, to have

Table 3.28 Peruvian copper. Production, prices, workers, 1910–1921. Export tax on copper 1916–1920

	Production mt	Production £p	Price £ s d/ton	All mine workers
1910	27,374	1,414,124		
1911	27,734	1,411,416		
1912	26,970	1,867,855		18,610
1913	27,776	1,814,266		19,515
1914	27,090	1,530,344	64/0/0	20,335
1915	34,727	2,447,277	56/12/6	21,480

	Production mt	Production £p	Price £ s d/ton	All mine workers	£p	% of tax raised
1916	43,078	4,800,900	86/2/6	22,759	266,664	6.8%
1917	45,176	5,059,000	133/5/0	23,738	315,609	8.8%
1918	44,414	3,948,157	110/5/0	21,310	242,189	6.2%
1919	39,230	2,879,983	112/0/0	22,000	128,129	2.4%
1920	33,982	2,358,243	116/2/0	22,500	121,465	1.6%
1921	33,284	2,175,407		21,000		

Sources: Extracto estadístico 1918, Extracto estadístico 1925, The Economist, 21 February 1921, p. 445.

Table 3.29 *Peruvian trade. Percentage shares of major trading partners 1910–1920*

	Exports to				Imports from			
	UK	US	Germany	Chile	UK	US	Germany	Chile
1910	36	29	5	13	34	19	16	3
1911	36	29	8	17	32	23	17	1
1912	34	28	7	11	27	23	18	4
1913	37	34	7	13	26	30	17	4
1914	37	35	4	15	28	33	13	2
1915	26	45	—	21	21	48	3	3
1916	18	63	—	11	17	59	—	3
1917	20	59	—	13	14	65	—	3
1918	32	47	—	13	16	54	—	7
1919	31	47	—	12	14	62	—	6
1920	36	46	—	10	15	55	2	6

Source: Extracto estadístico 1925.

accelerated the dual process of foreign takeover and monopoly control of copper mining in Peru. Although levels of returned value were quite high in comparison with foreign mining companies elsewhere, the capital drain and the exclusion of local entrepreneurs from this lucrative sector had an overall detrimental effect on the Peruvian economy by reducing retained earnings and opportunities for domestic enterprise and accumulation.[224]

The same problems arose with regard to petroleum, the production of which was dominated by the International Petroleum Company, a Canadian subsidiary of Standard Oil of New Jersey. But the negative effects of petroleum exploitation were, if anything, greater than that of mining, for returned value was only between a quarter to a fifth as large as that from copper mining, and the company itself was far more aggressive in its dealings with the Peruvian government. For example, during the war the IPC successfully defied the government's authority to impose taxes on reassessed oil claims and escalated the dispute into a major diplomatic row and a heated domestic political issue.[225]

As well as a substantial increase in US direct investment, the war period also witnessed the strengthening of trading ties between the two countries. These were already considerably more advanced before the war than in the other three countries. By 1913 the US was supplying almost 30% of Peru's imports and taking 33% of her exports (Table 3.29). Much of this had to do with the powerful position of the US merchant house of W.R. Grace & Co. within the Peruvian economy. Not only had it become by the war years the most important foreign trading company in the country, but Grace also owned a major sugar estate, controlled by (1918) almost half of the cotton textile industry, and was actively involved in banking, insurance, and many other local business ventures.[226] The growth of US investment in mining and petroleum was another important factor in fostering a closer trading relationship. During the war the US share of both imports and exports rose (Table 3.29), while German trade was destroyed and the British position was quickly eroded. The latter was to recover somewhat after the war, especially with respect to agricultural exports,[227] but with regard to imports, exports, and investment the United States easily maintained its economic domination of the Peruvian economy, a domination greatly augmented during the First World War.

V

It was the combination of the strong position of US exports in the Peruvian market and the rapidity and sustained quality of the country's export boom which probably accounts for the fact that the quantum of imports had recovered its prewar level by 1916. Even though the terms of trade were generally unfavourable, the unprecedented surge in export earnings led to a substantial improvement in the capacity to import. Peru was the only country where this happened, except for a two year period in Chïle. Although an import quantum index is not available, both import figures (adjusted to give a constant quantity measure) in Table 3.30 and the data for the four countries' imports from the US and Britain (Table 3.31) show clearly that, especially in terms of consumer goods, Peru did not experience shortages during the war. This had an important negative effect on local industrial development.

VI

On the whole the war tended to accelerate trends already apparent in Peru before 1913. The most conspicuous aspect was the solidifying of the economic position of the United States. Because the war brought such a high degree of prosperity to the native export elites and because imports continued to be available, there was little reason for them to be displeased either with foreign takeovers, many of which put money in local pockets, or with the export orientation of the Peruvian economy.

Table 3.30 *Peruvian imports 1911–1918 (adjusted values)**

	(000 £p)							
	1911	1912	1913	1914	1915	1916	1917	1918
Food & drink etc.	805	987	890	676	680	997	1,285	1,193
Manufactured consumer goods	1,893	1,954	1,975	1,493	915	1,922	2,419	1,718
Fuel	299	202	395	319	150	433	366	300
Raw materials	202	85	77	88	35	88	72	77
Semi-finished goods	823	850	1,036	860	557	968	880	905
Producer goods	1,037	889	1,458	1,212	664	1,068	1,139	1,171
Other[†]	330	174	256	283	102	1,172	2,798	102
Total	5,389	5,141	6,087	4,931	3,103	6,648	8,959	5,466

Sources: Calculated from *Estracto estadístico 1919.* *From 1910 to 1915 the official values given to imports remained the same. In 1916 and again in 1917 these were adjusted upwards, in the first year by an unknown amount, in the second by an average of 21.46%. On the basis of a small random sample the 1916 figures given above were deflated by 25%. This is at best a very rough measure.
[†] "Other" includes live animals, "diverse goods" and, most importantly, gold and silver.

Table 3.31 *Indices of Latin American imports from Britain and the United States 1912–1920*

	(at 1913 prices) (1912 = 100)			
	Peru	Argentina	Brazil	Chile
1913	115	108	97	100
1914	85	64	52	69
1915	78	63	52	54
1916	112	68	57	32
1917	123	59	52	95
1918	109	57	45	101
1919	121	72	70	73
1920	192	90	90	74

Share of imports from UK & US imports in 1912

54%	66%	60%	66%

Source: Thorp and Bertram, *Peru*, p. 128.

If anything, the wartime experience strengthened faith in this orientation, as capital poured into cotton and sugar estates. Except for the unseemly battle with the IPC, there were also fewer manifestations of economic or cultural nationalism than in other countries. Everything did not, however, proceed smoothly. A glaring contradiction in these years was that while exporters and business in general seem to have done remarkably well, the great mass of Peruvians did not share in the war's bounty. If anything real wages fell.[228] This led, as it did in the other countries, to mounting social unrest. In Peru this was found not only among urban workers and certain sections of the middle class, but also among rural workers both on the coastal plantations and in the mines. Faced with these challenges, and already politically divided and vulnerable, the export elite, who had profited handsomely during the war, were unable to maintain their oligarchic state once the conflict had ended.[229] Although during Leguía's *Oncenio* (1919–30) there was no attack on their economic position, the political authority of most leading Civilistas was substantially undermined and the economy, especially what were to become its most important export sectors, came increasingly under the sway of US capital.

Conclusion

What does the course of foreign trade and the varying fortunes of the different countries during the First World War tell us about the nature of Latin American capitalism? Did the events of this period bring about any significant changes which shaped subsequent development?

Because primary export sectors were the main engines driving these peripheral capitalist economies, it was not particularly surprising that the initial dislocation of the world economy caused by the outbreak of the war should have caused such massive disruption. However, the widespread nature of this disruption and the rapidity with which it spread was a painful reminder of the extent to which so much of economic life had become directly and indirectly dependent on foreign trade. But problems arose not simply because these were primary producers tied to the international economy. As noted above, there were other countries in a roughly similar position. It was the extent to which the economic fabric of these societies had been woven by and remained under the powerful influence of foreign merchants, banks, insurance companies, railways, public utilities, etc., which made the trade dependence such a fundamental liability in terms of both economic stability and a more thoroughgoing capitalist transformation.

Trade dependence was also apparent in that the economic recovery that occurred in the four countries varied for the most part with the relative success of their export sectors. This was a clear continuation of prewar trends. As regards exports, the war did not represent a loosening of Latin America's ties with the metropolitan countries. If anything, the reverse was true, particularly as the character of the trade revival was determined by Allied demands for specific primary commodities. As Gravil has argued in the case of Argentina, and as seems to have been true in varying degrees with all the countries, the metropolitan powers exerted a particularly blatant form of coercion with respect to trade during the war. Control of shipping, bulk purchasing, blockades, blacklists, and direct threats for failure to comply with Allied demands all served to limit the economic sovereignty of the four republics. Of course, it might be argued that the exigencies of war forced the Allies to take these steps. This is partially true. Nonetheless, it seems clear that in many cases the war served as a convenient pretext for holding down commodity prices by creating and enforcing monopsonies and using blacklists to cripple German economic interests so as better to control Latin American trade in the postwar period. On the whole external economic intervention probably did not in most cases create insurmountable problems for exporters, for prices did rise. However, it is unlikely that such intervention did not reduce the extent of export prosperity. Furthermore, the very fact that during the war the central pillar of primary export capitalism could be so easily manipulated against the interests of the exporting countries attests to the essential weakness and vulnerability of their economic structures, structures which were in place largely to perpetuate a particular brand of capitalist development geared to complement but not replicate the more progressive industrial capitalism of the United States and Europe.

This weakness and vulnerability is further underlined if what happened to imports and the terms of trade is considered. Export prices and profits may have risen, but in most cases import prices rose more. Even when this was not the case and the terms of trade improved, both import and export prices increased steadily. This created hardship for workers and the urban middle classes, partly because of dearer imports and partly because the Allies' demand for food reduced domestic supply and drove up prices. Of course, these movements were not determinant, they simply set the stage. Who was to bear the burden of inflation was a matter decided by class struggle, and in all countries this became particularly bitter during and immediately after the war. In those cases in which terms of trade declined, this represented a transfer of economic surplus to the metropolitan countries, although the extent of this drain was mitigated to some degree by the physical difficulties in obtaining needed imports. Finally, the shortage of strategic imports, especially capital goods and fuel, was another major drag on economic advance in the region, for growth in the prewar years was predicated on the easy availability of these commodities and they could not be quickly or cheaply replaced.

The preceding arguments might seem to suggest, as the diffusionists would have it, that economic growth is best served when the links with the world economy are strongest. This is true, but only because these economies were largely shaped, by external forces and their respective elites, to fit in with the international capitalist system developed in the nineteenth century. When this system was working smoothly it was to be expected that it would generate growth, although as has been argued, this growth was not laying the basis for materially progressive capitalist advance. Also, the war effectively destroyed the nineteenth-century world economy. The new version of this economy constructed in the interwar period was a much more fragile affair, partly because a protectionist United States replaced free trade Britain as the principal creditor nation. Under the new rules of the game the chimerical vision of "modernization" through export-led growth was to prove increasingly difficult to sustain. It became virtually impossible in the 1930s. However, by looking only at foreign trade no conclusion about the success or failings of capitalism in the republics can be reached. What has to be considered is how trade was linked to the evolution of socio-political and economic structures. This issue will be considered in the final chapter after more pieces of the puzzle have been examined.

With regard to the second question posed at the beginning of this conclusion – what wartime changes in foreign trade were important after 1918 – there were three of major significance. The first was the quite drastic alteration in the world economy outlined above. This effectively altered both the basic international context as well as many of the key variables which had guided the course of Latin American development before the war. The second change brought in by the war was closely allied to the first, the much greater involvement of the United States. This took two principal forms. As a market and a supplier of imports the US massively increased its share of Latin American trade. While the conflict in Europe was an undoubted help, this move was in progress before 1914. It was also strongly encouraged by the US government, in what came to be a major campaign to capture the region for the US business. Along with trade came increased investment. This was most evident in Peru and Chile where large US firms consolidated their position in mining and petroleum. Although similar takeovers of export sectors were not seen in the other countries, here too US investments began to increase markedly. The trend of greater trade and investment which became so pronounced during the war was to be strengthened in the interwar period. The shift of the metropolitan centre from Britain to the United States was to lead to a significantly different and, in many respects, more insidious form of foreign domination and economic deformation.

Finally, despite Allied machinations, high profits were being earned in most export sectors during the war period. This caused many domestic as well as foreign entrepreneurs to increase substantially their investment in export production. For reasons outlined above, this was most apparent in Peru, Chile, and Brazil and somewhat less evident in Argentina. The extraordinary demands of the war years, therefore, served to make primary export more attractive, and in this way rather than providing a period of isolation from external pressures or an opportunity for economic diversification the experience of the First World War tended to reinforce the prewar pattern of primary export capitalist development. But, as will be argued, this reinforcement brought with it strong countertrends. The manner in which the pattern of development was strengthened, the social unrest and costs associated with it, together with the war's stark illumination of Latin America's woeful lack of economic independence provoked the beginnings of a strong, albeit diverse, nationalist backlash which was to offer political and economic alternatives to primary export dependence. This was to prove one of the most important legacies of the First World War for Latin America.

4

Seeking financial solutions

Introduction

I

The dislocation of Latin American finances brought about by the outbreak of war was savage but, given that the region's economies had been so closely tied to the international system, this was to be expected. Similar events were repeated throughout the world not only in dependent primary exporters, but also in such a powerful industrial country as the United States. The question pursued in this chapter is not so much whether or not crises were initiated in the centre and then spread to the periphery, but rather how by looking at events during the war we can begin to understand more clearly how the course of peripheral capitalist change was influenced by the nature of the various domestic financial systems, and how these systems themselves were, in many important respects, shaped by external forces. These are issues which, surprisingly, have received little critical attention. Scholars have identified particular problems, such as reliance on capital imports, or the key role played by foreign banks, but capitalism creates and comes to rely upon an integrated financial structure for its development and these structures in Latin America have not been systematically investigated. By "financial structure" is meant not only institutions such as banks, insurance companies, the stock exchange, etc., but also the framework which conditioned the formation of governments' fiscal and monetary policies as well as the larger international financial network, including in this the massive inflow of foreign capital. Although the latter is not strictly part of the structure, it is included here because of its strong pervasive influence on Latin American finance and economic growth in the decades before the war.

A full-scale analysis of the entire financial system is, however, beyond the scope of this study. Such an investigation would demand, among other things, detailed surveys of governments' fiscal and monetary policies, the movement of foreign capital, the provision of short-term credit, as well as the operation of the insurance companies, the banking system, and local capital markets. Given the relative paucity of secondary works on these topics,[1] especially the latter three, a comprehensive picture of the financial system would require a separate study for each country based on extensive primary research. What is offered here is no more than an outline of how some of the main elements of the financial systems functioned during the war, with special emphasis on the state sector, its revenue, expenditure, and borrowing. Attention is also given to foreign capital and the lending activities of the banks, in so far as these can be gauged from the official figures. All were important factors which strongly conditioned economic performance. The particular concern here is to see how these factors were in turn influenced by external constraints. Before doing this, some more general points need to be made about how these constraints affected the operation of Latin America's financial structures.

II

With their economies oriented *hacia afuera*, the high degree of direct and indirect foreign domination of Latin America's financial structures is not too surprising. This took many forms. The dependence on capital imports is one of the factors most commonly discussed, probably because it was of such concern to both investors and politicians at the time and is also central to most classical theories of imperialism. In the prewar years the massive inflows of foreign capital financed a wide range of infrastructural projects, the most important of which was the railways. They also served to prop up free-spending governments and helped these countries maintain their balance of payments positions, in many cases in difficulty because of the increasing burden of servicing previous debts. Immediately before the war direct investment in productive enterprises also grew. This was particularly evident in Peru and Chile where large US firms moved into mining, and in the former country, into petroleum.

The advantages from such a flood of capital were obvious, the disadvantages less so. The principal benefit to Latin America was that foreign investment allowed a much higher rate of capital accumulation, so central to any capitalist transformation. The building of extensive rail networks, ports, and public utilities would all have taken much longer without external assistance. However, a price was exacted for this more rapid growth, and in the end it may have been too high.

Triffin has argued that although in the long run the balance of payments position was assisted by capital imports, this was paid for by "perverse fluctuations in the availability of such capital" which contributed, together with other factors, to the instability of exchange.[2] The primary export economies could also not protect themselves against the cessation of lending during cyclical downturns and the amplitude of such cycles therefore tended to be more extreme than in Britain, the principal investing country, which during a crisis, such as that of 1913, was able to shift part of the burden of its balance of payments adjustment to its debtors.[3] A crisis could also be triggered by local events such as harvest failures, an overextension of credit or political upheavals, but the effects of these were made considerably worse by the growing intrusion of externally generated financial constraints.

There were other more long-term costs associated with high levels of foreign borrowing. Firstly, much of the profits from the investment flowed out of the countries, thereby limiting continued and expanded levels of capital formation. Large amounts of foreign capital, by dominating certain areas of investment, may have dulled the local propensity to invest and in this way served to slow the rate of domestic capital accumulation. For example, Quiroz argues that in the years before the war the excessive import of capital to a limited Lima market "...forced the displacement of scarce native capital from secure investments without offering alternative opportunities for the uprooted funds... Local sources of capital formation were wasted as a result and not adequately served or channeled."[4] The ability to borrow abroad also greatly reduced the pressure on governments to modernize taxation. Finally, in terms of the impact on the economic structure, it can be argued that in Latin America because heavy dependence on foreign capital became a deep-rooted rather than transitory phenomenon (as it had been, for example, in the United States) it became an important factor tending to reinforce reliance on primary exports. This was because, not surprisingly, much of that capital went into projects directly or indirectly related to export production. Furthermore, the need to earn foreign exchange to cover mounting foreign debts generally served to enhance the already powerful position of the primary export sectors, especially in terms of government policy. It is for this reason that Saes and Szmrecsáyni's observation on Brazil is more widely applicable. They write that during the years 1880–1930, foreign capital in Brazil "...at the same time as contributing to the mobilization and the development of the forces of production, also represented an obstacle to this same mobilization and development."[5]

Given the aforementioned conditions, the cutting off of foreign loans during the war should have devastated most Latin American economies. It did not. There were, of course, innumerable problems of external and internal economic adjustment, but these did not prove insuperable. For example, balance of payments positions were on the whole not compromised because of inordinately large falls in imports and, with the exception of Brazil, substantial increases in export earnings. Ordinarily, the latter would have induced a rise in imports, but this did not occur due to the problems of shipping and supply caused by the war. Domestic adjustment was not as easy. Again, because of the special circumstances created by the war, many "normal" adjustment mechanisms were inoperative. Each country's experience varied, but generally it seems that the burden, in the form of rising prices and in some cases high unemployment, fell most heavily on the workers and urban middle class. Much of this had to do with the nature of governments' monetary and fiscal policies. These were in turn strongly influenced by exogenous forces.

The weaknesses engendered in the financial structure by the reliance on foreign capital was compounded by the fact that about 50% or more of central government revenues were derived from import duties. When there was a downturn in trade, government income would, therefore, fall and if, as often happened, exchange too was adversely affected, the cost of the external debt would increase at the very time when it was most difficult to pay and when foreigners were likely to be least interested in new investment. Either expenditure would, therefore, have to be cut and domestic activity reduced or deficits carried, financed by internal loans or money would have to be printed with the likelihood of generating inflation, putting further pressure on exchange and worsening the debt position. Matters were significantly complicated because the export elites in all countries generally favored exchange devaluation as it gave them higher commodity prices in local currency. The regressive taxation system also worked to their immediate advantage. All this led to a contradictory situation in which the same conditions which created the government's financial fragility could strengthen the economic position of export elites who controlled the state which ultimately they depended upon to protect their interests. It must be emphasized, however, that although these elites were politically dominant, government policy did not always mirror their immediate interests, if those interests were such as to threaten the overall stability of the state.[6]

From 1914 imports, and with them government revenue, were drastically cut. Together with the sudden drying up of foreign loans this put an almost intolerable strain on government finances, and it took some time before solutions could be found. While these varied considerably, in most cases it involved a degree of deficit financing, the inflationary effects of which, along with increases in excise taxes, more expensive imports, and the Allies' strong demand for foodstuffs made a major contribution to the rise in the cost of living. With wages held down, this became the spark that ignited the wave of labor unrest and urban middle-class discontent which swept through the region from the latter years of the war and helped to undermine the absolute political power of the landed elites.

The final major external intrusion in Latin America's domestic financial structures was the strong presence of foreign-owned banks. Their relative position varied over time, but in 1913 they controlled between 26% and 28% of deposits in Peru and Argentina, about 46% in Brazil and 40% in Chile.[7] British banks predominated, but there were also some important German and French institutions, and from 1914, with the change in US law, North American banks began to be established.[8] If the experience of the British banks in Argentina is representative, by the 1900s policy was being made in London and was closely attuned to changes in the City and the interests of the shareholders.[9] The actions of the foreign banks were, therefore, delimited, if not determined, by economic conditions outside Latin America. To the extent that these institutions played a leading role in local financial affairs they directly transmitted and substantially reinforced the exogenous financial pressures already brought to bear on Latin American economies by their dependence on primary exports, foreign capital and the London money market.

The main concern of these banks, specifically the British ones, but also other foreign and many local private banks, was with financing foreign trade. Although they had begun to diversify somewhat in the immediate prewar period and were providing financial accommodation for certain industrial and infrastructural projects,[10] generally they pursued fairly conservative policies which tended overall to reinforce the existing pattern of primary export-based growth. Interestingly, however, they were usually reluctant to offer long-term loans to agriculturalists, probably because of the high risk of such investment. It was this behavior combined with the fact that they drew their deposits from local pools of savings, and that they made and remitted abroad tremendous profits (the British banks paid dividends twice to four times the average of other Latin America investments) which created such bitter feeling against foreign banks in Latin America.[11] Furthermore, their very strength may have tended to weaken the local banks, many of which concentrated on riskier development loans. Weakness was engendered because in times of crisis depositors would tend to switch their money to what they perceived as the more secure foreign banks,[12] and secondly, because these banks dominated the relatively safer end of the financial market. This made it more difficult for the local banks to spread their risks over a wide range of projects. While their careful methods may have served as a useful model of financial propriety it can be argued that paradoxically the foreign banks helped create an unbalanced and therefore fragile banking structure. At the same time they were instrumental, together with the foreign merchant houses which extended credit, in solidifying these countries' export orientations and the political systems by which they were supported. Charles Jones comments that the British banks, "...lent a semblance of stability to inherently unstable national economies... All in all, they had proved a powerful agent in the maintenance of the political status quo during a period of turbulent economic change."[13] Their performance during the war was little different, but their dominance began to be eroded by increasing nationalist sentiment and greater direct government support for official or semi-official banks such as the Banco de Chile, the Banco do Brasil or the Banco de la Nación in Argentina.

All the above-mentioned factors demonstrate the high degree of external orientation and dependence which, in general, characterized Latin American financial structures. These structures seem to have suffered from an extreme form of what Hyman Minsky has identified in the more recent period as "systemic fragility."[14] That is, weaknesses engendered in the financial system not by accident or government policy, but rather by the normal functioning of that system. For example, Quiroz shows that while there were many factors which influenced financial conditions in Peru, it was those directly associated with the international economy, such as the export–import trade, exchange rate movements and foreign capital flows, which had the most telling effect on the domestic financial system.[15] This contributed to the chronic instability of the entire economy.

Another important weakness was that these structures tended to be fragmented in that, although backing was given to certain industrial projects, financial institutions were set up essentially to support the import–export trade and not producers looking to the domestic market. This might mean, for example, that an importer of particular goods would find it easier to obtain credit than a local manufacturer of the same product, or that a farmer raising cotton for export would get an advance from a foreign merchant, whereas he could get no financial support if he wanted to grow food crops for the nearby urban market. This clearly did not rule out the development of such locally directed projects, it just made that development more difficult. The problem was expressly recognized in many countries and was the basis for the continual and strong demands from farmers and industrialists for the creation of financial institutions which would meet their needs for both credit and long-term finance. McKinnon has argued[16] that in recent years excessive government intervention has contributed to the creation of fragmented capital markets in many Third World countries and that this "...causes the misuse of labor and land, suppresses entrepreneurial development, and condemns important sectors of the economy to inferior technologies." But up to the First World War it was not government policy which created this fragmentation, but the "normal" operation of the classically liberal international financial system. This provides further evidence, if that was needed, of the limitations of the theory of comparative advantage, a theory which is often adduced in support of the idea that the export of primary commodities reflected the optimal use of resoures in Latin America.

III

As outlined in Chapter 2, the initial impact of the war on Latin American finances was devastating and by and large fairly similar. The timing and character of recovery varied considerably, however. In Argentina conditions had more or less returned to normal by the beginning of 1915, whereas in Chile there was little improvement until later in the year when nitrate sales picked up once more. Although Peru's exports had bounced back fairly quickly and a strong balance of trade was recorded in 1914 and 1915, it was not until 1916 that the financial situation was more or less normalized and exchange reached par. This was due, among other things, to political uncertainty (resolved by the election of José Pardo in August 1915), public reluctance to accept paper money and a crisis in government finance. Brazil faced probably the worst financial difficulties during the war because of a weak trade position compounded by a heavy burden of both foreign and domestic debt. Maybe it was because conditions were so bad here that the government turned to the printing press to resolve its problems. Against all orthodox expectations this seems to have worked fairly well, at least as long as the war lasted.

The basis for the reestablishment of some form of financial order in Latin America was linked directly to the Allies' need for the region's commodities. By December 1914 the blockage in international foreign exchange had been cleared.[17] The reopening of the acceptance market in London, a greater contribution by the New York discount market, telegraphic sales and direct government purchases all facilitated the revival of trade. The pegging of the sterling–dollar exchange rate in January 1916 brought about greater international financial stability, and as Brown observed:[18] "The preservation of the sterling–dollar–franc nucleus introduced into economy of the Allied countries a volume of imports whose whose cost was less than it would have been had the exchanges not been pegged." This increased the effective demand for the products of the neutral countries, while at the same time subjecting them to a degree of inflationary pressure. Brown concludes:[19] "In this way the burden of financing the war was transferred from the banking systems of the Allies to the banking system of the United States and in less degree to those of smaller neutrals by the mere fact of relatively stable exchanges." The overriding importance for the Allies of maintaining exchange also led to the accumulation of sterling balances in London and credit-exchange agreements such as that concluded between Britain, France and Argentina for the sale of grain in January 1918.[20] The power to manipulate the international financial system was a major weapon in the Allies' wartime economic arsenal, but it remains unclear to what extent Brazil, Peru, Argentina and Chile were adversely affected by this, for although the problems associated with the ubiquitous foreign links remained, the effective suspension of both the gold standard and the "normal" functioning of the international financial system insulated the peripheral countries to some degree from sanctions and increased their freedom of action in the conduct of their domestic financial affairs.

Although the response of each country was unique, this newfound freedom remained, on the whole, unexploited. Domestic capital was not mobilized to replace foreign loans. Instead projects, such as railway building or public works, which had relied on external financing, were greatly reduced or suspended. Governments made only marginal changes in their fiscal or monetary policies, while banks and merchant houses retained, and may have even increased, their essentially conservative approach to lending and credit. All this is not particularly surprising. The War delivered a major shock to the export economies, created social and political upheaval, and raised doubts about the efficaciousness of export dependence for long-term development.

But this shock did not really provide the opportunity for fundamental economic change. This being the case, Latin America's
financial structures, both a product of her primary export capitalism
and an essential element in maintaining that system, were hardly likely
to undergo radical alteration. Nonetheless, by studying the wartime
crisis and the varying responses to it much can be learned about the
strengths and weaknesses of some of the principal components of these
structures, how they influenced the pattern of the region's economic
development and were in turn influenced by the character of that
development.

Brazil

According to Williams,[21] during the war the financial difficulties
facing Brazil were worse than in either Argentina or Chile. This was
due, he claims, to a combination of a lackluster export performance,
the burden of heavy prewar borrowing, and the ending of capital
inflows. One manifestation of this was the adverse movement in
Brazilian exchange (Table 4.2). The value of the milréis fell dramatically
from 1914–15 and even though some improvement began in 1917, it
remained below par throughout the war. This contrasts with the other
countries under review where exchange was more often at a premium
over these years. Williams' analysis of exchange rate movements is,
however, questionable because it was precisely at the time when
Brazil's export trade was at its worst that exchange began to improve.
This apparent paradox is discussed below. Whatever the causes, the
devalued milréis increased exporters' earnings and afforded protection
to local industry but made the foreign debt more onerous. At the same
time the Brazilian government had to cope with a much lower income
level as imports fell. Although for the war years there are only figures
for budgeted rather than actual expenditure, it seems that spending was
not significantly reduced, partly because of the heavy burden of debt
servicing and partly because fixed capital formation by the state, while
falling in real terms, was maintained at a reasonable level (Table 4.6).
The result was substantial budget deficits (Table 4.3), albeit with large
reductions in the amount of annual shortfall after 1915. Unable to
cover these by foreign borrowing, as it had done before 1914, the
government was forced to issue interest-bearing Treasury instruments
and a great deal of paper currency. This gave a boost to inflation and
also put pressure on exchange rates, already troubled by the
precipitous drop in capital imports. During the war, federal, state, and
municipal borrowing was cut to almost nothing and, although private

Table 4.1 *Brazil: Main identifiable balance of payments items*[a]

Year	Exports	Imports	Trade balance[b]	Interest on public debt[c]	Balance of current account	New Long-term public loan[d]	Amortization of Public debt	Balance of capital account	Total balance
					(£ millions)				
1913	65,451	67,116	−1,715	7,596	−9,311	19,133	6,913	12,212	2,901
1914	46,803	35,473	11,060	7,505	3,555	4,200	1,498	2,252	5,807
1915	53,951	30,008	23,863	4,977	18,886	—	2,616	−2,616	16,270
1916	56,462	40,369	16,093	5,417	10,676	270	1,435	−1,165	9,511
1917	63,031	44,510	18,521	6,540	11,891	—	3,078	−3,078	8,903
1918	61,118	52,817	8,351	8,264	87	—	5,212	−5,212	−5,125

Source: Fritsch, "Great War," p. 48.

Notes: [a] The balance of payments given here is only a rough estimate as it excludes, most importantly, the movement of private foreign capital and remittances. [b] Approximates trade plus freight and insurance as exports valued FOB and imports CIF. [c] Includes commissions and fees. [d] Loans net of discounts and commissions. Excludes funding loans.

foreign investment continued, especially from the United States, it did so at a much lower level. Despite the massive decline in the inflow of foreign capital and the deficit on the capital account which it apparently caused from 1915, because of the great reduction in imports and a positive trade balance, the balance of payments seems to have remained healthy until 1918 (Table 4.1). The banking system too was affected by the war. Between 1913 and 1915 credit was restricted, the value of bills discounted fell by 17.4% and advances on current accounts were reduced by 11.6%.[22] However, as more money was printed, credit eased and interest rates fell, from 11% in 1915 to between 6% and 6.5% in the following year.[23]

The aforementioned factors were both complex and closely inter-related with each other and, of course, with the performance of the export sector. But the aim here is not to present a detailed technical treatment of Brazilian finance. Rather it is to see how domestic financial conditions were influenced by external pressures and how these conditions in turn affected the general level of economic performance. The connections are traced starting with the problems facing the government because of the collapse of imports, the duties on which were their main source of revenue, and the difficulty in raising foreign loans. The solutions adopted are then considered, as are the wider economic and political impact of these solutions. Although it is difficult to understand any one facet of the financial system in isolation, for the sake of clarity it is necessary in the first instance to consider them separately.

Brazil conformed to the general Latin American pattern of a narrowly based and vulnerable government revenue structure. This was compounded by the fact that the states too were heavily dependent on foreign trade for their income, export taxes providing the largest single element.[24] In 1915 J.P. Wileman commented[25]

It is commonly asserted that taxation is exhausted, and so it is if by taxation is meant further burdens on the poor. Imports and Exports can bear no more and it is the richer classes, that have benefitted by the financial orgy of the last few years, to whom the administration should look to provide resources not only to meet current expenditure, but to amortise actual and perspective issues of paper money.

However, the rich, in control of the state, did not choose to tax themselves and the "burdens on the poor" were made heavier. A slight increase in import duties was effected by raising the proportion which had to be paid in gold from 35% to 40%. With the milréis at 12d this

Table 4.2 *Brazilian exchange rates 1913–1918*

	1913	1914	1915	1916	1917	1918
			[par: milréis = 16d]			
January	16.26	16.06	13.87	11.56	12.00	13.75
February	16.22	16.05	12.75	11.67	11.89	13.42
March	16.14	15.89	13.01	11.73	11.84	13.34
April	16.08	15.83	12.20	11.64	12.05	13.11
May	16.09	15.86	12.28	12.05	13.31	13.05
June	16.05	16.05	12.42	12.30	13.66	12.98
July	16.06	15.81	12.83	12.59	13.36	12.22
August	16.08	13.53	12.31	12.56	13.05	12.28
September	16.08	11.95	12.09	12.36	12.86	12.14
October	16.08	12.56	12.25	12.19	13.05	12.51
November	16.08	13.59	12.25	12.00	13.12	13.51
December	16.08	14.05	12.09	11.97	13.69	13.70

Source: Fritsch, "Great War," p. 47.

represented about a 5% rise in the effective rate.[26] For the mass of the population it was the higher excise taxes which were more worrying. These were raised on a whole range of goods including (in order of their yields) drink, tobacco, textiles, matches, boots, salt.[27] While the receipts from import duties had fallen by 50% between 1913 and 1918, excise collections were up by 46% and their share of total revenue had become substantial (Table 4.3). There was a slight rise in direct taxes due to a temporary (1915–17) increase of the amount taken from civil servants' wages, but at its peak the total contribution of direct taxation was never more than 4% of revenue.[28] Therefore, although there was a lessening of dependence on the external sector the ruling class insured that their relative share was not increased and taxation remained highly regressive. In doing this they tended to exacerbate another problem, for higher excise duties could not help but give a further twist to the inflationary spiral which was to spark off such violent social unrest at the end of the war.

Before the war the government had relied on continued inflows of foreign capital to cover its increasing deficits. By 1914 its external debt had reached £103,500,000.[29] Together with state and city liabilities (£48,200,000) this was almost twice the amount registered eight years before,[30] and represented the highest ratio of government debt to export earnings in the whole of Latin America.[31] With such a large

Table 4.3 *Brazilian Federal Government revenue and expenditure
(budgeted) 1910–1920*

Year	Revenue	Expen-diture	Balance	(1000 contos de réis) Revenue from:	
				Import duties	Excise taxes
1910	524.8	623.5	− 99	288.7 (55%)	54.6 (10%)
1911	563.5	681.9	− 188.4	317.7 (56%)	59.8 (11%)
1912	615.4	789.2	− 173.8	348.2 (57%)	62.6 (10%)
1913	654.4	763.0	− 108.6	344.3 (53%)	65.0 (10%)
1914	423.0	766.0	− 343.0	195.1 (46%)	52.2 (12%)
1915	404.0	688.0	− 284.0	152.6 (38%)	67.9 (17%)
1916	478.0	686.0	− 208.0	184.3 (39%)	83.8 (18%)
1917	537.0	801.0	− 264.0	158.4 (30%)	117.7 (22%)
1918	619.0	867.0	− 248.0	171.4 (28%)	119.7 (19%)
1919	626.0	932.0	− 306.0	212.7 (34%)	131.8 (21%)
1920	922.0	1227.0	− 305.0	348.9 (38%)	175.6 (19%)

Sources: *Anuário estatístico do Brasil*, VII, Rio, 1946, p. 457; Villela and Suzigan, *Government Policy*, pp. 346–7.

debt to service it is not surprising that the international crisis of 1913–14 created immense financial problems for Brazil, leading to negotiations with a consortium of European banks for a large funding loan. These talks collapsed in July 1914.[32] The 1914 Funding Loan of £14,500,000 from Rothschilds, agreed to in October, relieved the immediate strain somewhat. Interest payments on sixteen previous loans (about 85% of the country's external debt) were effectively suspended for three years as they were to be met with the Funding bonds and amortization on most of these loans was put off until 1927.[33] The previous funding loan of 1898 (£8,245,950), also with Rothschilds, was not included nor was the 1903 Rio Port Improvement Loan (£7,698,100), although amortization on the latter was postponed.[34] There were numerous attempts by the federal government to raise money abroad, particularly in the United States,[35] but only one seems to have been successful.[36] Economic stringency was thereby forced on Brazil and by 1920 the total foreign debt (including state and city debt) had been cut to £151,353,559.

States and cities also faced severe financial problems, but there was considerably less they could do about them as they could not print money. In 1916 their total external debt, much of which had been issued in France, stood at about £38,000,000 and £16,500,000 respectively.[37] To this was added over 400,000,000 milréis in funded internal debt and an unknown quantity of floating debt. The *South American Journal* reported that in 1914 of all states only Rio and São Paulo were able to service their debts fully.[38] Elsewhere in the country many cities and states defaulted and had to arrange funding loans. This made it virtually impossible for them to borrow additional sums during the war. Only the city of São Paulo, which had met its previous obligations, was able to raise a substantial loan in these years. In November 1916, it borrowed $5,500,000 for 12 years at 6% and issued at 86% of face value from the Equitable Trust Co. and Morris Imbrie both of New York.[39] If such harsh terms were being demanded generally it is little wonder more loans were not negotiated in Brazil.

Besides loans to government, there was also substantial foreign private direct investment in Brazil. Between 1860 and 1913, about £292,000,000 had been invested by foreign companies operating in Brazil.[40] Although it is impossible to say with any assurance how much of this was outstanding by the First World War, Abreu estimates the figure at £255,900,000.[41] To this sum must be added the unknown quantity of foreign capital invested in Brazilian companies. More than 60% of investment which can be calculated was from Britain, but with the 1916 Order in Council prohibiting foreign capital issues, there was probably little new investment from here during the war.[42] French and German investments seems to have fallen even more sharply. Capitalists from the United States were more active, especially in meat-packing, banking, and paper manufacture,[43] but there was still a marked decline. For example, between 1909 and 1913, thirty-seven United States firms with an average nominal capital of $1,673,000 were officially authorized to operate in Brazil (some never did begin operations), whereas from 1914 to 1917 the number had dropped to twenty-two and the average capital to only $288,159.[44] The fall in investment by foreign companies together with the precipitous drop in loans to government undoubtedly fed through to reduce the level of economic activity generally and in the case of the latter decline, social overhead projects in particular.

Barred by circumstance from international markets, and needing to cover the record deficits, the central government, besides trying to cut expenditure, resorted to two expedients, increasing the internal debt and printing money. Between 1914 and 1918 the former rose from 758,673 to 1,012,138 contos.[45] This caused a great deal of comment at

Table 4.4 *Brazil's servicing of central government debt 1910–1920 and expenditure on gross fixed capital formation*

	External debt			Internal debt	Total	As % of expenditure	Gross fixed capital formation
	Interest	Amort-ization	Total				
1910	96,764	17,170	115,461	44,315	159,776	25.6	113,587
1911	81,625	5,003	87,765	39,342	127,107	18.6	138,173
1912	76,172	20,482	97,519	35,990	133,509	16.9	188,899
1913	88,964	20,402	114,437	44,885	159,322	20.3	171,665
1914	15,445	77,413	93,249	36,952	130,201	17.0	165,747
1915	24,376	108,796	133,172	36,977	170,149	24.7	148,872
1916	22,611	180,025	202,636	58,635	261,271	38.1	148,434
1917	22,350	183,022	205,527	69,719	275,246	34.4	174,450
1918	20,250	123,498	143,896	73,806	217,702	25.1	213,843
1919	21,384	138,352	160,155	89,501	249,736	26.4	239,563
1920	30,005	194,124	224,372	106,519	330,531	27.0	295,728

(Contos de réis)

Source: Villela and Suzigan, *Government Policy*, pp. 344–5, 350–1. Also see Table 4.3. *Note:* figures for 1915–20 estimated from budgets. The total for external debt service included commissions and brokerage fees, and internal debt serving includes interest, amortization and commissions and brokerage.

the time, for although the annual rate of increase was only slightly higher (7.5%) than in the four years leading up to the war (6.2%), in 1915 and 1916 there was a sudden jump of about 20%. Because the internal funded debt was made up of various kinds of interest-bearing treasury bills, when a great quantity came onto market it tended to depress their price and, therefore, gave rise to complaints from the business community, who had to accept these bills in payment of government debts. Conditions in early 1915 were particularly fraught, for in February 150,000 contos of renewable one-year treasury bills were authorized to pay off the government's deficit. These were augmented in March and May by further issues so that within the next two years the equivalent of 266,438 contos paper was made available, representing a potential increase in the internal debt of 35%. Matters were complicated by the fact that about 96,000 contos (£5,054,521) were in gold milréis at 5% (Treasury Bills or "Sabinas," named after the then Minister of Finance, Sabino Barroso), issued to cover government debts contracted in gold, while the remainder were in paper (Internal Bonds or *apólices*) and carried 6%.[46]

There was an immediate outcry from the government's creditors who demanded payment in cash. The Associação Comercial of Rio de Janeiro had a stormy meeting and then went to see the Finance Minister to demand the bonds be made legal tender.[47] This complaint went unheeded and the creditors were forced to accept the bonds. Their fears were soon realized for by July "Sabinas" were being traded at a 25% discount. However, by April of the following year this had fallen to between 7% and 8.5%, and there was a further reduction by 1917 when large-scale redemption began.[48] The government paid off the holders of "Sabinas" half in cash and half in new Internal Bonds. There was resistance to this by some large US companies such as United States Steel, the Baldwin Locomotive Co. and the American Bank Note Co., but they could do very little about it. The Brazilian government stood firm, partly because of the extreme anxiety over what unrestricted submarine warfare, begun by the Germans in 1917, would do to shipping and also because a bumper coffee crop was expected.[49] By early 1917, 80% of the holders had accepted the terms. Many of the large companies did most their business with the state and could not afford to push their objections too far.[50] Brazil was, therefore, clearly not powerless when dealing with foreign firms. By early in 1918 only £89,000 of the more then £5,000,000 of "Sabinas" remained outstanding and 140,000 of the 170,000 contos of Internal Bonds issued under the 1915 decrees had also been redeemed.[51] However, this was only carried out by issuing yet more Internal Bonds (191,000 contos to March 1918) and a great deal of inconvertible paper currency.

Up to the war Brazil, through the Caixa de Conversão, established in 1906 partially as a means to arrest the upward movement in exchange, had been steadily redeeming the stock of inconvertible paper with convertible notes.[52] This was brought to an end by the war when redemption was suspended to protect the country's stock of gold. The process then began to be reversed. In August 1914 the first major issue of 250,000 contos of inconvertible paper money was made. This was seen as an emergency measure only, not as part of an expansionist monetary policy.[53] That met with only partial success and a year later a further 350,000 contos had to be authorized. Most was used to cover the state's current expenses, but some was earmarked for particular projects, such as help for agriculture (11,000 contos), general loans to

Table 4.5 *Brazil notes in circulation. In banks and held by public*
1912–1918

	Notes in circulation			In banks	%	Held by public	%
	Incon- vertible	Con- vertible	Total				
December							
1912	607	397	1,004	209	20.6	804	79.4
1913	602	295	897	214	23.9	682	76.1
1914	833	158	981	311	31.7	669	68.3
1915	982	95	1,077	341	31.7	735	68.3
1916	1,123	95	1,218	340	27.9	877	72.1
1917	1,389	95	1,484	387	26.1	1,097	73.9
1918	1,679	21	1,700	462	29.4	1,108	70.1
1919	1,729	19	1,748	—	—	—	—
1920	1,829	19	1,848	—	—	—	—

The values above are in units of (1,000 contos).

Sources: WBR, 3 December 1918, p. 1143; Charles A. McQueen, *Foreign Exchange in Latin America. A Survey of Conditions since 1914.* Supplement to Commerce Reports, Trade Information Bulletin 316, Washington DC, 1925, p. 52. *Note:* the figures for holding in 1912 and 1918 have been calculated using McQueen's data for total issue and Wileman's percentage figures.

the banks (100,000 contos) and an advance to the Banco do Brasil (50,000 contos) to begin rediscounting operations.[54] In August 1917, a further 300,000 contos was authorized, half of which was to finance the São Paulo coffee valorization.[55] By the end of December 1918, there were 1,679,176 contos of inconvertible paper in circulation, an increase of about 1,000,000 from August 1914 (Table 4.5).[56]

The massive increase in paper currency had a potentially important impact on the rate of domestic inflation and the movement in exchange. It is hardly surprising that in Brazil, with foreign trade the critical sector of the economy and an extremely large external debt that had to be serviced in sterling, the movement of the exchange rate should have had a powerful impact on the domestic price level and also have been such a major political issue. Although the coffee interest generally favoured a devalued milréis, as Fritsch has shown,[57] in the prewar years despite their immense political power they were not always able to sway government policy in their favor. There is also some question as to the extent to which policy was able to influence the movement in exchange. These issues were highlighted by wartime experience.

It was widely held that the greater quantity of money together with the similarly steep rise in the internal funded debt would lead to a fall in the rate of exchange.[58] Williams and Redfield argued that this was in fact what happened during the war.[59] But, although the value of the milréis did fall, it is impossible to disentangle the relative weight of the various factors that brought this about. To one of the most informed contemporary observers, although there was an apparent connection between the growing quantity of paper and devalued milréis, this was not as clear-cut as might be thought. In February 1917, J.P. Wileman wrote,[60]

Painful experience has impressed but too deeply on Brazilian imagination the fact that, however, laudable the intention, overissue of paper money can never be indulged in with impunity. Anxiety as to what may be the effect of late additions to the currency is, however, tempered by astonishment at the apparent failure of existing conditions to respond to the most cherished of all exploded theories, accepted hitherto almost as an axiom – the quantity theory of money!

That between July, 1914 and May, 1918, exchange should have dropped from 16d. to 12d. seemed according to that theory, only the logical and inevitable consequence of the issue of paper money to value of Rs. 250,000:000$ in 1914. But what puzzles candid observers is that although as much again has been issued and the Government is, apparently, preparing to issue more, exchange scarcely budges, and for nearly two years has oscillated within the narrowest limits, around 12d. per milréis!

He went on to argue that although inconvertible currency had almost doubled, the stock of convertible notes was greatly reduced so that overall the supply had only increased by 22.7% since 1913. This ignores the difference in terms of the confidence in and, therefore, the value of inconvertible and gold-backed currency. He also maintained that the strong export performance and positive balance of payments had helped stabilize exchange. Wileman remained uneasy about using the printing press to solve the country's financial plight. Not only did it mean putting off finding a "real" solution, and burdening posterity with the debt, but it also meant higher prices and more social unrest. "Financial jugglers and ministers may gull the public for a time, but not always, and gradually the fact that debt must be paid by labor and labor alone is gradually being brought to the comprehension of the proletariat."[61] This was a most perceptive observation, but there is some question as to the accuracy of his analysis of exchange movements, for it was in 1917 and 1918, when coffee was at its lowest point, when the terms of trade and capacity to import became substantially more adverse (Table 3.2), and while new issues of both Internal Bonds and currency continued to be made, that the value of the milréis began to improve (Table 4.2). This is difficult to explain. Villela and Suzigan contend it was entirely because of the new regulations to control speculative exchange dealings imposed in July 1918 (Decree 13,110),[62] probably basing this on a similar claim made by the Banco do Brasil.[63] But while these may have helped maintain a better rate they did not initiate improvement. It had begun in mid-April 1917, following the United States declaration of war and the consequent heavy buying of coffee as well as other Brazilian exports.[64] There was a drop in the rate in July 1918 and then a sustained improvement from October. The timing of change, therefore, does not support the argument about the significance of the 1918 decree. Finally, although exporters clearly gained when exchange fell, during the war official policy decisions were aimed at trying to resolve the government's fiscal difficulties and overall it seems that it was external pressure which was in the end the most potent factor influencing movement in the value of the milréis.[65]

What were the economic effects of the movement in exchange and government fiscal and monetary policies? This a difficult question because of the many variables and the fact that there was continual interinfluence between financial and real factors. Some initial impressions can be gained by looking at the performance of the banks, taking this as one indication of wider economic activity. The impact of the war is immediately apparent in the statistics. The volume of discounted bills and loans fell, and the cash/deposit ratio rose dramatically as banks became very cautious. At the same time there was a substantial increase in the proportion of the total currency held by the banks, further confirming the reduction in economic activity. Fritsch writes[66] that, by increasing cash reserves and reducing credit, the banks "... wiped out the temporarily expansionary effect of the emergency note issue of late 1914 and the money supply resumed its falling trend during the first half of 1915." The data point to there being an improvement from 1916 and that it gathered strength in the following year at the very moment when the export and import trades began to experience a severe contraction. Government deficits and the printing of money may, therefore, have injected sufficient life into the economy from 1917 to counteract the effects of the depression in foreign trade, especially as it seems that spending on fixed capital formation began to increase significantly from 1917 (Table 4.4). Haddad's work on the growth of production per capita gives some support to this conclusion, showing a 3.4% rise between 1916 and 1917, although it also shows a small drop of .37% in the next year when the bank figures continue to indicate expansion.[67] This question cannot be satisfactorily resolved until we consider in detail the growth of manufacturing industry during the war.

It is interesting to compare the performance of national and foreign banks during the war, as it is indicative of the problems created by the strong presence of the latter within Brazil. Although they worked with money deposited by Brazilians, their policy was made in London or other European capitals, in the interests of their shareholders and influenced strongly by financial conditions in the City of London. Given these basic constraints it is hardly surprising that they both transmitted and accentuated European crises. The greater caution of the foreign banks at this time is obvious with their cash ratios soaring in 1914 and staying well above those of local banks throughout the period. It was this conservatism together with their reluctance to support local agriculture or small-scale industry which fueled national- ist hostility against them, and may have been a factor encouraging the government to bolster the Banco do Brasil, which was in effect its financial agent. Another reason for government intervention was the long-term dissatisfaction with the inelasticity of the banking system, especially the substantial seasonal drain to the cash-holding rural areas where there were few banks.[68] The Banco do Brasil received 50,000 contos in 1915 to develop its lending and discounting operations and much of the paper currency issued was channeled through it.[69] Twenty-two branches were opened in 1916, two years later there were thirty-seven established in all parts of the country[70] and total assets grew from 345,000 contos in 1914 to 1,145,686 in 1919, more than twice the total of the next largest bank. Topik argues that the financial dislocation brought by the war forced the government to assume a more interventionist role in the banking system through direct loans to banks (100,000 contos in 1914), its greater involvement with the Banco do Brasil and increased regulation. All this, he maintains, strengthened the domestic banks as against their foreign rivals.[71]

A number of seemingly contradictory conclusions follow for the preceding brief analysis of financial conditions in Brazil during the war. The crisis at the outbreak of the war provided a dramatic

Table 4.6 *Selected Brazilian banking statistics 1913–1919*

Year	(Foreign banks [for.] and National banks [nat.]) (1000 contos)						
	Sight deposits	Term deposits	Bills dis- counted	Loans	Mort- gages	Cash	Cash- deposit ratio
1913	475	253	295	440	108	214	29.4%
for.	(162)	(131)	(114)	(192)	—	(108)	(33.3%)
nat.	(313)	(122)	(181)	(248)	(108)	(106)	(24.4%)
1914	389	261	262	392	67	312	48.0%
for.	(170)	(125)	(67)	(171)	—	(173)	(58.6)
nat.	(219)	(136)	(195)	(221)	(67)	(139)	(39.2)
1915	440	274	243	390	111	342	47.8%
for.	(248)	(129)	(74)	(175)	—	(185)	(49.1)
nat.	(192)	(145)	(169)	(215)	(111)	(157)	(46.6)
1916	576	350	332	462	120	340	36.7%
for.	(269)	(118)	(98)	(190)	—	(165)	(42.6)
nat.	(307)	(232)	(234)	(272)	(120)	(175)	(32.5)
1917	711	356	417	550	132	387	36.3%
for.	(286)	(142)	(129)	(215)	—	(181)	(42.3)
nat.	(425)	(214)	(288)	(335)	(132)	(206)	(32.2)
1918	1059	500	566	802	128	492	31.6%
for.	(474)	(206)	(170)	(354)	—	(274)	(40.1)
nat.	(585)	(294)	(396)	(448)	(128)	(218)	(24.8)
1919	1196	713	708	1091	118	571	29.9%
for.	(608)	(249)	(181)	(470)	—	(280)	(32.7)
nat.	(588)	(464)	(527)	(622)	(118)	(291)	(27.7)

Sources: Comércio exterior 1913–1914, Comércio exterior 1915–1919.

demonstration for the Brazilians of the limitations and vulnerability of a financial system so dependent on foreign capital, foreign trade and foreign banks. Perhaps it was this demonstration, the extraordinary circumstances brought by the war, and being somewhat isolated from the "normal" sanctions of the international financial system and/or simply having few other options, which convinced the government to liquidate its debts with Treasury bills, to print money, and directly encourage expansionary banking. State intervention should not, however, be seen as out of character for Brazil. There had been previous attempts to assist industry and agriculture, the government had been active in promoting railways and immigration, and the apparent success of the 1906 valorization must have given further proof of the benefits of intervention. The Brazilian government seems successfully to have defied prevailing financial orthodoxy, and although its policies might be seen as a blow against foreign domination, in effect they represented no more than an attempt to strengthen government finances, the export sector and links with the world economy in a way consistent with the extreme conditions of the period. It was the only way they could overcome the difficulties created by the sudden collapse of foreign investment. Finally, it was neither foreigners nor the Brazilian elite who had to bear the burden of these measures. As always, internal economic adjustment to meet the externally generated crisis was carried out at the expense of the mass of the population who suffered from the rising prices brought about by the increased export of foodstuffs, higher excise taxes, and inflationary financing.

The essence of the contradictions in Brazil's financial experience during the war was, therefore, twofold. In order to weather the economic tempest of the war the ruling class adopted fiscal and monetary policies which did not cause, but clearly helped to fuel, violent class conflict, a conflict which posed a threat to their position and forced them after the war to seek a political accommodation with sectors of the middle class.[72] Secondly, although it might be assumed that the dominant role of foreign interest and influence within Brazil's economy generally and its financial system in particular would have imposed severe limitations on the state's freedom of action, as it seems to have done in 1898, in fact this was not the case. However, this "freedom of action" was itself limited by the entirely understandable perception of the Brazilian elite that primary product export still held the key to the country's economic success and progress. As radical as their financial measures may seem, at the most they wanted to use them to improve Brazil's position *vis-à-vis* the international economy not to change it.

Argentina

Argentina's wartime financial condition seems to have been far better than that of Brazil. After the initial crisis had been weathered, the peso remained above par and then late in 1916 its value began to rise until by the end of 1917 it was at a premium of about 13%.[73] To stop a further appreciation, which would have reduced exporters' peso earnings still more, credit-exchange agreements were made with Allies. This meant that Argentina in effect loaned money to France and Britain so that they could buy Argentine goods.[74] The basis for the almost too healthy state of exchange was the country's positive balance of payments, brought about mainly by a strong trade position. This more than compensated for the virtual cessation of foreign capital inflows. The high value peso also made external debt servicing less burdensome. Nonetheless, because of the drop in imports and therefore customs duties, government revenue fell by about a third, and the attempts to reduce expenditure were only moderately successful. The result was substantial deficits. The issuing of paper money was not resorted to in order to solve this problem as in Brazil. Note circulation did increase by over 40% between 1914 and 1918, but this was backed by a large (about 70%) gold reserve.[75] In terms of domestic inflation gold backing seems to have made little difference, and Argentina suffered much the same rate of inflation as Brazil. This was probably due to the fact that the unprecedented Allied demand for foodstuffs was pushing up prices throughout the world, and the war also made imports very much more expensive. The Argentine deficits were financed by a series of short-term loans floated both internally and abroad, mainly in the United States. Tulchin maintains[76] that domestic government borrowing soaked up both savings and the wartime windfall profits, and that because state spending was primarily on current expenses the policy damped down economic activity and helped "...maintain the financial status quo...." This is an extremely provocative argument, and if correct, provides a possible answer to why with exports booming and an excellent balance of payments position the Argentine economy seemed to be so sluggish during the war. However, the failure of local interest rates to rise suggests that government borrowing in itself may not have crowded out private investment. This question is taken up below. The degree to which foreign influence could be brought to bear on the Argentine economy through the financial system is also investigated, as well as the longer-term issue of the relationship between that system and the apparent rigidities in the structure of Argentine capitalism. However, it must be remembered that Argentina's wartime financial history is immensely complex and could easily support a separate monograph. The following account is, by necessity, very selective.

As in Brazil, government revenue was badly hit by the massive fall in imports (Table 4.7). The resulting fiscal crisis galvanized some members of Congress to push for major tax reforms. As the Budget Commission in the Chamber of Deputies noted in 1919 "The

Table 4.7 *Argentine Federal Government revenue and expenditure*
1913–1920

				(million gold pesos)		
					Revenue from:	
	Revenue	Expenditure	+/–	% Import duty	% Excise tax	% Export duty
1913	163.2	177.5	−14.3	53.7%	15.7%	
1914	124.2	184.6	−60.4	42.0%	17.2%	
1915	111.4	176.0	−64.6	37.5%	24.4%	
1916	112.2	164.8	−52.6	41.0%	21.5%	
1917	111.9	171.4	−59.5	38.0%	22.9%	
1918	145.2	185.3	−40.1	27.0%	19.8%	16.5%
1919	180.9	188.3	−7.4	30.9%	19.1%	17.9%
1920	228.2	214.6	+13.8	34.4%	17.0%	19.5%

Source: Peters, *Foreign Debt*, pp. 71, 73.

European war has served to show the fallacy of a taxation system
which puts the weight of public charges almost exclusively on
consumption and bases its revenue system on customs duties."[77]
However, while some changes were eventually made, such as the
imposition of an export tax and a slight increase in the land and
inheritance taxes, potentially the most important and radical new
departure, an income tax, was narrowly voted down. The failure to
achieve any substantive reform was due not only to the fact that the
Radicals lacked a majority in the Congress throughout most of the
period, but because they were not committed to such reform. They
had come to power without an economic program and only towards
the end of the war when the condition of government finances became
critical did they begin concertedly to push for change, and then it was
by adopting ideas which had been advocated mainly by the Socialists.
But the Radicals' interest in reforms was nothing more than a product
of crisis, and when by 1920 this seems to have passed, with the increase
in import duties, so did any attempt at devising a fairer and more
effective system of taxation. In the end, despite the levy on exports,
which did make a significant contribution, taxation remained highly
regressive, reflecting both the essentially traditional upper-class origins
of the leaders of the Unión Cívica Radical, and their lack of concern
for any fundamental change in the structure of the domestic economy.

Table 4.8 *Argentine government expenditure. Percentage distribution 1910–1921*

Year	Public Works	Public Debt	(Percentage) Defense	Pensions	Admin.	Salaries
1910	22.7	15.3	20.6	2.4	19.1	20.0
1911	23.2	15.6	19.7	3.0	19.4	19.1
1912	18.4	18.3	16.7	3.2	20.1	23.2
1913	17.3	19.9	14.7	3.6	20.7	23.8
1914	17.7	19.2	12.6	3.5	22.5	24.4
1915	16.7	20.5	12.8	4.3	23.0	22.6
1916	8.5	22.3	13.2	4.2	27.4	24.4
1917	4.3	24.0	13.0	4.9	31.3	22.5
1918	3.9	28.1	13.7	5.6	29.3	19.3
1919	3.8	29.7	14.5	4.2	27.2	20.7
1920	5.8	23.0	15.2	3.6	31.5	20.9
1921	6.8	22.4	16.5	3.9	25.2	25.2

Source: Argentina, Dirección General de Estadística, *Los gastos publicos*, Informe 7, serie F, no. 3, 1923. Reproduced in Karen Remmer, *Party Competition in Argentina and Chile. Political Recruitment and Public Policy, 1890–1930*, Lincoln and London, 1984, p. 157.

Government expenditure was slightly lower during the war, and there was a substantial reduction in spending on public works such as railway and port improvements (Table 4.8).[78] There was a belated effort to counter this and relieve urban unemployment when in 1918 19,600,000 paper pesos (m/n–*moneda nacional*) was budgeted for public works. By 1920 the sum had risen to over 35,000,000 pesos.[79] But this represented a small proportion of the budget and, although the percentage devoted to public works rose in this year, the impact was not sufficient to excite much contemporary comment. After administrative expenses, the single most important item was debt service which accounted on average for about a third of budgeted expenditure and, according to Bunge's calculations, 45% of actual revenues between 1914 and 1918.[80] These percentages are at considerable variance with those in Table 4.8. This may be explained by the fact that there are no reliable or agreed upon figures for Argentine government expenditure in this period.[81] Whatever the exact breakdown was, it is clear that notwithstanding the moderation in

Table 4.9 *Estimated foreign investments in Argentina 1910–1920*

| | (in millions of £) | | | |
	1910	1913	1917	1920
Great Britain	293	383	387	363
United States	4	8	17	15
Germany	40	50	55	53
France	81	94	92	81
Others	30	111	114	114
Total	448	646	665	626

Source: Phelps, *International Economic Position*, p. 246. The original gold peso figure has been converted at .1986 pounds per peso.

expenditure, deficits were substantial. Unable, before the imposition of an export duty in 1918, to increase its income through tax reform, the government was forced to look for loans. Before considering government debt and wartime borrowing it is important to place it in perspective by looking briefly at the total amount, the composition and the cost of the country's foreign liabilities.

There are a number of different estimates of the size of Argentina's foreign debt in 1913. Phelps has carefully sifted through these[82] and his figures (Table 4.9) offer probably the best estimate available. This shows Argentina to have been by far the largest debtor in Latin America, total liabilities being about 25% greater than the highest estimate for Brazil. There are no reliable estimates for composition of investment in 1913, but detailed figures prepared by A.B. Martínez relating to December 1911 (Table 4.10) show railways accounting for the greatest single share and government taking only 30%. An important reason for this is that unlike Brazil and Chile, where many of the railways were state-owned (61% and 56% respectively)[83] and much government borrowing was linked to these lines, in Argentina private British railways were dominant, in 1915 controlling over 70% of the mileage.[84] As for costs, although total foreign debt-servicing rose slightly during the war, as a proportion of export earnings it fell as the latter increased and the value of the peso appreciated (Table 4.11). Together with the drastic reduction in imports this helps explain why the Argentine economy was able to withstand the choking off of foreign investment without experiencing a balance of payments crisis.

Although the balance of payments position was secure during the

Table 4.10 *Composition of Argentine foreign debt December 1911. Percentage shares*

Public (Total)		30.4%
a. National	18.2	
b. Cedulas	4.0	
c. Provincial	6.3	
d. Municipal	1.8	
Railroads		36.4
Banks		1.4
Ports		0.8
Tramways		3.5
Refrigerating plants		0.4
Public utilities		2.1
Mortgage companies		9.1
Miscellaneous		1.4
Mortgages		7.3
Commerce and credits		7.3

Source: Calculated from A.B. Martínez, *Annuaire Economique et Financier de la Republique Argentine*, 1913, pp. 155–8, reproduced in Phelps, *International Economic Position*, p. 243.

Table 4.11 *Cost of servicing the Argentine foreign debt 1913–1920*

	(million gold pesos)						
	Total	Public debt	Cedulas	Private			% of Export value
				Mortgages	Rails	Other	
1913–14	139.3	50.0	10.0	17.0	38.3	24.0	34.5%
1914–15	138.1	46.7	10.2	20.0	37.2	24.0	24.8%
1915–16	146.2	48.5	9.9	18.0	45.8	24.0	28.9%
1916–17	148.5	49.8	9.9	16.8	40.0	32.0	24.8%
1917–18	146.1	49.9	10.5	14.0	38.7	33.0	19.3%
1918–19	157.8	44.4	5.5	20.1	44.6	43.2	17.5%
1919–20	152.0	42.5	3.9	9.9	42.8	52.9	13.0%

Source: Phelps, *International Economic Position*, facing p. 238. Based on yearly balance of payments account calculated by E. Tornquist.

war the government's financial position was not. Large deficits and the impossibility of placing long-term foreign loans, as it had done before the war, forced it into short-term borrowing abroad and, from 1917, increasingly at home (Table 4.12). In 1913 Argentina was in the middle of a program of public works which the federal authorities intended to finance temporarily with advances from local banks and then fund with a large foreign loan.[85] However, the Balkan crisis was in full swing when this loan was sought and it proved impossible to obtain in the City of London at a rate considered reasonable in Buenos Aires. Instead early in 1914 two issues of one year 6% Treasury bills were placed in London for a total of £13,000,000.[86] In June, London bankers finally agreed to a £16,000,000 loan but in the end could only come up with £5,000,000 for a year. After poor results from another short-term flotation in London, Argentina turned to New York where between 1914 and 1917 over $110,000,000 in various forms of short-term securities was raised, much of it being used to pay off previous short-term loans. By the end of 1917 all but $25,000,000 had been repaid, mainly by borrowing the money from Argentine banks. After the US entered the war the entire burden of dealing with the government's borrowing needs fell on the domestic banking system, and by 1918 the internal floating debt, which according to Tornquist did not exist four years earlier, had reached over 542,500,000 gold pesos (Table 4.12). Funded internal obligations had also grown, although much of this was held by foreign investors. Moreover, the country's "official" debt was considerably larger than indicated in Table 4.12 because it does not include either numerous non-federal internal loans, *cédulas* (bonds of the Banco Nacional Hipotecario which were guaranteed by the federal government), or external provincial and municipal loans. In 1914 the last three totaled 150,700,000 gold pesos, and by 1917 the amount had risen to 194,500,000 gold pesos.[87]

To get a rough idea of how much of the debt was held in Argentina we can assume that almost all the external liabilities were in foreign hands, that the internal floating debt was mainly in the country, and then using Tornquist's 1917 estimate that of federal internal funded debt, that 92% of the paper and 27% of the gold were owned by Argentines.[88] This would mean that between 1914 and 1919 the government, excluding provincial and municipal authorities, had borrowed domestically the equivalent of about 375,000,000 gold pesos. Was this sum, which included advances made by the Banco de la Nación to the government, enough to cause the dearth of investment

Table 4.12 *Argentine Federal Government debt 1910–1918*

	Internal paper	Internal gold	External gold	Total funded debt (in gold pesos)[a]	Floating external paper	Floating internal paper[b]
			(000,000)			
1910	121.4	92.5	306.9	452.8	nd	nd
1911	139.7	161.4	303.7	526.6	nd	nd
1912	167.6	159.8	298.0	531.5	nd	nd
1913	177.5	157.8	308.9	544.8	nd	nd
1914	174.1	156.0	312.4	545.0	140.6	—
1915	169.2	153.8	309.3	537.6	181.7	95.0
1916	214.2	151.3	301.3	546.9	258.2	234.3
1917	223.3	202.5	294.6	595.4	116.2	471.6
1918	219.1	199.0	282.8	578.2	116.2	542.5
1919	214.2	196.2	275.0	565.4	116.2	534.8
1920				553.3	116.2	368.6

Source: Ernesto Tornquist & Cia, *The Economic Development of the Argentine Republic in the Last Fifty Years*, Buenos Aires, 1919, pp. 302–3.

[a] Paper pesos were converted to gold at 1 paper = .44 gold.
[b] Except for 1914 and 1915, all the floating debt figures are from Argentina, Ministerio de Hacienda, *Memoria del Departamento de Hacienda correspondiente al ano*, for years 1917 to 1920.

which Tulchin argues was the root cause of economic stagnation? To begin to provide an answer we need first to look at the behavior of the banks.

Except in 1915 and 1916, the banks did not overall follow a particularly restricted lending policy throughout the war, at least in comparison with the previous period (Table 4.13). Furthermore, the disaggregated data on discounts and loans shows that the decline here was due entirely to a falloff in the former, a reflection of trade conditions, whereas advances continued to increase (Table 4.14). Many loans, especially from about mid-1916, were made to the state, and, therefore, the category "Government documents" understates the government's share. For example, by October 1916, the government had borrowed 99,000,000 m/n on six-month loans from the banks in Buenos Aires, and by August of the following year this sum had grown to 219,000,000 m/n. At about the same time (April 1917) the

Table 4.13 *Argentine (Buenos Aires) banks: capital & reserves,*
deposits, discounts & advances, cash 1908–1919*

	(000 paper pesos)					
	1	2	3	4	5	6
	Capital & reserves	Deposits less current accounts	Total deposits	Discounts & loans	Cash	Cash ratio %
1908	289,383	445,244	753,710	760,762	274,910	36.5%
1909	361,777	551,433	988,616	936,797	394,511	39.9%
1910	363,473	657,284	1,135,099	1,149,642	391,014	34.4%
1911	425,126	697,943	1,174,090	1,314,527	392,331	33.4%
1912	487,991	749,102	1,275,932	1,384,495	438,250	34.3%
1913	506,318	847,098	1,215,576	1,421,197	399,287	32.8%
1914	512,736	731,943	1,076,773	1,256,248	375,901	34.9%
1915	510,177	824,356	1,223,880	1,258,037	512,005	41.5%
1916	512,916	957,986	1,389,063	1,310,870	519,800	37.4%
1917	517,803	1,126,843	1,559,428	1,547,613	476,891	30.6%
1918	527,341	1,506,783	2,082,627	1,982,621	460,322	22.1%
1919	541,882	1,602,249	2,214,027	2,207,759	424,102	19.2%

Source: Argentina, Dirección General de Estadística de la Nación, *Veinte años de estadística bancaria de la República Argentina 1908–1927,* Buenos Aires, 1928. **Note:* Covers 13 Buenos Aires banks and their provincial branches, which together accounted for between 80% and 90% of capital, deposits, and cash. There is a listing in the statistics for 27 banks, but it runs only from 1912.

Banco de la Nación had allowed the government an overdraft of 73,700,000.[89] By the end of 1918 the loans from local banks had reached 305,000,000 m/n and the overdraft at the Banco de la Nación stood at 128,000,000 m/n.[90] On the basis of these figures it seems that between 1916 and 1919 the government took respectively 23%, 41%, 32% and 29% of total bank loans (not including discounts). On the face of it this seems to lend support to Tulchin's contention about the impact of government finance on the ability of the banks to support private ventures. However, if such crowding out was really a problem, interest rates should have risen and, except for a relatively short-term rise at the beginning of the war, both the discount rate and that on advances either fell or remained stable from 1915 to 1919. [91]

Although the government borrowed heavily from the banks, there was a great deal of contemporary complaint that large balances were being simply left to accumulate in bank vaults. This may seem paradoxical, but presumably meant that the public was not taking government paper in sufficient quantities, and it was falling to the banks to make up the difference through short-term loans. It was claimed that in 1915 about half the money in circulation was in the banks,[92] which offers a sharp contrast to the Brazilian case where at the same time 70% of the paper currency was in the hands of the public.[93] In August 1916, *The Economist* reported[94] that although the Banco de la Nación had reduced interest rates on savings and fixed term accounts to induce depositors to invest in *cédulas* and other government paper, not much success was anticipated. "The depositors in the saving department care more for the security of their small capitals and for the certainty of being able to withdraw the full amount when money is needed than for the interest paid on deposits." Furthermore, the report continued, people were waiting for the best moment to buy land, and generally economic conditions were creating a great deal of uncertainty. This high liquidity preference was also commented upon by W. Henry Robertson, US Consul General, who wrote in 1916 and again in 1918 that money was lying idle in the banks.[95] In the latter report he wrote, "...banks have been seething with idle deposits during the last three years, without the slightest effort being made towards using these for developing the country or even for the floating of an internal loan for paying off its foreign debt or for meeting the ordinary running expenses of the government." It was true that the average annual rate of increase of deposits was higher between 1914 and 1919 (17.0%) than from 1908 to 1913 (13.7%), but then the rate of growth of loans was also considerably higher in the second period, 25.3% as against 15.6%, although much of this did represent loans to the government. Nonetheless, although the state did make increasingly heavy demands on the banks, judging by the stability of interest rates this demand did not result in a squeeze on the private sector. The evidence presented above, while far from conclusive, suggests instead that most Argentines judged war time conditions too uncertain to merit the risk of substantial investment. Also, the banks, traditionally reluctant to provide long term loans, especially to industry, may have restricted loans to this sector, seeing the opportunities for import substitution as a temporary phenomenon.

There was a massive decline in capital imports and, with loan repayments and the Allied grain deal, even though some new foreign investments were made during the war, particularly by the United States, overall Argentina became a net exporter of capital in these

Table 4.14 *Argentine (Buenos Aires) banks:* *Breakdown of loans*
1912–1919

	Discounts	Overdrafts	(000 paper pesos) Govern-ment documents	Other loans	Total (less discounts)
1908	560,082	149,620	—	51,060	200,680
1909	673,315	193,015	—	70,467	263,482
1910	831,504	232,018	—	86,120	318,138
1911	933,235	278,024	—	103,268	381,292
1912	1,025,308	255,836	—	103,351	359,187
1913	1,005,402	274,499	—	141,296	415,795
1914	836,433	241,568	—	178,247	419,815
1915	726,876	308,258	10,150	212,753	531,161
1916	712,234	356,911	22,803	218,922	598,636
1917	721,972	481,819	59,913	283,909	825,641
1918	762,208	461,583	87,500	671,330	1,220,413
1919	911,194	567,494	69,981	659,000	1,296,475

Source: Same as Table 4.13. **Note:* These figures cover 13 Buenos Aires banks and their branches.

years. Total foreign indebtedness, according to Tornquist's calculations, showed a net decrease of £78,000,000 between 1915 and 1919.[96]
Much of this decline was due to the appreciation of Argentine
exchange which, when it reached its high point between 1918 and early
1920, reduced the peso value of foreign debts to such an extent as to
encourage the repayment of mortgages held abroad as well as the
re-import of *cédulas* and government securities.[97] Although the figure
in Table 4.15 must be treated with considerable caution, the general
direction and magnitude of the change in levels of investment are
probably correct. It was construction which seems to have been
hardest hit, especially those projects such as railways, port and urban
improvements, etc. which had relied on foreign capital.[98] It seems
likely that because it was so important for the Argentine economy, a
falloff in foreign investment by reducing the general level of activity
would lead, at least in the short run, to a reduction in domestic
investment. This seems to have happened. In Buenos Aires the value of
building permits fell by 80% between 1913 and 1915, and throughout
the war amortizations in the city consistently exceeded new

Table 4.15 *Investment as a percentage of*
Argentine GNP 1913–1920

	Foreign investment	Domestic investment	Total
1913	22	17	39
1914	10	17	27
1915	9	7	16
1916	4	10	14
1917	—	12	10
1918	—	10	10
1919	3	9	12
1920	—	20	20

Source: Tulchin, "Argentine Economy", Part II,
p. 966.

mortgages.[99] As a further measure of the generally depressed economic conditions, the scale of business failure doubled in 1914 and although subsequently there was some improvement the level remained high throughout the war (Table 4.16). Finally trading activity on the Buenos Aires stock exchange was greatly reduced from 1914, particularly of company issues, and prewar conditions were not recaptured before 1918.

The preceding discussion makes clear that although, as Tulchin has suggested, there was in effect something of an internal drain of capital in Argentina during the war, this in itself did not make it markedly more difficult for domestic investors. It did, however, show up some of the weaknesses in the country's financial structure. The roots of this can be traced to the government's profligate prewar foreign borrowing, much of the proceeds going to cover budget deficits, combined with a narrow tax base that relied far too heavily on import duties. The crisis-induced vulnerability of the latter proved to be synchronous with that of foreign lending and so led to prolonged financial difficulties for the government in these years. This not only reflected the dangers of excessive dependence on external finance, but, as importantly, how this dependence was cultivated by the ruling export elite through their active encouragement of foreign investment and by their refusal to devise a more effective, not to say more equitable, system of taxation. For the government, therefore, the availability of

Table 4.16 *Argentine business failures and stock market transactions*
1910–1919

	Business failures	Value of securities traded on the Buenos Aires Bolsa de Comercio	
	(000 pesos m/n)	Government bonds & cédulas (000 pesos m/n)	Joint-stock shares (number)
1910	53,953	183,316	3,724,636
1911	68,837	214,814	2,160,824
1912	93,110	305,164	1,584,057
1913	198,386	226,373	1,692,847
1914	440,078	204,195	209,232
1915	197,825	128,763	703,530
1916	106,533	157,272	823,978
1917	106,354	207,439	1,027,080
1918	55,188	217,560	2,718,731
1919	40,042		

Source: Tornquist, *Economic Development*, pp. 213–14, 231.

foreign capital offered short-term advantages but at the same time helped create a chronically unstable fiscal system.

The aforementioned instability permeated the entire financial structure for, when foreign lending dried up, the government turned to the banks to cover the shortfall. It is important to note that while the developmental aspect of banking was often forcefully advocated by Argentines, Charles Jones has argued that during the nineteenth century in countries such as Argentina it was the fiscal needs of the government which were paramount in guiding official policy towards the banks and, therefore, the latter's principal orientation.[100] This orientation was substantially strengthened during the war by the unprecedented demands made by the state. Because of this the banks were not forced to seek new, alternative outlets for their mounting deposits. But even if the government's borrowing requirements had been more modest, it is unlikely that the banks would have acted very differently in these years. The pattern of their activities and the expectations of domestic capitalists had already been firmly established. Except for the mortgage companies and such public institutions as the Banco Nacional Hipotecario, the Banco de la Nación or the Banco de la Provincia de Buenos Aires all of which lent against land, the vast majority of bank business, for both foreign and local private banks, was in discounting and making short-term loans to finance trade or the harvests. This they continued to do during the war, but some contemporaries felt that domestic capital should have been more willing to take up the investment role previously carried out by foreigners and to help industry or the small farmer, neither of whom were served by the existing financial system. However, the strong position and influence of foreign banks combined with the great influx of foreign capital had helped create a fragmented financial system in which it was expected that different projects would be virtually the exclusive preserve of distinct groups of investors, and some projects would find no institutional support at all. In the short-run neither the system nor the Argentine investors could adjust to the new conditions brought about by the war. The financial structure had developed in response to the peculiar demands of Argentina's export economy and its purpose was to strengthen and maintain that type of eviscerated capitalist economy not to facilitate its transformation into a more independently dynamic capitalism.

Chile

Chile's financial position during the war differed quite markedly from that of either Brazil or Argentina. Conditions were extremely bad in the first two years, but once nitrate sales picked up there seem to have been on the whole fewer serious problems until the postwar collapse of exports in 1919. Much of this had to do with the fact that although debt servicing did absorb a large proportion of public expenditure (Table 4.19), the government did not rely so heavily on foreign borrowing to balance its budgets. In 1914 the ratio of public foreign debt to export earnings was 3.51, 1.91 and 1.45 for Brazil, Argentina and Chile respectively.[101] Direct foreign investment was of greater importance in Chile than in the aforementioned countries. It was mainly, although not entirely, in nitrate and copper mining, but the high profits enjoyed by both these industries probably meant that during the years of conflict either they continued to attract capital or they were able to finance what improvements were made by reinvestment. The flexibility of the country's monetary system and the particular structure of government revenue were also instrumental in preventing serious financial difficulties. The fact that the currency was already inconvertible allowed Chile to meet the monetary difficulties caused by the war with relatively greater ease, although by the last year the appreciation of exchange had reached such a level as to create unease among exporters, and there were moves, as in Argentina, to try to curb the rise. Finally, the high proportion of revenue which came from the tax on nitrate exports (53.5% in 1910–13) meant that once this trade revived there was no income problem because of falling import duties, and neither the Brazilian solution of printing money or the Argentine one of extensive domestic borrowing was necessary. However, this situation of financial ease was transitory, resting as it did on the increasingly unsound foundation of nitrate sales. When these faltered in 1919 so did the country's finances and the entire economy.

In the years immediately preceding the war Chile had carried a moderate deficit. If the losses incurred from the operation of the state railways are included, and officially they were until the railways were placed under a semi-autonomous body in 1914, the total is higher. But compared to Brazil or Argentina, Chile's budget deficits still appear to have been of relatively manageable proportions, the average in the years 1910–13 being only 7.4% of total revenue (railways included), as against 21.2% and 25.9% respectively for the other countries.[102] Although the government did borrow abroad, the cessation of foreign loans did not, therefore, present such a grave fiscal threat. Nonetheless, during the first two years of the war state revenues were seriously compromised (Table 4.17). The collapse of exchange (Table 4.19) created an additional burden as it increased the cost of servicing the foreign debt. The reasons for all this are clear. 87.2% of government income (1910–13 not including loans) came directly from foreign trade and trade was depressed until the last months of 1915. The situation in these years was serious enough to force the first major revision of the 1897 tariff. Some duties were raised, but the main aim of the 1916 law was to change the basis from an *ad valorem* to a specific rate so as to increase the effectiveness of collections.[103] There were also moves at about the same time to deepen and broaden the domestic tax base with increased levies on alcohol and the banks and new taxes on property, securities, and inheritance.[104] These made some difference, but the external sector, particularly the export tax, continued to provide the lion's share of government income (Table 4.18).[105] The Chilean tax system, therefore, tended to be less regressive than those in most other countries. In the prewar years it was through monetary rather than fiscal policy that the working and middle class had suffered as the

Table 4.17 *Chilean government revenue, expenditure and railway results 1910–1920*

Year	Government (ooo gold pesos)			State railways (ooo gold pesos)		
	Revenue*	Expenditure	Surplus + Deficit −	Revenue	Expenditure	Surplus + Deficit −
1910	145,901	163,963	− 18,062	30,084	36,364	− 6,280
1911	155,263	159,218	− 3,955	32,357	39,718	− 7,361
1912	170,689	191,398	− 20,709	36,840	42,591	− 5,751
1913	182,929	169,238	+ 13,691	38,283	48,781	− 10,498
1914	132,380	165,847	− 33,467	32,294	38,703	− 6,409
1915	122,577	131,315	− 8,738	37,386	32,648	+ 4,738
1916	168,211	148,126	+ 20,085	44,231	40,544	+ 3,687
1917	198,976	172,184	+ 26,792	52,033	50,971	+ 1,062
1918	218,510	181,726	+ 36,784	75,972	85,096	− 9,124
1919	119,969	171,971	− 52,002	63,912	77,768	− 13,856
1920	192,488	228,061	− 35,573	76,348	96,606	− 20,258

Source: McQueen, *Chilean Public Finance*, pp. 9, 18. *Revenue is exclusive of loans.

Table 4.18 *Chilean state revenues (excluding loans). Percentage contributions 1910–1918*

	Export duties	Import duties	Direct taxes	Indirect taxes	Other
1910	55.2%	33.5%	1.6%	2.7%	7.1%
1911	53.8%	34.1%	1.7%	3.3%	7.1%
1912	52.0%	34.5%	1.7%	3.2%	8.5%
1913	52.8%	32.9%	1.8%	4.2%	8.3%
1914	49.3%	30.6%	1.9%	4.1%	14.1%
1915	55.2%	17.5%	11.0%	4.6%	11.7%
1916	60.6%	21.9%	5.3%	4.0%	8.2%
1917	50.6%	26.4%	5.9%	5.5%	11.6%
1918	50.4%	24.5%	10.8%	2.9%	11.5%

Source: Calculated from Chile, Oficina Central de Estadística, *Anuario estadístico de la República de Chile 1918*, vol. vi (Hacienda), p. 15.

Table 4.19 Chilean public expenditure 1911–1918. Percentage shares of major ministries and exchange rates[a]

	1911	1912	1913	1914	1915	1916	1917	1918
Finance[b]	24.3%	26.9%	29.3%	31.0%	34.6%	33.3%	29.0%	28.7%
(Public debt)	(26.0%)	(28.1%)		(21.6%)	(25.7%)	(24.1%)	(21.0%)	(18.6%)
Defense	26.0%	28.1%	27.1%	25.4%	24.7%	25.7%	27.7%	25.8%
Education	13.3%	14.0%	12.8%	12.5%	11.6%	11.6%	12.4%	13.7%
Industry & public works (excluding railways)	8.2%	9.9%	9.3%	10.0%	8.1%	7.0%	6.7%	7.5%
Exchange rate (pence per peso)	10.625	9.750	8.968	8.250	9.469	12.739	14.591	10.783

Sources: Calculated from McQueen, *Chilean Public Finance*, pp. 22–8. Using conversion of paper to gold pesos as employed by McQueen.

[a] These expenditure figures include both budget and "special" expenditure and the total is therefore slightly greater than that shown in Table 4.17 above. Furthermore, except for public works, the percentage shares are significantly greater than those presented by McQueen on p. 28. Possibly this is because the above are ministry figures and the others are more disaggregated. Finally, the expenditure on railways has been deleted because the railway accounts were separated from the national accounts in 1914. A small amount continued to be spent on railways by the government and this is included under public works from 1914.

[b] Before 1914 it was difficult to find reliable data for debt payment and so statistics for both the Ministry of Finance and public debt expenditure are given. Exchange rates from McQueen, *Chilean Public Finance*, pp. 65–6.

inflationary effects of an inconvertible and generally depreciating currency, which tended to favor exporters, eroded real wages.[106] Fetter comments:[107] "The ruling classes in Chile prospered under paper money, and convenient theories were developed to justify it."

In the years leading up to 1914, Chile had borrowed abroad fairly liberally. Between 1905 and 1913 the external debt had almost doubled from 241,124,429 gold pesos to 457,987,072. During the war there were no overseas loans negotiated and debt was steadily reduced, reaching 403,553,867 by 1918.[108] There were also few major new internal loans during the war. A couple of school and park bond issues were floated, totaling only 10,550,000 paper pesos,[109] and 35,000,000 paper pesos of interest-bearing *vales de tesorería* (treasury notes) were emitted in 1916 to cover current government expenditure and repay the debt owed to the Banco de Chile.[110] By the same law 20,000,000 gold peso treasury bonds were also authorized for the completion of the Santiago water system and the port works at Valparaíso and San Antonio.[111] There was, however, difficulty in floating this loan, and it was never placed.[112] Possibly the improvement in nitrate sales and the greatly increased revenue this brought in made it unnecessary. The only other official borrowers were the Chilean cities, and their debt remained more or less stationary or declined slightly between 1914 and 1918.[113] In short, Chile's external debt position substantially improved during the war and because of the large export revenues the state did not have resort to extensive domestic borrowing.

Despite the healthy state of government finances, including budget surpluses from 1916, public works expenditure was reduced during the war. On balance, the government followed an extremely conservative spending program and, except for the first years of the conflict, it does not seem that the state injected any added life into the economy. This is not to suggest, however, that it was not actively interventionist. It was and precisely at the time when it was most financially hard-pressed itself. As mentioned above, in 1914 it paid for the movement of more than 30,000 workers and their families from the northern deserts and tried to find them work. It also stepped in to support the banks and tried at the same time to help the nitrate producers.

These projects were greatly facilitated because the country was operating under a system of inconvertible paper currency. This system, which had been used, with a short break between 1895 and 1898, since 1878, had created innumerable problems for the economy and was the source of continual and bitter political debate,[114] but was, for all its faults, reasonably flexible in a crisis. This flexibility was built in mainly through a law passed in 1912 which allowed the banks to draw additional currency under certain conditions. Subercaseaux, a strong proponent of paper money, argued[115] that if Chile had had a gold-backed currency or one which was convertible there would have been a serious run on the banks. While withdrawals were much heavier than usual, there was little reason to hoard paper currency and consequently for most banks there was no need to close. One factor which helped was the moratorium declared on debts contracted in gold before August 1914. Initially imposed for 30 days it was extended in modified forms until September 1915. More important for the banks was the government's depositing, under the provisions of the 1912 law, £1,500,000 in London for the account of three major banks. This allowed them to draw an emergency issue of about 30,000,000 pesos from the Oficina de Emisión. Eventually, a little over 55,000,000 pesos was emitted, although by mid-1915 about half of this had been retired. Two laws passed at the beginning of August provided further aid in the form of non-interest-bearing treasury notes (*vales*). The banks took about 25,000,000 of these, but most had been withdrawn by the end of September. In an attempt to keep some *oficinas* open, the same type of notes were loaned to the nitrate industry, secured against existing stocks. Over 20,000,000 pesos were provided, most of which was taken between August and December 1914. All but about 4,000,000 pesos had been repaid with interest by August 1915.[116]

At the beginning of the war there had been calls for meeting the revenue crisis by printing money. There was, however, very strong public feeling against the issuance of more paper money and the powerful sound money lobby in the government, including the President, successfully resisted these efforts.[117] But for the temporary use of treasury notes, monetary policy remained unadventurous throughout the war. The amount of currency in circulation decreased from its short-lived expansion in 1914 and only began to rise again significantly in 1918 in response to the fear that exchange was about to go over 18d (the nominal par value of the peso). To understand this, the dramatic developments in exchange during the war must be considered.

By the end of 1914 the value of the peso had hit a historic low of 7.5d.[118] It was not until August, 1916 that it reached 9.5d, its July 1914 level. From that time exchange steadily improved as exports boomed and imports were restricted. The upward movement in exchange gave rise to renewed efforts at monetary reform. There had been a growing agitation for such reform in the years following the crisis of 1907, and in 1913 a comprehensive scheme, modeled on the Brazilian and Argentine conversion programs, had been strongly supported but finally abandoned because of the outbreak of war.[119] The proponents of stabilization felt that with exchange at between 11d and 12d it was an opportune moment to implement the 1913 proposal.[120] But there was fierce opposition from those who saw an increasingly strong peso as an indication of national prosperity. Labor groups also opposed the idea of a conversion fund fearing that to halt the rise in the peso's gold value would adversely affect real wages. The proposal was defeated and exchange continued to rise. By June 1918 it had reached 17.168d, an increase of 125% in three years. In the prewar period this would have spelled ruin for both exporters and industrialists, but the rise in the value of the peso was compensated for the former by the extraordinary rise in export prices and for the latter by the restricted importation of competing goods. Wartime conditions also made it difficult and inordinately expensive to ship gold and, when in 1917 the Chilean government decreed that duties had to be paid in gold or its equivalent, this increased demand and began to drive up the gold premium. This provoked fear that exchange would rise above the 18d par value and emergency legislation was brought in permitting the issuance of fiscal bills in exchange for gold. This explains the sharp rise in the amount of currency in 1918 (Table 4.20). But this was a stopgap measure not a reform. The problem of inconvertibility remained. It was not to be successfully tackled until 1925 when the gold standard was adopted and a central bank established.[121]

All that has been said might suggest that Chile escaped the financial shock waves of the war. It did not. Government support for the banks dampened, but could not prevent the financial panic which began in August 1914. Most banks weathered the storm but the Banco Italiano, still not completely recovered from the 1907 crisis, could not and went under.[122] To give some idea of the severity of the situation, in the week between 29 June and 5 August the cash balances of the Anglo-South American Bank in Santiago fell from 1,697,692 pesos to only 539,616 pesos.[123] The immediate reaction of the banks to the war was the same in Chile as elsewhere, loans were reduced and the extension of credit sharply curtailed. This process had been to some extent proceeding before the war in response to the rather indifferent performance of nitrates, but it was stepped up from August 1914 (Table 4.21). It is curious, but probably no more than coincidence, that the percentage drop in loans and advances (11.6% in gold pesos) was exactly the same

Table 4.20 *Chilean currency in circulation at end of each year*
1910–1919

| | Fiscal bills | | Treasury notes | | |
	Fixed emission	Gold-backed	To banks	Nitrate	Total
1910	150,000,000				150,000,000
1911	150,000,000				150,000,000
1912	150,000,000	18,481,764			168,481,764
1913	150,000,000	33,822,354			183,822,354
1914	150,000,000	45,000,000	6,800,000	21,256,000	223,056,000
1915	150,000,000	12,054,227	9,970,000	3,857,000	175,881,227
1916	150,000,000	18,145,000	274,000	8,708,000	177,127,000
1917	150,000,000	24,898,649	7,803,000	1,679,000	184,380,649
1918	150,000,000	70,558,253	705,500	4,614,500	225,878,253
1919	150,000,000	57,104,383	1,584,500	41,239,000	249,927,883

Source: McQueen, *Chilean*, p. 60. Does not include small and diminishing quantity of old fiscal bills.

as that experienced in Argentina and Brazil (11.6% and 11.1% respectively). Rowe claimed[124] that, as elsewhere, foreign banks were far more restrictive than their native counterparts. He writes that "This was a source of a widespread feeling of complaint and led to a marked feeling of opposition toward the foreign institutions." The dislocation caused by the war brought into sharp focus the pervasiveness of foreign interests and so gave a boost to economic nationalism, a growing intellectual force in Chile before 1914.[125] While there were, of course, considerable differences, this is not unlike the experience in Argentina and Brazil.

Although nitrate sales began to improve in 1915, because of uncertainty about the effects of the war, banks continued to follow a restrictive policy until the second half of 1916 and it was not until a year later that lending showed a substantial increase. This was also true of deposits. The discount rate went to 9% at the end of 1915 and it was late the following year that it fell to 7½%.[126] All this suggests that to the extent that the level of bank lending is indicative of the state of domestic investment this did not increase markedly before the second half of 1917. This in turn may have held back to some degree the growth of domestic industry, although there were a number of other

Table 4.21 *Chilean banks loans and advances and deposits 1913–1918*

| As of end of: | Loans and advances (to the public) | | Total deposits | |
	000 paper pesos	000 gold pesos	000 paper pesos	000 paper pesos
Dec. 1912	575,927	48,534	429,614	51,975
June 1913	564,819	58,193	420,373	58,842
Dec. 1913	566,086	56,408	410,667	61,102
June 1914	553,607	55,277	405,306	55,101
Dec. 1914	502,544	48,828	391,554	68,669
June 1915	542,932	41,785	427,275	63,230
Dec. 1915	549,110	45,402	432,486	65,952
June 1916	538,673	44,409	452,404	74,980
Dec. 1916	551,580	54,090	467,495	86,462
June 1917	586,872	59,487	498,794	107,283
Dec. 1917	620,168	78,772	499,558	121,001
June 1918	667,382	74,924	543,246	181,134
Dec. 1918	706,124	150,957	669,526	237,019

Source: Anuario estadístico 1918, vol. x, p. 131.

important factors at work and the banks were not particularly disposed in any case to make long-term loans to industry.[127] Therefore, the banking data may be indicative of general economic conditions, but tells us nothing about access to private sources of capital, the amount of reinvestment, or direct foreign investment, especially important in copper mines and nitrate *oficinas* but also of considerable significance for domestic industry.[128] Presumably all these must have been tapped to some degree by local industry, for from 1915 there seems to have been a steady rise in the volume of capital invested in industrial enterprise. But the evidence is very scanty and a great deal more primary research would be needed to establish the level of investment in Chile during the First World War.

Compared to the other countries reviewed here Chilean public finance seems to have been considerably sounder during the war. This meant less state imposition on the private sector, and the latter was able, after some time, to function more or less normally. Part of the strong relative position was due to the fact that the scale of government budget deficits was not large enough to create the severe problems experienced in Brazil or Argentina. This was a real strength. But it was dependent on another which was not real, or at least was not reliable – nitrate exports. Because of the growth in production and sales from the 1880s the state had been able to cover a great deal of its quite extensive spending on public works and education without having to rely as heavily as many other countries on foreign capital. Interestingly, Conoboy argues[129] that it was its favorable debt position and relatively sound fiscal behavior which allowed the Chilean government to follow such an unorthodox monetary policy, a policy which was strongly opposed by the British and their domestic allies. While this suggests a substantial degree of economic autonomy, it was a position built upon a dangerous degree of external dependence nonetheless, that of nitrate exports. During the war the demand for nitrates was so buoyant that the dangers continued to be masked.

Monetary policy, particularly the regime of inconvertible paper currency, a long-standing issue of bitter political conflict and major socio-economic significance was on the verge of substantive reform when the war erupted. During the conflict because of the unusual conditions affecting trade and gold movements the system seemed to function reasonably well. For instance, Fetter maintains[130] that because of the combination of an appreciating peso and the declining international purchasing power of gold, "...Chile enjoyed during the war a currency remarkably stable in terms of internal as well as of external purchasing power." Reform was not, therefore, pursued, and when the war ended, monetary instability and inflation once again emerged as serious problems for the Chilean economy. As was the case with trade, and very much because of the continued success of nitrates, existing Chilean financial structures, especially those of the state, were generally reinforced during the war. There was little if any pressure for substantive change.

Peru

A brief glance at the statistics seems to suggest that Peru was the most financially and monetarily sound of the four republics in 1914. Although the government had been carrying budget deficits these were even less than Chile's, at between 3.1% and 5.5% of revenue (1910–13) (Table 4.23) The state's foreign debt was also extremely small, consisting primarily of two loans totaling £1,800,000[131] and the ratio of foreign public debt to export earnings was only 0.57%, about a third of the Chilean figure and a sixth of the Brazilian.[132] Since 1897

Table 4.22 Peruvian government revenue and expenditure 1910–1920

	Ordinary expenditure (£p)	Ordinary revenue	Current* Surplus + Deficit –	Sources of revenue (% share)				
				Import duties	Excise tax	Export duties	Direct taxes	Other
1910	2,927,546	2,795,775	– 8,276	44.5%	32.5%	—	4.2%	18.8%
1911	3,339,670	3,227,417	– 45,988	45.1%	33.0%	—	3.6%	18.3%
1912	3,711,320	3,535,877	– 175,443	44.3%	34.4%	—	3.3%	18.0%
1913	3,720,600	3,549,283	– 171,317	39.1%	36.6%	1.6%	3.4%	19.3%
1914	3,289,090	3,069,451	– 219,639	33.2%	40.2%	0.7%	4.3%	24.6%
1915	2,821,957	2,837,881	– 15,924	24.6%	45.9%	1.0%	5.6%	22.9%
1916	3,193,610	3,942,383	+ 748,773	27.0%	35.4%	12.8%	3.8%	21.0%
1917	3,330,484	4,510,435	+ 1,179,951	27.0%	38.5%	13.7%	3.6%	17.2%
1918	4,693,343	4,892,461	+ 199,118	21.6%	31.2%	20.9%	4.0%	22.3%
1919	5,799,981	6,154,171	+ 354,190	20.3%	28.2%	24.1%	3.3%	24.1%
1920	7,481,303	8,087,297	+ 605,994	23.5%	23.9%	30.0%	3.3%	19.3%

Sources: McQueen, *Peruvian Public Finance,* pp. 43–4, *Extracto estadístico 1919,* pp. 91–6; *Extracto estadístico 1920,* pp. 35–9.
Note: This excludes deferred and extraordinary items.

the country had been solidly on the gold standard and there was no paper currency in circulation. Despite all this, Peru was the poorest and least developed of the four republics. But in this case at least, there was no contradiction between financial probity and relative economic backwardness.

One indication of the weakness underlying the statistical strength was that it took Peru almost eighteen months to recover financially from the impact of the war. Using exchange as a rough measure, it appears that it was not until February 1916 that the sol was at par.[133] This was even though there had been a strong positive trade balance in the previous year and the government's deficit had been greatly reduced. The delay was caused by a number of factors. The country was already in poor financial shape when the war broke out. Budget deficits had been fairly high by Peruvian standards in 1912 and 1913. The political upheaval before and after the coup against Billinghurst in February 1914, combined with the tense international situation to create additional financial uncertainty.[134] This was exacerbated by the general economic disruption caused by the war and the widespread suspicion and unpopularity of the paper currency issued as an emergency measure in 1914. But possibly the most important reason for the slow recovery was the political uncertainty which continued to plague the country. There was a need for a strong government to deal with the wartime crisis, particularly the severe fiscal problems, and this was not forthcoming until the August 1915 election of José Pardo.[135]

Pardo was faced with a serious fiscal crisis brought about in the main by the massive fall in import duties, from £p 616,491 in the first half of 1914 to £p 568,351 in the following twelve months.[136] A foreign loan was unsuccessfully sought, and although local banks and some foreign firms made short-term advances, these were not enough to shore up the state's finances. The new President, therefore, moved immediately to increase government revenues. Some import duties were raised as were the official values upon which certain tariffs were calculated.[137] The excise on alcohol and tobacco was increased,[138] and a modest inheritance tax was introduced. Most importantly, a tax was imposed on the country's principal agricultural and mineral exports. This was an extremely successful, albeit controversial, measure and together with a revival of imports from 1916 made for strong government finance throughout the remainder of the war. But although successful, the tax on exports was not easily accepted and gave rise to bitter controversy.

Up until 1915 only rubber had been forced to pay an export duty.

The new tax went some way to redress the manifest injustice of the Peruvian taxation system, under which, as Rowe observed,[139] "...the laboring classes are compelled to bear the heaviest burden of taxation whereas the wealthy escape with a totally inadequate contribution to the public treasury." The "wealthy" were not, however, in favor of this tax reform even though its cost was easily absorbed by high export prices, and its being based on a sliding scale meant when prices dropped the incidence of the tax also fell. There were strong protests from the mining and agricultural interests in 1915 and again in 1917 when the rates were increased.[140] It is important to note that the government's move did not represent any official antipathy toward mining or export agriculture. Pardo himself was a sugar *hacendado*. It was simply that there was no other resource that could be as easily and quickly tapped. Recognizing this, some exporters reluctantly went along with the scheme. For example, the Sociedad Nacional Agraria lodged a protest in 1917, but two years earlier on the grounds of national need had not opposed the move,[141] and the Aspíllagas, owners of both sugar and cotton estates, although agreeing that the tax would harm their industry commented that[142] "...these arguments cannot be taken into account because of the critical situation of the country's finances."

The debate over this tax is interesting on two counts. It demonstrates that when in power, members of the export elite were often forced to take decisions which imposed burdens on their own class in order to maintain the integrity of the state. In this case, despite the agonized complaints, the burdens were easily borne. Secondly, the campaign against the tax demonstrated how divided the export elite was, not only between different producing groups, but within each group.[143] This greatly weakened their political clout in the Congress. All this suggests that it is wrong to see either the primary product exporters as if they were a single homogeneous group or the state as if it represented their immediate interests at all times and at all levels. This applies to Peru as well as the other three countries, but does not gainsay the power of the export elites in all the countries to determine the overall externally directed, primary product orientation of economic growth.

As income improved so government expenditure, which had been cut back in 1914 and 1915, was slowly increased. Spending on public works was greatly reduced and did not begin to recover until 1917. But with the export sectors booming there was probably little need for this added stimulus, although there were many improvements which were needed, including irrigation schemes and road construction. Further-more, given the chronic labor shortage on the coast[144] such projects may only have drawn workers away from expanding cotton and sugar plantations. The one major change in the pattern of expenditure was that the proportion devoted to debt servicing fell. The 1915 figure was unusually low because the government was unable to meet all its obligations in this year. Subsequently, budget surpluses were used to repay many short-term loans, and the amount needed to service the debt was substantially reduced. By 1918 both the actual payments and proportion of total expenditure given over to the debt had fallen by about 60% (Table 4.23). This was by far the best record of any of the four countries. How had it been possible for Peru to achieve this?

At the outbreak of the First World War the Peruvian government's foreign debt was extremely small by Latin American standards. However, a lack of debt in itself is not necessarily a sign of economic strength. In fact, it can be associated with stagnation. Under the best of circumstances public debts in Latin America were contracted with a view to undertaking projects such as railways, irrigation works, or port improvements which would eventually facilitate the expansion of exports. Problems arose either when loans were contracted for non-productive purposes and/or when debt servicing began to absorb a disproportionate share of government income. In Peru the foreign public debt was so small primarily because the extraordinarily large backlog of nineteenth-century obligations, estimated at almost £50,000,000 (both principal and unpaid interest) in the late 1880s,[145] had been consolidated and settled by the 1890 Grace Contract. Under its provisions the Peruvian Corporation was created. In return for the cancellation of the country's debt, mainly held in Britain, the government turned over to this new company most of Peru's railways as well as the franchise for commercial navigation on Lake Titicaca, the steamers then in operation, a sizable yearly quota of guano, a cash annuity, and 500,000 undeveloped acres in the remote Perene Valley. The country lacked a large foreign debt because her creditors had already foreclosed.

There were no foreign loans negotiated during the war, although the government did attempt to borrow $15,000,000 from the National City Bank in 1915.[146] However, the prospective lenders demanded concessions on both oilfield and petroleum export tax, most of the fields being controlled by the International Petroleum Company, a subsidiary of Standard Oil. There was a public outcry against this and there were also pressures to block the loan from the Peruvian

Table 4.23 *Peruvian public expenditure. Proportion of major categories 1913–1919*

	1913		1914		1915		(£p) 1916		1917		1918		1919	
Debt servicing	1,338,809	24.8%	747,304	18.2%	191,769	5.9%	659,789	18.6%	836,919	17.6%	564,306	10.5%	648,845	9.9%
Army & navy	1,072,913	19.9%	747,930	18.2%	586,342	18.1%	492,490	13.9%	531,207	11.2%	632,288	11.8%	870,241	13.3%
Police	308,095	5.7%	314,380	7.7%	287,778	8.9%	293,427	8.3%	275,864	5.8%	374,174	7.0%	447,053	6.8%
Education	259,998	4.8%	210,400	5.1%	203,468	6.3%	263,027	7.4%	267,852	5.6%	352,211	6.6%	415,633	6.3%
Public works	109,499	2.0%	26,844	.7%	46,059	1.4%	42,762	1.2%	153,961	3.2%	382,615	7.1%	502,292	7.7%

Source: McQueen, *Peruvian Public Finance*, p. 60.

Corporation unless their claims against the government were made a first charge on the proceeds. The money was never raised. In 1914 and 1915 the government scrambled about to find money from local sources, as it had in the immediate prewar years.[147] In return for the right to build their own port at Malabrigo, Gildemeister & Cia, owners of the massive sugar estate Casa Grande, lent £p 44,000 in 1914. £p 500,000 was forced from the banks as part of the issuing of *cheques circulares* in the same year, and other small short-term loans were also raised to meet government current expenses. However, advances to the government remained a small proportion of total bank loans and there was, therefore, no internal capital drain as occurred to some degree in Argentina. Once revenues began to recover, the debt was steadily reduced (Table 4.24), although the floating debt seems to have remained fairly steady. In 1918 many outstanding obligations were consolidated by a £p 2,000,000 internal bond issue.

Peru's budgets and debts were kept well under control during the war and so, by and large, was monetary policy. Initially, however, there were problems with the £p 2,500,000 of *cheques circulares* issued in 1914. In a country which had been on gold for such a long time and where the political situation was unsettled, the suspicion which greeted the new paper money was understandable and Rowe writes that, "The inevitable result has been the gradual depreciation of the Peruvian paper pound. In August 1915, this depreciation amounted to sixteen per cent."[148]

It was not until the beginning of 1916 that conditions became more stable.[149] Silver coins soon began to disappear from circulation because the bullion value became greater than the currency value. In response to this in 1917 the government issued £p 260,691 of gold certificates of 5 and 50 centavos. A further £p 170,346 was added in the following year together with five, ten and twenty cent nickel coins. As exchange rose, gold was imported and began to be minted once again in substantial quantities. This tended to hold down the rise in exchange, which was high but remained fairly steady throughout 1917. However, on entering the war, the US put an embargo on gold exports, and the premium on the sol (on 90-day London bills) skyrocketed from 7% in November 1917 to 17% by the following June. The solution to this was to allow the Lima banks to issue more *cheques*, up to £p 3,000,000, against gold deposits held abroad resulting from export sales. The operation was successful. The amount of money in circulation rose and the premium fell back to about 7% where it remained for almost a year. In terms of the amount of money held by

Table 4.24 *Peruvian debt 1913–1919*

	1913	1914	1915	1916	1917	1918	1919
				£p			
Internal debt	3,640,215		3,105,612	3,690,267	3,602,681	3,487,886	3,556,742
Bonded debt	1,853,630		1,971,997	1,998,787	1,783,445	1,592,672	1,037,665
Local bank loans	539,800		1,102,642	1,098,193	871,868	822,386	762,830
Tax collecting co. loans	1,493,346		1,579,069	1,576,335	1,543,082	1,488,320	1,488,198
Various	32,500		116,680	110,234	39,516	37,493	20,379
Total	7,559,491		7,876,000	8,473,816	7,840,592	7,428,757	6,865,814
Floating debt	71,250		1,866,436	1,959,415	1,959,415	1,857,052	2,035,180

Source: McQueen, *Peruvian Public Finance*, p. 81; 1915, Halsey, *Investments*, pp. 322–3. [*Note*: these figures have been reworked because they contain many errors]. 1916–19, *Extracto estadístico 1918*, p. 128, *Extracto estadístico 1919*, pp. 107–8, *Extracto estadístico 1926*, pp. 195–201. [*Note*: The data on the floating debt is questionable as each source gives a different figure for the same year. It would seem that the 1913 figure from McQueen is too low as he did not include balances from previous budgets, a sum included in other years. There is also a discrepancy between the debt figures in the three *Extractos*. Part of this was because the debt was reclassified in 1926. In the table earlier figures are used in order to maintain comparability.]

Table 4.25 *Peruvian monetary statistics and exchange rates 1912–1919*

	Net gold imports	Gold minted	£p Cheques circulares and gold certificates			Average exchange rates	
			In banks (accumulated total)	In circulation	Total	(US$ per £p)	(% premium on 90 day London bills)
1912	98,150	65,799	—	—	—	4.81	−.25%
1913	67,807	79,016	—	—	—	4.77	+.50%
1914	108,987	124,312	1,167,448	812,158	1,979,606	4.72	+1.25%
1915	2,530	91,984	1,085,796	1,230,416	2,316,242	4.23	+8.25%
1916	948,886	582,477	1,045,212	1,259,453	2,304,665	4.82	−2.75%
1917	2,775,109	1,930,452	748,848	1,955,762	2,704,610	4.99	−6.25%
1918	73,920	602,558	1,576,676	3,533,194	5,109,870	5.275	−11.0 %
1919	299,971	737,655	2,350,108	4,454,796	6,804,904	4.92	−11.75%

Sources: Extracto estadístico 1920, pp. 38–40; Exchange Rates: McQueen, *Peruvian Public Finance*, p. 106.

the public, Peru after 1915 compares favorably with Brazil, and while a rough measure, this suggests that there was not the financial stringency here that was found in Argentina. A review of banking policy does not, however, lend much support to this view.

The effect on and the reaction of the banks in Peru to the outbreak of the European war was the same as in other countries; confidence faltered, deposits fell, advances and loans were cut back and profits were reduced. Once the economy settled and the export boom got into full swing, deposits began to recover as did bank profits, but lending policy remained extremely conservative (although the discount rate remained constant over the period at 8%, except for a brief fall in mid-1915 and a .25% rise in 1919)[150] as indicated by the high cash ratios and the relatively low quantity of advances. It was not until June, 1918 that loans (in current soles) reached the levels obtained four years before and this against a considerably greater volume of deposits. If these figures are deflated by the retail price index, bank performance looks considerably more feeble (Table 4.26). Why this should have happened while the economy was apparently so healthy is not entirely clear. One factor may have been that because their profits were so great, exporters, at least, did not need to turn to the banks, although it

Table 4.26 *Peruvian banking figures 1912–1919*

	Deposits (real index)*	Advances & discounts (real index)	£p Cash ratio	Profits of national banks	Ratio to capital & reserves	Mortgages from mortgage banks
1912	7,663,964	6,389,357	20.4%	157,520	9.99%	762,392
1913	8,107,567 (100)	6,612,997 (100)	13.8%	156,682	9.93%	840,014
1914 (June)	7,776,922 (93)	6,483,168 (95)	14.2%	—		
1914 (Dec.)	5,373,739 (64)	6,148,735 (90)	27.9%	123,316	7.13%	855,627
1915 (June)	5,047,217 (57)	5,630,358 (78)	33.4%	—		
1915 (Dec.)	4,378,976 (50)	5,270,442 (73)	35.1%	89,431	6.01%	820,158
1916 (June)	4,820,648 (50)	5,210,552 (66)	34.4%	—		
1916 (Dec.)	5,768,602 (59)	5,032,364 (63)	38.8%	100,940	6.75%	882,840
1917 (June)	6,521,219 (57)	5,127,709 (53)	40.0%	—		
1917 (Dec.)	7,902,909 (69)	5,496,610 (57)	40.2%	160,469	10.67%	915,952
1918 (June)	8,376,483 (62)	6,449,859 (58)	25.0%	—		
1918 (Dec.)	10,053,877 (74)	6,265,757 (57)	28.8%	221,187	14.58%	969,926
1919 (June)	11,186,308 (73)	6,934,173 (55)	31.8%	—		
1919 (Dec.)	14,481,963 (94)	7,758,432 (62)	28.9%	332,357	17.51%	1,099,499

Source: Extracto estadístico 1919, pp. 46–8. *Real index: 1913 = 100 deflated by price index.

seems that during the war the banks began actively to seek the custom of the now-affluent cotton and sugar growers.[151] Furthermore, much of the incredible windfall profits made, at least by the sugar producers, was held outside the country and so did not go to swell the coffers of the local banks.[152] As in other countries uncertainty about what would happen in the postwar period may have deterred potential investors. Quiroz, whose work on the Peruvian financial system is the most detailed to date, puts part of the blame for the lack of expansion on the collapse at the end of the war of the blacklisted Banco Alemán Transatlántico, but most weight is given to the banks' traditionally "conservative banking and monetary policies," partly a function of their abiding concern with liquidity.[153]

It is interesting to note that although foreign banks were apparently less prominent in Peru than in the other countries, the largest "native" bank, the Banco de Perú y Londres, had a majority of British and French shareholders and foreign directors from 1907 to 1921.[154] The only purely foreign banks were the Banco Alemán Transatlántico and the new (1916) American Mercantile Bank of Peru.[155] There was also what Quiroz refers to as a "foreign-resident bank," the Banco Italiano, which in 1915 could claim 17% of the country's banking assets and 20% of its capital and reserves, the "native" banks controlling 58%

and 67% respectively.[156] By 1920 three new foreign banks had been established and this, together with a substantial increase in share taken by the Banco Italiano (28% of assets and 33% of capital and reserves), reduced local control substantially (39% and 45% respectively). Direct foreign control of the banking sector was, therefore, considerable, although it was to decline markedly in the 1920s.

Judging by the banking returns, the extent of domestic investment may have been constrained during the war. The data on the imports of capital equipment also indicates that it was after the war that the most expansive new development occurred.[157] Furthermore, the domestic industrial sector did not enjoy particularly buoyant demand during the war and so the need for investment here was probably limited. There was, however, a good deal of expansion in the export sectors. A lot of local capital went into agriculture, but much was used to buy out established concerns and did not represent an addition to the country's capital stock.[158] The increase in mortgages, including both urban and rural properties, does indicate that at least the land market was fairly active in the latter part of the war (Table 4.26). With respect to foreign investment there is little direct information. In 1915, Halsey estimated that a total of $200,000,000 of foreign capital, both direct and portfolio, was to be found in the country.[159] Thorp and Bertram provide figures for British and US direct investment which show that between 1910 and 1919 the amount increased from $84,000,000 to $161,000,000,[160] but much of this probably came in before 1914. Immediately before the war US capitalists had virtually taken over the lion's share of the mining and petroleum industries.[161] Oil production, which jumped 40% between 1914 and 1915, stagnated during the remainder of the war as an intense political conflict with the government created fears of expropriation and stopped new development. However, in mining, the output of copper, the most important mineral, did increase during the war, US firms continued to buy out local operators and invest in new projects.[162]

The general soundness of Peruvian government finances during most of the war period was largely, although not entirely, illusory. In terms of the public debt, things looked good only because the country had been forced to part with important national assets in order to liquidate debts and had been such a poor credit risk that it found it difficult to raise further capital abroad. To the extent that this slowed the development of infrastructure and, therefore, Peru's capitalist transformation, the country suffered, but the lack of borrowing also had positive implications. For example, the country avoided the kind of pressure on the balance of payments felt by Argentina and Brazil because of their heavy debt burdens, and fiscal difficulties were not unduly complicated by onerous levels of servicing. These difficulties were resolved by shifting the burden of taxation onto exports at a time when prices were so remunerative that it meant little real hardship for exporters. But this was to prove a precarious dependence when prices began to fall in the mid-1920s. As had happened, particularly in Chile, and to a lesser extent in the other two countries, the war, by giving a massive boost to exports in Peru, tended at the same time to strengthen those financial structures and expectations which had been developed to support the existing pattern of development. Overall these structures, especially with respect to government fiscal and monetary policies, were reinforced. The same thing can be seen in the banking sector, where, during the war, export agriculture became a favored area for lending and in the 1920s many prominent estate owners invested in and became directors of banks.[163]

Finally, although Peru, more than any of the other countries, experienced the direct takeover of key sectors by foreign capital before and, to some extent, during the war, there seems to have been none of the nationalist outcry against foreign financial manipulation found elsewhere. One reason was that although foreigners dominated banking, the largest bank, the Perú y Londres, was still nominally a local institution with Peruvian directors, and the rest of the financial sector was mainly controlled by Peruvians or, as in the case of the Banco Italiano, immigrants. Another was that nationalist agitation was more easily directed at that large foreign companies such as the Peruvian Corporation, Cerro de Pasco, or the International Petroleum Company, which directly exploited the country's resources, whereas in Brazil or Argentina production remained mainly under local control and the limitations of the banking system could, therefore, be more clearly identified as a source of foreign influence. This was also the case in Chile. Here foreign-owned enclaves were, of course, of major importance and a target for nationalists, but there were vocal groups, such as the industrialists, who also felt their interests were compromised by the extent of foreign dominance of the financial structure.

Conclusion

What did the events of the First World War reveal about the character of Latin American financial structures? How did these structures relate to the way in which primary export capitalism functioned and was able or unable to transform itself into a more independent and progressive capitalism? Because only some selected aspects of finance have been touched upon, and because it is apparent that a great deal more detailed research is necessary, particularly with respect to the actual problems faced by Latin American entrepreneurs in raising money, it is possible to offer no more than some tentative answers to these questions. Furthermore, generalizations must be made with some care because of the immense diversity of experience shown by the four countries. Their reliance on foreign capital varied, as did the influence of foreign financial institutions, and each government seems to have tackled their fiscal problems in a unique way. Despite these and other differences that have been emphasized it is worth while teasing out some common factors which may help us understand the nature and extent of foreign financial domination and the impact it had on these economies.

As with foreign trade, and in many ways directly connected with it, the initial impact of the war demonstrated in dramatic fashion the substantial external vulnerability of all peripheral capitalist financial systems to the "pull" from the City of London. This had, of course, been evident before and during the periodic metropolitan financial crises, but never had the disruption been so extensive or penetrated so deeply into the economy. Government revenues, the largest part of which came from import duties, were drastically cut. This was due primarily to the collapse of world trade, but the problem was exacerbated by the sudden halt in the inflow of long-term capital which not only compromised state finances but also put a stop to many construction projects, thereby exacerbating the problem of unemployment caused by the paralyzation of trade. With respect to the availability of credit, the long chain of financial dependence can be seen running from London to such far-off places as Peru's Cañete Valley. When the bankers in Britain shut up shop, within a very short time there was not enough ready money to pay Peruvian agricultural workers. This was not, of course, simply a problem of inadequate credit. The crisis, like the one faced by governments, was due to the disruption of trade. The point is that systems of domestic credit had become to a large extent creatures of foreign commerce, designed to facilitate it and dependent upon it. The outbreak of war starkly illuminated this and the many other externally induced financial constraints on Latin America's economies.

Once the initial crisis had passed, some degree of financial normality was restored. This was restricted mainly to commercial credit, needed if the Allies' demands for primary goods were to be met, and it was based on the necessary changes being made in London and New York. However, this did not lead to an immediate easing of financial conditions or substantial domestic economic expansion. Although there was considerable variation, banking data suggests that, in general, discounting and bank loans remained fairly restricted throughout the war, especially if the degree of export growth is taken into account. Some of this can be attributed to the conservative policies of foreign banks, but local banks too seem to have been cautious. The reasons for this are unclear, but perhaps it was due to the unsettled nature of the world economy and uncertainty about the future. It may have been this uncertainty, rather than restrictive bank lending policies (interest rates do not seem to have risen during the war) which dissuaded local businessmen from borrowing more. It must be remembered, however, that many banks confined their lending activity mainly to export-related activities, and low rates of interest did not mean that capital was necessarily available for other purposes.

The fact that foreign capital remained cut off also had a generally negative impact on economic activity as work on major infrastructural projects undertaken by foreign-owned railways or on public utilities came to a virtual halt during the war years. The effects of the falloff in construction on employment and demand were made worse because governments' incomes were sharply cut by the fall in import duties and because of the difficulty of obtaining the foreign loans upon which they had become so dependent. This forced them to adopt a variety of extraordinary measures for increasing revenue, and also to reduce their expenditure. It was spending on public works which was generally worst affected, tending to further depress demand. This was part of the price paid for having been able to ignore fiscal reform by relying on externally derived sources of income and loans.

It would appear, however, that, despite the many difficulties, there was a degree of resilience in the region's financial institutions which enabled them to adapt to the changed conditions brought by war. How else could these economies, most of which were so habituated to continual inflows of foreign capital, survive the period's immense financial dislocations? Does this not suggest that rather than creating self-limiting structures, the nineteenth century had seen the development of a more vigorous system then we have allowed for? This is possible but unlikely. The reestablishment of commercial credit was no more than a necessary extension of the revival of trade. Furthermore, potentially one of the most serious consequences of the flow of foreign capital being shut off, pressure on the balance of payments, was easily avoided during the war mainly because imports were hard to obtain and export earnings reached unprecedented levels. These special circumstances, which crucially distinguish the external shock of the First World War from that delivered in the 1930s, made external adjustment relatively straight-forward, whereas internal adjustment came mainly through rising prices and/or higher unemployment. The former was to make a major contribution to mounting social unrest in the last years of the war.

There was little indication during the war that the financial structures were able to accommodate or encourage changes in the region's primary export orientation. In one sense this was to be expected for the systems developed essentially to serve economies in which the central generating force was overseas trade, and with certain exceptions that trade was buoyant during the war. Furthermore, to the extent that financial structures reflect demands for specific kinds of services, then one would not expect changes here to precede changes in the productive base. Once in place these structures also undoubtedly helped perpetuate the existing system. It is interesting that during the war local capital, the accumulation of which was undoubtedly increasing because of highly profitable exports in at least three of the four countries, showed little interest in taking up the role which foreign capital had assumed in the prewar years. On the whole, infrastructural projects languished, most investment went into expanding export production and, in Chile and Peru, local miners sold out to the powerful United States corporations. It would seem that the fragmented character of the capital market was maintained and to some degree extended. Reliance on foreign capital was not a transitory phenomenon as it had been, for example, in the United States, but had marked out certain areas as virtually the exclusive domain for overseas investors. This tended both to sap local initiative and reduce the scope for domestic capital accumulation. There was a nationalist reaction to this as well as to the dominance of foreign financial institutions during and immediately after the war, but on the whole it made little difference. In the following decades US capital became increasingly powerful, exercising a direct and pervasive influence on economic life, particularly in the west coast republics. As has been argued with respect to trade, the war did not really provide an opportunity for changing direction. It helped rather to extend and consolidate primary export capitalism and to increase the dominance of foreign capital.

5

The War and the growth of manufacturing industry

Industrialization has been the main focus for most recent debates about the impact of the war upon Latin America. Up until the early 1960s it was assumed that the external shock delivered by the sudden and substantial reduction in imports gave a push to local manufacturing and that in these years there was a significant degree of industrial expansion based on import-substitution, at least in the more advanced of the Latin American countries. André Gunder Frank, accepting this argument, used it in support of his contention that:[1]

If it is satellite status which generates underdevelopment, then a weaker or lesser degree of metropolis–satellite relations may generate less deep structural underdevelopment and/or allow for more possibility of local development ... satellites have typically managed such temporary spurts in development as they have had, during the wars and depressions in the metropolis, which momentarily weakened or lessened its domination over the life of the satellites.

In a recent summary of the work on wartime industrial development in Peru, Chile, Colombia, Brazil, and Argentina,[2] Rory Miller explicitly challenged Frank's position and concluded that, "... in none of these five countries can the wartime period be distinguished as one of significant and lasting initiatives in manufacturing industry, but rather as one of windfall profits and limited expansion on the basis established before 1914." This he claims was mainly because of a combination of falling real incomes, and the impossibility of importing vital capital equipment, raw materials, and semi-finished goods. Rather than strong links with the international economy forestalling industrial development, the general conclusion seems to be that the latter's success depended on a healthy export performance and close links with the world system.

This may have been true, but in many crucial respects the entire debate has been misconceived. For example, as shown with respect to the export trade the nature and degree of Latin America's isolation during the war is not self-evident and has to be carefully reassessed in light of the strong Allied demands for most exports and these governments' direct interference in the region's economic affairs. Secondly, if industrialization was less than robust, does this support the contention that industrial growth as well as economic development generally was a function of strong trading ties? Again, possibly it does, but a relatively indifferent industrial response can also be interpreted as a reflection of the structural weaknesses inherent in the form of prewar capitalist development. This development had been based on the volatile fortunes of primary exports which were extremely sensitive to the changing needs of the advanced countries as well as being dominated by the relatively conservative logic of merchant capital. In this light, if there was slower industrial growth during the war this may not be a vindication of efficacy of the pre-1914 pattern of development but rather a testament to its weaknesses and limitations. This issue as well as Miller's argument and the works upon which it is based will be considered at length in this chapter, but it is first necessary to discuss some of the assumptions which inform the entire controversy and some of the empirical and conceptual problems encountered.

The major implicit assumption for both sides of the "external shocks" debate is that the growth of manufacturing industry can be equated with materially progressive capitalist development. Is this true? For Europe, North America and Japan it clearly was, but for Latin America and many other Third World regions, there is some doubt about accepting such an easy equation. For instance, there was considerable opportunity within a system of primary export dependence for the establishment of certain industries, without there being the prospect of breaking free from that dependence and moving towards an integrated, more dynamic industrial capitalism. In all four countries there was a substantial degree of industrial growth before 1914. However, in general it was of a very particular kind, either being directly linked to primary product exports, such as sugar *ingenios*, flour mills, and packing plants, or heavily concentrated on basic consumption goods, mainly food processing or clothing, for the local market. Intermediate and producer goods industries were weak or nonexistent. Furthermore, almost all the technology which served as the basis for modern industry was developed abroad and had to be imported, generally in the form of machinery and equipment. It is mainly because of this that Frank's belief that some viable form of autonomous capitalist growth was even possible, especially in the short run, is a historical illusion which ignores both the structural formation of the Latin American economies, to say nothing of the internal balance of class forces, and the fact that it is continual changes in technology which help drive the capitalist system forward. As Kay has argued,[3] the industrial development that occurred in regions like Latin America was partial in that it was confined to a narrow range of goods, failed to absorb much labor, and did not succeed in ending dependence on primary exports. In short, industries were developed but this did not lead to industrialization. Nonetheless, it is important to investigate the phenomenon of industrial growth more closely in order to see if in fact its ability to transform the Latin American economies was limited and if so, why. Such an investigation cannot be, as most have been, a simple counting exercise, rather the strengths and weaknesses of the industrial structure have to be assessed and the relation of manufacturing industry to the dominant export sectors clarified.

There are a number of difficulties in undertaking such an investigation. First, how does one define industry? In Latin America there were many enterprises classed as "industrial," which were not factories, but small workshops carrying out repairs or very basic processes. Artisans were also often included in the industrial category. Among the firms there was a great variation in numbers of workers employed, the level of technology, productive capacity, and output which makes it impossible to rely on figures for total numbers of industrial enterprises. Even when disaggregated data exists there is the question of exactly how one measures industrial growth. Is it in terms of output, number of establishments, productive capacity (usually impossible to determine), or capital invested? If all this was not enough, there is an even more insurmountable problem – lack of adequate statistical information. For example, there was no systematic industrial census carried out in Peru either before or immediately after the war. In Argentina there were censuses in 1895 and 1914, but none after the war, and in Brazil such surveys were carried out in 1907 and 1919, but once again the war period escaped direct measurement. Chile has the longest and most detailed run of yearly industrial inquiries, but even though there were surveys in 1914 and 1918, because of changes in the extent and manner of collecting data and the fact that 1914 was a time of economic recession, the two years are not easily comparable. Finally, and to an extent reflecting the differences in industrial performance and availability of data, there is extreme variation in the number of secondary studies of the manufacturing sectors in the different countries, with a great many works on Brazil, considerably fewer on Chile and Argentina and only a single major book dealing with industry in Peru. As this is by and large a work of synthesis, it tends to reflect this unevenness of coverage.

In order to judge the impact of the war on industry in Latin America it is essential to have a clear idea of the extent and character of prewar industrial growth. For this reason each of the following sections begins by reviewing the development of manufacturing up to 1914. In dealing with the war period the first concern is to try to arrive at some standard of measurement, and where this is not possible at least to spell out the various alternatives and their relative value. There is also the need to consider the way in which industry was tied to the external sector, whether through reliance on key imports, the processing of exports, or through the stimulus to domestic demand from export earnings. Finally, and most importantly, it is necessary to assay the industrial structure and the potential it offered for the development of a more dynamic, more balanced capitalism.

Brazil

I

Evidence of modern manufacturing in Brazil can be traced back at least to the middle decades of the nineteenth century, but the general consensus seems to be that significant progress in industrial development did not begin here until the 1880s. Writing in 1939, Simonsen maintained that the first major surge came between 1880 and 1890 and, using retrospective data from the 1920 Census, showed that during the decade at least 398 new firms were established.[4] Subsequent studies have tended to play down this period and argue that significant progress did not come before 1888–9 with the abolition of slavery, the massive influx of immigrants and the founding of the First Republic.[5] Versiani has questioned this and maintains that in terms of import-substitution the cotton textile industry, which because of its relatively high concentration of capital and labor dominated the country's modern industrial structure, had grown notably from the early 1870s.[6] In this he has essentially taken up and greatly elaborated Stein's argument that by 1892 cotton textile manufacture was embarking on its second stage of development.[7] This is an important point for, among other things, it makes the rapid industrial expansion of the 1890s more comprehensible. Unfortunately, there is no data on industrial production for this period similar to that available for some of the other countries.

It is clear that there was an industrial boom in the 1890s. The precise reasons for this are the subject of continued debate. For example, Fishlow has argued[8] that there was rapid expansion in the early 1890s because of the sudden increase in credit which followed the new, liberal banking legislation. This led to a rise in capital goods imports and subsequently when the progressive devaluation of the milréis made foreign equipment more costly, higher import prices acted as a shield for local industry. Versiani on the other hand claims that while inflation and devaluation were important, for textiles the high Brazilian tariff, although created to raise revenue, also afforded a significant degree of protection and was a crucial factor accounting for growth.[9] In fact, the general incidence of tariffs was extremely high in Brazil, and while it is usually claimed that revenue was the first consideration the great selectivity of duties (that is, higher rates on locally produced consumer goods) clearly demonstrates that special interest groups were able to obtain significant degrees of protection.[10]

The most important issue regarding Brazil's prewar industrialization was its link with coffee exports and the increasing concentration of industry in the southeast, particularly São Paulo. Of the many reasons for this, Cano claims[11] one of the most fundamental was the development of capitalist relations of production on the coffee estates, which differentiated São Paulo from most of Brazil's other regionally based export sectors. Combined with the massive inflow of immigrants this provided an expanding market for local industry, while at the same time permitting a substantial degree of local capital accumulation. The immigrants also contributed to increased urbanization and provided an industrial labor force. Furthermore, the growth of railways, built in Saõ Paulo mainly to extend the coffee frontier, served to open up the domestic market. Dean has made the strongest, most comprehensive case for there being a positive correlation between a healthy expanding coffee sector and industrial growth. He writes that,[12] "The industrialization of São Paulo depended from the beginning upon the demand generated by the growing overseas market for coffee...It is evident that the continued growth of Paulista industry was a result of the growth of the coffee trade." Cano[13] makes a much more detailed analysis of the way coffee exports stimulated industry, but disagrees with Dean regarding many specific aspects of the process, particularly the positive correlation between export prosperity and industrial growth. Versiani also takes up this last point and argues that although the "external shocks" hypothesis does not seem to apply to prewar Brazil, "...a direct association between export booms and the growth of industrial capital seems no more convincing nor warranted... it would be clearly inadequate to think of it [industrialization] in terms of the standard 'staple' models of growth and trade."[14] This issue will be explored in more detail when events during the war are considered.

It is not possible to give a precise picture of the state of Brazilian industry in 1914. With respect to its relative importance in the economy Leff, reworking Haddad's data, claims this had become substantial by 1908–14, when industry's share of value added in comparison with that of agriculture, transport and communications and government had reached 19.4%.[15] But, by its very nature, industry's proportion of value added is likely to be relatively high. A general picture of the structure of industry can be drawn from the 1907 Census, but it is important to realize that the collection of information was undertaken not by the state but by the Centro Industrial do Brasil, and by their own admission the coverage was only partial.[16] The survey showed 3,258 firms with a capital of 665,576,000 milréis, employing 151,841 workers and an output valued at 741,536,108 milréis.[17] Dean estimates that to gauge the true extent of industry in that year one would have to triple the number of firms and double the number of workers and the value of production.[18] Furthermore, Cano claims that between 1907 and 1913 industrial growth in São Paulo was extremely rapid,[19] making the 1907 Census even less representative of conditions six years later. Bearing these shortcomings in mind, Table 5.1 shows Brazilian industry was dominated by textiles and food processing, as it was to be twelve years later, with a reasonable share taken by intermediate goods but virtually no heavy industry recorded. There were a few of the latter, however. For example, the Census records 17 shipyards which employed on average 213 workers, 31 firms making transport material and numerous metalworking shops as well as some machinery makers or repairers, which have been listed as intermediate goods producers.[20] In 1898, Worthington[21] had noted that there was an important rolling mill and foundry near Rio employing 400 workers, a smaller enterprise in Porto Alegre which made steam engines, and four firms in the São Paulo area making coffee machinery and "water motors." The largest of these employed over 500 workers.

Judging from the relative structure of imports (Table 5.3), in terms of providing substitutes for consumer goods Brazilian industry had achieved a considerable degree of success by the First World War. The 1907 Census shows that of thirty major consumption items, including

Table 5.1 *Brazilian industry 1907: percentage share of production*

	% Share
Consumer goods	75%
Food	27.5%
Textiles	20.1%
Shoes	4.1%
Beverages	8.0%
Tobacco	2.7%
Matches	2.9%
Clothing	4.0%
Soap and candles	3.0%
Various	2.7%
Capital goods	1.0%
Shipbuilding	0.7%
Machinery	0.1%
Various	0.2%
Durable goods	4%
Furniture	1.6%
Various	2.4%
Intermediate goods	20%
Metal products	4.3%
Jute	3.0%
Woodwork	4.2%
Tanning	2.0%
Chemicals	1.4%
Transport materials	1.6%
Various	3.5%

Source: Calculated from Centro Industrial, *O Brasil*, p. 149. *Note:* These figures must be seen as no more than rough estimates, due both to the failings of coverage and the difficulty in assigning products to particular categories. For example, some of the goods listed as "Metal products" or "Transport materials" were probably capital goods. The breakdown in the census was not detailed enough to pick this up.

cotton cloths, shoes, hats, sugar, and beer, local industry was supplying about 80% of domestic needs.[22] This may be too low a figure given the incomplete nature of the survey, but it is probably offset by the fact that the list of items presented is itself only a sample and does not include such major imported items as flour or kerosene.

Finally, it seems that although the production of consumer goods was dominant, Brazil had made at least some progress toward industrial diversification.

II

In 1920, Arthur Redfield observed that, "Manufacturing in Brazil owes its present vigor to the war."[23] This can be said generally to have reflected contemporary opinion about the impact of the war on Brazilian industry. The many problems, most notably the shortages of coal and imported machinery and raw materials, were recognized, but it was felt that on balance these difficulties were outweighed by the country being cut off from foreign competition. The industrial census of 1919 seemed to add quantitative confirmation to the more impressionistic accounts. Of the 13,336 factories listed, 5,936 (44.5%) had been established between 1915 and 1919 (Table 5.2). This suggests a phenomenal wartime expansion, but in all respects these new firms were very considerably smaller than average. However, this is to be expected, as in general the older firms would have had to have been more hearty to survive and would also have had longer to accumulate capital. Furthermore, these newer establishments did account for about a quarter of capital, production and workers employed and a fifth of the power used.[24] To assess more adequately the significance of wartime changes what is needed is some measure of the growth of industrial production, capital, and/or labor. An initial attempt to provide the first of these was made by Simonsen in his 1939 study.[25] Using the excise returns for certain manufactured goods he created an index of industrial production, which he deflated by a cost of living index. This showed a substantial spurt of industrialization during the war years, the deflated index rising between 1914 and 1918 from 100 to 171 for Brazil and to 181 for São Paulo. Based on this Simonsen claimed that the growth experienced during the war period was of key importance in the country's industrial evolution. Until 1968, Simonsen's analysis of industry during the war was widely accepted and used as evidence by those, such as Frank, who advocated variants of an "external shocks" theory.

In 1968 Warren Dean published his important study of industrialization in São Paulo, an entire chapter of which is devoted to the First World War. In this he launched a telling attack on Simonsen's findings.[26] He rightly points out that because there was a recession in 1914 using it as a base year could not help but inflate the rate of growth and that, furthermore, the value of production was substantially

Table 5.2 *Relative size of industrial firms in Brazil*

Years founded	Number of firms	Average capital (milréis)	Average power (HP)	Average no. of workers	Average production (milréis)
Before 1899	1,560	437,000	74	64	593,935
1900–4	1,080	101,500	18	18	193,476
1905–9	1,358	166,122	30	25	271,771
1910–14	3,135	107,000	20	17	206,230
1915–19	5,936	73,881	11	11	133,300
Unknown	267	90,853	28	16	175,356
Total	13,336	136,110	23	21	224,143

Source: Brazil, Ministério de Agricultura, Indústria e Comércio, Directoria Geral de Estatística, *Recenseamento do Brasil*, vol. iv, Rio, 1920, p. lxix.

increased by more costly inputs and did not simply reflect an increase in value added. Finally, Dean maintains that Simonsen's cost of living is inaccurate and, more importantly, that to use such an index as a deflator for one of industrial production is inappropriate because the former did not reflect the movement in manufactured goods' prices. Most increases in production were found in the export processing sector or were realized by utilizing excess capacity, for the sharp decline in the imports of capital goods and raw materials made it extremely difficult to expand the industrial plant (Table 5.3). Villela and Suzigan's indices of domestic steel and cement consumption give further support to this argument (Table 5.3). Dean makes a number of other important points, and then, consistent with his thesis that the health of industry depended on the health of coffee exports, he concludes:[27]

World War I increased considerably the demand for domestic manufactured goods but made it almost impossible to enlarge the productive plant to meet that demand. The fortunes that were made during the war grew out of new lines of exports, twenty-four-hour-a-day production, or out of mergers and reorganizations. New plants and new lines of manufacture were not significant. It might be asked if the industrialization of São Paulo would not have proceeded faster had there been no war.

Although the argument is made with references to São Paulo, because industrial development was so much more dynamic here than in the other Brazilian states it is reasonable to take this as a proxy for the

Table 5.3 Quantum indices of Brazilian imports 1901–1920, percentage share of different classes and cement and steel consumption

	(1939 = 100)								(1000 tons)	
	Consumer goods	(%)	Fuels	(%)	Raw materials	(%)	Industrial capital goods	(%)	Domestic cement consumption	Domestic steel consumption*
1901–5	137.0	(38.5)	23.5	(8.3)	49.8	(45.6)	46.0	(1.2)	76.7	59.5
1906–10	157.4	(31.9)	34.2	(8.2)	69.9	(47.9)	95.4	(3.1)	204.7	125.0
1911	194.0	(30.9)	44.4	(8.0)	90.7	(47.3)	153.6	(3.6)	268.7	171.0
1912	222.6	(30.2)	64.5	(9.0)	102.5	(44.9)	205.3	(3.8)	367.0	215.9
1913	217.1	(30.1)	60.1	(9.7)	104.4	(45.2)	152.6	(4.2)	465.3	251.2
1914	136.4	(34.0)	43.1	(12.3)	52.0	(42.9)	63.4	(3.3)	180.9	127.2
1915	92.8	(27.5)	37.9	(15.4)	46.5	(52.1)	25.2	(1.7)	144.9	82.7
1916	89.3	(24.2)	36.6	(16.2)	54.7	(54.0)	32.2	(1.9)	169.8	82.0
1917	79.6	(22.4)	28.5	(17.3)	39.8	(53.4)	32.0	(2.2)	98.6	74.4
1918	79.5	(23.1)	20.8	(11.9)	44.9	(58.7)	36.9	(2.6)	51.7	44.1
1919	99.5	(22.3)	39.9	(13.9)	61.0	(53.9)	64.6	(3.6)	198.4	126.4
1920	163.5	(25.5)	41.0	(11.3)	72.8	(51.5)	108.1	(4.2)	173.0	195.5

Source: Calculated from Villela and Suzigan, *Government Policy*, pp. 359, 363, 365. * Steel consumption does not include railway material.

entire country. If things were bad here they were likely to be worse elsewhere.

It took almost thirty years before Simonsen's views were questioned, but once they had been it was but a short time before a major debate was raging as to the course of Brazilian industrialization during the First World War. Nothing similar to this controversy has developed with respect to the other three countries and consequently much more is known about Brazil's wartime industrialization. However, greater knowledge, essentially the product of the debate, has not resulted in a new consensus on the war but rather has created continuing and ever more complex disagreement. Because of this the remainder of this section on Brazil will be given over primarily to a summary and assessment of the various arguments which have been advanced.

Fishlow's contribution has been one of the most telling and influential.[28] He agrees with Dean about the failings of Simonsen's analysis, but not over the importance of the war, which he sees as marking Brazil's second major period of import-substitution, the first being the 1890s. He points out that certain major industries such as textiles and iron experienced rapid rates of growth. The former's production rose by over 25% between 1911–13 and 1918 and from 1915 to 1918 pig iron output jumped from 3,500 tons to 11,700 tons. Dean maintains that much of the increased industrial production went for export, but Fishlow calculates that the figure was only about 20%. He also constructs a new industrial production index (excluding sugar and meat-packing). This shows an annual growth rate between 1911–13 and 1918 of 4.4%, which compares favorably with less than 4% achieved during the 1920s. A major point raised by Fishlow is that while it was difficult to obtain producer goods imports during the war, the high level of industrial profits provided the basis for postwar purchases and an increase in industrial capacity.

Dean's position has, however, continued to find outspoken and persuasive advocates. For example, Villela and Suzigan[29] essentially repeat his arguments and his conclusion. "...it may be appropriate to ask," they write, "whether the industrial spurt that seems to have taken place in the years 1905–1912 may not have led to a process of industrialization had World War I not occurred." In a later work Suzigan and Peláez[30] return to the attack, this time with a specific criticism of Fishlow's analysis.[31] A number of points are made, but the two most crucial are that Suzigan's index of industrial production is superior to Fishlow's, and shows a lower rate of wartime growth, and that capital formation was drastically cut. The first point is simply beyond final resolution as is any such argument about base years and weighting. The second seems to ignore Fishlow's clear distinction between wartime profits and postwar capital formation. Subsequently, this latter point seems to have been accepted by Peláez and his conclusions about the adverse effects of the war on industry somewhat tempered.[32] While still maintaining the position that the wartime conditions did not lead to an industrial boom, he concludes that, "It seems valid, in view of revisionist views on the origins of Brazilian industry, to raise serious doubts about whether adverse periods were *indispensable* for diversification of economic activities for the internal market."

A rather different tack has been taken by Versiani and Versiani, who although agreeing with Fishlow, point out that the debate has been rather inconclusive because one side regards an increase in production as important and the other feels an expansion of industrial capacity is what signifies meaningful development.[33] But, they observe, that for the textile industry both phases were necessary and complemented each other within the same model of industrial development. It is in this sense that they maintain for wartime, as they do for the prewar years, that neither an export-led nor an external shocks model can adequately explain Brazilian industrial development. Without the capital formation in the previous period the First World War could not have led to any substantial increase in industrial production.[34] Conversely, being protected from imports offered a valuable opportunity to employ capacity fully and to accumulate profits. This is an important observation which helps clarify, although it does not completely resolve the debate.

Just as Versiani and Versiani seem to have captured and dissected the elusive debate Cano has come along with an important new argument which once again throws the whole question open. In the part of his study of São Paulo which covers the war, drawing heavily on Fishlow, but also offering his own wide-ranging empirical critique of Dean's work, he maintains that productive capacity did not stagnate to the extent it is generally believed to have done in these years.[35] He claims that although machinery imports fell, in cotton textiles there was continued installation of new equipment during the war (Table 5.4). He also observes that the level of São Paulo's textile machinery imports was inordinately high in 1913, thereby exaggerating the subsequent fall. In the period 1913–40 a similar level was reached only in 1925 and 1938. Cano asks if perhaps there had not been over-investment

Table 5.4 *Importation of textile*
machinery and accessories 1913–1921

| | (tons) | |
	São Paulo	Rest of the country
1913	4,310	9,035
1914	778	nd
1915	861	1,333
1916	1,328	1,122
1917	786	1,216
1918	1,468	1,464
1919	1,292	1,461
1920	1,603	2,659
1921	2,822	3,473

Source: Cano, *Raízes,* p. 276.

immediately before the war and argues on the basis of this that textiles probably did not suffer very much from a shortage of equipment. This is a provocative point, but needs to be more firmly supported by additional evidence. It is true, however, that while total capital goods imports did clearly fall massively during the war, when seen over a longer time the years immediately preceding the conflict appear as particularly high and make the wartime decline seem more dramatic. Cano also argues that the fall in the imports of cement and structural steel was not so important for industry as for civil construction. Turning to demand, he questions whether it was as depressed as Dean suggests and shows that, as argued above, except for 1914, export earnings were not badly hit until the very end of the war. Unfortunately, the value of Cano's work is diminished by two major problems. The treatment of the war period is based almost entirely on modern secondary studies and a reworking of published statistical sources. The latter are notoriously inadequate for making fine distinctions and the former, with the notable exception of Dean's book, are generally based on the same questionable data. Secondly, the author fails even to mention the many other works which deal with the war, let alone to address the questions they raise.

Despite all that has been written, the extent of Brazil's wartime industrial growth remains an open question and one in need of more detailed primary research efforts. A few tentative conclusions can,

Table 5.5 *Brazilian industry. Index of*
manufacturing production and value
added 1900–1921

	Manufacturing production (1939 = 100)	Value added (000,000 milréis)
1900–4	12.8	
1905–9	15.5	
1909	18.4	400
1910	19.4	463
1911	20.7	404
1912	22.8	530
1913	22.8	490
1914	20.6	369
1915	23.3	542
1916	26.1	713
1917	28.4	1099
1918	28.1	964
1919	32.4	1147
1920	34.1	1378
1921	33.6	1055

Source: Haddad, *Produto Real*, p. 131.
Note: From 1901 to 1907 index is based
on cotton textiles, 1908–11 all fabric and
an index of food products were added,
1912–21 drinks, tobacco, shoes, hats, and
an index of chemical products.

however, be suggested. All indications are that over these years there
was an increase in the number of firms, employment, capital invested,
and production. Besides the 1920 Census there is other evidence of
this. For example, in São Paulo between 1915 and 1917, 323 new firms
were established with total capital of 14,087,624 milréis.[36] Most of
these were probably small and employed relatively few people, but as
argued above this is hardly surprising. Furthermore, the index of
manufacturing production as well as the amount of value added both
rose quite substantially during the war (Table 5.5). With respect to the
crucial iron and steel industry, Callaghan comments,[37] "In general, the
unavailability of imported iron and heightened demand by growing

Brazilian firms during the war years stimulated the rapid growth of the iron industry." Secondly, Fishlow's observation on the importance of wartime profits and the Versianis' idea about the necessary complementarity of alternating cycles of industrial expansion go some way toward resolving the issue of the apparently low level of wartime capital formation. Cano's contribution on this question is interesting but far from conclusive. On the whole the conditions brought about by the war, particularly the major decline in competing imports, did stimulate Brazilian industry, this development being constructed on the base laid down in the years from the 1890s. At the same time, the apparent dependence on capital goods imports limited the extent to which capacity could be expanded. In terms of demand, export earnings did not deteriorate before the end of the war and this, together with inflationary government finance, helped maintain the level of domestic demand. These findings cut across the positions taken by the opposing sides in the debate. Industry was given a boost by the First World War, while at the same time, it relied on imported producer goods as well as the stimulus to domestic demand given by a healthy export sector.

The fact that there was a growing industrial sector does not in itself indicate a broader materially progressive transformation was taking place. In the Brazilian case both the wartime expansion and the restrictions on the nature of that expansion showed that for all its size industry remained dependent upon and subservient to foreign trade. The weakness of this form of industrialization is also reflected in the country's industrial structure which remained completely dominated by nondurable consumer goods. According to Fishlow's reworking of the 1919 Census figures (Table 5.6) 80% of the total value added fell into this category, with food processing providing the largest single share. At the same time, there was a continued strong dependence on the import of producer and intermediate goods. Fishlow argues[38] that the figures substantially understate the extent of this dependence because "Foreign and domestic supply are not equivalent. The former represents a net addition to available factor resources and is more comparable to value added, than to gross sectoral production, whose sum exceeds national income." There is also the problem of calculating the tariff on competitive goods. Correcting for both of these factors he comes to the conclusion that imports represented about 40% of total value added.

Leff takes issue with Fishlow's analysis and argues that it is to be expected that early industrial development should concentrate on basic

Table 5.6 *Structure of Brazilian industry 1919*

	Percentage distribution of value added	Imports as a percentage of supply
Consumer goods	80.3	13.7
Textiles	24.4	6.2
Clothing	7.3	11.5
Food	32.9	23.8
Beverages	5.4	0.3
Tobacco	3.4	70.7
Rubber	0.1	57.0
Chemicals	4.2	32.0
Leather	0.2	40.5
Nonmetallic minerals	1.2	53.4
Miscellaneous	1.2	—
Consumer durables	1.8	
Electrical	—	100.0
Transport	—	53.5
Furniture	1.8	2.2
Intermediate goods	16.5	
Metallurgy	3.8	64.2
Nonmetallic minerals	2.8	40.5
Leather	2.0	32.0
Chemicals	0.8	57.0
Wood	5.7	6.1
Paper	1.4	58.3
Rubber	—	70.7
Electrical	—	100.0
Capital goods	1.5	
Mechanical	0.1	96.7
Electrical		100.0
Transport	1.4	53.5
Total	100.0	24.7

Source: Fishlow, *Origins*, p. 323.

Note: Federal excise tax deducted and food adjusted for inclusion of bakeries and sugar refining. Also in second column percentages refer to entire sector not specific use, which is why some are repeated.

goods for which there was both a substantial local demand and the requisite raw materials.[39] Furthermore, import substitution was far advanced by 1919. Using Fishlow's figures, he observes that 60% of the industrial value added was locally produced. This seems to be a disagreement over "whether the glass is half full or half empty." He also argues that early industrial growth was important in providing the basis for subsequent development, a point which by its nature is almost impossible to refute. However, the character of this development was not an unmixed blessing with respect to subsequent change as is attested to by Dean, who observes that in terms of providing protection,

the prior implementation of consumer goods industries may have retarded the development of more basic industry, because each consuming unit, whether the ultimate consumer or an intermediary, would tend to oppose an increase in the costs of his purchases...One is struck by the absence, in all the polemical literature of the industrialists between the wars, of any exhortations in behalf of new industries... During this period it was not the "entrepreneurs" but engineers, journalists, and bureaucrats who spoke in favor of the immediate creation of steel, petroleum, and chemical industries.

Leff does not, however, ignore the problems which plagued Brazilian industry. The most important of these in his opinion was not the dual dependence on the foreign trade sector, but rather the constraints imposed by the state of domestic demand. "The size of the market for manufactures was limited by the country's low income levels. These also determined a pattern of demand which was oriented mainly to food products and textiles."[40] This conclusion is a variant of the major leitmotif in his analysis of Brazilian economic growth. The reason for Brazil's relatively poor economic performance during the nineteenth century owed much, he argues, to the backwardness of domestic agriculture. There were numerous reasons for this, including inadequate transport, but Leff places particular stress on the fact that mass immigration created an elastic supply of labor which helped to hold down wages while at the same time perpetuating a dual economy.[41] This was a purely internal issue, and he explicitly denies that external links played any substantively negative role in Brazil's development.[42] "On the contrary, integration into the growing world economy enabled Brazil to achieve rising income, a more capable state apparatus, and improved infrastructure facilities. Those conditions in turn, promoted Brazil's transition to more generalized economic development and domestic industrialization."

It is beyond the scope of this work to begin a full critique of Leff's often elegant and powerful but always unrelentingly neoclassical analysis. A few brief observations must, however, be made with reference to the question of industry. Because he sees his principal intellectual adversaries as the by now straw men of the "stagnationist–dependency" school, it is easy to overturn their case by showing that considerable economic expansion had occurred and was associated with industrialization. What he fails to do is offer any substantive critical assessment of either the wider socio-economic transforming power of this industry or the close relationship between it and the external sector. For Leff, export expansion stimulated industrial development in the southeast but its volatility created no problems for that development. Any difficulties were purely internal ones. But were they? For example, if mass immigration was, as Leff contends, a negative factor and has to be understood in terms of a class and political analysis of nineteenth-century Brazil, it must also be seen as an integral part of the coffee complex which so dominated the country. This, as well as the European emigration, cannot be understood except within the context of the development of the capitalist world economy. In terms of historical comprehension it is not very helpful to sweep away criticisms of the character of industry by appealing to the subsequent "positive" changes which occurred, for these later developments, specifically the industrial growth in the 1930s, cannot themselves be taken at face value and also demand a critical evaluation. Furthermore, Brazilian industry's unsophisticated structure and heavy reliance on imports became a major political issue during and after the First World War. The agitation which developed over this played a major part in a new, more interventionist attitude of the state from the 1920s and so helped set the stage for the next phase of Brazil's industrial growth.

To clarify the last point a brief comment is called for on the relationship between industry and economic nationalism during the war.[43] A fairly strong economic nationalist sentiment had of course been present in the country throughout most of the nineteenth century, as evidenced by the various coordinated efforts made, particularly from the latter decades, to muster government support for industry through tariff protection.[44] There were many arguments advanced for the benefits of industry. One of the most prominent was that compared to the irregularity and precariousness of agriculture, industry offered a secure source of national properity. Another was that national "misery" was the result of a drain of wealth abroad which was contingent upon excessive agricultural dependence.[45] During the war the problems experienced in obtaining vital commodities, particularly steel and coal, gave such claims greater weight and so increased pressure for direct state involvement in industry. Topik writes:[46] "The lesson of the First World War to most of Brazil's decision-makers was that the government should stimulate 'industrial initiatives capable of liberating us from dependence on foreign markets'." Subsequent government intervention in coal, steel and petroleum was a direct response to the wartime experience. The war, therefore, not only stiumlated industrial production, but also high-lighted its weaknesses and external dependence and thereby helped alter the political climate in a way which favored subsequent industrial development.[47]

Chile

I

Until fairly recently it was believed that Chilean industrialization, as well as that in the rest of Latin America, was essentially a product of the 1930s.[48] However, as more research has been done on its history, so the date of the country's industrial genesis has been steadily pushed back. Both Ortega and Palma make convincing arguments for there having been a substantial degree of modern industrial growth from the 1870s,[49] although neither would claim that this worked a dramatic transformation on the Chilean economy. Kirsch, on the other hand, sees the War of the Pacific as the major turning point for industrial growth, not only in terms of the pace of expansion, but also in the new economic pattern he sees emerging after 1879 which was more conducive to industry.[50] He maintains that the war itself provided a powerful stimulus because of government demand and that subse-quently, "...urbanization, population movements to the north and the south, developments in transportation, agriculture, mining, and foreign commerce – operated to provide the preconditions for the implantation of a meaningful industrialization process in Chile." Tariffs also played an important part in this process, particularly the 1897 Tariff. Although primarily a revenue measure it was strongly influenced by protectionist pressures and did in fact give considerably, albeit selective, protection for industry.[51]

Kirsch may have underestimated the significance of pre-1879 industrial growth, but it is clear that from the War of the Pacific, there

Table 5.7 *Estimates of Chilean*
industrial production 1880–1913

	(1918 = 100)		
	Low	Most probable	High
1880	36	50	70
1885	39	55	77
1890	47	67	96
1895	47	71	101
1900	48	71	97
1905	52	75	108
1910	64	94	137
1912	64	94	137
1913	64	94	138

Source: Kirsch, *Modernization*, p. 26. Note:
The author warns that these figures do not
represent actual index values of production,
but rather a long-run trend in those values.

was an acceleration in the process, albeit an uneven one (Table 5.7).
The 1895 census prepared by the Sociedad de Fomento Fabril (founded
in 1883), showed a total of 2,449 factories and small workshops, 76%
of which had been founded in the previous 15 years.[52] The flourishing
nitrate fields, Chile's prize for victory in the War of the Pacific,
stimulated the development of a number of associated industries. Of
prime importance were the metallurgical industries and the construction of transport equipment, especially for the railways, which were
extended substantially from 2,747 kilometers in 1890 to about 8,000
kilometers in 1913.[53] By the decade following the end of the war, the
metallurgical works established by Lever were employing 2,000
workers and producing not only materials for railways but also
equipment for mining and warships.[54] In 1886 the first Chilean
locomotive was made, all the major parts, except the wheels, being
produced in the country. Subsequently, a small output was maintained
up until the First World War.[55] Although there was a heavy
dependence on imports of raw material, technology and capital goods,
before 1914 a reasonably integrated industrial structure had been
established.[56] Palma observes that by this time about 16% of the
economically active population was engaged in some form of

Table 5.8 *Structure of Chilean imports 1880–1913*

	Consumer goods	Raw materials	Capital goods & transport	Fuel	Other
	(average annual percentage share)				
1880–4	36.1	49.0	5.1	4.5	6.0
1885–9	36.0	47.2	7.7	4.1	5.1
1890–4	32.2	45.8	11.7	5.8	4.5
1895–9	31.6	45.9	6.2	9.1	7.2
1900–4	30.2	48.2	9.5	10.9	1.1
1905–9	26.8	42.9	16.8	13.0	0.5
1910	26.7	47.2	10.8	14.6	0.7
1912	28.8	42.8	15.4	12.2	0.8
1913	31.0	40.8	13.8	13.2	1.2

Source: Calculated from Kirsch, *Modernization*, p. 164.

manufacturing, although many would have been in small artisan workshops. The industrial sector was providing 80% of the country's immediate consumption requirements but only 20% of durable and intermediate goods needed.[57] This is clearly reflected in the structure of imports (Table 5.8) which shows a steady fall in and, in comparison with other Latin American countries, a relatively low percentage of consumer goods imports. In this respect Chile's industrial structure was somewhat similar to that of Brazil, with the important expection of cotton textiles.

Another view of Chilean industry on the eve of the Great War is provided by the 1914 Industrial Census. This census does, however, greatly underestimate the size of the industrial sector, for important, albeit unspecified, changes in collection and catagorization of data were introduced in that year, and compared to 1913 there was a most unlikely 46% drop in the number of firms enumerated.[58] Obviously, this census cannot, therefore, provide a reliable benchmark for comparison, but assuming that the omissions in its coverage were random, it does offer a fairly reasonable outline of the structure of Chilean industry at the outbreak of the First World War. The figures in Table 5.9 do not include the 2,470 small workshops which were listed separately, the assumption being they employed less than five workers.[59] The picture that emerges is one of an industrial sector characterized by an extreme concentration on consumer goods

Table 5.9 *Structure of Chilean industry
in 1914. Share of production*

	% Share
Consumer goods	81.8%
Beverages	4.3%
Food	52.7%
Clothing	4.6%
Textiles	3.1%
Shoes	6.5%
Paper	2.5%
Chemicals	5.1%
Tobacco	2.6%
Various	0.4%
Capital goods	1.2%
Shipbuilding	0.7%
Railway cars	0.5%
Durables	1.9%
Furniture	0.3%
Metal goods	1.6%
Intermediate goods	15.3%
Metal goods	2.3%
Wood products	4.9%
Tanneries	5.2%
Paper	1.1%
Various	1.8%

Source: Calculated from Chile, Oficina
Central de Estadística, *Anuario estadístico
de la República de Chile*, vol. viii, Industrias año 1914, Santiago, 1916. *Note:* We
have excluded gas and electricity generating
plants and the country's one meat-packing
plant.

production, a pattern common throughout Latin America. However,
there were some uncommon aspects of the Chilean industrial profile.
The textile industry was extremely weak, whereas in many peripheral
capitalist countries this was one of the first industries to be developed.
Kirsch ascribes this to the cheapness of intermediate goods imports

and the domination of weaving by local merchant houses who found it more profitable not to establish an integrated industry.[60] Secondly, although their share of total production was small, there were a number of important intermediate and capital goods industries, such as cement, leather tanning, shipbuiding and repair, metalworking factories, and heavy equipment producers. Finally, it seems that there was a degree of industrial diversification achieved but it was less marked in Chile than in Brazil. However, the numerous shortcomings of measurement in both countries make any meaningful comparisons on this point virtually impossible.

II

The debate over the experience of Chilean industry during the war has not yet developed to the same level of informative acrimony as that which continues on Brazil. There are, in fact, no studies devoted exclusively to the period. Instead there are five important works which deal with the war years as part of a longer term analysis of Chilean industrial development and in which, by and large, the First World War is not afforded very detailed coverage. A major task for all the authors has been to construct a reliable statistical measure of industrial production. Because this exercise is so fundamental and so problematic a summary and critique of the various indices of production, with special reference to the war period, is a necessary first step.

A relatively early attempt to formulate an index of industrial production was made by Ballasteros and Davis in 1963. They showed that the war years were essentially a period of stagnation, with a sharp upward movement only discernible in 1918.[61] But these findings were soon discredited,[62] as they had not used the available data for 1913–15 and had simply taken 1916 figures to be indicative of the entire period. It is little wonder that the war seemed such a sluggish time. Another estimate was made in 1971 by Carmaganini.[63] Using the 1895 Census as a benchmark and the 1906–7 Census as well, he came to the conclusion that the years 1910–18 were ones of extremely slow industrial growth (1.3% per year). The well-known deficiencies of these early unofficial censuses and the numerous methodological errors in key calculations have effectively discredited this analysis.[64]

Completely different conclusions as to the importance of the First World War period have emerged from the works of Muñoz and Palma. The former calculates that between 1914 and 1918 industrial production grew at an average of 9% per annum, represented the first stage in import substitution and was, therefore, a watershed in Chilean economic history.[65] Subsequently, industry expanded much more slowly, growing by less than 5% a year between 1919 and 1930. The author argues that the principal reason for this dynamic growth was the cutting off of competing imports. In a latter work, Muñoz, taking on board Kirsch's findings, gives more weight to prewar development in providing a base but continues to maintain that the war represented a major discontinuity in the country's industrial growth.[66] Palma's reworking of Muñoz's figures leads him to argue that the rate of growth during the war was even higher, industrial production increasing by 52.8% between 1914 and 1918, an average of 11.2% per year.[67] He is aware of the shortcomings of the 1914 data, but downplays this and cites additional qualitative evidence which seems generally to support there having been substantial expansion during the war. Although he upholds and strengthens Muñoz' contention about the significance of the years of conflict, Palma's conclusions are substantially different. He rightly puts much greater emphasis on the importance of prewar growth and also claims that the war marked the beginning of industry's breaking away from dependence on the export sector. From this point, he maintains, the fortunes of the two diverge increasingly.[68] This is a strongly revisionist argument and will be considered more fully at the end of this section. But first a more detailed assessment of the statistical basis of the entire case is necessary.

The importance ascribed to the war by both authors hinges largely on their use and interpretation of the 1914 Census. Although Chile has apparently the best run of statistics on industrial production, because of vague definitions and alterations in the methods of collection there are immense problems with this material. Kirsch feels that the difficulties in using the official returns for assessing changes in production up to 1918 remain unresolved. "This conclusion," he writes, "is based on the fact that not only are serious errors to be found in the data, but the nature of these errors varies erratically from one year to the next so that no basis exists for uncovering a systematic bias to which appropriate corrections may be applied."[69] This quote is cited and agreed to by Palma,[70] but whereas Kirsch is quite clear that he is referring to the years from 1910 to 1918, Palma suggests that he is only talking about the period up to 1914. This misunderstanding is important for it allows Palma to ignore Kirsch's well-founded opinion and go on to make unwarranted conclusions about the extent of wartime industrial growth. There are a number of problems in using the 1914 Census as a benchmark. It was the first year when large firms

Table 5.10 *Chilean industrial censuses 1911–1918*

	Number of firms	Capital (pesos)	Employees & workers	Production (pesos)
1911	5,722	471,287,333	74,618	535,037,093
1912	6,215	529,393,486	80,697	563,339,541
1913	7,841	no comparable data	85,008	654,837,495
1914	4,212	285,903,480	48,101	445,731,319
1915	6,692	500,019,817	61,005	580,996,077
1916	6,830	566,695,101	66,540	651,581,446
1917	7,982	612,283,332	74,943	720,919,430
1918	7,481	635,868,547	78,711	780,496,724

Sources: BSSF, vol. xxxvii, no. 10, Oct. 1920, p. 577; *Anuario estadístico* for 1911, 1912, 1913, 1914, and 1918.

were separated from smaller ones (the figures in Table 5.10 include both) and a warning is given by the compilers that many enterprises are not included.[71] Given that previous and subsequent years also had their problems, Table 5.10 shows how out of line the 1914 figures are. Furthermore, from this time the enumerator's net was spread more widely each year and a proportion of the increase can be put down to this progressively improved coverage. 1914 was also a year of severe depression, a depression which did not really begin to lift until nitrate sales picked up once again from about May 1915. It is interesting to note that 1913 was also a year when complaints were raised by the Sociedad de Fomento Fabril about adverse conditions and factory closures,[72] yet that year's census recorded a high point in terms of the number of industrial firms, employment and level of production. And, whereas for at least 5 months of 1915 economic conditions were not all that bright, the industrial census for that year shows a massive increase in all measurements. Finally, even by 1918, the Sociedad de Fomento Fabril estimated that the census for that year underestimated the size of the industrial sector by at least 10%, for they could see no good reason for the apparent drop from 1917.[73] For all the aforementioned reasons any analysis which depends on the 1914 Census must be looked on with considerable skepticism.

If we ignore the 1914 data, either because of the depression of that year, an argument used in the case of Brazil, or because of the failings

Table 5.11 *Chilean industry: large and small firms 1914–1918*

	Firms		Capital (000 pesos)		Production (000 pesos)		Workers	
	Large	Small	Large	Small	Large	Small	Large	Small
1914	1,750	2,462	266,135	19,768	445,731	no data	39,654	8,449
1915	2,406	4,286	482,992	17,028	564,805	16,192	52,922	8,083
1916	2,625	4,205	552,416	14,279	635,073	16,508	58,593	7,947
1917	2,738	5,244	596,266	16,018	701,362	19,557	64,660	10,283
1918	2,820	4,661	626,020	9,848	766,777	13,720	70,920	7,791
1919	2,871	5,024	702,819	11,490	905,152	17,586	71,464	8,089
1920	2,975	5,026	767,958	13,380	993,220	19,822	72,718	7,836
1921	2,981	5,167	936,966	18,754	1,014,277	21,288	71,829	10,112

Sources: Anuario estadístico, 1914, 1918 and 1921. Note: Large = firms with more than five workers, Small = firms with less than five workers.

of the census and begin in 1915 instead, a somewhat more realistic, although still an approximate, picture can be drawn of the impact of the war on industry in Chile. From this base year it appears that the increases were far more moderate. A breakdown of the firms by size also shows a quite small increase in the number of larger establishments (over five workers) of only about 17%. It is also clear that in the boom year of 1917 the vast majority of new enterprises were both extremely small and short-lived (Table 5.11), although as argued in the case of Brazil this was probably to be expected. There is scattered qualitative evidence of larger new enterprises being formed during the war and of existing ones increasing their output. For example, Cemento El Melón, the vegetable oil producer Compañia Industrial, the Compañia Refinería de Viña del Mar, the cotton knit manufacturer Compañia Chilena de Tejidos, and the Fábrica Nacional de Envases all were able to step up production to meet increased domestic demand, and in the case of the Refinería some foreign demand as well.[74] In 1916 the *Boletín de la Sociedad de Fomento Fabril* carried two long articles detailing all the different branches of industry which had been stimulated by the war,[75] although it is curious that if industrial expansion was so dramatic there were not more such laudatory articles in the *Boletín* over the years 1914 to 1920. The Sociedad never tired of beating the drum for "un Chile industrial."

Of the five studies, Kirsch's seems to be have the most accurate analysis of the First World War period.[76] His index of industrial production from 1914 is based on Muñoz' figures (in 1950 prices) and, therefore, probably understates the level of output in 1914. But it does suggest that although production was probably increasing, until 1917 industry was doing no more than trying to recover lost ground and overall industrial growth during the war was "favorable, if not entirely spectacular."[77] He points out that industry in Chile was hampered by a massive reduction in capital goods and raw materials, a fact which strangely has not been stressed by the other authors, although this a is major issue in the Brazilian debate. Kirsch contends that this situation eased from 1916–17 as higher export earnings permitted increased imports. However, this argument is based on value figures, and with import prices rising rapidly a disaggregated quantum index of imports (Table 3.23) shows that in fact the volume of all imports remained well below pre-1914 levels throughout the war. Raw materials recovered fairly well from the extremely low level reached in 1915, as did producer goods imports. However, for the latter the quantum dropped once again after 1917. This indicates that Chilean industrialists must have been facing very much the same type of difficulties as their counterparts in Brazil. Was the "Fishlow factor" operative in Chile? Did higher wartime profits make it possible to import producer goods and expand capacity after 1918? Greater profits may have been earned during the war, but probably because of the collapse of nitrate earnings imports remained low in the immediate postwar period suggesting there was not a marked increase in investment in this period.

This brings us to the question of the link between industry and the export sector. Kirsch and Muñoz assume that the changes in industrial production are closely correlated with the prosperity of the export sector in terms of the generation of domestic demand.[78] This is contested by Palma who sees the importance of the First World War as signaling a break with this essentially prewar pattern of development.[79] For the war years this hypothesis is of doubtful validity as once again Palma relies on the 1914 Census to show that manufacturing output rose more rapidly than export earnings. In fact, comparing the indexes of the two (Table 5.12) they seem to have moved more or less together during the war, except in 1919 when there was a massive collapse in export values. While it is beyond the scope of this study to evaluate Palma's arguments as they relate to the postwar period, they do seem to find more unambiguous support for these years from the statistics he presents.

Table 5.12 *Indexes of Chilean*
industrial production and export values
1912–1921

| | (1918 = 100) | |
	Industrial production	Export values
1912	94	49
1913	94	51
1914	68	39
1915	75	42
1916	86	66
1917	94	93
1918	100	100
1919	101	39
1920	96	102
1921	98	54

Source: Kirsch, *Modernization*, p. 26 and calculated from p. 162. The export values have not been deflated because they are given not in widely fluctuating paper currency but in pesos of 18d.

An important aspect of Palma's argument as well as those of Muñoz and Kirsch is that by the First World War Chile's industrial structure was already strong enough to respond to the challenge offered by the reduction in competing imports. In terms of the proportion of domestic consumption supplied this seems to have been true, but unless the 1914 figures are used, it also appears that there was little change over the war years in this regard.[80] It has already been seen that in 1914, industry was heavily dominated by consumer goods production and this orientation had not changed very much by 1918 (Table 5.13). In fact, while the detailed makeup of industrial structure was quite different, in terms of the broad product categories Brazil and Chile were virtually identical. This is true even though value added was measured in the Brazilian case and percentage of production in the Chilean. Kirsch argues that overspecialization on consumer goods remained a fundamental weakness in the structure of Chilean industry and limited its ability to affect a wider economic transformation. He makes the interesting point that "The vast majority of industrialists,

Table 5.13 *Structure of Chilean industry and proportion of local consumption provided by domestic industry 1918*

	Percentage of total production	Imports as percentage of supply
Consumer goods	79.3%	14.6%[*]
Beverages	4.8%	8.3%
Food products	41.7%	10.6%
Textiles	3.5%	79.3%
Clothing	9.9%	
Tobacco	3.2%	3.8%
Leather goods	6.2%	
Chemical products	4.9%	
Printed products	4.2%	
Various goods	0.9%	
Consumer durables	1.5%	Consumer durables Intermediate goods Capital goods 67.1%
Furniture	0.8%	
Metal products	0.7%	
Intermediate goods	17.5%	
Leather products	5.5%	
Chemical products	1.0%	
Paper products	0.7%	
Glass and bottles	1.0%	
Construction materials	1.9%	
Metal products	3.8%	
Wood products	3.6%	
Capital goods	1.4%	
Shipbuilding	1.0%	
Metal products	0.1%	
Railway vehicles	0.3%	

Source: Anuario estadístico 1918. Note: This excludes gas and electric companies and the country's one meat-packing plant. Also small firms are excluded so as to make this data comparable with that for 1914. Column 2, Palma, "Growth and structure," appendices 47–60. Much of his data could not be used because of differences in the construction of the tables. [*]This does not include textile production.

producers of light consumer goods, opposed protection to basic industry, feeling that in would increase their production costs and provide them with goods whose worth was unproven.[81] This is exactly the same argument made by Dean about the problems created for Brazilian industry by the early and heavy dominance of consumer goods production. Palma takes a completely different line. He argues that during, but more significantly after, the war producer goods output increased faster than that of consumer goods and the share of the former increased.[82] According to him this showed that Chilean industry was becoming more diversified and therefore better able to take a leading role when exports floundered in the 1930s. But Kirsch miantains that the development of heavy goods production before 1918 was not a permanent feature and that latterly although the metallurgical industries expanded at a rapid rate consumer goods accounted for up to 50% of output and much of the remaining production could not be considered as capital goods.[83] The disagreement over the evolution of the country's industrial structure is, of course, a key issue, but because it takes us well beyond the limits of this work cannot be explored here in the depth it requires.

Much more solid primary research is needed before we can begin to have a fuller understanding of the impact of the First World War on Chilean industry. For example, the question of the shortage of imported producer goods has not been adequately examined. Another unstudied area is that of domestic demand. There are indications that it may not have been particularly buoyant. Although export earnings soared from 1916, throughout the war government expenditure was restricted, foreign investment virtually eliminated, and real wages fell. Were these propitious conditions for an industrial boom? Finally, despite Kirsch's warning, is there no way in which the statistical problems can be overcome? The continued confusion over this remains a major obstacle to unraveling the truth about the war years. Given these and other problems any conclusions about this period must be seen as extremely tentative.

It does not seem on the basis of the available evidence that the war saw a massive increase in industrial production as postulated by Muñoz or Palma. Up until 1917 industry was doing little more than fighting to regain its former position. That it was able to do this and make gains by augmenting the already high levels of import-substitution reached before the war was a testament to the importance of pre-1914 development. It is difficult to say with complete assurance why the advances which were made were not more substantial. In the early part of the war before nitrate sales recovered, industry was obviously hurt by the collapse in export earnings. When these recovered, so did industrial production. Over the entire war period the strength of domestic demand was probably muted and the ability to increase capacity was also restricted because of the reduction in capital goods and raw material imports. Another factor was that the fall in the volume of consumer goods imports, the reason always cited for this having been such a powerful stimulus to local enterprise, was not in reality all that great, and the share of these imports increased during the war. Chilean industry was extremely successful, with the major exception of textiles, in producing substitutes for most consumer goods, but although expansion had been laudable by the end of the First World War it had still not broken the ties that wedded its fortunes so firmly to that of the foreign trade. It continued to rely heavily on imports and demand for its products depended to a very large degree on the prosperity of nitrates and copper.

Argentina

I

The first organization of Argentine industrialists, El Club Industrial Argentina, was established in 1875,[84] and although it comprised relatively few members, many of whom probably ran small work-shops, it is one indication of the beginning of an industrial awareness in the country. Another was the attempt in Congress at about the same time, first to get state support for industry and when this failed to get protective tariffs. The latter did achieve a degree of success and a modest tariff was imposed in 1877.[85] It is important to note that even in this formative period there was a distinct split, mainly over the question of tariffs, between the firms which processed agricultural products for export and those whose output was mainly for local consumption. For example, when the Unión Industrial Argentina was formed in 1887, from the Club Industrial and the Centro Industrial Argentino, which had separated from the Club in 1878, many agro-industrialists remained in their own sectoral organizations.[86] This division was to become more pronounced.

The 1890s saw the beginnings of quite pronounced industrial expansion, partly due to the greatly devalued peso, one of the legacies of the Baring Crisis, but more importantly to export growth, the massive influx of immigrants and extremely rapid urbanization, especially of Buenos Aires. Another important factor was higher import duties, imposed primarily to raise revenue, but which seem to have afforded a degree of protection to certain industries. However, the exact role of the tariff remains a highly complex and contentious issue.[87] A careful detailed analysis would be necessary to confirm it, but the incidence of import duties seems to have been considerably less in Argentina than in either Brazil or Chile. For example, a US Federal Trade Commission Report in 1916 argued that compared to these countries Argentina had by far the weaker system of tariff protection.[88]

By the first national industrial census in 1895 it would seem that substantial progress had been made. The way in which the survey was carried out suggests that there were many more industrial enterprises here than in Brazil or Chile, but this is only because of the inclusion of a great number of extremely small firms. There were a total of 24,094 (excluding gas and electricity plants) with a capital of 459,512,000 pesos (m/n) and employing 174,057 people. Of these meat processing plants, sugar *ingenios*, flour mills, wineries, distilleries and breweries accounted for only 7.8% of the firms but 16.3% of the workers, 38.2% of the capital and 50.8% of the installed power.[89] According to Guy,[90] links with agricultural or pastoral activities also characterized about 70% of the remaining factories and workshops. Most of these were small operations, but it is important to note that there were a number of substantial manufacturing firms as well. For example, in his report delivered in 1899,[91] Worthington recorded there being a few factories employing between 150 and 400 workers making textile goods, sacking, hats, boots and shoes, and a number of other products. There were important iron foundries, the largest being the Vasena Works, which employed about 500 workers, a major paper making firm, La Argentina, and a match company, Compañia General de Fósforos with 1,200 workers and a yearly output of a million gross of boxes.

In the years that followed, industry continued to expand rapidly. ECLA's figures, which are by no means precise, show an annual rate of growth of Gross Domestic Product of 6.3% between 1900–4 and 1910–14. Over the same period industry grew at 7.7%, total capital stock in industry by 10% and labor by 5.8% per year. By the First World War (1910–14) the manufacturing sector accounted for between 11.5% and 15% of GNP and employed about 20% of the active population,[92] although this last figure seems much too large given that it is based on there being 633,000 workers in industry whereas the census gives only 410,201.[93] This was still a strong performance, but a substantial part of it was due to the large, often

Table 5.14 *Argentine industrial census 1913*

(000 m/n)	Firms (000 m/n)	Capital	Production	Horse power	Workers
Extractive Industries					
Food	13,549	649,539	797,137	140,949	88,193
Of which:					
(sugar mills and refineries)	(44)	(120,130)	(140,598)	(57,511)	(14,685)
(friqorificos)	(13)	(92,991)	(268,247)	(24,287)	(14,687)
(flour mills)	(401)	(86,774)	(148,899)	(26,531)	(4,909)
Other extractive industries	1,164	145,290	116,209	30,333	37,005
Total	14,713	794,829	913,346	171,282	125,198
Manufacturing Industries					
Food	1,948	68,279	101,321	16,737	17,077
Clothing	920	43,623	86,567	4,142	22,611
Construction	2,600	39,312	72,119	11,842	23,807
Furniture	4,335	61,584	85,925	8,946	28,468
Artistic goods	159	4,153	5,693	375	1,641
Metallurgy	1,919	77,295	81,527	16,980	23,141
Chemical goods	555	36,564	55,186	4,782	9,719
Printing	62	817	848	69	538
Textiles	1,726	30,729	37,058	8,938	13,058
Various	570	92,459	142,547	19,282	16,747
Total	14,794	454,815	668,791	92,093	156,807
Non-manufacturing Industry					
Total	18,732	176,079	266,785	16,299	106,915
Total	48,239	1,425,723	1,848,922	279,674	388,920

Source: Tercer Censo, vol. vii, pp. 27–34.

foreign-controlled firms, listed under "extractive industries," which processed food and primary products, much of which went for export. This provides an important contrast with Brazil and Chile where most major industries tended to be geared toward domestic consumption. Although apparently more complex and obviously much expanded, Argentina's industrial structure (Table 5.14) in 1914 differed little from

Table 5.15 *Composition of Argentine imports*

	Consumer goods	(percentage share) Fuels and raw materials	Capital goods
1908	47.4	25.4	27.2
1909	48.5	22.6	28.9
1910	49.0	24.0	27.0
1911	48.2	24.6	27.2
1912	47.7	26.3	26.0
1913	46.8	27.3	25.9

Source: Smith and Collins, *Argentina*, p. 92.

Table 5.16 *Argentine industry 1913: percentage share of production*

Consumer goods		70.8%
Food & beverages	57.0%	
Clothing	5.5%	
Textiles (including hats)	2.3%	
Tobacco	3.7%	
Various	2.3%	
Durables		6.1%
Furniture, etc.	5.4%	
Various	0.7%	
Intermediate goods		21.5%
Construction materials	11.5%	
Tanneries	2.0%	
Metal products	3.3%	
Bags and boxes	2.6%	
Various	2.4%	
Capital goods		
Metal products	1.5%	

Source: Calculated from *Tercer Censo*, vii, pp. 27–34.
Note: Table includes both extractive and manufacturing industries but not non-manufacturing industry.

what it had been 20 years earlier. As was the case in 1895, although there were some sizable manufacturing firms which produced for the local market, most were small-scale enterprises and a high proportion were what is called in the census "non-manufacturing industries," such as bakeries (3,242), tailors (3,083), shoemakers (2,243), carpenters (2,028), and blacksmiths (2,460). Although admittedly a crude measure of import-substitution, the structure of imports suggests that in terms of consumer goods this process had not been carried nearly as far in Argentina as in the other two countries. But comparisons are difficult. In Table 5.16 the data has been reorganized to conform to the presentation of the Brazilian and Chilean statistics. However, because of the inclusion of the large export industries and the exclusion of many small ones (the non-manufacturing sectors have not been incorporated in the table) it is doubtful whether this can be used as a basis for making comparsions. It seems to show a more diversified industrial sector, but the capital goods production remained marginal and the intermediate goods category is inflated by the large (109,000,000 pesos) extractive construction materials sector. Describing Argentine industry in about 1913, a US Report noted:[94] "Except for meat packing, flour milling, the dairy industries and sugar refining, the manufactures of Argentina are comparatively trifling and are quite insufficient to meet local demands."

II

If the picture of events relating to wartime industry in Brazil and Chile remains unclear, what happened in Argentina is all but totally obscure. Although there are many studies of Argentine industrialization, only in Dorfman's work is the war period given any substantive attention.[95] There is no reliable statistical material, and no debate has developed over the impact of the war. This makes it extremely difficult, without a major effort of primary research, to offer an account of Argentina similar to that given above. There is, however, a generally accepted view of the war. That is that while certain branches of production were stimulated, for various reasons domestic industry as a whole was unable to take advantage of the apparent opportunity offered by the sudden reduction in competitive imports. For example, Dorfman observes,[96]

Our industrialists understood, perhaps, that finally they had a breathing space, that the sword of Damocles of foreign trade which had for decades been suspended over their heads had been withdrawn momentarily and they believed that they therefore had their hands free to do what they wanted. But like a child that doesn't know what to do during a moment of freedom, they were not able to do anything concrete.

But it was the circumstances which industrialists faced, rather than their being childlike (an assumption of cultural inadequacy) which prevented a more vigorous response during the war.

In Brazil, and to a lesser extent in Chile, there were many contemporary observers who argued that the war had given a tremendous boost to industry. There were some who held similar views about Argentina,[97] but there were also a good number who adopted a more pessimistic position. For example, a British Department of Overseas Trade Report stated,[98]

The lack of iron and coal, or water power, high returns from capital invested in land, livestock and cultivation; unwillingness to risk capital in industrial enterprise, and the scarcity of skilled hands, have retarded the growth of industry...Few new industries of any importance have appeared, and the progress in manufacturing during the war has in nearly all cases been of the development of industries already in existence which were favoured by the scarcity of imported goods for their excessive cost.

This was generally representative of informed foreign opinion[99] and was echoed by many Argentine critics.[100] The consensus was that some growth had occurred but by and large it was quite modest.

Argentina was distinguished by the dominance of food and primary product processing industries. In general these earned high profits during the war, particularly meat-packing, the single most important. In terms of production, fortunes were rather mixed (Table 5.17), sugar, flour milling and wine production all being hit by bad harvests. It is usually assumed that most of the output was exported, but of the food processing industries only the *frigoríficos* were major exporters. In 1913 they accounted for a third of the output of the so-called "extractive industries" engaged in food production. Both the sugar and flour mills, after meat-packing the two largest of these, produced almost entirely for the local market, as did the wineries and beer factories. Only about 13% of the wheat flour was exported (1912–17). Dairying, another important industry geared essentially for the domestic market, showed rapid growth. The number of creameries, butter and cheese factories rose from 1,289 in 1913 to 2,846 by 1918.[101] The production of quebracho extract (used for tanning), and the tanning industry expanded significantly. The former tripled the value of its exports (1913–1918) and seven new companies were established during the war.[102] Much of the leather was sold abroad,

Table 5.17 *Major Argentine food and raw material processing industries (excluding mining) 1912–1918*

	(000 tons and 000,000 gold pesos)						
	1912	1913	1914	1915	1916	1917	1918
Meat-packing							
Export	455	443	459	441	543	557	761
Export value	65	77	91	97	129	136	253
Sugar							
Production	147	278	336	149	84	88	126
Export (net)	−30	−76	58	54	−30	−160	−33
Flour milling							
Production	898	848	908	938	994	939	
Export	132	125	67	116	144	113	177
Export value			5	10	10	13	15
Wine (000,000 liters)							
Production	420	500	514	482	452	475	470
Export (net)	−46	−40	−27	−17	−6	−3	
Dairying							
Cheese production	6	6	6	7	9	16	
Butter production	10	10	9	10	11	15	
Quebracho extract							
Export	75	80	80	100	96	90	132
Export value	5	5	5	16	20	14	14

Source: Tornquist, *Economic Conditions*, pp. 46–7, 52, 61–2, 70–1, 112, 167–9, 183–5.

but an increasing, albeit unknown, proportion must have found its way into local production, because the boot and shoe industry expanded output considerably in the war years. A great quantity of manufactured leather goods, including footwear and saddlery were also exported.[103] Washed wool was another export, increasing amounts of which were used by the Argentine woolen mills. The output is not known, but between 1913 and 1918 the textile factories' consumption of washed wool doubled from 1,500 to 3,000 tons.[104] With other domestic users taking a further 1,500 tons, in 1918 27% of washed wool was being consumed locally, although the great majority of the clip (80%) continued to be exported unwashed. While unavoidably part of the country's generally outward directed rural sector it is important to understand that these industries were also either feeding the local populace or providing intermediate goods for domestic industry.

There were some notable exceptions to the views expressed about the failure of local industry to seize the initiative. The boot and shoe industry has already been mentioned, and was in sense a "natural" for import substitution because the country was such a large leather producer. An important breakthrough occurred in 1903 when the United Shoe Machine Company opened for business in Argentina.[105] Local manufacturers, always short of capital, were now able rent the most modern equipment and production subsequently rose. By 1913 there were 231 shoe companies with an output worth 50,000,000 pesos a year and employing almost 13,000 workers, making it the second largest manufacturing employer in the city of Buenos Aires.[106] It was claimed that "The shoe-manufacturing industry has reached a higher state of development in Argentina than in any other South American country."[107] On this eminently solid prewar foundation the industry was able to take advantage of the sharp drop in shoe imports. These fell from 123,620 dozen pairs in 1913 and to a low 10,384 dozen in 1918.[108] Other industries which did well during the war included cooking oils, various basic chemicals, woolen textiles, and paper making.[109]

Industrial growth was not, therefore, completely moribund during the war, but without reliable aggregate data it is impossible to assess the significance of these developments. The figures conjured up by ECLA (Table 5.18), which have been widely accepted, must be used with considerably more caution than has been exercised by Díaz Alejandro or Di Tella and Zymelman, who claim on the basis of this data that the war years were a period of industrial decline. This cannot be fully accepted. Besides the sources used being unspecified, the industrial production index is constructed using 1950 output weights.[110] This does not inspire confidence in its being representative of conditions thirty-five years earlier. For example, in the years 1910–14 at 1950 prices ECLA has food and drink comprising 36.3% of total industrial output,[111] whereas in fact in the 1914 Census they accounted for over 50%. Finally, when it is remembered what problems were experienced with the more comprehensive Chilean material, the relative value of the ECLA indices is put in proper perspective. The decline and relative stagnation shown might reflect the difficulties experienced by some of the food processing industries because of poor harvests and, therefore, tell us more about agriculture than industry, while at the same

Table 5.18 *Argentine industrial production: volume index 1910–1923*

	Total	Textiles	Metals (no machi-nery)	Chemicals	Food and drink	Leather products
			(1950 = 100)			
1910	20.7	5	10	20	28	30
1911	22.2	5	11	24	34	34
1912	21.0	5	11	22	31	36
1913	22.3	7	12	29	31	38
1914	20.3	7	10	25	32	38
1915	18.2	8	7	28	28	45
1916	18.7	3	8	31	30	44
1917	18.5	11	8	24	33	43
1918	22.1	14	6	30	39	53
1919	23.0	13	9	30	39	55
1920	23.8	10	12	29	37	48
1921	25.1	12	10	29	42	48
1922	27.9	12	12	32	45	54
1923	32.6	11	16	43	53	64

Sources: Di Tella and Zymelman, *Las etapas*, p. 309; Díaz Alejandro, *Essays*, p. 450.

time offering a reminder of how the latter remained dependent on the former.

There is one further statistical source which should be mentioned, that is the preliminary findings compiled, but never published, by Alejandro Bunge.[112] He shows a substantial increase of about 35% in production and 24% in labor employed between 1913 and 1918. But the sample of only sixty-nine firms is extremely small (0.15% of those listed in the 1914 Census) and even though they accounted for a disproportionate share of capital (2.4%), labor (2.3%) and ouput (2.1) the results must be treated skeptically. It may have been because of the inadequate coverage that the prolific and methodologically meticulous Bunge never officially released the study.[113] With all its shortcomings it does suggest that at least among the larger firms there was some progress made in these years. Another indication of this, albeit only a very rough one, is that after a deluge of business failures between 1913 and 1915, the following years saw a substantial improvement (Table 4.16).

Despite Bunge's data, and the clear evidence of growth in some

Table 5.19 *Gross fixed investment in Argentina 1911–1922*

	Agri-culture	Industry	Transport	Com-merce	Govern-ment	Total
		(000,000 1950 pesos)				
1911	733	1,374	2,018	4,471	1,480	10,076
1912	686	1,616	1,440	3,434	1,039	8,215
1913	867	1,426	1,759	3,442	837	8,331
1914	1,112	774	1,009	1,515	753	5,163
1915	837	466	365	943	489	3,100
1916	839	354	284	887	379	2,743
1917	655	315	261	649	193	2,073
1918	731	291	195	730	144	2,091
1919	724	424	219	940	138	2,445
1920	1,009	785	509	2,016	218	4,537
1921	951	892	703	2,297	405	5,248
1922	950	867	1,124	2,781	439	6,161

Source: Di Tella and Zymelman, *Las etapas*, pp. 293, 313, 346.

sectors, both informed contemporary opinion and the ECLA statistics point to at best only modest overall expansion during the war. Further evidence for this is provided by more ECLA data on levels of investment. This shows an apparent decline, which given the massive fall in producer goods imports was undoubtedly the case, although once again it must be stressed that these statistics are not particularly reliable. On the whole it seems that Argentine industry did not do very well in these years, and while national comparisons are at best very conditional, it also appears that the industrial performance here was not on par with that in either Brazil or Chile.

There is a long list of reasons that have been given to account for the sluggish response of industry in Argentina. It is easy to set them out. It is not so easy to assess their relative importance, although comparing them with similar conditions in Brazil and Chile is instructive. It seems that domestic demand was fairly muted during the war. This was due partly to falling real wages and high levels of unemployment.[114] It was further exacerbated by a major drop in investment throughout the economy. This in turn was linked in some degree to the internal capital drain contingent upon the restrictive nature of government fiscal policy, as well as the caution demonstrated by local entrepreneurs.

Finally, the very marginal rise before 1918 in export earnings was probably not sufficient to generate the degree of effective demand needed to overcome the aforementioned retarding factors. While Chile and Brazil suffered from falling real wages, generally there seems to have been a greater degree of buoyancy in both economies caused in part by a short-lived export boom in the former and a high level of deficit financing and public works expenditure in the latter. Another element working against the Argentine industrialist was that the fall in consumer goods imports was not as extensive or prolonged as is often imagined.[115] There was a substantial reduction in some, such as leather shoes, but for the single most important consumer good import, cotton textiles, there was only a temporary drop and by 1916 prewar levels of fabric imports had been regained.[116] The small degree of tariff protection was also eroded by the improvement in Argentine exchange,[117] although the adverse effects of this were marginal as the quantity of most imports were cut by the lack of shipping and/or foreign supplies.

Like all Latin America, Argentine industry also suffered from a severe scarcity of raw material and producer goods imports, as well as crippling fuel shortage.[118] The lack of coal has often been cited as a major reason for the relative backwardness of Argentine industry, but under "normal" conditions coal had been cheaply and easily imported and no problems had arisen. It was only with the crisis of the war years that the country's vulnerability was clearly exposed. Once it had been, there was the emergence of what Solberg has dubbed "petroleum nationalism," a form of economic nationalism which was to play a major role in the 1922 reorganization and strengthening of the state oil company, Yacimientos Petrolíferos Fiscales.[119] While not a time of industrial breakthroughs, the crises of the war, such as that over fuel, served as an object lesson for many Argentines about the true nature of their economy, and therefore helped sow the seeds of subsequent change.

Another key problem was finding capital and credit. The chronic difficulty of financing industrial ventures does not seem to have eased during the war and if anything probably became a more serious obstacle for entrepreneurs. For instance, writing in 1919 about the country's shoe industry a US investigator commented that it was difficult for industry to find the necessary capital because, "Up to the present the tremendous growth of agricultural and stock-raising industries yielding relatively prompt and large profits has absorbed nearly all the surplus capital in Argentina."[120] Dorfman points out that there was not sufficient technical expertise nor the stock of machinery of raw materials to permit local entrepreneurs to move into new or weakly developed industries.[121] Probably the most important of these, in terms of its import share (21% of consumer goods imports 1913–15), was cotton textiles. The industry had not made significant progress before 1914 and with almost no local production of raw cotton and only an extremely short-lived fall in imports, there was little chance of wartime growth.[122] However, in a manner somewhat similar to that identified by Solberg for petroleum, the impact of the war heightened the awareness of the need for a stronger and less dependent cotton textile industry and this led to changes which helped put the industry on its feet from the 1920s. One of the most important of these was the extension of cotton cultivation. A small output of 713 metric tons of fiber in 1916–17 had risen to 5,535 by 1920–1.

Different wartime experiences or policies may afford a partial explanation of why Argentine industry seems to have fared less well than either Brazil's or Chile's, the latter's performance in any case not having been all that spectacular. However, the most important limiting factor was that prewar industrial development had been much less extensive in Argentina and the base upon which to build was, therefore, shakier here than in the other countries, not only in terms of physical plant but also in that industry had attracted far less direct state support than it had in Brazil or Chile. The problems of narrowness, rigidity, and external dependence which characterized the structure of prewar industrial development in all these countries was, therefore, probably relatively more serious in Argentina.

Looking at what he considers to be the decline in industrial growth during the war, and closely following the arguments made by Díaz Alejandro and Gallo,[123] Gravil concludes that,[124] because Argentina was experiencing a form of "staple development" that, "The First World War is more correctly interpreted as an interruption of this process than as a growth opportunity." Although the Allies did try to impose their economic will on Argentina, this had little to do with the country's indifferent export performance. Furthermore, it is perfectly true that a prosperous export sector, the foreign investment it attracted and infrastructure it called forth were positive stimuli to industrial development. However, it was a particular type of development which tended to be self-limiting. As Lucio Geller comments, "...the growth of Argentine industry was the product of the effect of agricultural production, and at the same time was limited by the lack of export diversity."[125] As Gallo himself admits,[126] virtually the whole of

Argentine industry remained a dependency of the export sector. To the extent that it did, it was bound to suffer either directly or indirectly from the vulnerability and volatility of the harvest and of foreign trade. Rather than demonstrating the strength of prewar development, the war showed instead how partial it had been and how little it had established any meaningful degree of independence.

This was more or less the conclusion reached by a number of influential Argentine thinkers for whom, much the same as for their counterparts in Brazil, the war-induced crisis highlighted the country's economic frailty and subservient international position, thereby calling into question the primary product export model of growth.[127] "The war," wrote Enrique Ruiz Guiñazú, "has revealed a national emptiness, the lack of a positive independence. Nothing is more urgent than a political economy of intensification to make us self-sufficient, guaranteeing industry and commerce a certain stability."[128] This strain of economic nationalism found echoes in the increasingly popular cultural nationalism which had developed in the decades before the war and the growing anti-imperialist sentiment which was focused most strongly on the British-owned railways.[129] The war years themselves may not have been a time of great industrial progress in Argentina, but by dramatically demonstrating both the weakness and dependence of the national economy in general and of industry in particular as well as the perfidiousness of the international economy, the First World War acted as a powerful ideological catalyst which was fundamentally to alter perceptions about the nature of economic progress.

Peru

I

From at least the 1880s all the countries under review had national industrial associations. In Peru it was not until 1896 that the Sociedad Nacional de Industrias was established.[130] This is a minor point but indicative of the fact that of the four countries, Peru undoubtedly had the weakest industrial sector. A variety of reasons could be adduced to explain this relative backwardness. A lack of immigration, only limited urban growth, the fact that about two thirds of the country's small population remained in subsistence or petty commodity production in the *sierra*, and relatively low real wages all contributed to lessen the force of domestic demand. For example, in 1908 Lima had but 140,900 inhabitants, whereas at about the same time Santiago had 333,000, Buenos Aires 1,300,000 and São Paulo over 500,000 (in 1920). By 1910 only 5.4% of the Peruvian people lived in cities of over 20,000, while the figures were 28.4, 24.2 and 9.8 respectively in Argentina, Chile and Brazil.[131] Brazil's low percentage was counterbalanced by the rapid expansion of large urban areas, especially in the southeast. In terms of demand and, in some sense a crude indication of relative standards of living, it is interesting to note that in the prewar period almost all of Brazilian and Argentine sugar production went to supply the domestic market, while over 80% of the output of Peru's coastal *ingenios* was exported and about half of this went to the Chilean refineries in Viña del Mar. In 1914 per capita consumption of centrifugal sugar was 26.8 kilos in Argentina, 22.6 kilos in Chile, but only 7.5 kilos in Peru.[132] This is not, however, an entirely fair comparison because many Peruvians continued to consume *chancaca* (a crude boiled sugar), not surprising as most lived in rural areas.

Against the aforementioned argument has to be set the strong case made by Thorp and Bertram[133] that there was a major expansion of domestic demand in Peru from the mid-1890s to about 1920. Without a detailed comparative analysis it is impossible to resolve this issue, but it seems likely that however powerful the growth of demand was in the Peruvian economy over these years, because of the important differences listed above it could not compare in either weight or depth with what was going on in the other countries.

Despite what can be identified as comparative limitations on the size of domestic market local demand did become more significant and there were clear signs of industrial growth, particularly from the mid-1890s. The sugar industry was in the forefront of this development. Sugar is generally considered as "export agriculture," possibly "agro-industry" but rarely as part of the industrial sector *per se*. This is probably because the factory process is so closely associated with the growing of cane. In Peru the two were usually combined in the same company. However, with respect to the capital employed and the technical sophistication required, the sugar mills were one of the most modern of industrial enterprises. For instance, in 1914 Argentina's forty-four sugar mills and refineries had sixty-four times more capital than the average extractive or manufacturing firm and produced on average about 10% more value added.[134] While its agricultural links and export orientation are key factors in assessing its role in local capitalist development, it would be wrong not to see it, in the same way as meat-packing or flour milling, as part of industry.

Table 5.20 *Number of factories in Peru 1905 and 1918*

	1905	1918
For domestic market		
Textiles and clothing	24	30
Tanneries	17	35
Shoe factories	1	7
Candles and wax	10	19
Furniture	3	11
Construction materials	8	12
Soft drinks	5	71
Wines and liquors	4	33
Breweries	5	10
Food and food processing	85	128
Other	42	79
Sub total	204	435
Export processing		
Cottonseed oil	8	25
Sugar mills	55	33
Oil refineries	2	2
Cocaine	22	10
Sub total	87	70
Total	291	505

Source: Thorp and Bertram, *Peru*, p. 122.

Thorp and Bertram,[135] make a compelling case for there having been a substantial expansion between the end of the civil war in 1895 and the recession of 1907. During this relatively brief period diverse circumstances combined to create excellent conditions for industry. The infrastructure was elaborated with the expansion of the financial system and the setting up of numerous public utility companies throughout the country. Demand was stimulated by the growth of export earnings, most of which were returned to the economy because key sectors were predominantly locally owned. At the same time a marked devaluation of the sol and high revenue tariffs, which inadvertently gave protection to local industry, improved relative prices for Peruvian manufacturers. Because of the aforementioned factors these years witnessed an important degree of import substitution in a wide range of goods including beer, cigarettes, soap, candles, shoes and furniture. The most significant development was probably in cotton textile production. To the Vitarte mill, in operation before 1890, six new factories were added by 1902 and production increased from 1.5 million yards in 1891 to 25 million yards by 1908. In the latter year the output from Peruvian factories accounted for 47% of local supplies. One measure of the overall success of Peruvian industry in this period was that as a proportion of total imports consumer goods (excluding foodstuffs, which makes it impossible to compare this figure with those given for the other countries) fell from 54.3% in 1897 to 39.0% in 1907. However, with all the apparent growth, in 1905 Alejandro Garland recorded only 173 urban-based factory-sized (an unexplained category) firms.[136]

This buoyant period of expansion came to an end in 1907, and although subsequently new factories continued to be established, the rate of growth slowed considerably. No official industrial census was conducted in Peru in these years, and to get some idea of the structure of industry it is necessary to use Garland's private survey made in 1905 (Table 5.20). This shows that although there were clear differences in the size and complexity of industry in Peru when compared to the other three countries, a similar general pattern is apparent.

II

The fact that there is but one secondary study on Peruvian manufacturing industry during the war years makes it impossible to give more than the briefest account of this country's industrial growth. There are also few contemporary works which even mention the subject and no detailed, reliable census data. All this is a reflection of the relatively minor role played by this sector within a national economy concerned overwhelmingly with developing mining and agricultural exports.

The evidence of industrial progress is extremely scanty. The best compilation of the available data is that done by Thorp and Bertram.[137] They have not only brought together all the various private industrial surveys, but have revised them and arranged the material so they are more readily comparable. Unfortunately, as is the case with Brazil, the two reports which straddle the war are too far apart to be able to pick up the change which took place in these years. There is the additional problem that the coverage in the 1918 report was very much better than Garland's 1905 study and included many more small-scale firms, thereby tending to greatly accentuate the degree of change. Finally, having only the number of firms tells us nothing about their size. In the case of sugar, for example, the fall in numbers does not indicate a decline in this industry but instead a major concentration of production. Sugar output increased by 75% over these thirteen years. The authors conclude that what modest industrial development there was came almost entirely in the years 1911–13 and 1916–19 and was confined to textiles, tanning, shoes and beverages. There were neither new lines of production nor heavier industries established.

This view of the lack of wartime industrial activity finds support in the comments of contemporary observers. For instance, in a speech given in May 1918, Alberto Salomón, Peru's Minister of Justice, referring to a recent article in a Lima newspaper about industrial growth in Chile wrote, "...our capitalists, who lack sufficient enterprise to even start new industries, which, together with the indifference of our authorities, has prevented our industrialization from awakening. The war and the days of transient bonanza will pass, and Peru will return to its miserable existence and to its dependence on other producing countries..."[138] Salomón's view was repeated in what seems to have been the only major Peruvian study of the war in which manufacturing industry is discussed, Hernando de Lavalle's, *La Gran Guerra y el organismo económico nacional.*[139] He also claimed no new industries had been established and bemoaned the fact that the opportunity presented to local industry by the war had been totally lost.

But did the war really present such a great opportunity for substantial industrial development? Probably not. When comparing the Argentine experience with that of Brazil and Chile it was argued that a key factor in accounting for the lack of growth in Argentina was the relative weakness of prewar development. Without a firm base, not only of physical plant, but also of easy access to finance and government support, the short-lived competitive breathing space could not be exploited. This applied even more strongly to Peru where, despite the initial burst from the mid-1890s and the relative success of cotton textiles, domestic manufacturing remained weak and unsophisticated. On the supply side Peru does not seem to have suffered as severely as most other countries with regard to the import of machinery and raw materials. It is difficult to be precise about this because the official valuation of imports was raised in 1916 and again in 1917, and before that there were no quantity figures provided for machinery. The data in Table 3.30, which have been adjusted to

provide a constant measure of change, show that although the high
levels of 1913 were not regained, imports of fuel, raw materials,
semi-finished and producer goods had all made a substantial recovery
by 1916. The statistics do not distinguish between machinery for
industry or mining, but given the US control of the latter and the
increases in mineral exports, it is reasonable to assume that much of the
new equipment was imported by the mining companies. There was a
great deal of money being made by exporters, but as Salomón
observed, the extraordinary profitability of the export sectors attracted
Peruvian capital at the expense of domestic manufacturing industry.

The demand for domestic manufactures may also not have been all
that strong in Peru during the war. The most immediate cause of this
was the steady rise in food prices and the fall in real wages. The decline
in competitive imports was also extremely short-lived. By 1916 these
had recovered substantially. In fact, as explained in chapter 3, of the
four countries, Peru was unique in that, except for 1914 and 1915, the
level of total imports was more than maintained (Table 3.30). It is not
immediately apparent why this should have occurred. The reasons
offered by Thorp and Bertram, appreciating exchange, decreased tariff
protection, and domestic inflation,[140] were also found in Chile and
Argentina, where the drop in imports was more sustained, although in
the last two years of the war Chilean imports did recover. A more
persuasive argument,[141] is that by 1913 the United States supplied a far
greater share of Peru's imports (30%), than it did for any of the other
countries.[142] This meant that the commercial contacts were better
developed and US exporters could move into the market more easily.
There was also the phenomenal increase in export earnings which led
to an improvement in the country's capacity to import.

Why was there no attempt to fight against this by Peruvian
manufacturers? Particularly, why was there no reaction to the decline
in tariff protection? Once again, the most telling points are made by
Thorp and Bertram. They write,[143] "By the 1910s, ... there were no
longer many manufacturing ventures in which the ruling class had a
direct interest; élite figures had withdrawn from manufacturing, or
relegated their industrial interests to secondary importance. Enterpreneurs who remained in manufacturing did not constitute a social
group either powerful or cohesive enough to influence policy." Not
only was this group weak but unlike what happened in the other
countries, except for the grumblings of those like Salomón and
Lavalle, the war does not seem to have stimulated any surge of
economic nationalism in Peru. Although the export elite suffered

serious political reversals, their vision of Peru's economic destiny remained virtually unchallenged. The massive bonanza of export earnings and the availability of imports meant that rather than shaking confidence in this vision the war strongly reinforced it.

Conclusion

Manufacturing industry is the heart of modern capitalism, and it has been used as the touchstone for the success of economic development in Latin America, as well as elsewhere in the world. The preceding chapter has demonstrated that by the First World War manufacturing sectors of different levels of sophistication had appeared in all four countries. Even in Peru, in most respects the least advanced, an industrial sector had been firmly established by the outbreak of the First World War, and an industrial working class was beginning to make its voice heard. The rapid expansion of primary exports in these countries had led to the growth of a number of major industries for processing those exports, and firms producing a wide variety of consumer goods for the local market had also appeared. This latter type of development is not surprising, for domestic producers enjoyed a substantial comparative advantage over many imported goods because of considerations of weight, perishability, or local tastes. To this was added, in some cases and at varying times, the shelter of a depreciating exchange as well as differing degrees of tariff protection, even though in most instances this was little more than a by-product of government's need for revenue. Furthermore, it is also clear that the rapid growth of export earnings was a major factor which stimulated industrial development, both in terms of income and indirectly by attracting immigrants and/or in fostering the extension of the transport network.

The extent and timing of industrial growth did vary considerably, but everywhere the general pattern of development was more or less the same. Non-durable consumer goods production was overwhelmingly dominant, and large-scale industry was mainly, although not entirely, confined to exports. Notwithstanding these biases and the weakness that they engendered, was the emergence of industry not a strong indication that there had been substantial and materially progressive economic change in the region during the decades before 1914? Critics may point to the lack of basic industries such as iron and steel and the continuing dependence on the import of fuel, semi-finished and capital goods, but could it not be argued, as Leff has with respect to Brazil, that industrial development proceeds in stages and it is unreasonable to expect a completely balanced, integrated system to emerge all at once? Furthermore, if, as it seems, industrial growth during the war was not as dramatic as has been thought, does this not support the contention that such growth was stimulated by closer ties with and not, as Frank has claimed, isolation from the metropolitan economies?

It is perfectly reasonable to see industrial development up to 1914 as a sign of progressive change. There is little basis for the cruder stagnationist claims that the period saw the development of under-development. Leff's point about the necessity for the industrial structure to evolve over time is also well taken. However, as both Dean and Kirsch have pointed out, excessive concentration on consumer goods production did create a number of serious obstacles to a more balanced industrial expansion. Weaver's observation on this issue is broadly applicable. He writes,[144] "The South American industrial bourgeoisie, as individuals and as a class, had but little stake in general industrialization; their position and interests had developed within a system of partial dependent industrialization and were tied to it."

Up to the First World War most Latin American industry was in one form or another dependent on foreign trade – whether for its markets, imports to supply needed intermediate and producer goods, or export earnings to generate income and therefore domestic demand. As Geller observed in the Argentine case, exports both stimulated industry and imposed limitations on its fuller development. These limitations took many forms, such as the foreign trade bias of the financial system, the greater political power of the export élites, or the latter's ability to impose their concept of externally oriented, primary product-based economic development on the country. Within this dominant world view manufacturing industry tended to be relegated to a secondary position. This was reflected and greatly reinforced by the particular and peculiar configurations of class interest which developed in these societies. This question is well beyond the scope of this study, but Kirsch's conclusion on the failure of industry's transforming power in Chile, is instructive on this point. He writes:[145]

From the onset the industrialists were intimately involved with the homogeneous economic elite which composed the dominant element of national life. A separate group united by a new economic activity and by the same aspirations did not emerge to make demands upon society which would imply transformation of traditional institutions. For this reason, the conflict between the entrepreneurial bourgeoisie and the existing oligarchy, commonly believed to be inevitable in the industrialization of a nation, did not occur.

These exact conditions were not found in the other countries, but a strong convergence of interests between industrialists and exporters with regard to the basic structure of the economy has been identified in all of them.[146] Firmly tied economically as well as ideologically and politically to an inherently unstable primary export sector the power of industry in Latin America to perform the revolutionary transforming role it had in Europe was critically diminished.

The question that must be asked, therefore, is exactly what kind of industrial growth was taking place? To what extent was it allowing industry itself to move away from reliance on imports and the economy as a whole from its dependence on primary exports? In order to answer these questions it is necessary first to summarize exactly what happened during the war with respect to both industrial production and links with the metropolitan economies.

Any conclusions about Latin American industry during the war must be qualified by the fact that many key issues relating to wartime development remain unresolved, mainly because of a lack of reliable statistics. This is the case even for Brazil, the country for which we have the most extensive literature dealing directly with the impact of the war on industry. Keeping these difficulties in mind, it appears that during the war there was an appreciable increase in industrial production in Brazil, a reasonable, albeit on the whole fairly moderate, increase in Chile, and in Argentina and Peru, although there were certain industries which did expand, overall there was little positive change. Some of the key reasons for these different experiences have already been considered, but there were also similarities which in terms of understanding the nature of industry in Latin America are perhaps more important.

Firstly, all countries except, somewhat paradoxically, Peru, suffered from a shortage of needed imports, which probably limited the growth of productive capacity. This might be taken as an argument for the efficacy of strong external ties, but it can also be seen as an aspect of the region's partial capitalist transformation. To pay for these imports demanded an increased reliance on exports and/or capital imports, so reinforcing the existing structures of dependence. This was to become a critical problem during the later period of import-substitution industrialization. Secondly, although the output of various manufactured goods increased during the war, there was virtually no significant change in industrial structure. Those industries which processed exports expanded to meet Allied demand, and those which had enjoyed some natural, or in some cases tariff-assisted, advantage over imports prior to the conflict simply improved their share of the local market. Producer and intermediate goods production, on the other hand, showed little advance.

Does the lack of a more dramatic spurt in industrial production and the failure of substantive change in the structure of productive forces lend support to the argument outlined at the beginning of this chapter that industrial development proceeded more rapidly when ties with the metropolis were stronger? Perhaps it does, but only if we accept that the prewar pattern of industrial development was creating the basis for a break with, or at least a diminution of, dependence on foreign trade, and that the war was a time when the tentacles of world-capitalism relaxed their grip on Latin America. But industrial development up to 1914 fit rather well within the limited form of socio-economic transition set in motion by primary export capitalism and was in many ways reliant upon it. Also, during the war Latin America was not free from strong, pervasive external pressures.

The war led to only selective isolation from these pressures. Most exports were in great demand and the Allies showed little compunction in trying to control markets. Despite this interference, export earnings did increase in most countries, and this undoubtedly stimulated domestic demand. It also led to more investment in export sectors, which probably reduced the capital available for local industry. This problem was exacerbated by the fact that primary export orientation had led to the creation of a financial system which did not cater to the needs of industry. It should also be emphasized that demands was probably adversely effected by the ending of capital imports and the unemployment and higher prices which were, at least in part, aspects of the internal adjustment to this. To the extent that the demand for foodstuffs was relatively inelastic, the increase in food prices, which can be linked to the irresistible pull of foreign demand, not only led to falling real incomes, but also reduced spending on other commodities. It is, however, difficult to quantify the differential impact of the various countervailing factors. The decline in imports also seems to have had somewhat contradictory effects. The rise in the price and the fall in the quantity of consumer goods did increase demand for local products, while at the same time the difficulty in obtaining producer goods reduced the extent of capital formation. It was really only with respect to imports that the region can be said to have been "isolated" during the war. Even here there were exceptions. By 1916 the quantity of Peruvian imports was higher than prewar levels, in Chile the inflow of consumer goods showed some signs of recovery, and one of Argentina's most vital imports, cotton textiles, was back at its 1913 level three years later. It is, nonetheless, broadly correct to see the war as a period in which the scarcity of certain imports offered an opportunity for local industry to expand its output. But this opportunity was substantially limited in various ways by the continued, and in many respects enhanced, dependence on primary exports and capital goods imports.

In short, the debate about industry and the war has been misconceived on a number of counts. The first, and most important has been the failure to distinguish between different forms of industrial development. Sufficient attention has not been given to the question of whether the prewar manufacturing sector was providing a viable alternative to primary export capitalism. There is also the continued confusion about whether the debate should be over increases in output or productive capacity, although Fishlow's and the Versianis' observations suggest that these need not be mutually exclusive considerations. Thirdly, during the war Latin American economies were not free from powerful external influences which continued to confine what industrial growth there was into recognizable channels which posed little threat to the prevailing economic systems or the hegemony of those who dominated them. That hegemony was, however, being challenged, and it is the most powerful component of that challenge, the upsurge in working-class militancy, which is now considered.

6

The War and the workers

Introduction

The development and spread of primary export-based capitalism in Latin America from the latter decades of the nineteenth century was characterized by many of the phenomena associated with the rise of industrial capitalism throughout the world, such as improved communications, a more up-to-date financial system, urbanization, industrial growth, and the extension of railway networks. These revolutionary changes in the material forces of production called forth an equally if not more revolutionary transformation in the relations of production. From the early to middle decades of the nineteenth century such a transformation had begun to take place in most Latin American countries. It should not, however, be imagined that this was simply a function of the supposed technological or market imperatives of industrial capitalism. It was a much more complex process. From Independence systems of servile labor in Latin America had been under attack from a number of quarters. The most potent force underlying all the various strands of the anti-slavery movement was the liberal ideology thrown up by the process of capitalist change taking place in Europe. This ideology not only influenced many Latin Americans, but also lay behind the vigorous and largely successful anti-slave trade policy of the British government. Slaves became more expensive, the systems decayed and alternatives had to be found. There was, however, great variation in the character and timing of change. In Peru slavery was abolished in 1856, but semi-servile Chinese coolie labor continued to be used on coastal plantations into the 1880s. Slavery was not ended in Brazil until 1888, while in Chile and Argentina this form of labor had never been very important. Although changes in productive relations are rightly seen as the result of the local circumstance and class conflict, in Latin America external forces, both material and ideological, played a major role. This influence would continue to be felt.

There had always been wage labor in Latin America, the difference was that by the late nineteenth century it had become the dominant form of labor exploitation within the respective economies. Free labor, a growing proportion of it skilled or semiskilled, was needed to run the trains, to operate the new machinery in the factories, to keep the increasingly complex cities functioning, and, of course, to produce the exports. Up to the First World War the growth of a proletariat was most pronounced in the cities. Wage labor was employed in agriculture and mining, but there were still extensive areas where either non-capitalist relations of production persisted, such as on many *haciendas* in the Peruvian *sierra* or on estates in central Chile, or where peasant subsistence or petty commodity production continued. Furthermore, many workers labored under systems which can be seen as transitional, combining capitalist and non-capitalist forms of exploitation, such as some of the many types of sharecropping or the systems of temporary migrant labor used on Argentine and Peruvian sugar estates.

No attempt is made here to discuss all sectors or facets of labor in the four countries. The focus will be mainly, although not entirely, on the urban workers, for the principal concern is with the development of organized labor and the growth of overt, modern class conflict. The latter became increasingly bitter from about the turn of the century. This was a function of the far-reaching and rapid economic changes which were taking place and creating tensions which increasingly could not be contained within the more slowly evolving social and political structures. These structures, under pressure in the immediate prewar period, were profoundly shaken, and in many ways fundamentally changed, by the events of the war, particularly the explosion of working-class unrest which occurred between 1917 and 1920–21. This was one of the most significant features to come out of the war period–the ushering out the era of uncontested oligarchical political authority and the beginning of mass politics. The key question to be answered is why the war should have seen the elite's political power challenged at the same time as its vision of the region's economic destiny seems to have been so strongly reinforced. What was the relationship, if any, between the external constraints to which Latin America's primary export capitalism was subject and the development of class struggle? Before trying to tackle these and other issues which arise when considering wartime events, it is necessary to offer a brief general outline of the growth of organized labor and class conflict in Latin America.

In all the countries under review the first stirrings of worker organization can be dated from about the 1850s when artisan groups in the cities formed mutual benefit societies, offering various forms of benefits, such as money for sickness or burial, to their members.[1] These societies were to remain a significant force through the First World War, but from the 1890s their relative importance was overshadowed by the emergence of more militant *sindicatos* established in specific trades, in factories, the railways or the docks. These organizations generally came into existence during the disputes between labor and capital, which became increasingly common from the 1890s. Those *sindicatos* set up by skilled workers, such as printers or shoemakers, or the unions set up in sectors vital for foreign trade, such as the docks or railways, were generally fairly strong because of the scarcity or strategic economic position of labor. But even here defeats generally outnumbered victories. Most unions were financially weak, were vulnerable to the use of scab labor, and could not survive the frequent cyclical economic recessions. Furthermore, unions were rarely granted official recognition, and although at times employers were obliged to negotiate in order to end disputes, the permanent existence of *sindicatos* was strongly and violently resisted by employers and the state.

Needless to say, the development of workers' organizations was viewed with alarm by the local elites, who wanted economic change but not the social upheaval with which it was invariably associated. They seem to have believed that class conflict was an aberration, a foreign import, the work of European agitators, in short anti-national, anti-patriotic. This view was strengthened by the fact that, in order to make sense of the position they found themselves in, workers, many of whom, especially in Argentina and Brazil, were immigrants, embraced current European ideologies such as Anarchism, Syndicalism or Socialism. Because the political systems were generally not open to them, it was the first two, with their disdain for parliamentary solutions and their advocacy of direct action, which became dominant and were adopted by many Latin American workers' groups in the prewar years. This may seem to give credence to the claims that class conflict itself was a "foreign import," but as James Morris has noted,[2] "The conditions for worker revolt or adaptation to the industrial order are made at home, and if foreign models are successfully transplanted, it is because they fit these conditions in a greater or less degree and not because they have created them."

Although there were some very modest social reforms brought in

before the First World War, the most common response of employers
and the state to the challenge to their authority represented by unions
and revolutionary ideas was the use of force. This was employed
liberally. Strikers were frequently dispersed by police or troops, "free
labor" was given police protection, during serious strikes the workers'
publications were often banned, printing presses smashed, and labor
leaders arrested. In Brazil and Argentina these leaders could be
deported under stringent laws passed to rid the countries of "foreign
subversives." It is interesting that of the four countries it was in Chile,
with its long tradition of political stability, where repression seems to
have been most brutal. In October 1905, 300 people were killed in the
aptly titled *Semana roja* in Santiago, in the following year forty-eight
people lost their lives during a rail strike in Antofagasta, and in 1907 more
than 1,000 workers, their wives and children (and according to some
estimates up to 3,000) died in a hail of machine gun bullets in the grounds
of a school in Iquique.[3] It is not immediately apparent why official
violence should have been so relatively excessive here.

For all countries except Chile the immediate prewar years saw
substantial setbacks for the labor movement. The recession in 1913
and then the chaos and widespread unemployment brought by the
conflict in Europe further undermined workers' strength and confidence. Measured by strike action, it was not until late in 1916 or 1917
that it began slowly to return. For example, in the last months of 1916
Argentine workers began to strike with increasing frequency and their
actions continued to grow until the massive general strike in January
1919 and the bloody *Semana trágica* which followed. There was
continued unrest in the country well into 1921. In Peru, there were a
great many rural strikes from 1917 as well as two general strikes in
Lima in 1919. In the same year sugar estate workers began to win
demands for better wages and conditions, their agitation culminating
in a prolonged strike in the major sugar producing valleys of the
northern department of La Libertad in 1921. Strike activity increased
in Rio de Janeiro and São Paulo from 1917, and two years later there
was a series of general strikes in many parts of the country. Chile too
saw countless strikes and in August 1919 100,000 people gathered in
Santiago to protest against high food prices. Events similar to those
mentioned above were recorded during these years in Colombia,
Ecuador, Bolivia, Uruguay, and Cuba.[4] It is clear, therefore, that
although the growth of working-class movements in each country was
distinctive, as Spalding has observed, and as the war dramatically
demonstrated, "The impact of external events and domestic–foreign

interactions determined that broad trends emerged at roughly the same time throughout Latin America."[5]

The dramatic upsurge in militant labor struggle in each country during and immediately after the war was not only part of a larger class war being fought throughout Latin America, it was also part of an uneven, generally short-lived, but worldwide, workers' uprising unleashed by the First World War and given heart by the success of the Russian Revolution. To what extent these outside forces directly influenced the specific actions taken by Latin American workers or their leaders is open to question, although even a small sample of the extensive workers' press shows that the course of events in Russia, as well as in Europe and Mexico was followed in great detail and with much interested comment. At May Day rallies the Russian workers' victory was recounted and praised. While the general feeling that the workers' time had come probably did exercise a powerful influence on Latin America's labor movements, more specifically, it was the crisis which convulsed international capitalism, especially the functioning of the world economy and, therefore, the Latin American economies, which materially helped to ignite working-class unrest.

Inflation and falling real wages were the way in which the international economic crisis manifested itself in Latin America and throughout the world in the war and immediate postwar years. However, the workers' reaction to this cannot be seen as a simple rebellion of hunger. The most bitter struggles occurred at the end of the war when wages were rising and employment was high, whereas the relatively depressed years from 1913 through 1915 saw the workers economically battered and unable to mount a concerted defense. Furthermore, to explain the unrest mainly in terms of falling living standards, even when that was a major issue, is to confuse the spark with what was set alight. For instance, few strikes were solely concerned with achieving higher wages. Also prominent in the workers' lists of demands were shorter hours, better conditions, union recognition, broader political concessions, no post-strike victimization and many other issues. These broad sets of demands and the avowedly political nature of the general strikes demonstrates that while still at a formative stage and suffering from all kinds of intra-class divisions and ideological rivalry, the class consciousness which had begun to coalesce before 1914 was rekindled and forged anew in the bitter battles of this period. This had important implications for the future course of organized labor.

The wave of wartime working-class agitation also posed a direct threat to the political authority of the ruling elite. In most cases this threat was met by savage repression, but because by the end of the war these societies had become socio-politically more complex, force alone was not enough, and in every country some form of political compromise had to be found in order to blunt the edge of the workers' challenge. For the most part this was done by a minimal degree of social legislation together with the political co-option of sections of the middle and working classes. This represented a major watershed in Latin American history. In some countries there were attempts to meet the workers' challenge by propping up the cultural–ideological hegemony of the ruling elites through campaigns to promote a more active, aggressive nationalism. This was not, however, a simple or straightforward process. It had strong prewar roots and in many instances it was sectors of the urban middle classes which were the most vociferous in the propagation of nationalist values. This was no doubt welcomed by the export elites to the extent that nationalism could be used as weapon against "subversive foreigners" (that is, leaders of organized labor) and their imported ideologies.[6]

The nature of worker unrest during these years seems to have been remarkably similar in each country, although the immediate and long-term social and political significance of the struggle did vary considerably, depending to a great extent on how the different labor movements had developed in the prewar years. For this reason it is important to look rather closely at the development of organized labor up to 1914, before detailing the events of the war period. Furthermore, it should be made clear that what is offered here is an extremely modest, partial, and abbreviated exercise in comparative working-class history. Even for a single country the writing of a history of the working class would be a monumental undertaking. Rather what will be considered is the growth of organized labor, whether in established *sindicatos*, union federations or informal and transient strike committees, the development of class conflict, and what all this meant in terms of wider socio-political change. In other words, how the relatively sudden emergence of a combative working class, mainly, but not entirely, in the cities both reflected and at the same time helped to shape the brand of capitalism and the political systems which were being developed in Latin America. It is also vital to try to unravel the links between these developments and the many aspects of the region's manifest external dependence. In trying to understand this complex process, strikes and the formation of unions are used as a crude proxy for the emergence of the working class. It is crude because as

Thompson has argued[7] class consciousness is the way in which workers deal in cultural terms ("...traditions, value-systems, ideas and institutional forms.") with their experience as proletarians. Disputes and formal organizations are but one aspect of this experience, and although it is true that consciousness is raised and extended through struggle, by looking only at this part of workers' lives we have taken only the first step towards understanding the formation of the working class in Latin America.

Argentina

I

To understand the genesis of the Argentine labor movement it is first necessary to know something of the dramatic demographic changes which took place from the last decades of the nineteenth century. The two main features of this were mass immigration and rapid urbanization. The major surges of immigration came in the years from the mid-1880s to the Baring Crisis and again from 1905 to the First World War, coinciding almost exactly with the periods of most active foreign investment (Table 6.1). According to the three national censuses in 1869, 1895 and 1914 the total population grew from 1,737,076 to 3,954,911 to 7,885,237. In the latter year about 30% were foreign-born.[8] This was the highest proportion of immigrants of any major nation.[9] At the same time the cities expanded rapidly. By 1914, 57.4% of the population was living in urban areas, although only 38% were in the 49 cities of more than 10,000. In the largest of these, Buenos Aires, 49.4% of the 1,575,814 inhabitants were immigrants. It was also here that the most important developments in the labor movement occurred. The fact that immigrants comprised such a large proportion of the work force not only in the federal capital, but also in the pampean provinces (35.4% of the population) was extremely important. Because of it the rise of the labor movement and the question of Argentine nationalism became tortuously intertwined. The latter, comprising a number of varying strands, was essentially used as a weapon against the former. In many ways the subsequent course of the country's history was markedly influenced by this explosive combination.

The country's occupational structure reflected the high degree of urbanization. The data from the 1914 Census is, however, problematic, for there are a great many inconsistencies in the categorization of

Table 6.1 Net immigration into
Argentina 1880–1914. Five-year
average

1880– 4	41,252
1885– 9	127,922
1890– 4	20,976
1895– 9	54,327
1900– 4	49,043
1905– 9	154,766
1910–14	121,781

Source: Calculated from Tornquist, Economic Conditions, p. 15.

employment.[10] With this limitation in mind, it appears that by the First World War 26.0% of the employed work force was in industry and services, 16.4% in agriculture and 12.5% in transport and commerce. The proportion of workers in industrial and service employment was so high because it included about 185,000 seamstresses and dressmakers, 108,000 who washed and ironed clothes, 14,600 barbers, 23,400 tailors, 23,600 bakers, 71,600 bricklayers, 52,800 carpenters, and a host of similar trades.[11] There were also a great many small workshops and only relatively few sizable manufacturing firms which employed many workers. A large number of peones and jornaleros were not classified in any particular sector, and 1,793,661 workers were apparently unemployed. The unclassified workers were those who moved between agriculture, primarily harvest work, and construction or other temporary jobs in the cities. The figure for agricultural employment is, therefore, greatly underestimated. Alejandro Bunge calculated that about 300,000 workers, including 100,000 golondrinas (literally swallows–those who came from Europe for the harvest and then returned), found seasonal employment during the harvest.[12]

The transient nature of such a large proportion of the work force is an important feature of the Argentine labor market and goes some way to explain why during the war despite net out-migration there were no labor shortages in agriculture and levels of urban unemployment were high. With the inflow of foreign capital stopped and government spending sharply curtailed, both private construction and public works were massively reduced and this meant little work for almost

Table 6.2 *Argentine occupational structure, 1914*

		% of those employed
Agriculture and livestock	529,866	16.4%
Industry and services	841,237	26.0%
Commerce	293,646	9.1%
Transport	110,774	3.4%
Public administration	108,852	3.4%
Domestic service	218,619	6.8%
Education	83,814	2.6%
Jornaleros and *peones*	813,912	25.2%
Others	232,533	7.2%
Sub total (employed)	3,233,253	
Unemployed	1,793,661	
Total	5,026,914	

Source: Argentina, *Tercer Censo nacional,* vol. iv, pp. 383–95.

25% of the labor force during the months from February to July. Assuming Bunge's figures applied during the war years, even without the *golondrinas*, no more than 300,000 workers would have been needed at harvest time, leaving over 500,000 to find jobs in the depressed building and public works sectors.

Only a small proportion of the country's work force either took part in direct confrontations with their employers or were organized in any way, although this probably did not distinguish the Argentine workers from those in most other countries. Hobart Spalding estimates that by 1912 between 20% to 30% of the labor force "...belonged or had belonged to some resistance society, workers' federation, social centre, mutual society, or workers' political party."[13] But sheer numbers were not all that significant, for during strikes, especially the frequent general strikes, a great many non-organized workers were drawn into the conflict. During the 1907 General Strike, of the 93,000 workers who took part only a third were associated with *sindicatos*, and of these there were but 10,000 paid-up members.[14] What was important, in terms of the economic and political impact of labor, was the groups of workers who had organized. Some of the earliest workers to band together were those in the small-scale urban industries such as bakers, shoemakers, tailors, waiters and other hotel workers, cigarette makers, bricklayers, printers, carpenters, etc.[15] Objectively they did not have a great deal of economic muscle, but their strikes could disrupt urban life and thereby the peace of mind, not to mention the comfort, of the elite. Their example was also important for other workers. One group that did have considerable power was the railway footplatemen's union, *La Fraternidad*, established in 1887. In the years of most active strike action, between 1900 and 1910, a great many other groups of workers organized, including those in the railway workshops, the docks, the flour mills, the packing plants, as well as maritime workers, tram drivers, gas plant workers, and those in numerous other trades and services. As the ability of labor to disrupt the export sector increased so did their power and influence.

Besides the many *sindicatos* and working-class political societies there were also a number of union federations put together before the war. The first to actually get off the ground, the Federación Obrera Argentina (FOA), was set up in 1901 in a rare and short-lived cooperative endeavor between the Anarchists and Socialists.[16] The Socialists left a year later because of unresolvable ideological and tactical differences with the Anarchists, and in 1903 established the Unión General de Trabajadores (UGT). The FOA, which changed its name to the Federación Obrera Regional Argentina (FORA) in 1904, remained the stronger of the two with 7,360 members to the UGT's 1,780.[17] The UGT lasted about five years when it merged with the Congreso Obrero Regional Argentino (CORA). Before this the Syndicalists had taken over the organization and in 1906 ties with the Socialist Party were severed.[18] Attempts in 1909 to unify the movement failed as most Anarchists remained committed to the hard-line anarcho-communist position officially adopted by the FORA at its fifth congress in 1905.[19] In 1914 the Syndicalists abandoned the CORA and affiliated with the FORA. At the ninth congress held in April 1915 the new group in a well-managed coup ousted the Anarchists from the leadership and passed a resolution disowning the principles of anarcho-communism. The FORA, and effectively the leadership of the union movement, was now firmly under Syndicalist control. Subsequently, the Anarchists formed yet another separate federation, the FORA 5th Congress, but their influence was now greatly diminished.[20]

The Argentine workers' movement was ideologically split, with Socialists, Anarchists and Syndicalists vying for dominance. This is an extremely complex story for there were contending factions within the different camps, over time positions changed, and stated doctrines were often not adhered to in practice. The Socialist Party was established in 1894.[21] Its leaders were mainly middle-class professionals and it followed a reformist program, wanting to achieve power peacefully. While many members of the elite saw it as a threat, for most workers excluded from the political process until 1912, (even after the Sáenz Peña Law non-naturalized immigrants were barred from voting) Socialism could not answer their immediate demands in the workplace. It they could vote, workers probably gave their support to the Socialist Party, but it was to Anarchism and Syndicalism that they turned for ideological sustenance in their struggles with capital. Anarchism became a potent force among Argentine workers from the 1890s with its policies of internationalism, direct action, and class struggle.[22] In Argentina, where the movement was for a time one of the most important in the world, the individualist strand was displaced by a more collectivist approach which was important in facilitating the Anarchist domination of the union movement. The Anarchists' principal weapon was the general strike, which was seen as a necessity in situations where unions were weak and alternative sources of labor (provided by the continued influx of immigrants) plentiful. Syndicalism, which began to gain adherents from about 1906, also advocated class struggle but its aims were directed more at achieving immediate economic demands. Because of this less revolutionary, more "practical" orientation it was the Syndicalists who moved into a position of dominance in the labor movement during the First World War. The preceding descriptions are broadly accurate, however, they do tend to break down when actual practice is considered. For example, Socialists did support strikes, including general strikes, and Anarchists frequently compromised, acted as normal trade unionists, and made deals to end disputes.[23] Therefore, while the ideological positions were adopted and bitterly contested it should not be thought that this necessarily meant hard and fast application on the field of battle.

There was a great deal of activity on this field in the prewar years and it was through these conflicts that the workers' movement described above was created. It is impossible here to provide any more than the number of disputes, and this simply does not convey the real scale or impact of the movement. Table 6.3 shows that activity increased in the 1890s and then exploded from the turn of the century until about 1910. This year marked a high point for the workers, in that strike victories vastly outnumbered losses for the first and,

Table 6.3 *Strikes in Argentina 1881–1904 and Buenos Aires 1907–1920*

	Total	Won	Lost	Partial success	Number of workers	Number of workers according to outcome		
						won	lost	partial
In Argentina:								
1881–5	9	1	4	4	na			
1886–90	39	15	16	8	na			
1891–6	58	26	24	8	na			
1901–4	142	–na–						
In Buenos Aires:								
1907	231	39	161	31	169,017	4,366	163,473	1,178
1908	118	18	88	12	11,561	1,945	9,546	70
1909	138	36	97	5	4,762	527	3,713	522
1910	298	185	47	66	18,806	13,499	3,395	1,912
1911	102	7	92	3	27,992	4,216	20,534	3,242
1912	99	25	68	6	8,992	1,627	6,702	663
1913	95	18	62	15	23,698	775	19,154	3,769
1914	64	18	42	4	14,137	6,277	2,216	5,644
1915	65	17	42	6	12,077	1,605	9,482	990
1916	80	19	46	15	24,321	9,600	2,891	11,830
1917	138	26	74	37	135,605	22,924	36,666	76,015
1918*	196	71	83	41	133,042		–na–	
1919	367	145	147	74	308,967	31,064	88,877	39,026
1920	206	66	103	20	134,015	17,867	96,005	9,228

Sources: 1881–1902, Godio *Historia*, pp. 74, 124, 193–4, 219–20; 1907–18, *Boletín del Departamento Nacional del Trabajo*, no. 42 1919, pp. 89–96, 247–50; 1919–20, *Revista de Economía Argentina*, año 2, no. 22, April 1920, p. 310; año 3, no. 34–5, April-May 1921, p. 342. Note: In 1918, one strike remained unresolved; in 1919, one strike listed 150,000 workers as "returned to work," in 1920 seventeen strikes involving 10,915 workers were unresolved.

seemingly, the only time. In addition to the many strikes by separate groups of workers for high wages, shorter hours, better conditions, etc., there were also more than ten general strikes between 1900 and 1914, and in 1907 a massive rent strike erupted in the slums of Buenos Aires and then spread to Rosario, Bahia Blanca and other cities.[24] The reaction to this wave of unrest varied. At times agreements were reached with employers, although in most cases the workers were simply not strong enough to win their demands. During the clearly political general strikes the state moved in and the risings were crushed, generally with a great deal of bloodshed. Often unofficial "patriotic" organizations were allowed to take a hand in smashing the workers' printing presses or burning down their headquarters. In 1902 the government passed the Ley de Residencia which gave them the power to deport suspected "agitators," mainly foreign Anarchists.[25] This was in line with the widespread conception that the trouble was caused by a handful of politically motivated foreigners and if they could be removed the problem would go away. It clearly did not go away. Following the brutally suppressed 1910 General Strike there was a suspected Anarchist bombing of the Colón Opera House in the capital. This reignited upper-class hysteria and precipitated another draconian measure, the Ley de Defensa Social. Among other things, this law made anarchist meetings and demonstrations specifically illegal and banned the entry into the country of "undesirables."[26] There were many strikes after this, most importantly the maritime strike in 1911–12 and a major railway strike in 1913,[27] but the strength of the Anarchists had been broken and it was not until about 1917 that within a broad-based movement the workers once again began to make their strength felt politically.

The prewar development of the labor movement in Argentina had been spectacular. Some critics have argued that the Anarchists were spoilers because their tactics brought down the wrath of the state against the workers.[28] But this suggests that peaceful means to redress grievances would have been successful, which is highly questionable as non-anarchist unions were also suppressed, the "peaceful" Socialists were seen as a grave threat by the ruling class and before 1912 the political system remained closed. Furthermore, a great many workers were immigrants, who had no vote even after 1912, and for whom the Anarchists' revolutionary rhetoric coupled with their commitment to organizing unions and fighting for better conditions was immensely appealing. As Munck writes,[29] "For a long time the anarcho-syndicalist theory did fit closely with the reality of a bourgeois state impervious to workers' demands, but in which the possibility existed for gaining real victories through 'direct action', because of a certain degree of employer disorganization." If the Anarchists made a tactical mistake it was underestimating the power of the state to suppress dissent forcibly and at the same time the ability of the economic and political system to change in such a way as to make their particular call to the barricades increasingly less attractive. Furthermore, the appeal of the militantly internationalist Anarchists was seriously undermined by the rising tide of Argentine nationalism, a weapon initially forged by the elite to defend their position against the specter of social change, but increasingly finding adherents among the middle and working classes.

An important key to the political aspect of this change was the Sáenz Peña Law of 1912.[30] This reform was an attempt by the elite to protect its position essentially by allowing the middle class a greater political role. For the workers the change was less important for only native-born and naturalized men were enfranchised, and in order further to limit working-class participation the elite made sure that it remained extremely difficult to obtain Argentine citizenship.[31] Nonetheless, in the first by-elections in 1913 Socialist candidates won in Buenos Aires, and in 1914 they captured seven of ten congressional seats in the city.[32] This alarmed both the Conservatives and the Radicals. It became obvious that under the new electoral system the working-class vote was important, especially in Buenos Aires. This became a major factor influencing the seemingly more conciliatory labor policies of Hipólito Yrigoyen's administration from 1916. In order to dish the Socialists and draw the teeth of the Anarchists, the Radicals embarked on a policy of trying to co-opt sectors of the working class. This had an extremely important impact on the course of labor struggle during the First World War.

For all the many problems and setbacks, by the outbreak of the First World War both politically and organizationally the Argentine workers' movement had made major gains and was probably the most advanced in Latin America. Significantly, this applied entirely to the urban working class, for in the rural areas, where the bulk of the country's wealth was generated, the only major incident of unrest had occurred in 1912 in the famous *Grito de Alcorta*. This was not, however, a workers' protest but one of *colonos*, angry over high rents and unfavorable contracts.[33] It was not until the war period that rural workers began to organize, no doubt spurred on in part by the example provided by the extremely strong resurgence of the workers' movement in the cities. While built on the substantial foundations laid down before the 1914, this resurgence marked a major turning point in the character and fortunes of the workers' cause in Argentina.

II

The organized working class in Argentina had developed to an impressive degree by 1914. Nevertheless, its relative weakness, and by extension that of Latin America's working class generally, was demonstrated by the immediate response to the severe crisis brought about by the outbreak of war. In Argentina, where the movement was most advanced, there was virtually no response at all. Food prices and unemployment soared, but neither individual *sindicatos* nor the federations mounted any protest. The crisis was so sudden and the effects so devastating that it clearly overwhelmed the ability of the divided and still demoralized workers to react. Furthermore, although by international standards workers in Argentina were relatively well-off, like most of their compatriots throughout the world it did not take much to push them into poverty. The mass unemployment ushered in by the war, when combined with the other adverse conditions under which organized labor suffered, therefore, effectively limited the scope for immediate or concerted action.

Although the Argentine export economy soon recovered from the early effects of the war, the workers continued to face serious problems. The rate of unemployment which doubled in 1914, rose steadily, reaching a high point of almost 20% in August 1917. In Buenos Aires conditions seem to have been substantially worse (Table 6.5). This occurred despite a net out-migration to Europe. High unemployment was the result of the cessation of public works, railway expansion, and building activity generally. This can be tied directly to the ending of foreign investment. The harvest failure in 1917 further reduced the demand for labor. The cost of living also went up sharply. This was an international phenomenon during the war, and compared to most metropolitan countries inflation in Argentina was relatively modest. For example, between 1914 and 1920 the cost of living in France, Britain, and the United States had risen by 270%, 169% and 98% respectively compared to 86% in Argentina.[34] While interesting, these comparisons would have been of little comfort to workers in Buenos Aires whose real wages had fallen 37% by 1918 (Table 6.4). Furthermore, using 1914 as a base year tends to understate the extent of wartime inflation as there was an extremely sharp upward movement in prices in the last months of that year.[35]

Why, with exports doing well, did the standard of living of the workers fall so drastically? This is a difficult question which demands a fuller analysis than can be offered here. A few tentative reasons can, however, be suggested. In a time of inflation wages tend to be sticky in any case, and, if the Departamento de Trabajo figures are reliable, or at least indicative of the general movement, in Argentina money wages (of men in Buenos Aires) did not reach their 1914 level before 1918

Table 6.4 *Argentina: cost of living and real wages 1914–1920*

Year	Cost of living	Food	Rent	Clothes, etc.	Average daily money wage. Men in Buenos Aires (pesos)	Real wages (1914= 100)
			(1914 = 100)			
1914	100	100	100	100	3.81 (m/n)	100
1915	107	108	93	114	3.64	90
1916	115	108	87	145	3.66	84
1917	135	127	89	178	3.70	72
1918	169	132	116	265	4.02	63
1919	160	141	115	250	5.06	83
1920	186	163	130	273	6.19	88

Sources: A.E. Bunge, *El costo*, 7.21. For wages 1914–17, *Boletín del Departamento Nacional del Trabajo*, no. 42, 1917, p. 9.

Table 6.5 *Unemployment in Buenos Aires and Argentina and net migration 1912–1919*

Year	Buenos Aires per cent unemployed	Argentina per cent unemployed		Net migration
1912			5.1%	213,700
1913			6.7%	143,300
1914	15.3%		13.7%	− 62,000
1915	18.0%		14.5%	− 64,500
1916	24.8%		17.7%	− 50,000
1917	30.12	1917 (Aug.)	19.4%	− 31,000
		1917 (Dec.)	13.0%	
1918	20.8%	1918 (Mar.)	10.3%	− 8,400
		1918 (Aug.)	12.0%	
1919	17.5%	1919 (Aug.)	7.9%	12,350
1920	16.8%	1920 (Aug.)	7.2%	40,000
1921	18.2%			

Sources: Revista de Economía Argentina, año 4 no. 42, December 1921, p. 488. Figures for Buenos Aires Robert E. Shipley, "on the outside looking in: A social history of the porteño workers during the golden age of Argentine development, 1914–1930," PhD thesis, Rutgers, 1977, pp. 346–53, quoted in Charles Bergquist, *Labor in Latin America. Comparative Essays on Chile, Argentina, Venezuela, and Colombia*, Stanford, 1986, p. 114.

(Table 6.4). With high unemployment and a weakened labor movement the ability of workers to resist cuts or force up wages was significantly impaired. Finally, the war served to bid up both the price of imports and of food. Workers in Argentina, as elsewhere in Latin America, could not easily compete with the demand from the more advanced capitalist countries, especially with the Allied governments organizing and supporting purchases of beef and grains. This was probably the most important material external factor (as distinct from, for example, the morale boost given by the Russian Revolution) influencing the course of labor unrest throughout the region. It also provides at least part of the answer to the apparent paradox of why the war saw both the strengthening of export sectors and the weakening of the political authority of the export elites. In all of Latin America the rising cost of living and lower real wages became major issues during and immediately after the war. Governments became so concerned about higher prices not only because they were seen as a cause of working-class unrest, but also because this was an issue which temporarily united the workes and urban middle class. Politically this proved to be a dangerous combination for the ruling elites.

Despite its worries the government did relatively little to alleviate the situation. There were essentially two courses open, to control prices or the export of foodstuffs and/or to create jobs through public works schemes. In August, 1914 the Provincial Government in Santa Fé provided 100,000 pesos for public works, but this did little to reduce unemployment.[36] When the Radicals came to power in November 1916 there was speculation that money would be spent on public works, but because of financial stringency this did not happen.[37] From 1918 increasing sums were budgeted for this purpose, but it is not clear whether they were actually used and, if they were, what impact they had.[38] At the outbreak of war when inflation soared spectacularly there was legislation passed to control the price of bread, but this never seems to have been applied.[39]

The only significant move during the war was taken following the harvest failure in 1917, when the government imposed controls over wheat exports for almost a year.[40] Once again, it is difficult to isolate the effect of this measure, however, between 1917 and 1918 bread prices fell from an average of .29m/n per kilo to .264 m/n.[41] In 1920 prices moved sharply upward and the government felt compelled to take some action to control food prices. Although they did manage to impose rent control in Buenos Aires, their attempts to moderate price rises were a failure and revealed, "... a greater sensitivity towards the producer interests in the province of Buenos Aires than it did towards the consumers in the city."[42]

For the reasons given above, the deterioration in living standards brought by the war did not elicit an immediate response from the workers. Strikes did continue, but the numbers declined and there were no major incidents. Marotta writes,[43] "The account of the workers' struggles for almost a year and a half after the Ninth Congress (of the F.O.R.A. in April, 1915) does not take up much space." Yoast argues that this was mainly because union organization still had not recovered from the defeat in 1910.[44] From the last months of 1916 all this began to change. In November a major strike occurred among the maritime workers, organized by the Syndicalist FOM (Maritime Workers Federation). The new government stepped in almost immediately, refused to allow troops and police to harass pickets or protect blacklegs, as was the usual practice, and due largely to this the strike was successful.[45] The following March, the Compañia Argentina de Navegación Nicolás Mihanovich disputed the arbitration agreed with the FOM in December and attempted to set up a yellow union for those working on its ships. The FOM struck again. Troops were sent, but fearing a general strike by the FORA, the government recalled them, and within a month the workers emerged victorious once more.[46]

The victories of the maritime workers seemed to open the floodgates of discontent. In 1917 the number of strikes in Buenos Aires increased by about 70%, the number of workers taking part by over 450%, and more days were lost in disputes (2,100,269) than in any previous year.[47] The level of unrest increased in the following year. The underlying conditions had not changed, real wages continued to fall and unemployment remained high. The difference now was the growing confidence of the workers and, most importantly, the seemingly more liberal attitude of the authorities. It is also significant that of the 334 strikes in these two years, only about 40% were classified as being about wages, while 33% were over questions of union recognition, unfair dismissals and in support of other workers.[48] Therefore, although immediate economic motives were important, the wave of strikes also represented broader, more long-term demands and an enhanced level of both consciousness and organization on the part of the urban working class. The latter is clearly shown in Table 6.6.

To understand fully the unrest it would be necessary to analyze each major dispute in detail. This is clearly beyond the scope of this study. But in order to gain some feel for the turbulence of these years mention

Table 6.6 *The syndicalist F O R A 1915–1921*

	No. of affiliated unions	Total dues-paying members		Monthly average of dues-paying members
1915	50	21,332	(8 months)	2,666
1916	70	41,124	(12 months)	3,427
1917	199	158,796	(12 months)	13,233
1918	232	428,713	(12 months)	35,726
1919	530	476,203	(12 months)	39,683
1920	734	749,518	(11 months)	68,138
1921	—	240,101	(9 months)	26,678

Sources: Rock, *Radicalism*, p. 160.

of at least some of the more outstanding events should be made. There was a strike of municipal workers in the capital in March 1917 which was settled favorably after the FORA threatened the government with yet another general strike.[49] In the last months of the year workers struck at US-owned meat-packing plants in Berisso, near La Plata and Avellaneda. In this instance the government adopted a hard line, either because, according to Rock, there was nothing to be gained politically from supporting the workers or, as Smith has argued, there was intense pressure from foreign interests and the Sociedad Rural.[50] Marines were used, blacklegs hired and the workers defeated. In 1918 there were successful strikes in shoe factories, which had grown considerably because of wartime reduction in imports. The Unión General de Obreros en Calzado emerged from these battles greatly strengthened.[51] In the same year there was a prolonged strike (2 May to 17 August) of flour mill workers and also one of telegraphists and postal workers. The former was successful, while the latter was smashed by the government.[52]

The most significant series of disputes in 1917–18 were those affecting the railways.[53] A general rail strike jointly planned for the end of 1917 by La Fraternidad and the Federación Obrera Ferroviaria (FOF), was preempted first by a violent struggle on the Central Argentine Railway in Rosario over the reinstatement of dismissed workers, and subsequently by other strikes on different parts of the rail network. The government's refusal to use troops and the pressure they put on the companies to settle led to the workers gaining concessions in almost every case. Not surprisingly, there was an outcry against this from local business and foreign capital. The *Review of the River Plate* complained,[54] "The strikers have triumphed. Foreign capital has been humiliated. The government is now acclaimed as protector of the poor." The general railway strike which began in September and lasted about three weeks led to further gains by the workers, although this time the government took a less pro-labor stance. They were finding their role as "protector of the poor" an increasing burden as the trouble on the railways continued, and they came under pressure, both from the agricultural interests anxious over exports and the Allies anxious over continuity of supplies, to adopt more repressive measures. The British, along with many unsympathetic Argentines, believed that the strikes were the work of German agitators, and following a renewed series of stoppages in February 1918, Sir Reginald Tower, the British Minister in Buenos Aires, threatened to cancel the recently signed wheat deal and impose a shipping boycott unless normal working was resumed.[55] This proved the final straw for a beleaguered government. They now turned on the railwaymen, a decree was issued against further strikes and armed force was used to back it up. This provided a clear example of the how foreign pressure could be brought to bear on the Argentine government's labor policies.

But, the government's labor problems were only just beginning. In Argentina, as in the rest of Latin America and throughout the world, 1919 was to prove a year of unprecedented labor rebellion as the disruption caused by the war in Europe continued to unsettle world markets and governments. Furthermore, the Russian Revolution was providing a potent example for oppressed workers everywhere. This and the upsurge of labor unrest in many European countries was closely followed in the Argentine workers' press, and helped create an atmosphere of imminent revolution not only among certain groups of workers but also among many capitalists.[56]

Despite the recent clampdown on the railwaymen, at the beginning of 1919 the Argentine workers were still confident and combative. A strike at the Pedro Vasena Metal Works in January which resulted in the shooting by troops of four workers proved to be the spark which set off a massive general strike, mainly among the industrial workers of the capital. This was the beginning of the famous *Semana trágica*, in which between twelve and fifty workers were gunned down by the authorities while attending the funeral of their comrades, and upper and middle-class vigilantes were given free rein to attack the Jewish quarter of the city because they believed Russian Jews were about to lead a Bolshevik revolution.[57] It was a bloody and confused week in Buenos Aires. Katherine Dreier, a visiting American sympathetic to the workers' plight, described the mood of the city during this upheaval:[58]

I could not but have a feeling of admiration for the men who organized this strike. So thorough was it, that in a city of one million and a half people there could not be found enough strike breakers to counteract the general organized labor...Mounted police dispersed all gatherings and, as I watched the streets from my balcony or took a daily walk in my section, I was struck by the serious expression on the faces of the men as well as their quiet dignity.

The Anarchists saw the *Semana trágica* as the opportunity for a full revolutionary rising, but the Syndicalist FORA together with the government quickly moved to prevent this and bring the situation under control. Yrigoyen put pressure on the Vasena Company to come to terms with their workers, and soon thereafter the FORA, after consultation with the government, officially called off the strike. The federation did not, however, have full control. Many rank and file members ignored its call and the Anarchists remained active. Consequently, strikes and violence continued for some time. Furthermore, the official and unofficial intimidation suffered did not quash the workers' struggle. During the remainder of the year there were numerous strikes throughout the country, and union membership soared, rising from 79,800 in December 1918 to 118,200 a year later.[59]

It is important to note that these years saw major changes not only in the relative power of those groups which vied for the allegiance of the working class, but also in the relation between the state and labor. Although they had a brief revival in 1919, the Anarchists, who had been such a leading force in the prewar labor movement, were now completely marginalized. They had been increasingly eclipsed before this by the Syndicalists, who by appealing to immediate economic interests, steadily extended their control over the major *sindicatos*. A few days into the *Semana trágica* the Anarchists found themselves entirely isolated. They were abandoned by the Socialists and Syndicalists, who saw them as spoilers whose actions would undermine their reformist ambitions. The Anarchists, dubbed "Maximalists" for their revolutionary pretensions, therefore became the main target for government and vigilante repression.[60] The Syndicalists on the other hand went from strength to strength. But much of this was done by an increasing reliance on the direct or indirect support of the Radicals.

They in turn were currying favour with the Syndicalists partly in order to undermine the electoral support of the Socialists, and partly to co-opt the labor movement so as to control it in the interests of promoting the social harmony they perceived was needed for the smooth functioning of a "modern" capitalist system.[61] The alliance was, however, not very stable and social harmony was never realized.

This latter failure was due to the imminent and essentially irresolvable conflict between labor and capital and to the violent reaction on the part of sections of the upper and of the middle class to the upsurge in labor militancy. Immediately after and in response to the *Semana trágica* the anti-union, anti-immigrant Liga Patriótica Argentina was established (19 January 1919). Although born out of the wartime crisis its roots can be traced back to the socio-political tensions associated with the country's rapid economic development of the previous forty years.[62] The Liga sought to uphold their version of Argentine nationality against the immigrant left which they claimed, "... was evil and anti-Argentine because it pitted class against class, deriding the nation and undermining authority. A natural hierarchy of intelligence, culture, and wealth existed in every society. To destroy this hierarchy, as the left proposed, would be disastrous for the nation, for it would lead to the rule of the ignorant over the rest of society."[63] Not only did the Liga threaten workers but it, together with foreign capital and the military, posed a political threat to Yrigoyen's government whose policy towards labor was not nearly strong enough for these groups. Bowing to this pressure, from about April the Radicals began to employ a far harder line against strikers. But it was not until about 1921, when the postwar boom collapsed spectacularly, that the power of the union was finally smashed, and the five years of buoyant militancy and attempts at government co-option were brought to an end.[64]

On the whole, workers seem to have been more successful both in organizing and in their contests with capital when exports were doing well. At these times employers had more room to maneuver and more to lose by suffering strike action, while lower levels of unemployment strengthened the workers' negotiating position. Greater external demand for Argentina's food exports which led to greater profits also fueled local inflation, thereby making demands for higher wages more likely. All these were important aspects of the link between external forces and the course of domestic class struggle, and may, at least partially, help account for the striking convergence of labor uprisings throughout the region.

The war and immediate postwar years were clearly crucial for the Argentine labor movement. They also marked a major change in both the country's political structure and the balance of class forces. It is completely legitimate to claim, as Rock has done, that the Radicals' handling of labor in these years was an exercise in political opportunism. His argument that the General Strike in January 1919 was "In broad terms...more a series of unarticulated riots than a genuine working-class rebellion."[65] is also sound. But the level of militancy and union organization from 1917 was impressive, and to imply, however obliquely, that there could have been a more coherent "revolutionary" response by the working class is perhaps asking too much given the low level of purposeful political mobilization, and the dominance of reformism among Socialists and Syndicalists. Furthermore, to see only political maneuvering (in fact Rock's analysis does take in a much broader sweep) is to lose sight of a more important feature of these years—that from being primarily an object of crude repression, the urban working class, propelled by the world and domestic capitalist crises brought by the war, had fully emerged as a legitimate and powerful factor in the Argentine political equation. This was a major blow to the landed oligarchy, who had believed that through electoral reform they could foil the Radicals and continue to exercise direct authority. Their world, or at least some of the more "stable" features of it had disappeared. The First World War had finally shattered their assumptions, already rather shaky before 1914, of an international economy of harmonious interdependence and of domestic growth without class conflict. The more strident cultural nationalism and the formation of the sinister Liga Patriótica were the most obvious reactions to this new situation.

Brazil

I

Like Argentina, Brazil experienced a considerable degree of militant working-class unrest in the decades before the First World War. However, the workers here were unable to sustain as strong an organized movement or mount as effective a challenge to the elite. There seem to have been far fewer *sindicatos* established, they were usually short-lived, and with the exception of a few isolated trades, labor's gains were virtually nil. The relative weakness of the labor movement in Brazil may seem somewhat paradoxical for industry here was more advanced that in the pampean republic. But industrial development cannot be equated in a simple or direct fashion with the growth of overt class conflict or consciousness. It depends very much, among other things, on the structure of industry, the composition and experience of the work force, and the nature of the political system. In Brazil none of these were particularly favorable for the creation of a powerful or effective working-class movement.

In percentage terms immigration and urbanization were far less significant in Brazil than in Argentina. Between 1891 and 1920 almost two million immigrants had settled in the country, but according to the Third National Census, in 1920 only 5% of the country's 30,635,605 inhabitants were either foreign-born or naturalized.[66] A decade earlier less than 10% of the population lived in cities of more than 20,000.[67] Nonetheless, the impact on Brazilian society of the increasing concentrations of immigrants in a few large cities, especially São Paulo, Santos, and to a lesser extent Rio de Janeiro, was immense. For the most part it was these new arrivals who made up and led the first modern labor unions. By 1920, immigrants accounted for 35.5%, 35.6% and 20.8% respectively of each city's population, and a higher proportion of those in work.[68] For example, in the state of São Paulo, 51% of the industrial workers and 58% of those in transport were immigrants, and Maram argues that these are underestimates as the figures include employers and administrators.[69] While the working class had also begun to find its voice elsewhere in the country, it was in these southeastern cities with their large immigrant populations where it was heard the loudest. This was a function of rapid expansion of coffee production which attracted mass immigration in the first instance, the considerable urban development which followed as many foreigners, finding work as coffee *colonos* hard and unrewarding, filtered into the cities, and the growth of industry, most of which was developed to supply the local market.

Compared to the land-extensive wheat and cattle economy of Argentina, Brazilian agriculture tended to be much more labor-intensive and this together with the existence of a large subsistence sector meant a relatively far greater rural population and higher proportion of workers engaged in agriculture than in either Chile or Argentina (Table 6.7). But, although Brazil was famous for its massive and dramatic rural rebellions, such as those at Canudos or Joazeiro, working-class organization was almost entirely an urban phenomenon. For example, it seems that in the state of São Paulo there was but one rural strike before 1914, and that was near to an urban

Table 6.7 *Structure of Brazilian employment 1920 compared with Chile and Argentina*

Country	Agriculture mining, etc.	Industry	Transport	Commerce	Administration	Liberal professions	Domestic service	Total
Brazil	6,421,530 (70.50%)	1,189,357 (13.0%)	253,587 (2.77%)	497,548 (5.44%)	226,242 (2.47%)	168,111 (1.87%)	363,879 (3.98%)	9,120,254
Brazilian States								
São Paulo†	882,559 (63.9%)	229,280 (16.6%)	51,594 (3.7%)	87,675 (6.3%)	35,786 (2.9%)	38,229 (2.8%)	45,447 (3.3%)	1,382,207
Rio de Janeiro (including Federal District)	371,936 (24.1%)	212,680 (13.8%)	60,701 (3.9%)	114,643 (7.4%)	73,476 (4.8%)	34,742 (2.3%)	108,541 (7.0%)	984,438
Argentina*	531,251 (24.07%)	847,237 (38.11%)	110,828 (5.02%)	294,140 (13.32%)	118,641 (5.38%)	92,482 (4.91%)	218,619 (9.91%)	2,213,198
Chile	548,469 (42.94%)	326,224 (25.54%)	70,114 (5.49%)	119,568 (9.36%)	38,355 (3.0%)	41,556 (3.26%)	132,923 (10.41%)	1,277,209

Source: Recenseamento do Brasil 1920, vol. vi, pt 5, pp. xviii-xix, xxx.† Note: São Paulo also had 11,637 people listed as living on rents (*rendas*) and Rio had 7,719 in the same category. *Note: As mentioned above, the Argentine figures greatly underestimate agricultural employment and exaggerate industrial employment, and the data given here excludes the over 800,000 laborers who moved between jobs in the city and the *campo*.

centre.[70] The overwhelming dominance of rural employment may have acted as an obstacle to workers' organization, for even in those states where industry was strongest, São Paulo and Rio de Janeiro (including the Federal District), agricultural workers were still the single most important group, accounting for 63.9% and 24.1% respectively of the work force (Table 6.7).

The weakness of labor in Brazil has also been attributed to the dominance of immigrants among the urban proletariat. Hall claims[71] that in São Paulo strong organization was made difficult because of fierce national rivalry among immigrant groups as well as conflict with Brazilian workers. Furthermore, he contends, contrary to accepted opinion, the majority of immigrants had no previous industrial experience nor had they been exposed to political or union affairs. Most were from rural areas in southern Europe, and had come to "make it in America" and then return home. They had little interest in militant collectivist endeavors which might jeopardize this goal. Maram also catalogues the various ways that the labor movement was compromised because of its immigrant base, including the nationalist xenophobic campaigns directed against it, and the wholesale deportation of union leaders and other "undesirable" militants under the Adolfo Gordo Law of 1907 and its more draconian 1913 version. However, Maram argues persuasively that these factors alone could not account for the problems which plagued Brazilian labor.[72] The Argentine working class was similarly dominated by immigrants, but was stronger, and in Brazil the movement was more vital in São Paulo and Santos with their large numbers of immigrants than in Rio de Janeiro where Brazilian-born workers were in the majority.

A somewhat more persuasive reason for the relative weakness of the labor movement is the particular structure of Brazilian industry, specifically the central role of cotton textiles, which because of the extent of its development made the country's manufacturing sector seem relatively advanced as compared to other Latin American countries.[73] In the prewar years more strikes occurred in the mills than anywhere else but almost all were unsuccessful, and not until late in the war was a stable union established. This failure was immensely significant because the textile workers composed by far the largest part of the country's factory proletariat.[74] A number of reasons have been offered for the failure of organization, including the extreme fluctuations in production, the relative physical isolation of the mills and the pervasiveness of paternalism, the use of force by both employers and the state, the unskilled and semiskilled nature of the work and therefore the ability easily to replace striking workers from the ample reserves of labor, and finally the high proportion of women and children in the labor force. In a 1911 survey of thirty-three São Paulo mills it was found that 72% of the workers were female and 30% of the entire work force was under sixteen years of age. The 1920 Census shows that these two groups accounted for over half those working in the textile industry. While women did take an active role in many strikes, their low wages and the all-round oppression they suffered within Brazilian society made it very difficult to withstand the considerable hardships entailed in striking and trying to organize and sustain a *sindicato*. However, with a few exceptions, most male workers in textiles as well as other occupations were faced with a similar lack of success. Maram writes,[75]

Labor's inability to organize the largest and most important manufacturing industry left it isolated and without significant power in Brazilian society before World War I. There is almost a direct correlation between organizational success in textiles and the strength of the labor movement. The inability to organize textiles was paralleled by the weakness of labor as a whole prior to 1917.

Maram goes on to argue that the relatively greater success of the Argentine workers was due, among other things, to there being more skilled and semiskilled workers and relatively fewer women in the labor force. However, this point cannot be taken too far. The strength of the Argentine movement should not be exaggerated. There were more strikes in Argentina and the unions were more numerous and tended to survive longer, but with rare exceptions, the workers' defeats far outnumbered their victories (Table 6.3). Secondly, while such groups as printers, bakers, or construction workers did go on strike with some frequency, the real muscle of the Argentine labor movement was in the railways and the docks, areas which were presumably as open to organization in Brazil. Finally, when in 1917 Brazilian workers began to confront their employers with renewed vigor it was the textile workers who were in the forefront of the battle. There was, therefore, nothing about the character of the industry itself which necessarily blocked the mobilization of labor.

In Brazil the dominant working-class ideology was anarcho-syndicalism. There were not the same divisions as witnessed in Argentina, for although there were competing movements they were never of major significance. A number of "labor parties" were set up immediately after the Republic was established, but these were essentially middle-class reformist efforts with little support from that class and virtually none from the workers.[76] They quickly disappeared. While somewhat more successful, the politically oriented, reformist strand of Socialism also seems to have had little impact in the prewar period. Contrasting this experience with the stronger showing of the Socialists in Argentina, Fausto argues[77] that the political system in Brazil was not as open or well-developed, that there was little need to placate the urban sector and that the weakness of Anarchism and the workers' movement made the moderating role of a reformist party unnecessary. There was occasionally a politician in the federal Congress, such as Lauro Müller, Nicanor Nascimento or Maurício de Lacerda, who spoke up for the workers, but although they were able to introduce some reforms, most importantly the creation of the Departmento Nacional do Trabalho in 1917, theirs were isolated voices.[78] There was an attempt by the government of Hermes da Fonseca (1910–14), during the time of the 1911–13 wave of strikes, to co-opt the workers when his son, Mário Hermes, and a fellow army lieutenant, organized a workers' congress in Rio in November 1912.[79] This proto-corporatist move failed, and the Anarchists, whose position among the workers it was meant to usurp, remained in effective control of organized labor. They did so because their battles to form unions, their call for direct action, and rejection of political solutions was immediately appealing to the disenfranchised and oppressed immigrant worker.[80] However, despite Anarchism itself being an "imported" ideology, these workers did not arrive in Brazil as Anarchists, "...it was the experience of working in Brazil which brought them to that philosophy."[81]

Anarchists were active in Brazil from the late 1890s, but it was not until 1906 and the First Workers' Congress that the anarcho-syndicalists assumed the leading role in the workers' movement. The first major union-led strike had been in Rio in 1902 against a shoe manufacturer and a year later there was a general strike in the capital followed by the formation of the syndicalist-inspired Federação das Classes Operárias.[82] From that time to about 1908 there were an increasing number of unions formed and strikes held. Among the latter were a major dock strike in Santos in 1904 which was supported by groups in Rio and São Paulo, two strikes against the Rio docks in 1906 and 1907 and a widespread general strike for the eight-hour day in São Paulo, also in 1907. A year later the Confederação Operária Brasileira was formed. The power of organized labor seemed to be building, but the gains were for the most part only temporary. Although many

sindicatos were set up as a result of the surge of militant action most of
them were extremely weak and tended to fold when a strike was
defeated, as the majority were in these years. With the onset of
unfavorable economic conditions in 1908 and continued savage
repression by the authorities, including the deportation of many labor
leaders, the movement went into decline until 1911. For the next two
years there was a brief resurgence of strike activity, and, according to
Maram,[83] it was during this period that a high point in union
membership of 60,000 was reached. But once again the state moved in
to crush the strikes, there were mass arrests, and deportations were
stepped up under a more stringent Adolpho Gordo Law rushed
through in 1912–13. When the war broke out a year later the
organized working class in Brazil was severely debilitated and
demoralized. Not until 1917, also a fateful year in Argentina, was
there to be a recovery.

II

The initial impact of the war upon the Brazilian workers and their
response to it was remarkably similar to that of their Argentine
comrades.[84] Food leaped up in price and tens of thousands were
thrown out of work. The authorities, quite reasonably, feared mass
unrest, but except for a few scattered incidents, there was little trouble.
The workers were simply in no position to stage any effective
resistance for the Brazilian movement was generally quite fragile, and
had recently suffered a major setback. Also, as was the case in
Argentina, it proved extremely difficult for labor to resist the wage
reductions or fight against the higher prices because high levels of
unemployment made mobilization almost impossible, at least before
1917. There were only five strikes in the city of São Paulo between
1914 and 1916,[85] and but two stoppages in Rio in 1915.[86] It is hard to
say exactly what role unemployment played in maintaining this quite
remarkable degree of worker passivity for there are no figures, but at
least in São Paulo, unemployment remained a serious problem well
into 1917.[87]

The main difficulty facing the workers, and the reason most
frequently cited for their eventual uprising, was the rapid increase in
the cost of living coupled with falling real wages—a situation similar to
that found in Argentina, and for that matter throughout the continent.
Food prices rose steadily until 1918, while industrial and rural money
wages fell precipitously in 1915 and did not regain their 1914 level until
after the war (Table 6.8). The cost of living apparently increased by

Table 6.8 *Brazil: indices of food prices, cost of living, wages, and real wages 1914–1919*

	A	B	C	D	E	F	G	H	I
	Food prices	Cost of living (Min. Fazenda)	Industrial wages	Rural wages	Railway wages	Real wages [Industrial]	Cost of living (Simonsen)	General wages (Simonsen)	Real wages [General]
			(1914 = 100)					(1915 = 100)	
1914	100	100	100	100	100	100	—	—	—
1915	117	109	75	95	101	69	100	100	100
1916	119	117	86	97	101	74	107	101	94
1917	132	128	86	94	104	67	118	107	91
1918	148	144	130	102	122	90	132	117	89
1919	146	149	160	107	119	107	137	123	90

Sources: Columns A, C, D, E—Cano, *Raízes*, p. 171. Columns G & H, Dulles, *Anarchists and Communists*, pp. 539–40. Column B, Dean, *Industrialization*, p. 92.

49% between 1914 and 1919. However, this index, devised by the Ministério da Fazenda, (Simonsen's is derived from it) is unreliable because it does not include key imports such as wheat, wheat flour, salted cod, and kerosene. Further, because of the social unrest of the period, the figures may have been deliberately understated.[88] Simonsen's wage index may be similarly suspect. Finally, because 1914 is used as a base year there is the same downward bias imposed on the price rises as noted in the Argentine case.

The rise in prices was not a novel phenomenon for Brazil. Throughout most of the nineteenth century the country had suffered from chronic inflation, albeit with substantial periods of remission. According to Leff,[89] this was brought about by a combination of the government's monetary policies and price inelasticity of aggregate supply, particularly the backwardness of domestic agriculture. He concludes from this that, "... the causes of Brazil's inflation during the nineteenth century must in general be sought internally rather than in the country's external sector." This analysis does not seem to be applicable to the war period, which compared to the preceding years saw a very much higher level of inflation, at least with respect to food prices (Tables 6.8 and 6.9). Also, the worldwide nature of price rises points to the importance of external pressures. Contemporaries argued that there were a number of causes for higher prices; inflationary government fiscal and monetary policies, dearer imports, speculation by local merchants, and increased exports of food goods to meet

Table 6.9 *Index of food prices in Rio 1900–1920*

	(1914 = 100)
1900	117
1901	96
1902	89
1903	91
1904	96
1905	86
1906	105
1907	100
1908	102
1909	97
1910	90
1911	100
1912	108
1913	106
1914	100
1915	142
1916	150
1917	182
1918	217
1919	285
1920	304

Source: Recalculated from Eulália Maria Lahmeyer Lobo, et al., "Evolução dos preços e do padrão de vida on Rio de Janeiro, 120–1930—resultados preliminares," *Revista Brasileira de Economia*, vol. 25 no. 4, Oct.—Dec., 1971, pp. 260–3. *Note:* these figures were originally 1820 = 100 and are constructed using 1919 weighting. They are made up of nine commodities, sugar, rice, salt cod, coffee, jerked beef, wheat flour, manioc flour, beans, and butter. The extremely high figures in 1919 and 1920 may be due to the fact that they were constructed using the prices of only three commodities.

greater Allied demand.[90] The first may have been important, but food prices rose almost as rapidly in Argentina, and the cost of living to a greater extent and here government financial policy was extremely conservative. Wileman, who continually railed against the effect he believed that the excessive issue of paper money was having on domestic prices and exchange, admitted that the link between the two phenomena during the war years was far from clear. He wrote,[91] "Since the outbreak of war in 1914, prices and the cost of living have,

Table 6.10 *Brazil: import (−) and export of selected foodstuffs*
1911–1918

| | (Tons) | | | |
	Rice	Beans	Potatoes	Maize
1911	− 16,400	− 8,058	− 17,846	− 3,798
1912	− 10,189	− 9,388	− 28,971	− 6,262
1913	− 7,728	− 8,540	− 29,800	− 8,892
1914	− 6,532	− 5,310	− 18,970	− 1,119
1915	− 6,945	1,042	− 8,757	− 2,066
1916	410	44,599	− 4,526	3,551
1917	44,603	93,402	4,401	23,867
1918	27,914	70,883	4,766	12,976

Source: Villela and Suzigan, *Government Policy*, p. 106.

all the world over, risen incessantly, even in countries like Uruguay, where credit has not been abused and there has been no material increase in the amount of money available."

It has been argued in chapter 4 that domestic fiscal and monetary policies probably exacerbated the increase in prices, but the evidence presented above strongly suggests that on balance it was external factors such as shipping restrictions and the demand from the Allies which were of greater relative importance in accounting for the rising cost of living. For imports this was clearly the case. Brazil's depreciating exchange made things that much more difficult. With respect to Leff's argument about price inelasticity of supply in domestic agriculture, this does not seem to have applied during the war, when exports of food crops increased at an unprecedented rate (Table 6.10). Dean maintains that in the state of São Paulo higher levels of exports meant less for the home market and thereby stimulated higher prices.[92] This point has been disputed by Villela and Suzigan and by Cano,[93] who contend that the increase in food goods was sufficient both to meet domestic requirements and leave an increasing surplus for export. However, there are no reliable figures for agricultural output before 1920, and although some of the data given by Cano[94] does indicate that increases in production of a few crops in São Paulo may have been great enough to supply both the domestic market and export demand, the evidence is not sufficient to overturn the argument made by almost all observers at the time that the export of foodstuffs was a major factor contributing to the high prices which were causing such severe problems for Brazilian consumers.

The federal government was extremely slow to respond to the problem. It was only after the strikes of 1917 that thought began to be given to some form of control. But it was in the state of Rio Grande do Sul that the first measures were taken. After the strikes in Porto Alegre in mid-1917, the president of the state, Borges de Medeiros, issued decrees controlling exports, and when the unrest continued a further decree to regulate prices was made.[95] In November, the mayor of Rio de Janeiro was considering a system of controlled sale and fixed prices,[96] but it was not until the following year that a Commissioner of Public Food Administration for Rio was finally established. An inventory of the stocks of food and other basic goods was ordered and this was followed by decrees fixing the maximum price for a great number of commodities, including coal, candles, flour, beans, rice, sugar, kerosene, dried meat, etc.[97] In September, similar controls, together with the power to control exports of certain commodities, were set up throughout the country.[98] The reasons for these moves were clearly spelled out in the preamble to the decree for the Federal District, which stated that "...the increasing cost of articles of prime necessity aggravates the position of the working classes and gives rise to dangerous perturbations of order...this has already given rise to disturbances that it is the duty of the Government to put a stop to by utilizing the powers conferred upon it."[99]

It is not clear to what extent these measures reduced price rises. Most food exports fell in 1918, but this may have been because of bad harvests. Except for the Rio index, there was a slight fall in food prices between 1918 and 1919, and the cost of living also showed only a very modest increase. It is impossible to gauge the role of the regulations in this, but Wileman strongly believed that they had achieved a degree of success and were vital to maintain social harmony. When *O Paiz* welcomed the news that Congress was considering the abolition of controls, he wrote,[100] "This is a peaceful community, but there is one thing they can't stand for long, that is the hunger that speculators would condemn this population to if advisers like "O Paiz" had their way!" Congress, under pressure from agrarian interests who complained their business was being adversely affected, did pass a law ending the regulations, but this was vetoed by the Vice President. According to the British Minister in Brazil, no advocate of government intervention, the Vice President was correct in recognizing the beneficial impact that the controls had had. He had also taken the advice of Rio's chief of police "...that if Food Control was abolished the laboring classes would certainly become disaffected, and in view of the tumult in Argentina which displays features of anarchy which are attributed to the spread of Bolshevism, he felt that this warning could not be disregarded."[101]

As significant as higher prices were in contributing to the mounting wave of unrest it would be a mistake to equate strikes with rising prices in a mechanical, one to one fashion, as Dulles does. Rising prices were of undoubted importance, but in themselves cannot bear the entire weight of explanation for the wave of strikes between 1917 and 1920. Fausto points out[102] that the workers had to put up with high rates of inflation between 1922 and 1925, and there was no uprising. Furthermore, it seems that by 1919, when the most serious outbreaks took place, price rises had moderated somewhat and both money and real wages were increasing.

While control may have slowed price rises, it did little to stifle working-class unrest. 1919 was a year of exceptional, unprecedented militancy, especially in São Paulo. But, purposeful resistance had begun two years before.[103] Activists had been trying to mobilize workers, and they finally began to have some success when, in March, daily meetings were held in the working-class districts of Rio de Janeiro to protest against the high cost of living. Union organization also began to recover as industry, especially cotton textiles, picked up. It was in these factories that major strikes erupted in both São Paulo and Rio in May. These were swiftly crushed by the police. At the beginning of June the workers struck for higher wages and improved conditions at Cotonifício Crespi's cotton mill in São Paulo. By the end of the month the strike had spread to other factories and soon to other industries as well, with workers striking both for improved wages and in solidarity with Crespi's workers who had been fired and/or arrested. A coordinating committee, the Comitê da Defesa Proletária was established and a comprehensive list of demands drawn up. As had happened during the *Semana trágica* in Argentina, it was the shooting of a worker which transformed a strike into a vociferous mass protest. On 9 July, a young Anarchist shoemaker, Antônio Martinez, was shot by police in front of the Mariangela textile works. After his funeral, attended by thousands, there was widespread rioting and eventually 7,000 troops had to be brought into the city. While force was used, the general strike was brought to an end when some of the most important employers, under some pressure from the state government, agreed to a 20% wage raise as well as a number of other demands made by the

Comitê. Although the workers were not completely successful, nonetheless they had achieved a considerable victory.

Similarly adverse conditions and the important example given by the São Paulo workers (detailed coverage was given in the regional press) sparked off strikes throughout the country. There was a general strike in Rio de Janeiro which eventually involved 50–60,000 workers and resulted in some workers gaining a small raise in wages and others a reduction in hours. Less comprehensive strikes took place in the states of Minas Gerais, Paraná, Bahia, Pernambuco, Santa Catarina, and Rio Grande to Sul.[104] In Porto Alegre, in the state of Rio Grande do Sul, strikes began at the end of July on the railway and by August a general strike was in progress.[105] Force was used, particularly against the railwaymen, but this was uncharacteristic of the state government's handling of the unrest. To bring the strike to an end an extremely conciliatory line was taken by the authorities, who issued decrees to control prices and the export of basic consumption goods and forced local firms to grant a 25% wage increase and the eight-hour day. Bodea argues that this policy was in line with the brand of corporatist positivism advocated by Júlio de Castilhos, and was the first instance of the type of "gaucho populism" which was to be effected country-wide after 1930 by Getúlio Vargas. The reason why it was first implemented here he ascribes to the particular complex of social forces which allowed a dissident sector of the oligarchy to join with the urban and industrial interests and together co-opt the working class in an alliance against the local agrarian elite. The course of events in Rio Grande do Sul is important in showing the immense socio-economic diversity within Brazil. Even in Rio and São Paulo, the working class exhibited distinctive characteristics and reactions.[106] This all points to the limitations of country-wide generalizations about either the working class or the structure of class relations within Brazil.

Despite the concessions made and the force used, strikes continued. In São Paulo the government adopted increasingly repressive measures against strikers and unions. These were directed particularly at the Anarchists, many of whom were arrested and deported. This was in line with the widely held belief here, as throughout Latin America, that the explosion of working-class discontent was being "artificially" fomented by "foreign agitators." With Brazil's declaration of war on Germany in October, state of siege powers were given to the President and these were used to stamp out the expanding labor movement.[107] The government had some success in São Paulo (Table 6.11), but in Rio the workers continued to put up active resistance in 1918. A strike

Table 6.11 *Brazil: number of strikes 1917–1920*

	São Paulo (city)	São Paulo (interior)	Rio de Janeiro
1917	7	4	12
1918	1	2	27
1919	64	14	17
1920	37	12	7

Source: Fausto, *Trabalho urbano*, pp. 162–3.

of textile workers in November was defeated because they chose the wrong moment. Employers were able to withstand the stoppage because of a slump in demand and swollen inventories, while the government, linking an armed Anarchist uprising with the strike, was able to take extremely harsh measures against the workers.

The strikes in 1919–20 marked both the apogee and defeat of the early Brazilian labor movement. The Russian Revolution and the uprisings in Europe were of special importance during these years for the Brazilian workers. The events were followed in great detail in the workers' press and provided a stimulating example as well as helping to create a feeling of optimism in the possibility of a workers' revolution.[108] Even in 1918 the impact was being felt. "The celebrations of May Day in that year in Rio de Janeiro differed from two years before. The workers celebrated the triumph of their brothers in Russia. Turning a day of protest into a celebration of solidarity and fraternity with the first workers' republic.[109] Similar sentiments were loudly expressed on 1 May 1919.

Fausto puts great stress on this factor.[110] While in no way undervaluing the importance of local conditions and the historical evolution of the movement, he claims that it was the international dimension of class conflict which not only accounted in large part for the tenor and timing of Brazilian events, but also helps to explain the fact that the workers' struggle was intensified at almost the same time in such diverse countries as Brazil, Bolivia and Argentina.

After mass parades during May Day celebrations in 1919, 20,000 factory workers in São Paulo came out on strike. This time police repression was particularly brutal, but still the workers were able to gain some concessions, including wage increases for streetcar workers and the eight-hour day for most textile factories. In the following

Table 6.12 *Brazil: reasons for strikes 1917–1920*

Wages	Conditions	Strikes over: Solidarity	Union recognition	Hours	Other
		São Paulo (city)			
55	37	23	14	12	9
		São Paulo (interior)			
18	7	6	5	6	4
		Rio de Janeiro			
27	13	9	13	15	7

Source: Fausto, *Trabalho urbano*, pp. 170–2.

month a major stoppage began at mills throughout the state of Rio de Janeiro. The employers were intractable and the police used every means to smash the union. By the end of June the workers had been defeated, and although strikes continued in all parts of the country[111] this was the beginning of a major rollback in labor's wartime gains.

The working class was not only under constant threat from the authorities but also from the press and mobs of middle-class students and vigilantes. As had happened in Argentina, xenophobic nationalism was worked up to fever pitch during the war and directed against immigrants, Anarchist-led trade unions or any sign of social disaffection. The press was full of blood-curdling stories of diabolical Maximalist plots and most papers fully supported the government's use of force against strikers. Such groups as the Liga da Defesa Nacional or Ação Social Nacionalista, established during the war, were very similar in aims and tactics to the Argentine Liga Patriótica. These organizations could trace their intellectual origins back to the nineteenth century, but all were born out of the intense socio-economic crisis and the violent explosion of class struggle which characterized the war years. These mainly middle-class organizations represented more than simply a reaction to working-class unrest. They signaled the emergence of a more complex configuration of class forces within Argentine and Brazilian societies.

The official and unofficial repression of the workers' movement marked not so much a change in attitude, as one of tactics. It had been thought that through modest concessions and reforms it would be possible to placate the workers and separate them from the Anarchists. It did not work. But official reforms were never pursued with any real conviction. Direct repression proved far easier and, as it was more familiar to them, also more popular for the ruling class. Most importantly it was consistent with their deeply held conviction that the unrest was due mainly to the machinations of labor agitators. Once these people had been removed social harmony would be restored. Just as the Russian Revolution gave hope to the workers, it provided a justification for the authorities to see the strikes as part of a sinister Bolshevik plot and, therefore, use force to suppress them. Washington Luís summed up the attitude of both the elite and much of the urban middle class when in 1920 he commented,[112] "...the labor question is a question which is more a matter of public order than social order, it represents the state of mind of a few workers, but not the state of society."

In 1920 textile factory owners in São Paulo defeated a strike over the collection of union dues and at the end of the year reintroduced the nine- and ten-hour day. Almost every strike was now being either directly suppressed by armed force or scab labour were given full protection to break strikes. Union offices were raided by the police and a great many key leaders were deported. Maram writes that "...by 1920 the general strike had become a weapon of the police, for it exposed labor's flanks and allowed the state to effect further massive arrests and deportations, thereby intimidating the rank and file and eliminating layer after layer of the leadership cadre, until finally the movement was crushed."[113]

The final defeat of the workers is relatively easy to explain. Although they put up a spirited fight, neither they nor their organizations were strong enough to withstand the combined assault from the employers and the state. Furthermore, the lack of national political parties and the country's extreme federalism seem to have made the Brazilian state less vulnerable to pressure from either the workers or the urban middle class than it proved to be elsewhere. The state was not, however, immune. In 1919 Rui Barbosa launched an unsuccessful presidential campaign (his second) against the oligarchy's candidate Epitácio Pessoa, in which he tried to appeal to the many sectors of the disaffected urban population. Stronger challenges to the oligarchic state were to be mounted in the 1920s following the *tenente* revolt in Rio de Janeiro in 1922.[114]

Explaining why the years 1917–20 should have seen such an upsurge in labor militancy is more difficult. Rising prices and falling real wages provide only part of the answer. Judging from the workers' press and the speeches made at rallies, the October Revolution was of major importance in creating the feeling that the time was ripe for proletarian risings. But this feeling could not function in a vacuum. The working class, or at least key sectors of it, had to have developed a sufficient degree of consciousness and organization to be able to respond. This had happened to some extent in the prewar years, but at the outbreak of war the movement was at an extremely low ebb. Maram argues that during the war this changed because the attitude of many immigrant workers changed. "By now the cherished dream of social mobility and return to the homeland in wealth had been shattered by long years of struggle on barely subsistence wages. Many came to accept Brazil as their permanent home, and racked by inflation, pragmatically viewed their labor involvement as necessary for their survival in much the same way they had pragmatically eschewed the trade unions previously."[115] In short, while external factors, both material and ideological, were important in accounting for the timing and something of the character of the wartime working-class revolt, it was the workers' experience and expectations as well as the particular socio-political culture of the country which gave form and content to the class conflict in Brazil.

Chile

I

The working class in Chile shared a number of features common to working-class movements throughout Latin America. However, in the years after the First World War, the Chilean labor movement came to differ markedly from those in the other three countries under review. In Chile the movement became more independent, self-directing, and less susceptible to attempt by the state to integrate into the existing political framework, unlike its counterparts in Brazil and Argentina.[116] Furthermore, it manifested a distinct unwillingness to subordinate itself to the populist blandishments of largely self-appointed leaders such as happened with Billinghurst and Leguía in Peru and was to happen later under Vargas and Perón. The reasons for these important differences must be sought in the particular characteristics of capitalist development in Chile, the origins and composition of the working class, and the way in which the elite comprehended and attempted to deal with the growth of organized labor.

It was primarily during the years of rapid nitrate-led economic growth from the 1880s that the modern Chilean working class began to be formed. The expansion of nitrate production in the north and of industry in the centre of the country drew workers in from rural areas to swell the populations of the cities, especially Santiago, Valparaíso and Concepción, as well as the nitrate provinces of Tarapacá and Antofagasta. For example, in 1885 the latter increased their population from 45,086 and 21,213 respectively, and to 110,036 and 113,323 by 1907.[117] The number of people residing in the capital increased from 150,000 in 1875 to 333,000 in 1907, by which time 10.3% of the country's total population lived there. Over the same period the proportion of the population living in centres of 20,000 or more (excluding Santiago) rose from 6.9% to 11.9%.[118] The more generous definition of "urban" used by Hurtado (Table 6.13), gives Chile an even more urban cast. It was in the large cities and the northern nitrate *oficinas* that the organized working class started to make its presence felt.

Unlike Brazil or Argentina, immigration played a very minor role in the growth of the Chilean proletariat. In 1907, only 4.1% of the population was foreign-born, compared to Argentina's 30% seven years later.[119] Furthermore, whereas in Brazil immigrants accounted for a similarly small proportion of the total population as in Chile, absolute numbers were far greater and their concentration in the south east, especially in the city of São Paulo made them a dominant force in the labor movement. In Chile, on the other hand, there were relatively few immigrant workers in the principal cities, and only 3.8% of industrial labor force were foreign-born. Immigrants were more important in the nitrate fields. Peruvian and Bolivian workers made up about 40% of the work force in Tarapacá and 15.7% in Antofagasta in 1907. However, they were essentially temporary migrants, the first to leave for home when the industry went into one of its frequent slumps. It is interesting to note that despite their small numbers, and the fact that labor leaders were Chileans, whenever there were major incidents of social unrest, foreign agitators were still blamed for stirring up discontent. All this is not to say the immigrants did not have a powerful impact on Chilean society, but this was mainly as entrepreneurs not as workers. For example, in 1914 immigrants owned over 30% of the country's commercial establishments and about 50% of the industrial firms.

Table 6.13 *Distribution and growth of Chilean population according to rural and urban residence (2,000 or more people), 1875–1920*

	Rural population			Urban population			Total population	
	Number (000)	% of total population	Growth rate	Number (000)	% of total population	Growth rate	Number (000)	Growth rate
1875	1,536	74.0	0.8	540	26.0	3.1	2,076	1.4
1885	1,790	71.4	1.5	717	28.6	2.9	2,507	1.9
1895	1,774	65.8	0	922	34.2	2.6	2,696	0.7
1907	2,009	62.2	1.1	1,222	37.8	2.4	3,321	1.5
1920	2,132	57.2	0.5	1,598	42.8	2.1	3,730	1.2

Source: C. Hurtado, *Concentración de población y desarrollo económico—el caso chileno*, Santiago, 1966, tables 2, 3 and 8. Reproduced in Kirsch, *Modernization*, p. 8.

More than 30% of the employed population were in transport and industry by 1920 (Table 6.7). These figures are, however, somewhat misleading. Mining is not listed separately, and in 1920 there were more than 23,000 nitrate workers as well as 30,000 miners in other areas.[120] Also, as in Argentina, the industrial category is swollen by the inclusion of such essentially non-industrial occupations as dressmakers (63,301), launderers (45,215), carpenters (34,589) and masons (14,720). While the figures for industrial employment, which in any case refer to the postwar period, must be treated carefully, it is clear that from the latter decades of the nineteenth century there had been a substantial increase in rural migration to urban areas and the mining regions and consequently a rise in employment in transport, mining, and manufacturing industry. It was out of these key economic sectors that organized labor erupted forcefully onto the national scene.

Most studies of the formation of the Chilean working class have tended to ascribe to the nitrate workers the vanguard role in the formation of a militant, politically conscious labor movement.[121] This view has, however, been strongly challenged by De Shazo who argues that, "... urban workers, especially those of Santiago and Valparaíso, were the driving force of the organized labor movement in early twentieth century Chile, ... the role of the nitrate miners was small by comparison."[122] A full assessment of this important debate is beyond the scope of this work. It is sufficient to note that whatever their relative strengths, the workers in the northern desert and the industrial and transport workers of the major cities, were the main components of organized labor in Chile.

The dualism mentioned above was to be reflected in the differing organizational forms adopted by Chilean workers. But, the country's first labor organizations, the mutual benefit societies (*socorros mutuos*), grew out of the artisan-dominated nature of industry in the years before the War of the Pacific. These societies did not seek to effect any social or political change, rather they worked within the existing framework in order to provide a basic degree of social security. The first society was established in printing in the early 1850s. By 1902, there were 168 legally recognized societies, generally craft-based, throughout the country with about 20,000 members.[123] As in other Latin American countries, artisans played a leading role in the early development of organized labor and, as elsewhere, their subsequent decline reflected the growth of more large-scale capitalist enterprise and the new relations of production which this brought. It is important to note, however, that throughout the years under consideration these groups represented more workers than any other working-class organizations, at times they did take part in strikes, and they continued to play an important role until the 1930s. Furthermore, the first union federation, the Gran Federación Obrera de Chile, (FOCh), formed in 1909, acted very much as a mutual society, eschewing strike action and adopting a legalistic approach to labor relations.[124] But, despite their greater numbers, the mutual societies had far less impact on the political formation of the Chilean working class than other more militant groups.

One of the most important of these groups, the *mancomunales* (brotherhoods) were established in the nitrate provinces. Whereas the early mutual benefit societies, with their emphasis on welfare provision, corresponded to the generally individualistic concerns of Chile's artisans, the new *mancomunales*, which agitated over wages and conditions, were indicative of the greater community of interest developed by workers thrown together in the northern deserts. The *mancomunales* generally sought to unite all workers in a particular area. The first was established in Iquique in 1900, and four years later the Primera Convención Mancomunal de Chile was held in the city, representing fifteen societies and 20,000 workers.[125] Subsequently similar organizations were set up in most other parts of the country. Their road was far from smooth, however. As Alan Bangell observes,[126] "... they were weak and constantly subject to harassment by state and employer, which made their existence temporary and dangerous, but because they represented the demands of the labor force they were constantly reappearing." This was less true after the savage repression of the Iquique workers in 1907, but there were other more activist organizations through which the struggle was continued.

These were the resistance societies, which in their espousal of strike action were far more militant than the *mancomunales*. They were strongly influenced by Anarchism, a growing force in Chile from the 1890s. In contrast to the Anarchist movements in Argentina or Brazil, the leaders and rank and file were Chilean, a reflection of the low level of immigration from Southern Europe. De Shazo argues,[127] that this tended to strengthen the movement in Chile as the elite was unable to use the issue of nationality to divide the workers, as they tried to do in Brazil and Argentina. This did not, however, prevent virulent xenophobic reactions to most major outbreaks of social unrest, and in 1918 the passage of a Residence Law similar to those used against "undesirables" in Argentina and Brazil.[128]

The first resistance society was established in 1898 among metal-workers in the state railway yards of Santiago. By 1930, tram workers, printers and bakers in the capital and metalworkers and merchant seamen in Valparaíso had formed their own societies. The movement was decimated in the wave of repression following the strikes and unrest of 1907, but from 1909 to the outbreak of war there was significant rebuilding of organizations in Santiago and Valparaíso.[129] During the first decade of the twentieth century the resistance societies were in the vanguard of working-class unrest, and on many occasions were able to extract significant concessions from employers.

Most of the working-class organizations mentioned above were forged in the bitter clashes between labor and capital which broke out with increasing ferocity from 1890. In that year the country was engulfed in a wave of over 300 separate disputes, in some areas amounting to general strikes.[130] They seem to have been more or less spontaneous, beginning in the nitrate fields and eventually spreading as far south as Valparaíso.[131] The unrest was settled by the use of troops, a pattern which was to become all too familiar. The period of most intense conflict before the First World War was between 1902 and 1908 when eighty-four strikes were recorded. Interestingly, of the sixty-nine strikes for which an outcome is known, 81.1% were settled through conci-liation or arbitration.[132] There were, however, some which ended rather less amicably. For example, the maritime strike in Valparaíso in 1903 ended in riot and arson, with at least 100 workers being killed and several hundred more wounded by police and troops.[133] Two years later 300 people died in Santiago during riots over high food prices, particularly of meat.[134] In 1906, forty-eight striking workers were gunned down in the central plaza in Antofagasta. But the worst massacre happened a year later in Iquique, during a strike of 20,000 nitrate workers when at least 1,000 men, women, and children were murdered in the grounds of the Escuela Santa María by troops with machine guns. This type of extreme repression and the economic crisis of the same year, brought the first stage of labor agitation to a close. From about 1909 there was a recovery in labor organization and strike action, especially in Santiago and Valparaíso. Between 1911 and 1913 there were forty-five strikes involving over 25,000 workers,[135] the most significant of which was the general strike in Valparaíso in 1913 in which more than twenty unions and 10,000 workers took part.[136]

It was not only through strikes and labor organization that the Chilean workers were making their presence felt before the First World War. There was also an important political dimension to their struggle. The Partido Democrático, established in 1887, was a populist party with an artisan and *petit bourgeois* base. It was essentially a liberal reformist party, although it did champion the workers' cause and attracted their votes. Also, for some time it maintained close relations with European Socialist parties and was a corresponding member of the Socialist International.[137] The party's general position was similar to the mutualist societies, and this proved too passive for some of its more militant members who, lead by Luis Emilio Recabarren, broke away in 1912 to form the Partido Obrero Socialista in Iquique.[138] The new party did not hold its first national congress until 1915, and it was only from this time that it began to have any impact on the workers' movement. In short, before the war the direct political participation of the Chilean workers was minimal, somewhat greater than in Brazil, but considerably less than in Argentina.

From about the mid-1880s onwards the growth of the organised working class and the perceived threat their increasing militancy posed to the status quo of Chilean society became a persistent cause for concern on the part of the ruling elite. On many occasions Congress debated the so-called "Social Question."[139] Because inflation was seen to play such a major role in formenting unrest, tariff and monetary policies were also frequently discussed with regard to their impact on the workers.[140] As was the case in the rest of Latin America, this all reflected a growing preoccupation with the social consequences of capitalist development. This was not the analysis favoured by the Chilean elite. In common with their compatriots elsewhere, they tended to see social unrest as the result of "their" workers being misled by subversive agitators, both domestic and foreign.[141] Intermittent repression, therefore, became a principal means of maintaining order. There were some reforms, but these played only an extremely marginal role.

By the First World War the Chilean working class had evolved into a particularly combative force. In terms of organization, militancy, and class consciousness, Chile's workers compared favorably with those in other Latin American countries. Only in Argentina could the organized working class claim to represent a more potent force. Despite a number of bloody setbacks and the ideological and organizational divisions common to labor movements throughout the region, the working class in Chile had mounted a severe challenge to the authority of the ruling elite. This challenge was significantly strengthened during the war and immediate postwar years.

II

Reviewing the effects of the First World War, the *South Pacific Mail* noted that,[142]

There can be no doubt that the World War has profoundly modified conditions in Chile as in every other country of the world. Attempt to conceal it as we may, class distinctions based on wealth and poverty have become accentuated, and the enormous increase in the cost of living has weakened the middle class and laid a heavy burden on the masses. Industrial unrest has permeated the country and labor has become, for the first time in Chile, conscious of its organized power.

These observations were fully justified. In the latter part of the war and the years immediately afterwards, the Chilean working class, together with a frustrated and disaffected middle class, demonstrated as never before its ability to play a decisive role on the nation's political stage. The war proved to be a watershed in the development of organized labor in Chile. It was out of this period that the labor movement emerged with the consciousness, political ideas, and organizations which were to define the character of working-class politics in the country for many years to come.

However, the war years should not be seen simply as a period during which the mettle of organized labor was tested. In many respects these were troubled times for workers and their families. In common with their counterparts in Argentina, Brazil and Peru, they were forced to endure a steady deterioration in their living standards

Table 6.14 *Cost of living in Chile and Santiago 1913–1921*

	1913	1914	1915	1916	1917	1918	1919	1920	1921
Chile									
Light and fuel	100	106	108	106	101	108	128	151	174
Food (local)	100	116	128	109	112	110	132	165	151
Food (imported)	100	112	136	144	141	151	238	256	230
Drink	100	100	100	106	110	110	110	127	136
Clothing	100	102	128	140	147	155	177	207	208
Transport	100	101	111	109	107	106	110	112	126
Average	100	108	120	117	118	121	143	168	169
Santiago*									
(weighted average)	100	115	135	115	130	129	152	195	180

Sources: *Sinopsis estadística 1924*, p. 117; De Shazo, *Urban Workers*, p. 61.
*These figures may not be exact as they had to be read off a graph.

through severe bouts of unemployment, falling money wages, and largely persistent inflation. That they came through all this to shake the foundations of elite rule in Chile was a reflection both of the significance of wartime developments and of the progress in organization and consciousness which had been made up to 1914.

Because of the heavy concentration of workers in the northern desert where there was no work except that related to nitrate production, the outbreak of war and the virtual suspension of exports had a devastating effect on labor here. Hardship was not confined to the North, for when nitrates slumped so did the entire Chilean economy. In Santiago and Valparaíso it is estimated that in the last months of 1914, unemployment reached 44% and 35% respectively.[143] Conditions were made significantly more difficult for all workers by the forced exodus of thousands of nitrate miners and their families to the centre and south seeking jobs. Not only did unemployment reach staggering levels, but the cost of living also increased sharply (Table 6.14). The final blow was delivered when many employers, judging correctly that those in work would want to protect their jobs at all costs, cut money wages. In 1914 and 1915 wages were reduced by between 10% and 30% in the two largest cities, and there was little if any tendency for wages to rise before 1917, in some cases not until the following year.[144] This roughly parallels the movement of wages in Argentina and Brazil.

All the aforementioned setbacks evoked a relatively muted response from Chilean workers, who had seemed to be such fire-eaters just before the war. The reasons for this behavior are not hard to find. It has been noted that in Argentina, the working class, despite the impressive political and union strength which it had developed, could be reduced to complete impotence by a major economic crisis. This clearly happened in Chile, where the militancy of labor seems to have been quashed at a stroke. Much of this was due to the workers' lack of financial reserves, the organizational weakness of the resistance societies, but most importantly to the effects of mass unemployment, which historically has tended to deprive workers in any economy of the ability to engage in effective collective action. There were only fifteen strikes recorded in 1914 and 1915, as opposed to fifty-three in the proceeding two years.[145]

Nonetheless, Chilean workers were not completely quiescent. For example, Anarchists organized rallies in Santiago to protest about unemployment in August, and two months later they were the guiding force behind demonstrations demanding rent reductions both here and in Valparaíso.[146] At the beginning of November there were almost daily protests of unemployed workers in the capital, and in December there were days of serious rioting in Valparaíso over increased tram fares. Trouble flared here again the following February.[147] But as serious as some of these outbreaks were, they remained isolated incidents, and the organized working class seems to have remained largely demoralized.

It was not until an upturn in demand for Chilean exports, especially nitrates, that that balance of forces between labor and capital began to show signs of change. Reviewing the events of 1916, *The South Pacific Mail* observed that, "The new conditions, of course, have not been brought about without a few little flaws showing in the fabric of state. An epidemic of strikes that spread along the coast was a distressing factor showing the weakness of certain parts under the strain of extra work."[148] With industry returning to full production, demand for labor picked up and because of this the working class began to regain its confidence and its taste for struggle. The number of strikes increased in 1916 and in the next five years workers' militancy reached unprecedented levels (Table 6.16).

A major factor underlying this was the increased cost of living, a problem common throughout the continent and the world during the war years. Inflation was also a long-standing and bitter political issue in Chile, having been directly responsible for, among other incidents of social unrest, Santiago's bloody *Semana roja* in 1905. The wartime inflationary trend is shown in Table 6.14, although because it is an unweighted average it probably understates the hardship experienced by the working class who spent most of their money on food. Also there is no provision in the index for rent. De Shazo's figures for the cost of living in Santiago, which show a somewhat greater degree of inflation, are weighted, and because of this, inspire more confidence than the official returns.

Most contemporary critics argued that high food prices, which were the principal focus for protest, were caused by the export of foodstuffs, especially the important Chilean staples of wheat and beans, to meet increased Allied demand.[149] A similar complaint was heard in all four countries under review, but in the Chilean case there are strong grounds for doubting these claims. In the first place, the output of most key foodstuffs increased during the war. Although the production of wheat fell in 1914 from the extraordinary heights reached during the bumper harvests of 1912 and 1913, production remained reasonably adequate and by 1917 had virtually returned to prewar levels.[150] In that year the United States government reported that Chile had an extremely large grain surplus, and exports rose.[151] Secondly, exports fell to extremely low levels in 1914 and 1915, recovered from 1916 and dropped sharply again in 1919 and 1920.[152] Except for 1917, when both exports and prices increased, at least in Santiago, the two variables seem generally to have moved in opposite directions.

Given that there were good harvests throughout the war, it is somewhat difficult to account for the apparent inverse correlation between prices and exports. One answer could be that even if the quantity of exports did not rise, the world price may still have helped to push up domestic prices and if these reached a sufficient level there would have been no need to export. Without much more detailed research this can be no more than conjecture. This is, however, a central issue because it has been argued in the case of other countries that it was the extraordinary foreign demand which was a major cause of higher local food prices, and that this in turn was an important feature of Latin America's unequal position within the international capitalist system. If in Chile prices were not pushed up by a greater volume of exports, despite insistent claims at the time that this was happening, could this not have been equally true elsewhere? It is possible, but each country's agrarian sector and its performance during the war was quite different, and although the Chilean case does raise serious questions, it cannot in itself overturn the conclusions reached

Table 6.15 *Per capita consumption of key foodstuffs in Chile 1913–1921*

	Wheat	Potatoes	Beans	Rice	Sugar
	(Kilos per inhabitant)				
1913	140.6	41.6	6.0	5.0	24.5
1914	126.3	37.9	5.4	3.5	22.6
1915	144.0	43.4	9.4	5.7	18.7
1916	127.3	60.3	7.7	3.3	19.7
1917	133.6	55.9	4.4	4.8	22.0
1918	108.7	49.8	9.7	3.4	21.4
1919	103.2	44.0	4.6	1.9	21.6
1920	144.5	75.1	11.9	3.2	17.8
1921	133.9	73.9	7.8	2.5	17.5

Source: Sinopsis estadística, 1918, p. 130; 1923, p. 136.

on events elsewhere. Finally, it is significant that only in Chile were there no official measures taken to control prices and/or the export of foodstuffs, even though the power was given to do so in 1914. Either the authorities were more complacent than in other countries or they felt the problem was not one of excessive export.

Whatever the cause, it is clear that prices did rise. By today's standards the increases may not seem very great, but for workers with absolutely no margin in their budgets and many of whom, at least before 1916 or 1917, had had their money wages slashed, the effect of such price increases was devastating. This is shown perhaps most clearly in the figures for the per capita consumption of basic foodstuffs (Table 6.15). The particularly extreme conditions in 1918 and 1919 show why the high price of food should have provoked such a massive popular outcry in these years. Of course, lower real wages were a problem throughout the period, but as witnessed during the first two years of the war, they were not in themselves sufficient to ignite an organised, concerted working-class response. Furthermore, although demands for higher wages were always a prominent feature of industrial disputes, during the war many strikes were over union recognition or the sacking of colleagues, a pattern somewhat similar to that found in Argentina. It is, therefore, wrong to see the wave of strikes which began in 1916–17 primarily as affairs of the stomach, they very much involved the head and heart as well.

From 1916 to 1921 it seems that almost every important group of workers was involved at some point in strike action. It was through this action that the union movement gained in strength and coherence, as many resistance societies, crushed early in the war, were rebuilt and new workers' federations were organized. Furthermore, the FOCh, the mutualist workers' confederation, was taken over by the Socialists in 1917 and moved steadily to the left, finally coming under the control of the Chilean Communist Party in 1921. In 1916 there were, among the more than twenty strikes, those involving railway workers, El Teniente copper miners and glass workers in Santiago. The following year saw nitrate miners, port workers and bakers all taking action, and in 1918 shoemakers, tram drivers, teachers, and a host of other workers engaged in major strikes. 1919 was a crucial year, with a record number of strikes as well as mass popular mobilization against high food prices. Although 1920 was somewhat quieter in Santiago and Valparaíso, in the country as a whole official figures suggest that unrest was at an all-time high. Subsequently, activity declined as government repression increased and economic conditions deteriorated. Table 6.16 gives three different accounts of the number of strikes and of the workers involved. It is interesting to note that in Santiago and Valparaíso, although police and troops broke some strikes and scabs were used in others, about 50% of disputes ended in compromise, a substantial improvement over the 31% in the previous wave of strikes between 1902 and 1908.[153] Agreed settlements increased after the government decree in December 1917 ordering provincial intendants to engage in non-binding arbitration. It would be impossible to discuss all the many strikes of the war and immediate postwar years, but a few key disputes merit at least brief mention.

The first major wartime strike was by smelter workers at the Braden Copper Company's El Teniente mine in February 1916. They do not seem to have made any headway with demands for improved wages, working conditions and the eight-hour day.[154] Neither did their fellow workers at Braden's other mine at Rancagua, who came out on strike at the end of March. Somewhat more successful was the national railway workers strike in February and March of the same year. They had come out in protest at the fact that while their wages had been cut by 15% at the outbreak of war, a substantial share of profits was said to have been recently distributed to administrators and high officials. When the strike ended in mid-March, wages were improved, but the workers' other demands, including the ubiquitous eight-hour day, were not granted.[155]

In 1917 militant activity by workers increased substantially.

Table 6.16 *Strikes in Chile, 1912–1920*

	1	2		Santiago and Valparaíso 3
	Barrera-Barría Number	Official Number	De Shazo Workers involved	Number
1912	26	18	11,154	—
1913	27	17	10,490	—
1914	8	5	829	—
1915	7	no data		—
1916	21	16	18,523	—
1917	18	26	11,408	39
1918	18	30	24,392	48
1919	71	66	23,529	92
1920	58	105	50,439	22

Sources: 1. M. Barrera, "Perspectiva histórica de la huelga obrera en Chile," *Cuadernos de la realidad nacional*, no. 9, September 1971, pp. 125, 133, cited in De Shazo, *Urban Workers*, pp. 136, 165. 2. *Boletín de la Oficina del Trabajo* no. 18, 1922, p. 263, cited in Loveman, *Chile*, p. 227. 3. De Shazo, *Urban Workers*, p. 165.

Probably the most dramatic event was the strike which began in April among the Valparaíso port workers over their refusal to accept identity cards, an issue which figured prominently in the railway strike of 1913.[156] There were also other claims, including higher wages and the eight-hour day.[157] The first phase of the dispute, which involved almost every major port in the country, lasted from 2–19 April when it was called off without having achieved anything. After a meeting of workers at the end of July, a second, and this time, a full general port strike, was called. It soon spread to other groups of workers throughout the country, who either expressed support for the port workers or who struck on their own behalf.[158] The strike lasted until the end of August, and although the port workers did not achieve their principal aim of getting the identity cards abolished, their pay was increased and the militant example of the strike undoubtedly spurred other workers to seek improvements.

The following year saw a slightly greater number of strikes but, according to the official figures, with many more workers taking part.

In 1918 the teachers throughout the country struck, the first time this had happened in Latin America.[159] They had a good deal of public support and within a few days the government had acceded to their demands. Subsequently the teachers established a nationwide resistance society.[160] The formation of such societies and of workers' federations was one of the most significant features of the growing number of strikes during the war years.[161] Federations and resistance societies were set up in Santiago and Valparaíso among shoe workers, bakers, printers, furniture makers, painters, plasterers and bricklayers, tailors, coopers, foundrymen, tannery workers, and glass makers. Probably the most important federation was the Federación Obrera de Chile (FOCh), which in 1917 was taken over by Socialists. Its mutualism gave way to a policy of direct action. The FOCh was able to organize a wide variety of workers, including tram drivers, tinsmiths, glass blowers, tobacco workers, hatters, metalworkers, and those working in the food processing and textile industries. Success varied, but the fact that so many workers' organizations were being born out of struggle shows clearly that the wartime crisis had stimulated not only discontent with material conditions, but also widespread and purposeful militancy among the Chilean working class. This was not confined to the workers, as is attested by the following comment in the *South Pacific Mail*:[162]

The recent conflict has brought to light the cohesion among the working classes; and the proofs afforded of discipline and combined action warrant the assumption that class consciousness is on the increase... Nor is the phenomenon in question peculiar to the lower strata of society; the middle class, feeling the same economic pressure, is forming an association to study ways and find means of easing the economic pressure which becomes more burdensome day by day. The case of the struggling employee or of the miserably paid teacher who have to keep up appearances is worse than that of the average mechanic, but the class to which the latter belongs has evolved some sort of leadership and has a code which severs it from the classes above it.

This militancy was stimulated and given direction by the pervasive influence of anarcho-syndicalism and Socialism among the workers. During the war many resistance societies espoused Anarchist principles and the US-based Industrial Workers of the World (IWW) became a potent force among certain groups of workers. A counter-tendency, although one which was not seriously to divide the workers' movement until 1921, was Recabarren's Partido Obrero Socialista, which dominated the FOCh. De Shazo observes[163] that despite the conflict between Socialists, Anarchists, and Syndicalists, of greater importance in these years was the rejection by the Chilean workers of mutualism's passivity.

By 1919 the foundations of oligarchic rule throughout Latin America were being shaken by a massive wave of working-class unrest. This happened in Chile as well, but here economic conditions were considerably worse than elsewhere. Whereas in most other countries 1919 was a boom year for exports, in Chile nitrate sales collapsed and the value of exports plummeted. As had happened at the beginning of the war, although not on such a scale, workers and their families where transported south from the nitrate workings. However, unlike the early war years, workers were now better organized and their spirits tempered in the conflicts of the previous two years. The result was an explosion of strikes throughout Chile, in almost every trade and every city. The official figures show that unrest was even more severe in 1920. What was possibly a greater threat to the elite than this strike action, was the alliance of the working class and elements of the urban middle class in the popular agitation over the high cost of living. The Workers' Assembly on National Nutrition (AOAN) was set up in 1918,[164] by a number of workers' organizations, after two years of protest against rising prices. They were joined, in what became progressively larger rallies, by such groups as the Federation of the Middle Class and the Chilean Students' Federation. In November 1918, between sixty and 100,000 people demonstrated in Santiago, a 50,000 strong rally was held the following January in Valparaíso and the largest protest was mounted in August in the capital when 100,000 people took part. De Shazo argues that little of value was achieved by the AOAN sponsored actions, but he concedes that the political impact was considerable. Such mass actions demonstrated the power of the workers and the importance of the "social question" as a key election issue.

Faced with such an unprecedented threat to their authority, the Chilean elite adopted three main tactics. The first was an old standby, repression. This became particularly evident in the last year of the Sanfuentes administration, a time when the elite feared that revolution was imminent. Troops were used against strikers, many labor leaders were arrested and many working-class newspapers were shut down by police raids.[165] The second and third tactics, reform and conciliation, were less well-tried. But increasingly, and especially after the mass demonstrations of 1918 and 1919, at least some sections of the elite were drawn to the view that a degree of social reform was needed in order to safeguard stability and the existing social order. For example, in 1919 the Conservatives proposed legislation, which in the event was not passed, to regulate working conditions, collective bargaining and union organization.[166] It was in this atmosphere that in July 1920 the two parties of the Alianza Liberal coalition chose Arturo Alessandri as their candidate by a large majority. His program represented a radical departure from those of previous presidential candidates. He promised, among other things, a reduction in the cost of living, better living conditions for workers, the establishment of schools in rural areas, compulsory primary education, and a tax on inheritance.[167]

In his campaigning, Alessandri's demagogy, like that of Augusto Leguía's in Peru,[168] appealed to workers and middle-class employees, who believed his promise of a new social order. Because corruption was rampant during Chilean elections, on election day detachments of Alessandri's working-class supporters gathered at polling stations to prevent the sale of votes, and to intimidate opposition voters. As it happened, no candidate received a majority and so a Congressional Tribunal of Honour was convened to determine the winner. Much as had happened in Peru in 1912, Alessandri rallied crowds to support him, and there were threats of widespread violence if he were not chosen. Given the climate of unrest which had preceded the election, it is not too surprising that the Tribunal declared Alessandri elected (albeit by a majority of one). He took office on 23 December 1920.

Alessandri's accession to power was a clear sign that the elite was no longer able to wield power in its traditional manner. As in the other countries under review, after the war the export elite found that the working and middle classes had to be drawn into what was now a broader political equation. It can be argued that in many respects this elite continued to rule, but this rule was now placed discreetly behind a reformist façade.[169] For example, Alessandri was no revolutionary. Like Leguía, he wanted to promote social harmony in order to secure conflict-free capitalist development. He wrote,[170]

I believed that the moment had come to produce harmony between capital and labor on the basis of human solidarity and social justice, to thus defend public order and social salvation... In a word, I felt that it was necessary to have rapid evolution to avoid the revolution and the holocaust which in conformity with a reiterated historical law always takes place when evolution is retarded.

This goal was to prove unattainable. A reactionary Congress blocked his more progressive legislation, and in the second half of 1921, in the midst of an economic crisis and finding himself unable to reconcile conflicting interests (during a national maritime lockout and a general strike) Alessandri sided with the class whose interests he ultimately represented and began to take a hard line against the workers.

The war brought few lasting material gains to Chile's workers. Some gained increased wages or the eight-hour day, but unemployment and the rising cost of living brought widespread suffering. However, there were gains of another sort. The working class had made its presence felt and had helped force a change in the character of the elite's exercise of political power. There had been no revolution, but through the class struggles of the war years the balance of political and social forces in Chile was radically altered. Furthermore, a distinct class consciousness was formed which in the years to come was to enable Chilean workers to maintain their political independence, unlike their fellows in Brazil, Argentina or Peru.

Peru

I

Despite being relatively the least numerous urban working class of the four countries under review, partially a reflection of the weakness of Peruvian capitalism, in the years before the First World War Peru's urban proletariat were able to achieve, at least temporarily, a substantial degree of political influence. Although Uruguay's workers gained more under the populist–reformist administrations of José Batlle (1903–7, 1911–15),[171] in no other Latin American country did a politician claiming to represent working people become president, as Guillermo Billinghurst did in Peru. The prospect of a similar leader (referred to by the workers as "el primer obrero del Peru") holding such high office would have horrified the ruling classes in Brazil, Argentina, or Chile. It is apparent that the Peruvian elite was none too happy with the situation. Yet, it was divisions within their own ranks, probably more than the strength of Peru's workers, which had led to Billinghurst becoming President. It was not, therefore, a question of Peru having a particularly strong or effective organized working class, in most respects it was very weak. Rather the balance of class forces in the country was such that they were able to achieve a significant, albeit fleeting, victory two years before the outbreak of war. This was in many respects a hollow victory which ultimately weakened Peru's urban working class.

The vast majority of Peru's population was rural and most lived in the *sierra* isolated from the centres of political and economic power on the coast. There are no census data comparable to that available for the other countries, but with only an estimated 5.4% of the population in cities of over 20,000 in 1910, Peru was by far the least urbanized. In 1908 Lima had only 140,884 inhabitants. The next largest cities were Callao (1905) and Arequipa (1908) with about 35,000 each and Cuzco and Trujillo with 18,000 and 10,000 respectively.[172] Peru's industrial sector was also very small. By rough calculation between 1905 and 1908 there were but 28,000 artisans and workers in Lima and Callao, the number growing to 52,700 by 1920. Of the latter figure, only about 15,300 were factory workers, and many of these were probably in small workshops. The cotton and woolen textile industries, concentrated mainly in Lima, were the largest single employers of factory labor. There were an estimated 1,500 employed in 1905 and this had risen to 3,835 by 1918.

The most advanced sectors of the Peruvian working class were in the cities, but the largest numbers of wage laborers were in the rural areas, on the coastal plantations and in the mines (Table 6.17). These figures are, however, somewhat deceptive as many workers on the coast and in the *sierra* were contracted for relatively short periods. Over time, many settled and became permanent wage laborers, but by the First World War a large number still remained temporary migrants, who after their labors in the fields or down the mine, returned to their villages.[173] This continual movement meant that many rural workers were only "part-time proletarians" and, among other things, this must have hindered the development of class consciousness and made the task of organizing more difficult. However, this did not prevent rural labor becoming increasingly militant during and immediately after the war. Besides bad conditions and low pay, a major factor contributing to this militancy was the fact that the sugar estates and the mines saw the highest concentrations of workers in the country. Because a single *ingenio* often controlled more than one estate, the average number of workers shown in Table 6.17, does not adequately reflect the size of labor concentration on the sugar plantations. For example, Cayaltí, a medium-sized northern sugar estate, had about 1,000 workers in 1912, and a few years later three large plantations in La Libertad employed 1,500 workers each. The country's largest sugar producer, Casa Grande, had a work force of about 5,000.[174] Figures for individual mining companies are harder to find, but in 1917, the largest, owned by the Cerro de Pasco Mining Company, employed 1,200 miners and

Table 6.17 *Numbers of rural workers in Peru 1913–1920*

	Sugar		Cotton		Rice		Mining
	Workers	Workers per estate	Workers	Workers per estate	Workers	Workers per estate	
1913	20,942	233	—		—		19,515
1914	21,811	245	—		9,020	66	20,335
1915	24,443	284	20,514	91	9,471	74	21,480
1916	23,456	250	22,366	79	11,459	44	22,759
1917	22,835	243	27,358	41	13,133	93	23,738
1918	25,081	213	32,047		14,499	61	21,310
1919	28,860	247	35,877		11,733	43	22,000
1920	29,259	302	38,704		15,260	62	22,500

Source: *Extracto estadístico del Perú 1928*, pp. 122, 125, 129, 136.

another 1,300 men worked in the company's smelter, La Fundación.[175]

In common with other Latin American countries, and reflecting the dominance of artisans, the first workers' organizations in Peru were mutual benefit societies. The first of any significance was La Sociedad de Artesanos de Auxilios Mutuos, set up in the capital in 1860.[176] Subsequently similar organizations appeared throughout the country, and in the 1871 a federation was established. The latter was reorganized and renamed a number of times, in 1891 becoming the Confederación de Artesanos "Unión Universal." Artisans were also active politically. In 1896 a tailor, Rosendo Vidaurre, was nominated by Lima's workers and elected to Congress as a member of Piérola's Democratic Party. Later even the more conservative Civilista Party looked with favor on and tried to co-opt the leaders of the mutualist societies, especially when more radical elements began to emerge among the working class. Although the elite parties' political gestures were essentially token ones, they did show that the working class was becoming a power to be reckoned with. However, with the exception of the Law of Professional Risk (1911), by which workers were to be indemnified for job-related accidents, little was done for workers before Billinghurst came to power. The price exacted for such minimal political participation and results was inordinately heavy, in that the artisans had to court and depend upon the elite-dominated parties. This created divisions within the labor movement and bred a form of clientism which was inimical to independent working-class action.

Partly because of their political failure conservative artisanal organizations gradually lost their leading role among Peru's working class. But more important was the fact that as a modern capitalist economy developed, the social and economic base of artisan power was eroded. Furthermore, as their livelihoods came under threat, more artisans began to turn to Anarchism, which in its rejection of both capitalism and political solutions seemed to offer a viable alternative to conservative mutualism. In any case, mutualism proved unable to respond to the more militant mood in evidence around the turn of the century from an increasing number of Peruvian workers in occupations where there were few artisans, such as on the railways, docks, and in the textile mills.

As in neighbouring Chile, Peru's Anarchist movement was largely locally developed and controlled. Although even fewer immigrants came to Peru than to Chile, Blanchard suggests that the many Italians who settled in the former country between 1891 and 1901 may have had an impact on the Anarchist movement.[177] Most of the Anarchist leaders were Peruvians, and the father of Peruvian Anarchism was Manuel González Prada, a radical limeño intellectual who travelled widely in Europe in the 1890s and when he returned to Peru in 1898 became a fervent advocate of the philosophy he had adopted during this travels.[178] Initially his call was largely unheeded, except for some other intellectuals and a few dissident artisans. But as economic pressures on artisans increased from about 1900 and the urban proletariat grew so did the popularity of Anarchism. In 1904 the first Anarchist paper was published and Anarchists supported and took part in strike action, helping to establish resistance societies similar to those formed in Chile. They organized May Day demonstrations, and it was through their lead that the fight for the eight-hour day became a key demand which served to unite various sectors of the Peruvian working class.

In Lima and Callao there were an increasing number of strikes from about 1904 (Table 6.18).[179] There were a number of major strikes on the railways, in the Callao docks, among Lima's bakery workers, and from 1904 a wave of strikes hit the textile industry. Many other trades were also affected. The results were mixed. In some cases workers' demands were met, in others scabs were brought in or police and troops were used. It is interesting to note that although there was

Table 6.18 Strikes in Callao and Lima 1895–1911

	1895	1896	1897	1898	1899	1900	1901	1902	1903	1904	1905	1906	1907	1908	1909	1910	1911
Lima	2	4	2	1	2	2	3	—	5	8	2	2	10	5	1	3	12
Callao	2	2	0	1	5	4	2	—	3	8	0	6	9	6	9	0	2
Total	4	6	2	2	7	6	5	—	8	16	2	8	19	11	10	3	14

Source: Extracted from more detailed tables in Blanchard, *Origins*, pp. 68, 74–5.

official violence used against strikers, it was on an extremely small scale, at least in the cities, when compared to Chile or the other two countries. While the Chilean workers could claim many hundreds of martyrs, in Peru there seems to have been only one, Florencio Aliaga, shot and killed during the 1904 strike in Callao. There were in fact many more, but as they were murdered in the countryside, they remained nameless and their deaths made little impression on the urban working class or their leaders.

By 1911 out of the experience of struggle and leavened by the influence of the Anarchists, the workers in Lima and Callao had become more aware of themselves as a distinct class and were much better organized. This was demonstrated in the country's first general strike in April 1911. It began with a dispute in the Vitarte cotton textile mill in mid-March. After the strikers were forced out of their company houses and the strike committee arrested, a general strike was organized by various workers' groups in the capital. The President, Augusto Leguía, tried to talk the workers around to a compromise, but failed and the strike went ahead on April 10th. It lasted only two days, because most of the strikers' demands were met almost immediately. This represented a major victory for the capital's workers.

In the rural areas the prewar period was less eventful than in the cities. Working conditions were generally harsh and pay extremely low, but organized protest was difficult because plantation and mine owners were able to exercise a much greater degree of control over their work force than was possible in the city. Also, many workers were on the estates or in the mines for only a relatively short time, and were, because of this and their continued ties to land, not fully proletarianized. What is more, rural workers were relatively isolated, and unlike their urban counterparts it was only with great difficulty that they could make their voices heard by those in government. When their voices were raised, the usual response was to shut them up by force.

There were a number of minor strikes in the mines and the oilfields before the war. The one major mining dispute was at Backus and Johnson's mine at Morococha in December 1913. The workers here did manage to set up a strike committee, but it seems little was achieved. In the oilfields there were strikes in 1910 and again in 1913. In the latter Anarchists from the capital took a hand, and support came from workers in Callao.[180] On the coastal sugar estates there was a long history of spontaneous uprisings and acts of individual defiance whether by slaves, the indentured Chinese or the more recently imported (from 1899) Japanese contract laborers, but the first modern strikes did not take place until 1912.[181] They began on the large Casa Grande estate and soon spread to other plantations in the region. The disturbances were a mixture of general strike and general uprising, as the workers rioted, burning canefields, destroying machinery and looting company stores. To restore order troops were sent from Lima, and over 150 workers were killed on various estates in the area. This was by far the largest massacre of workers in the country's history. There was, however, also a more purposeful side to the conflict. Eventually a strike committee was organized and concessions wrung from the owners of Casa Grande. Although the official commission sent to report on the unrest, suggested strengthening the repressive apparatus so as to weed out and keep out "subversive elements," the *West Coast Leader*, recognizing the increasing conflict between labor and capital which the strike reflected, called instead for reform as the best means of safeguarding capital.[182] "We are not special pleaders for the proletariat, but in the interests of capital and its self-protection we strongly urge that our employers and labor accept the new, and coming conditions and remember the well-known axiom–that the well paid and well fed labor will give ample return for the increased wage total." This "axiom" does not seem to have been particularly "well-known" among Peruvian capitalists, but they were reluctantly being forced to give serious consideration to it as labor began to emerge dramatically onto the national scene. The successful 1911 Lima General Strike was followed a year later by the election of Guillermo Billinghurst, the workers' champion, as President of the Republic.[183]

Leguía was due to step down from the presidency in 1912. As was the custom, he chose his own successor, Antero Aspíllaga, a prominent north coast sugar *hacendado*, and traditional civilista.[184] However, Aspíllaga did not have the full support of his party because during Leguía's administration it had split into pro and anti-*leguiista* wings, and Leguía himself proved to be not particularly active in supporting his own candidate. Nonetheless, up until a month before the election it still seemed as if Aspíllaga would be easy victor. Then, quite without warning, from Cuzco the name of Guillermo Billinghurst, Piérola's first vice president (1895–9) and former mayor of Lima (1909–11), was put forward as a candidate. He was soon enthusiastically taken up by the Lima workers who remembered the many social, pro-labor reforms he had instituted when mayor. They took a very direct hand in his election, by calling a general strike on polling day and creating such disruption that no votes were cast in Lima or Callao, and the one-third turnout necessary for a valid election was not forthcoming. The burden was now placed on the Congress to choose a winner. With the dominant party still divided and fearing more social unrest if Aspíllaga was chosen, they voted for Billinghurst.

The new President was aware of his debt to the workers, and promised a program of substantial reforms, including sickness benefit, housing provision, and assistance for the unemployed. The workers, feeling that the government was now "on their side," became more insistent in their confrontations with employers and turned to Billinghurst for support. He did intervene in a number of strikes, including the one in 1912 among the Callao dockers during which he issued a decree establishing the eight-hour day in the docks. Subsequently, the right to strike was granted, although only under strict guidelines, which gave the state considerable control over workers' actions. This evinced no protest from the workers for whom a decree giving the right to strike was more important than the strings attached and who also seem to have been all too willing to defer to Billinghurst's leadership. One consequence of this was a weakening of the more traditional working-class organizations, which simply could not compete with the power of the President of the Republic. This loss of independence was the rot at the core of the workers' apparent victory. It was of considerable significance for a number of reasons. Billinghurst did have a genuine paternalist concern for the welfare of the workers, but, as with all paternalists, the concern was strictly measured. Essentially it was the "enlightened" containment of working-class unrest so as to promote conflict-free capitalist development. However, Billinghurst was unable to convince any of the ruling elite that this was a viable proposition, could not establish any political alternative to the existing system, and, therefore, was forced to rely on popular demonstrations to exert this authority with a hostile Congress. These demonstrations were important indications of the support he had among the masses, but did not represent the development of coherent effective working-class political organization. This was shown by the fact that there was little resistance when Billinghurst was finally toppled in a broadly based elite-sponsored military coup in February 1914.

In the two decades before the First World War the Peruvian working class had made impressive gains. But in the cities, particularly Lima and Callao, these gains were tempered by the fact that the workers had achieved many of them by giving in to the siren call of a populist leader. His overthrow left them leaderless and demoralized at the outbreak of the war. For example, reporting on the mood of workers in the months before June, 1914, a representative of the Peruvian Corporation reported, "There is considerably more willingness on the part of the men to do their duty than has been evident for some years past, in fact the agitating element would appear to have been practically eliminated."[185] It is impossible to assess the negative impact of the Billinghurst episode on the Peru's urban working class, it may account, at least in part, for the fact that on the whole the resistance of the urban workers during the war years was a great deal more muted here than in the other countries. It was not until the end of the war that they began to make their voice heard again with any effect. During the war it was the rural workers, less well-organized, but also less compromised by political involvement, who were to make their presence felt throughout the country.

II

In May 1919, the *West Coast Leader* reported that, "Lima awakened on Tuesday morning, May 27th, to find itself face to face with a labor situation which for a time threatened to assume the proportions of a social revolution. Repetition on a smaller scale of the Maximalist outbreak that swept Buenos Aires a short time ago was only avoided through the prompt decision of the Government to meet the contingency in the one and only manner possible."[186] This "prompt decision" resulted in five days of total disorder in the capital and Callao. One hundred people were killed, several hundred wounded, and between 300 to 500 imprisoned. These events represented the peak of working-class unrest in Peru and showed that much had changed since the Peruvian Corporation's report in 1914. Workers in the cities, in the mines and on the coastal estates displayed a degree of unity and class consciousness which resulted in their winning the eight-hour day and, perhaps more importantly, inflicting a serious political defeat on the oligarchy. Not since the election of Billinghurst had the working class seemed so powerful.

Yet the transition from the passivity of 1914 to the mass activism of 1919 was a slow and tortuous one, especially for the urban workers, who at the outbreak of war were leaderless and demoralized. As the harsh effects of the conflict in Europe spread throughout the country, demoralization rapidly became helplessness.

As in the other countries, high levels of unemployment were

undoubtedly a major factor in sapping the strength and confidence of the workers. There are no precise figures, but some idea of the extent of the problem can be gleaned from contemporary reports. For example, in the sugar-producing department of La Libertad 75% of the work force, both on the estates and in the nearby towns, were thrown out of work in August.[187] In the Cañete Valley many cotton estates shut down, and the one sugar *ingenio* reduced production and cut wages by 25%.[188] Similar conditions were found in the cities. In early August, there were reports of rising unemployment in Lima and Callao, and more sackings were noted in the following month in the port and in Pisco.[189] In Lima the El Inca textile mill cut wages by 35% in August and a further 20% in November, while the Vitarte mill reduced the working week by two days and in December wages were slashed 30%.[190] The mining companies also drastically reduced the number of workers employed.[191] To add to the country's difficulties, Peruvians working in the Chilean nitrate fields were the first to be laid off, and on 18 August an initial shipload of 1,500 were sent home.[192] They were to be followed by many of their compatriots as more *oficinas* suspended production.

Because of the relatively quick recovery of Peruvian exports, unemployment seems to have been relatively short-lived, at least in the rural areas (Table 6.17). In Lima and Callao, however, Blanchard gives the impression (no figures are available) that unemployment remained a problem throughout much of the war.[193] Added to this hardship was the rapid rise in the cost of living (Table 6.19), brought about by many of the same factors which were causing rising prices in the other countries.[194] This remained a major problem throughout the war and immediate postwar period, and was one of the principal underlying causes for the widespread upsurge in unrest in 1919. At the same time money wages either fell or at best rose very slowly. The only wage series available is that for sugar workers, and this, deflated by the Lima cost of living index (which gives only a very rough guide to changes in prices on the estates), shows a substantial fall in real wages during the war years (Table 6.19). This is all the more striking, given the fact that this was a booming industry and the *hacendados* were making inordinately high profits during these years.

The interim Benavides' administration, sensitive to the impact high-priced food would have on the urban workers, acted immediately in an attempt to alleviate the situation. Power was given to prohibit the export of foodstuffs and to regulate prices, although it does not seem either was done.[195] Subsequently a whole series of measures were

Table 6.19 *Indices of cost of living in Lima and wages of male field workers on Peruvian sugar estates 1913–1921*

	1914	1915	1916	1917	1918	1919	1920	1921
				(1913 = 100)				
Food	107	115	123	145	162	188	208	183
Housing	100	100	115	130	150	180	200	220
Clothing	100	117	129	146	192	223	268	291
Other costs	98	109	125	144	169	172	182	159
Cost of living*	104	112	123	142	164	188	210	199
Field worker's wage	98	101	88	106	124	142	126	143
Real wage	94	90	72	75	76	76	60	72

Sources: Oscar F. Arrus, *El costo de la vida en Lima y causas de su carestia*, Lima, 1925, pp. 15–20; Albert, *Essay*, p. 171a. *Note*: Cost of living weighted as follows: Food 55%, Rent 18%, Clothing 12%, Other costs 15%.

enacted in a vain effort to halt the rise in food prices. The government purchased and resold Argentine wheat, guano prices were cut for small farmers growing food crops, duties on certain food imports were ended, rice sales were regulated, and some cities were authorized to fix food prices.[196] From 1917 in the poorer sections of Lima basic necessities were sold cheaply by the state.[197] In Cuzco the municipal authorities went to great lengths to insure that foodstuffs were not exported from the region, and a Junta de Subsistencias was set up to sell foodstuffs cheaply.[198] In 1917 and 1920 laws were passed making it obligatory for estates producing export crops to plant a minimum acreage in food crops.[199] Finally, sugar producers were forced to sell a proportion of their output at a low price to the government and this meant that while the domestic price of sugar did rise, until 1919 it was well below the world price.[200] This last measure seems to have had some effect, but it is impossible to judge the overall impact of government regulation for food prices continued to rise throughout the war period.

Despite deteriorating conditions, workers in Peru were remarkably passive during the first two years of the war, even more so than their counterparts in other countries. There were no demonstrations as occurred in Chile and up until December 1915 there were only two strikes of any note. The first was by the Vitarte workers in December 1914 in protest at the drastic cut in wages. This was a violent dispute, which rallied the Lima workers' organizations behind their colleagues at Vitarte after troops had killed one striker and wounded six others.[201] The other strike was in the Lobitos oilfields in April 1915.[202] Although strikes became more frequent from 1917 in the capital and Callao, there were only twelve urban strikes between 1915 and 1919.[203] Blanchard attributes the apparent conservatism of the urban workers to prewar political defeats, unemployment, government repression of Anarchists, and the tendency of certain workers' organizations, mainly the revived mutualist societies, to rely on the good will of the government.[204] All these factors were, no doubt, of considerable importance but in themselves cannot fully explain the wartime quiescence of the capital's workers, for they all were more or less operative in 1918 when the tide began to turn.

While the urban working class was relatively subdued during the war, the rural workers became increasingly combative. In the mines there were a number of major strikes during the war, the most important being at Cerro de Pasco in May 1917.[205] The dispute was over pay and conditions and soon spread to other mines. Although some slight wage concessions were granted, as in most of the mining strikes, the employers called in police and troops and the strikers were forced to return to work.[206] On the coast demands for higher wages were a common element in all strikes, but the workers also pressed for better working conditions, educational and medical facilities, no post-strike victimization, and most significantly, a reduction in the working day. Some strikes even took on a clear anti-capitalist dimension and Anarchists were active in certain areas helping to organize and give a clear ideological edge to the workers' struggles. This new-found militancy alarmed the estate owners. For example, on August 18 1916, Antero Aspíllaga, failed presidential candidate and owner of Cayaltí, instructed the estate's administrator to insure the workers were treated with extra care.[207] He wrote, "... today's working class is not as before, as is shown by the strike and 'claims', which daily grow more serious and frequent." Within the next two weeks there were short-lived strikes by railway and port workers in Trujillo and Salaverry and on the Laredo sugar estate, and although these caused the Aspíllagas concern, it was the large-scale strike in the valley of Huaura in the following month which really scared them.

On 31 August 1,000 workers from two estates came out in the Huaura Valley demanding a 50% wage rise and shorter hours. They were soon joined by another 1,000 workers from other estates and also received the support of the port workers from Huacho. Four hundred troops were sent and during their efforts to "restore order" two workers were killed and ten injured. This did not end the affair. Soon the strikes spread to two large sugar estates, San Nicolás and Paramonga, in the neighbouring valleys of Supe and Pativilca. Here too the local port workers struck in sympathy. Soldiers prevented the Huaura strikers from coming to the aid of their compatriots, and the latter were forced back to work after gaining only a token 10% rise. In Huaura, however, despite persistent intimidation, workers stayed out until their claim went to arbitration in Lima. In the end many of their demands were met, but with respect to wages, only a 10% increase was granted. Commenting on the strike, *La Prensa* claimed that it had been,[208] "...an artificial phenomenon. The workers' protest has been in response to the calls of outside elements, it has been an imported strike." This was essentially the view of the Sociedad Nacional Agraria who blamed foreign agitators and called for an end to immigration. Like their counterparts in other countries, the oligarchy repeatedly raised the specter of the Anarchist agitator, and while it is true that Anarchists had been instrumental in setting up the Syndicate of Diverse Professions in Huacho in 1915, their influence only reflected the growing militancy of the workers. This militancy was spreading, and in June 1917 another series of strikes hit the main sugar-growing valleys in La Libertad. It ended when troops were brought in and strike leaders arrested. In Huaura another bitter strike broke out at about the same time. Once again troops were used, one hundred strikers were wounded, four killed, and Anarchists and strike organizers were arrested. As in the mines, although concessions were sometimes made, the employers and the state, having conveniently characterized most strikes as the result of outside agitation, felt free to use force to suppress them.

In some sense the militant stance adopted by the country's rural workers during the war makes the relative lack of activity in the cities more difficult to explain, because, in almost every respect they were at a disadvantage in comparison with their urban counterparts, and both suffered during the war from low wages, rapidly rising prices, and government repression. This in turn lends support to the argument that the urban workers' reliance on Billinghurst undermined their independence and thereby weakened their development. But the effects were not permanent. From the last months of 1918 the workers in the city began to go on the offensive once again.

The ending of the war in Europe unleashed a massive pent-up demand for primary products, and although this meant a bonanza for exporters it also probably contributed to forcing up the cost of living, which rose by almost 15% in 1918. This was the highest single yearly increase of the war, the next year saw a similarly steep rise and, coming after years of mounting hardship, seems to have been the last straw for many in the cities. In December 1918, workers at the El Inca textile mill in Lima struck for higher wages and the eight-hour day.[209] The initiative of the textile workers was quickly taken up by others, not only in Lima but throughout the country. Bakers in Lima, miners in Casapalca, and workers in the northern oilfields were all on strike at the end of 1918. The movement continued to gain momentum, and in Lima a strike committee led by Anarchists, who now assumed the leadership of the workers' movement, set about organizing a general strike.

In response to the unrest the government of José Pardo adopted a number of reforms aimed at improving conditions for the workers, but they were completely ineffectual as they did nothing to address the principal demands for higher wages, cheaper food, and the eight-hour day. This last demand, one championed by workers throughout the world since the late nineteenth century, and a central element in the program of Peru's Anarchists, served to unite workers throughout the country in common cause. On 13 January 1919 the General Strike began in the capital. It had widespread support and although some leaders were arrested and newspapers closed down, Lima and Callao were effectively brought to a halt. As the strike began to spread to other parts of the country, and some employers agreed to the eight-hour day, Pardo's resolve disappeared and within two days he issued a decree granting workers the right to demand the eight-hour day. But although the capital was soon back to work, because the new hours were not granted automatically, there was an outbreak of strikes throughout the country against employers who were slow or reluctant to implement the new conditions. Most of these were successful and the winning of the eight-hour day represented a considerable victory for the Peruvian working class.

However, shorter hours did nothing to alleviate the problems caused by rising prices and falling real wages, and the workers had to keep fighting for improvement. Throughout the early months of 1919, workers on the coastal estates were almost continually on strike and, possibly because sugar and cotton prices were so inordinately high and Pardo was now taking a more conciliatory line on disputes, the *hacendados* generally gave in to their demands without too much of a struggle. This was a complete reversal of the policy of repression followed during the war. In the cities there were also strikes, but the most important agitation here centred on the high cost of living. Anarchist-led "Committees for the Cheapening of Foodstuffs" (*Comité Pro-Abaratamiento de las Subsistencias*), similar to those set up in Chile were established in April, in Lima and Callao, as well as other Peruvian cities. These committees brought the various workers' organizations together for yet another general strike in the capital in May. This time the government response was more forceful, martial law was declared and troops and police broke up meetings and arrested strike leaders. After the strike had been brutally crushed the government moved against the Anarchists, providing for the closer supervision of foreigners and prohibiting Anarchist meetings. This followed the pattern established earlier in Brazil, Argentina and Chile. The other, softer, side of government policy was to introduce measures to bring down food prices, although like all such moves it was too little and too late. Strikes in the capital abated for a time, but rural strife continued and in October there was a general strike in the southern city of Arequipa.

It is against this stormy background that the rise to power for the second time of Augusto Leguía, on this occasion in a new populist guise, must be seen.[210] During the troubles of 1919 it became increasingly apparent that Pardo was unable to control the chaotic postwar situation in the country. The brand of *civilismo* which he represented was outmoded, no longer capable of ruling effectively in view of the new social forces which had erupted onto the national scene. To many in Peru Leguía seemed to offer the only solution. His conception of the country's predicament, basically the need to establish a more progressive and socially harmonious capitalist system, was remarkably similar to that of Alessandri's and, in its radical appeal to the workers and to the urban middle class, sharply differentiated him from the more traditional *civilistas*, represented in the 1919 election by Pardo's chosen successor, the luckless Antero Aspíllaga, who Leguía himself had picked to succeed him seven years before. Together with his strong popular appeal Leguía drew together a broad political coalition, including the newly formed Socialist Party, the Constitutionalists, Liberals, and even some dissenting elements from the Civilista Party.[211] Although he seems to have won the vote, because of fears that the electoral system, controlled by a hostile Congress, would give the victory to Aspíllaga, Leguía staged a bloodless and immensely popular coup in July 1919.

Having used working-class discontent to win the presidency, he partially repaid this support by including a number of important reforms in his 1920 Constitution, the foundation stone of his self-styled Patria Nueva. Also, in the first year of his rule, he attempted to settle labor disputes through arbitration rather than the wholesale use of force. But, in attempting to reconcile the interests of labor and capital Leguía was engaged in what proved to be an impossible balancing act. When world commodity prices began to collapse at the end of 1920, and with serious class conflict breaking out once again, especially in the sugar-growing Chicama Valley, Leguía found himself unable to continue wearing his reformist mask and finally moved to crush working-class unrest very much in the style of his predecessors. Once more, the Peruvian workers found themselves under attack from a hostile and repressive government.

The Peruvian working class emerged from the war immensely strengthened. By 1919, the feeling of optimism, largely lost after February 1914, had been rekindled, and through the struggles of these years the class collaborationist mutualist societies had been eclipsed by the more combative, often Anarchist-led, *sindicatos*. The war and immediate postwar years were a major period of union formation.[212] Indicative of this change was the transformation in 1919 of the Anarchist-dominated Comité Pro-Abaratamiento into the Federación Obrera Regional del Perú and its takeover of the headquarters of the conservative Confederación de Artisanos.[213] However, the Anarchists' ascendancy was only temporary. By the mid-1920s they had become a spent force.[214] Furthermore, as their support for Leguía shows, many workers were unable to break away from reliance on populist leaders. This weakness was to continue to plague the Peruvian labor movement in the following years, and was clearly demonstrated in the 1930s by the workers' attraction to both Sánchez Cerro and Víctor Raúl Haya de la Torre's Aprista Movement.[215] Whereas in Chile the ideas of Recabarren attracted a mass following, in Peru those of fellow Marxist José Carlos Mariátegui, developed in the 1920s, while fervently revered, were largely forgotten in practice for many decades.[216]

Conclusion

The preceding survey of the development of labor movements in the four countries before, during, and immediately after the First World War reveals considerable differences in national experiences. Attempts have been made to account for some of these, but to do this in any depth would require a much more substantial and closely focused comparative study than is possible here. In any case, the main concern is not the growth of workers' organization or class consciousness *per se*, but rather how the emergence of these phenomena was related to the course of capitalist development and how it affected political change in Latin America. Because of this, it is the underlying similarities which are of greater interest. These were many and significant. For example, the early dominance of the mutualist societies, the increase in more militant organizations and strikes from the last decade of the nineteenth century, the major influence of Anarchism, Syndicalism and, to a lesser extent, Socialism, and the use of force by the state to "restore order" were evident in varying degrees in all the countries and, in fact, throughout most of Latin America.[217] During the war, and in many ways due to the similarity of the external constraints imposed upon the region, the timing of working-class unrest also showed a remarkable degree of synchronization. The apparent passivity of the period 1914–16 gave way to a steadily growing wave of protest in 1917 and came to something of a peak in the first months of 1919, when general strikes seem to have broken out almost everywhere. The dramatic and often chaotic events of the war period served to reawaken working-class movements, all of which were able to build on the hard-earned experience gained in the bitter struggles before 1914. Modern class conflict was not something new, but the political impact and consequences of wartime unrest were unprecedented and marked a major turning point in Latin American history.

To explain these events is to explain a central feature of the development of primary export capitalism in Latin America and the contradictions attendant upon that development. The export elites in all the countries had sought to modernize their societies by linking their fortunes to that of the international economy. This entailed, among other things, the import of capital, technology, and labor. Another less tangible but equally important import was needed to draw these factors together. This was the ideology of progress, composed mainly of variants of European liberalism and positivism which were then adapted to suit local conditions. But the import of ideology was not the exclusive preserve of the elites. The emergent working class too was able to draw on ideologies, albeit proletarian ones, developed in Europe, and as the class struggle in Latin America became more intense, so these ideas were employed as important tools in helping to forge a purposeful response to the material implementation of the elites' ideology of progress. This was an import that the elites patently did not welcome, but the class conflict which provided fertile grounds for its propagation was a direct result of the kind of socio-economic transformation they were promoting.

Not only was class conflict unavoidable, but in many ways it became more intractable and, therefore, violent in Latin America because of the relative weakness of capitalism here. There are a number of aspects to this argument. First, the lower level of the development of the forces of production meant that in general the social productivity of labor tended to be lower in Latin America than in Europe or North America. This, together with the fact that the most significant wage goods, foodstuffs, were drawn directly and indirectly from Latin America to the more advanced countries (this problem becoming more acute during the war) meant that, all other things being equal, it took longer for labor to reproduce itself. That is, the ratio between necessary and surplus labor time tended to be higher. In general it seems that workers in peripheral countries are exploited (in the formal sense of their labor yielding a surplus for capital) to a lesser extent than those in countries where capitalism is more advanced.[218] This limitation on the rate of exploitation was a constant problem for Latin American capitalists and unless market conditions were particularly buoyant, as in the immediate postwar period, lower rates of exploitation could only be countered in the short-term by increasing the overt extraction of absolute surplus value–extending the length of the working day or intensifying the work regime. This was a tactic which could not help but exacerbate conflict with labor. The concealed exploitation afforded by an increase in relative surplus value through, for example, cheaper wage goods was largely denied to capital here because of the particular and, on the whole, subservient position of these economies within the world division of labor.

Furthermore, although local elites wanted "progress," in terms of their attitudes toward labor they were anything but progressive. They operated in societies which were essentially undemocratic and which had a recent history of the use of servile labor. In many areas various forms of non-capitalist relations of production were still being used. Having not yet established what could be considered as a hegemonic culture through which the exercise of elite control could be mediated relatively peacefully, there was a strong predisposition, virtually a necessity, to see any social unrest as subversive and meet it with force. However, although the problems imposed by weak primary export capitalism remained unresolved, and violent repression continued to be employed, the strength of the challenge mounted by the working class during and immediately after the war coupled with the discontent demonstrated by the urban middle class, in the various university reform movements,[219] new political organizations, or in protests over inflation, made wholesale repression alone an increasingly inadequate response. In order to maintain authority a new political approach was needed. This new approach has been outlined above, and the broader social, cultural, and economic changes stimulated by the European conflict are addressed in the chapter which follows.

7

After the War

I

If in the early 1920s James Bryce had retraced his steps through Latin America what major changes would he have noticed in the four countries he first visited right before the First World War? Had the years of conflict made any real difference to the political, social or economic life of the republics? Of course, in most respects the pattern of life for most of the people remained essentially the same. The massive inequality and grinding poverty, as well as the excessive degree of export and import dependence, had, if anything, probably become more acute because of the war. The keen-eyed Bryce would, however, have observed a number of major changes, changes which were to become of increasing importance for the region. Being British, he would have been painfully aware that the North American accent was now far more evident among the foreign communities and there were many more goods from the United States in the shops. Britain's prewar anxiety over German competition was being replaced by concern about the impact of US trade and investment. He would also have been forced to notice a very radical shift in the political climate in all the republics. No longer was elite domination to be taken for granted. The working class had revolted, the urban middle class was now more vocal and there was a greatly increased concern about the political ramifications of the "social question." Not only were political concerns very different, but the elites' fervent embrace of both the world division of labor and European ideas and culture, so apparent before the war, was beginning to loosen. In conversations with his Latin American friends, Bryce would have detected a variety of nationalist sentiments which were much more explicit and widely held than before 1914.

It is interesting and important that the war's reinforcement of export dependence should have been associated with the weakening of the political and ideological structures which had helped foster that dependence in the nineteenth century. This, and the shift in the centre of world economic power to the United States, were perhaps the most significant long-term consequences of the First World War for Latin America. Of course, there were many other changes brought about or stimulated by the war. For example, foreign influence over national financial systems became more of an irritant and began to be challenged. Manufacturing industry experienced some expansion, but came up against a number of constraints imposed by the fact that these economies were so heavily dominated by primary exports and dependent on imports. This in turn was important in fueling the economic nationalism which was eventually to offer alternatives to the pattern of nineteenth-century primary export capitalism. It would be impossible here to trace all of these factors as they worked themselves out in the 1920s. Only three will be outlined very briefly in this chapter: the growth of US economic dominance in the region and the changing character of world economy, the beginnings of mass politics, and the spread of nationalism. Understanding these changes is a first step to understanding Latin America in the interwar period.

II

At the first Pan American Financial Conference, held in Washington DC in 1915, Paul M. Warberg, Governor of the US Federal Reserve Board, commented,[1] "In August 1914, six European nations went to war. The anomalous consequence of this event was that all American nations were thrown into a condition of acute financial and commercial disturbance. Would it have been possible to avoid so disastrous an effect upon nations not directly involved in this struggle and thousands of miles removed from the fields of battle?" This was a calculated, rhetorical question, for as a prominent US banker, Warberg obviously knew that what occurred in non-belligerent countries in 1914 was neither an anomaly nor was it avoidable. During the nineteenth century the threads of industrial capitalism had been extended from Europe and had gradually drawn almost the entire world into an intricate web of economic interdependence. The dramatic crisis ushered in by the onset of the Great War was a harsh reminder to the countries of Latin America of their vulnerable position within this European-dominated framework.

It was the fact of this domination which Warberg was attempting to bring out, for he was one of the leading exponents of so-called

"Progressive Pan Americanism," which with strong government support and under the guise of cooperation sought to displace European interests and extend US economic dominance over the hemisphere.[2] Because of the massive and long-standing British involvement in these countries, the US campaign was only partially successful. Nonetheless, the United States' economic presence did grow substantially, marking a significant change in the character of the region's external domination. Trade with the US, which was growing before the war, received a tremendous boost during the conflict, and although the high percentage share achieved at this time was not always maintained after the Armistice, a permanent change had taken place in the region's pattern of trade. There was also an increased flow of capital from the United States, this being particularly important in Chile and Peru, where the mining sectors came to be almost completely controlled by large US corporations. The role of US capital in Brazil and Argentina was rather less important. In both these countries there was increased interest from the US in both government loans and in direct investment during the war,[3] but in terms of its share, British capital continued to play a dominant role up until the Crash of 1929. Although the figures in Table 7.1 provide only a very approximate measure, this dominance appears somewhat tenuous, for, except in Argentina, there was little increase in the amount of British capital invested in these years. On the other hand, US capital was much more dynamic and showed a massive surge during the 1920s.

The greater economic role of the United States in South America was one aspect of her rise to the leading position within the international economy in the postwar period. The change in the balance of world power that this represented was another important long-term effect of the war. The European conflict had shattered the nineteenth-century world order, and for Latin America the most important feature of this order had been the multilateral structure of trade and investment centred on the City of London. This structure had been effective in promoting an important degree of materially progressive, albeit self-limiting, capitalist transformation in the region. But, although the United States displaced Britain as the world's leading economic power, because it was both highly protectionist and a major producer of primary commodities it could not play the same mediating role within the system of multilateral settlements that Britain had done in the nineteenth century. There were, of course, a great many reasons why the "golden age" of the international economy was never recaptured in the interwar period, but this shift of the world's economic centre must be seen as one of the most important. It signaled

Table 7.1 *British and US investments 1913 and 1929 (000 US dollars)*

| | United States | | Britain | |
	1913	1929	1913	1929
Argentina	40,000	611,475	1,860,700	2,140,104
Brazil	50,000	476,040	1,161,500	1,413,589
Peru	35,000	150,889	133,292	140,897
Chile	15,000	395,733	331,691	389,749

Source: Winkler, *United States Capital*, pp. 275–83.

the beginning of fundamental changes in the working of the international economy, an economy upon which Latin America's elites had sought to "modernize" their respective countries.

The changes brought by the war in the structure of the international economy were important, but they did nothing to alter Latin America's primary export orientation. Rather than providing a rest from external pressures and an opportunity for more domestic-based growth, the war period saw the Allies extending their economic intervention substantially and the effect of this and high prices was to consolidate the position of primary export sectors within the four economies. Manufacturing industry did show some signs of growth, but on the whole this growth was consistent with prewar patterns and also fit in well with continued primary export dependence, rather than providing the basis for a break with that dependence. In short, the essential economic base of primary export capitalism was strengthened by the war. With some exceptions, this seems to have been true throughout the world.[4] The temporarily excessive demand for primary products during and immediately after the war led to a massive expansion in the output of most commodities. With demand growing relatively slowly in the 1920s and technical change leading to greater output and the development of synthetics (most importantly for nitrates and rubber) the result was a substantial weakening of the market for many primary commodities from about 1925. In this sense the war's reinforcement of primary export production nationally was a major factor contributing to its eventual international collapse.

III

At the same time as the primary export base was being consolidated, and in many respects as a function of the method by which this occurred—the more blatant exercise of foreign pressure and the increased externally dependent national posture—cracks in the social, political, and ideological superstructure, many of which had started to appear before 1914, began to widen appreciably.

The most obvious example of this was the explosion of working-class militancy during and immediately after the war. The reasons for this revolt are not hard to find. Higher prices and falling real wages, which, as has been argued, were to some degree a reflection of the relative weakness and dependence of Latin America's brand of primary export capitalism, were the most apparent immediate cause of unrest, but in themselves these particular grievances do little to account for either the timing or the character of the conflict which ensued. To understand this it is important to see the workers' struggle within the historical perspective of prewar working-class formation, as well as the profound influence exercised by the October Revolution. The victory of the Russian workers, probably the single most important international event of these years, fueled the hopes and aspirations of Latin American workers, as well as those throughout the world. It is notoriously difficult to assess a general mood among any group, but it would seem that the very idea that workers could achieve so much served as an important spur to working-class organization and action during this time.[5] This action had a profound impact on the political systems in three of the four republics.

It was not only the workers who were restive or influential during these years. Sectors of the urban middle class too began to push for change, and in some instance joined forces with the workers. Partly this was in response to higher prices, which affected both the middle and working class, but it also arose from more deep-seated and fundamental problems relating to the dissatisfaction with their social and political position in the elite-dominated states. This was shown most strikingly in the movement for university reform which began in Córdoba, in Argentina in 1918, and within a short time spread to Peru, Chile, and other countries,[6] although not to Brazil (probably because the first proper university, as opposed to specialized schools and institutes, was not established here until 1920.)[7] The initial student protests in Córdoba were over clerical control, the curriculum, and democracy, but as the movement developed so it became increasingly political and was soon allying itself with the workers' organizations. It was also taken up by other universities in the country, there were mass demonstrations, and in little more than a month Yrigoyen was compelled to give in to the students' demands for reform. In Peru, the

Federación de Estudiantes Peruanos had been formed in 1916, and under the leadership of Víctor Raúl Haya de la Torre (later to become leader of the Aprista Movement) it had been active in support of the workers.[8] Demands for university reform began to be made in June 1919, after the circulation of the *Manifesto liminar*, published by the Córdoba students, and speeches in Lima from the Argentine Socialist, Alfredo Palacios. The students strongly supported Leguía and were rewarded with reform soon after his election. In Chile a similar movement was formed in 1920 and backed the candidature of Alessandri. Portantiero writes that although there were many differences between the three countries,[9] "...university reform represented the most radical form of political participation found during the postwar awakening of the middle strata, shaken by a world in the process of revolutionary change." The student revolt was also associated with a broader ideological challenge to the elites' view of the world.

The effect of being "shaken by a world in the process of revolutionary change" did not produce a radical response among all the middle class. It also led to a more reactionary response, this being primarily directed against the rising tide of working-class agitation. This manifested itself in the Liga Patriótica in Argentina, and the Brazilian Liga da Defesa Nacional and Ação Social Nacionalista all formed during or immediately after the war.[10] These were groups led on the whole by members of the elite, but their shock troops were primarily middle-class. In Chile there was a similar backlash. The Liga Patriótica Militar, set up in 1907 to obtain better conditions for the military, soon campaigned for broader political objectives, including more resolute action against working-class unrest.[11] In 1920 patriotic leagues backed by the military were mobilized to harass the IWW, Anarchists, and the student Left.[12] In all countries these groups were supportive of the status quo (often receiving active or at least tacit government approval), generally anti-immigrant and extremely nationalist, although the particular strain of nationalism varied considerably from country to country.

The genesis of these diverse radical, revolutionary, and reactionary movements can be traced to the prewar years, in that they were indicative of the political and social ferment unleashed by the region's capitalist transformation. But the economic crisis of the war and immediate postwar period served to exacerbate the tensions within society and so precipitated head-on clashes among the sectors represented by these organizations and between some of them and the ruling elites. The socio-political costs of the elites' dream of export-led capitalist expansion, costs which had become increasingly evident before 1914, were now brought home with overwhelming force. Only in Brazil, where the extremely diffuse federal system dominated by a few powerful states paradoxically gave the central government more power to resist compromise, was it possible for the elite to maintain direct political control. However, even here Topik maintains[13] that after the war, and as a result of it, "...the ruling landed oligarchy could no longer make decisions independent of other classes." The 1922 *tenentes* revolt was the beginning of a mounting political challenge to the Old Republic.[14] Elsewhere political control had to be relinquished, although nowhere was the export oligarchy's economic position threatened, and in all cases the new regimes continued to follow the path of primary export-based capitalist development. Of course, there was considerable variation with regard to the timing and extent of political change. For example, in Argentina the oligarchic state was under pressure much earlier than elsewhere and there was a significant diminution of elite political representation by the early 1920s. In Chile on the other hand, despite Alessandri's victory, the political system proved far more resistant to such pressures and the social composition of the legislature was much slower to change.[15] Peru saw the most radical shift. Leguía wisely, from his point of view, disbanded the legislature and instituted a new constitution, which contained many innovative provisions, including major improvements in workers' rights, social welfare, protection for the Indian communities, and far-reaching educational reform.[16] Few of these were carried through. By 1922 he was moving strongly against the workers and students who had supported him, but under his regime sectors of the oligarchy, especially certain individuals, did suffer and the power of the Civilista Party was truly broken.[17] Regardless of their policies or the success they had, the fact that leaders espousing populist policies were able to win elections was a testimony to a major sea change, the beginning of mass politics in Latin America.

IV

The external shock delivered by the war in Europe, rather than creating the conditions for inward-directed capitalist development, tended to strengthen the central role of primary exports. Partly as a result of this, as well as the deep-seated and widely felt external economic vulnerability evidenced in 1914, and the naked forms of coercion employed by the Allies, the war witnessed a reaction against foreign economic domination and a substantial intensification of nationalist sentiment in most countries. This seems to have been a worldwide phenomenon, reflecting to some extent a reaction against European imperialist domination.[18] There was a long heritage of such thought in Latin America, the most recent (from 1900) and influential being found in the *arielista* movement,[19] which held that Latin America was the spiritual Ariel as opposed to the materialist Caliban of North America. This essentially idealist stance had undergone a fundamental change by 1920. Gerald Martin writes that, "After the First World War, the Mexican and Russian revolutions, and the 1918 Córdoba student revolt, such spiritual anti-imperialism would be supplanted by a keener perception of social and economic struggle, and art would take on a class character."[20]

The impact of the war made nationalism very much more prominent and broadened its appeal. Not only was economic nationalism given a boost, but cultural nationalism too became more popular, different variants being adopted and espoused by revolutionary and reactionary movements. It is important to understand the reasons for these differences, but whatever its form the nationalism that developed during the war and in the 1920s represented the growing disenchantment with the European social model so idealized by the Latin American elite before 1914 and the turning instead to a celebration of local culture and traditions. It is not surprising that this national cultural renaissance should have gained momentum during the war, for with the "advanced" nations at each other's throats it became difficult to sustain the idea that Europe represented a higher form of "civilization" or "progress." As Stabb has observed,[21] in the first two decades of the century,

...it became increasingly evident that European culture might not be as worthy of emulation as was once thought. The possibility that war, depression and totalitarianism might thoroughly exhaust the traditional centers of Western civilization gradually became quite real... In a world whose most valued goals were technical progress, material abundance, and a "rationally" ordered middle class society, Hispanic America might well feel inferior, but (Americanists) saw that these typically nineteenth century values were in retreat.

The war not only helped precipitate a greater degree of skepticism in Latin America about the nineteenth-century European values of rationality and progress. Faith in these values, already under attack in

Europe before 1914, was shattered by the war, which served to accentuate and spread the ideological disintegration. According to José Carlos Mariátegui, Peru's foremost Marxist theorist, this was a widespread phenomenon which affected the West as a whole. He argued that the war had rekindled ancient doubts about progress, as it demonstrated that humanity could survive factors greater than "Science" and against the interests of "Civilization."[22] He wrote,

The world war has not only modified and shattered the economy and politics of the West. It has also modified and shattered its thought and its spirit. The economic consequences... are no more evident or perceptible than the spiritual and psychological consequences. The politicians, the statesmen, will perhaps by experiment find a formula and a method to resolve the former, but they will surely not find a theory and a practice adequate to overcome the latter.

In this sense Latin American thinkers, although they turned increasingly to nationalist themes, were continuing to reflect the intellectual trends emanating from across the Atlantic.

There were also local factors which served to make nationalism a more desirable world view. For example, the elite found it convenient to abandon their erstwhile cosmopolitanism and whip up, or at least support, xenophobic nationalist sentiments in order to counter the threat posed by working-class unrest. This issue and those mentioned above need to be spelled out in somewhat more detail for, to the extent they reflected changing perceptions to a changing world, they are central to any consideration of the development of both Latin American society and of the primary export capitalism which was so central to that society.

Prewar Brazil, like the rest of Latin America, had been dominated by European cultural assumptions.[23] In his autobiography published in 1900, Nabuco wrote,[24] "We Brazilians—and the same can be said for the other American peoples—belong to America merely on a new and fluctuating layer of our mind, while we belong to Europe on all our stratified levels. As soon as we acquire the least culture, the latter predominates over the former. Our imagination cannot fail to be European, that is to be human." There were writers such as Manuel Bomfim, Alberto Tôrres, Euclides da Cunha, or Raimundo Farias Brito,[25] who vied against this type of self-imposed cultural imperialism, but not many of their fellow countrymen listened. Skidmore argues that the First World War changed all this as it served to stimulate a new form of nationalist thought in Brazil. He writes that Brazilians[26] "... began, for the first time on a large scale, to feel that they could change the role in which Social Darwinism and an inherited European culture were casting Brazil. For the first time the mainstream of Brazilian thought learned how to rebel against the framework within which European ideas had straightjacketed it–most importantly, to reject the determinism of racist thought."

An important feature of this new cultural awareness was the Brazilian Modernist movement, which can trace its origins to the controversial 1917 exhibition of Anita Malfatti in São Paulo, but really developed most fully from the early 1920s. Rachum has noted that[27] "Inasmuch as modernists attacked the conventional academic Brazilian art, they rejected an art which was in its form European as much as Brazilian. This led to an intransigent attitude against further subjugation to the European cultural metropolis, and as a result to the preoccupation with giving Modernism a genuine nationalist content."

As well as the beginnings of a greater national cultural awareness, the new nationalism also provided the ideological base for an attack on working-class militancy, something which had occurred earlier in Argentina, and was, in fact a common remedy for class conflict in all capitalist societies. When there were large numbers of immigrants in the work force, as in Brazil, Argentina or the United States, then this nationalism usually contained strong elements of xenophobia. This was the case in Brazil, where the Liga da Defesa Nacional, formed in 1916, espoused a particularly virulent form of anti-immigrant nationalism.[28] This can be seen as a reaction against social tensions associated with Brazil's capitalist transformation. There was also another equally reactionary variant which was directed against the Portuguese, especially the strong merchant community in Rio. This was associated with Afonso Celso and Alvaro Bomilcar, the journal *Brazilea*, launched in 1917, and the groups Propaganda Nacionalista and Ação Social Nacionalista.[29] Yet another reaction was the rise of economic nationalism. According to Topik,[30] "The lesson of the First World War to most Brazilian decision makers was that the government should stimulate 'industrial initiatives capable of liberating us from dependence on foreign markets.'" This is not to argue that a nationalist economic policy gained immediate widespread adherence among the elite,[31] but over time it did become a major feature of Brazil's economic programme.

Argentina shared almost all of the aforementioned forms of nationalism, although it would seem because the country was relatively more "advanced," the reaction against various foreign aspects of its capitalist transformation surfaced slightly earlier than in

Brazil. There were nationalist rumblings increasing from about the turn of the century,[32] but it is generally accepted that the first major statements of modern Argentine nationalism came with the publication in 1909 of *La restauración nacionalista* by Ricardo Rojas and *El diario de Gabriel Quiroga* by Manuel Gálvez in the following year.[33] Both were essentially arguments for the need to protect Argentine culture, usually seen as rooted in the countryside, from the pernicious influences of immigration. Gálvez even attacked the tango, which has since become so quintessentially Argentine, as a "lamentable symbol of our denationalization."[34] By 1914, the gaucho, who once represented the barbarism which was to be swept aside by the civilizing influence of European culture, had been elevated to the status of a national hero, and the poem *Martín Fierro*, published by Jośe Hernández in the 1870s, became a national epic. Solberg asserts that this change came about,[35] "...as intellectuals became increasingly aware that immigration was altering the social and economic patterns with which the upper class dominated Argentine life. Intellectuals who sympathized with the traditional social structure attempted to use the gaucho as a symbol to convince the public that the cultural values of the Argentine elites represented the true national character."

"World War I," writes Jesús Méndez,[36] "posed serious questions to Argentine culture. For one it confirmed previous suspicions that, at least in the cultural realm, positivistic concepts of continued, linear, progressively perfectible growth no longer survived." During the war the nationalist call was taken up, albeit in different ways, by the extreme right-wing Liga Patriótica Argentina and the university reform movement. For the latter it was Americanism rather than a narrow Argentine nationalism which they embraced. For example, Aníbal Ponce saw the war as "the greater liberator," creating a clear break with the past.[37] The war tarnished the European image of progress and civilization "...obliging a turning toward America, the Mexican Revolution accentuating the need for a nationalist consciousness, formed on the forge of anti-cosmopolitan romanticism, carrying a defensive and often provincial spiritualism."[38] This new consciousness was given an important radical dimension when the students joined with the workers to demand reform. It was this same upsurge in working-class unrest which the Liga was expressly formed to counter. However, for this group cultural nationalism represented less a rejection of European cultural norms, although they did reject them, than a weapon to be used against the immigrant working class.[39]

It would seem that on the whole, as Solberg has argued,[40]

before 1914 Argentine nationalism was cultural rather than economic. Nonetheless, in the decades before the war there was mounting criticism of foreign companies, especially the British-owned railways.[41] During the war Yrigoyen was publicly critical of foreign capital, seems to have taken the workers' part in their struggles with the railway companies, and was seen by many as anti-British. He clearly did not like the British, but on the whole his economic nationalism was for domestic political consumption. It was more rhetorical than practical.[42] For example, Solberg shows that Yrigoyen was firmly wedded to the economic links with Britain, and made no attempt to alter the country's externally dependent economic structure.[43] Furthermore, although he eventually pushed through the reorganization of the national oil company, Yacimientos Petrolíferos Fiscales, in 1922, a landmark of Argentine economic nationalism, this was only after years of indecision and delay.

The war did, however, stimulate the formation of a more genuine economic critique of the country's dependent economic position. Solberg writes,[44]

The wartime crisis...sparked a critical examination of the nation's economic structure among a small but influential group of Argentine intellectuals. The essayists and economic theorists who challenged the soundness of the traditional export-oriented economy made a profound impact on the evolution of twentieth-century Argentine economic thought. Their fascination with industrial power and economic independence places them among the intellectual precursors of modern Argentine economic nationalism.

Economic nationalism had been fully developed in Chile by 1914,[45] and war seems only to have confirmed the views of leading Chilean critics that a greater degree of economic independence was necessary. The monopsony control exercised by the Nitrate of Soda Executive and the wholesale takeover of the copper mines could not have been better illustrations of the extent to which the Chilean economy was at the mercy of foreigners. Chilean nationalists claimed that the increased US commercial penetration was a sign of the country's inferiority and decadence.[46] Monteón argues[47] that during the war "The rhetoric of economic nationalism was gaining at the expense of *laissez-faire*...Few political interests any longer accepted the arguments of free trade; the role of the state in the nitrate trade, in providing public services, and in protecting industry were too important to be ignored." Daniel Martner's views are more or less typical of the nationalist critique. Claiming that the disruptions caused by the war were creating the opportunity for a new direction in economic life, he argued that Chile must aspire to export manufactured goods, as do the developed countries.[48] "Being exporters of material made up in other countries weakens our economic and social independence and sovereignty and obstructs the road to prosperity and wellbeing." Although a patriotic nationalism was employed against students and workers in 1920, because there were so few immigrants among the working class there was little of the xenophobic cultural nationalism found in Brazil or Argentina.[49]

In Peru the reaction against European intellectual domination was slower to emerge than elsewhere. In fact up until the end of the First World War, with the exception of González Prada, Peruvian nationalism was predominantly associated with the Civilistas' desire to modernize the country along European lines and their revolt against "traditional" values.[50] This was very similar to the kind of positivist-inspired ideology which was coming under increasing attack in other countries. Such an attack was slower to develop in Peru, partly because of the defeat suffered in the War of the Pacific. In the years of civil war and national reconstruction which followed, it was argued by the ruling elites that defeat was due to the country's relative backwardness, and, therefore, what was needed was the reform of traditional institutions and the creation of a modern state.

There were, however, some dissenting voices. The most influential was that of Manuel González Prada, poet and anarchist, whose ideas about the need to bring the Indian masses fully into the nation, mark him out as an early *indigenista*. However, while his advocacy of social revolution clearly distinguishes him from most of his contemporaries, like them he too was imbued with strong positivist principles.[51] These principles were decisively rejected by another major Peruvian thinker, José de Riva-Agüero, whose romantic reverence for the country's Inca past was developed within an extremely conservative perspective. But it was not until 1919 that a major break came. It grew out of the workers' revolt and the university reform movement. It was from these conflicts that the radical anti-imperialism of Haya de la Torre and Mariátegui's revolutionary *indigenismo* were to arise in the 1920s.

The development of a new nationalist consciousness in Latin America during and immediately after the war was a complex and contradictory process, but in all its diverse forms it represented a mounting disquiet about, and in many ways a rejection of, the liberal assumptions which had underpinned the growth of world capitalism in the nineteenth century. This mirrored development in Europe, where, as Mariátegui argued, the liberal concept of progress dominated both bourgeois and proletarian culture before 1914. The war "... shattered the bubble of bourgeois complacency. The shock waves of the ensuing 'spiritual and psychological' crisis shocked the whole culture."[52] As with all the many different social, political, and economic changes that have been discussed, the revolt against European cultural and intellectual domination was not something that first appeared during the war. However, by showing the bankruptcy of the claims for European cultural superiority, destroying the international economy, and being the excuse for the Allies' often tactless meddling in the region's economic affairs the conflict served to stimulate a diverse, but powerful nationalist reaction. This reaction was further fueled by the two great revolutions of the period, the Mexican and the Russian. The latter demonstrated the possibilities of proletarian revolution, and so gave great encouragement to the embattled working class. At the same time, by creating panic among the ruling class it also helped to ignite an already smouldering nationalism, patriotic and often xenophobic, which was directed against workers. The Mexican Revolution, on the other hand, offered not only a symbol of national liberation, but also made heroes of the Indian and *mestizo* masses, offering a potent American cultural alternative to the tarnished, and in many eyes, discredited European model. As Portantiero writes,[53] "All of Latin America, which had built its links to the external world with its elites influenced by European manufactures and ideologies, felt the commotion of the war as the collapse of a historical cycle which brought with it the bankruptcy of cosmopolitanism and the rebirth of a nationalist preoccupation."

V

In many respects the war marked a major economic, political, social, and cultural watershed for Latin America. It also demonstrated a number of salient features of the region's brand of primary export capitalism. In the first place, there is little doubt that there had been substantial materially progressive change during the nineteenth century. Without it the export sectors could not have functioned. André Gunder Frank's stagnationist theory is, therefore, completely untenable. This does not, however, mean that a diffusionist perspective need be accepted. The capitalism that did develop in Latin America was both chronically weak and in many key respects excessively dependent. The two conditions fed on each other, the dependence engendering weakness and the weakness making greater economic independence difficult to achieve. The outbreak of war showed with startling clarity just how vulnerable and multidependent these economies had become. Furthermore, although developments during the remainder of the war indicated that the economic systems here were not totally devoid of independence, renewed prosperity continued to rely on the ability to export primary commodities financed by foreign credit and carried in foreign ships. In only very limited ways was Latin America isolated from outside pressures during the war.

But it is wrong to see these problems simply as the result of various forms of external imposition or control. The maintenance of primary export capitalism had relied and continued to rely on the complicity of the local elites. They freely collaborated because they prospered from this system, at no time more so than during the European war. It was this group who reaped the benefits of progress. E. Bradford Burns has recently maintained that in nineteenth-century Latin America:[54]

Economic growth, confined to a narrow economic sector involved in export, aggravated the inequalities of income and the differences in the qualities of life. An increasing rate of economic growth in that select sector further unbalanced income distribution by concentrating the wealth in fewer hands. The industrialization accompanying selective modernization likewise favored the wealthy at the expense of the poor...the elites' urge to export and to modernize exacerbated the position of the majority. So while the quality of life of the majority deteriorated, the lifestyle of the elites and to a lesser extent the emerging middle class improved, both to extremes previously unequaled.

This is a fair account of the period, but could as easily be a description of the early stages of the industrial revolution in Britain. In this sense it suggests that, however well-intentioned, it is wrong to argue as Burns does, that capitalist development is about the welfare of the masses. Historically, capitalism grew not by making everyone better off but through creating greater inequality. When later this began to be offset, or at least the worst aspects of poverty alleviated, in the more advanced countries, it was a product, among other things, of class struggle and political change, the efficiency of industrial capitalism, and the ability to increase real wages by drawing on cheap wage goods and raw materials from regions such as Latin America. These last two options were denied Latin America's primary export elites. During the war when the contradictions of dependent capitalist development were greatly magnified and the class struggle exploded, in order to maintain their hegemonic position they were eventually forced into varying forms of political compromise. Although there was little change in the structure of economic power within these societies, especially as export sectors were generally strengthened, this was the beginning of the end of the old political order. This existing economic order was to decay more slowly, awaiting the crisis of world capitalism in the 1930s for its most dramatic moment of transition.[55]

From the last decades of the nineteenth century the export elites in all four countries had different versions of essentially the same utopian dream. Their "barbaric" countries could be modernized by looking to Europe for capital, technology, labor, markets, and culture. By exploiting their "natural advantages" as primary producers they would benefit from the occasionally temperamental, but seemingly endless expansion of the British-dominated world economy. By the turn of the century the dream had begun to go wrong. Instead of the foreign presence being transient, there was growing foreign domination, whether by merchants or bankers, on the Argentine railways, or in the Chilean nitrate fields. And instead of obedient, docile labor the elite began to face an urban working-class movement, hesitant, but growing in confidence. The imperialist war in Europe brought the "golden age" of the international economy to a sudden and bloody end. By the early 1920s the elites' nineteenth-century vision of European-style progress lay shattered as much on the battlefields of Europe as on the smaller scale battlefields in the streets of Lima, Santiago, Buenos Aires and São Paulo.

Notes

Abbreviations

Boletín de la Sociedad de Fomento Fabril (Chile)	BSFF
Hispanic American Historical Review	HAHR
Journal of Latin American Studies	JLAS
US Bureau of Foreign and Domestic Commerce	BFDC
US Department of Commerce, Supplements to Commerce Reports	SCR
Wileman's Brazilian Review	WBR

Document references

All references to RG (Record Group) are to material held in the United States National Archives, Washington DC.

FO refers to British Foreign Office Documents in Public Record Office, London.

Cayaltí *mss.*, Palto *mss.*, SNA *mss.*, all in Archivo del Fuero Agrario, Lima.

Introduction

1 Bill Albert, *An Essay on the Peruvian Sugar Industry 1880–1920* (Norwich, 1976), p. 2.

2 See for example, Rory Miller, "Latin American manufacturing and the First World War: an exploratory essay," *World Development*, vol. 9, no. 8 (1981), 707–16.

3 André Gunder Frank, *Latin America: Underdevelopment or Revolution* (New York, 1969), pp. 9–10.

1 Before the war

1 Douglas Friedman, *The State and Underdevelopment in Spanish America. The Political Roots of Dependency in Peru and Argentina* (Boulder and London, 1984), *passim*.

2 Thomas E. Skidmore, *Black into White. Race and Nationality in Brazilian*

Thought (New York, 1974), p. 52. See also Carl Solberg, *Immigration and Nationalism. Argentina and Chile 1890–1914* (Austin, 1970), p. 29.

3 Robert Triffen, *The Evolution of the International Monetary System: Historical Reappraisal and Future Perspectives* (Princeton, 1964), p. 8.

4 Geoffrey Kay, *Development and Underdevelopment. A Marxist Analysis* (London, 1975), pp. 102–3.

5 See Elizabeth Fox-Genovese and Eugene Genovese, *Fruits of Merchant Capital. Slavery and Bourgeois Property in the Rise and Expansion of Capitalism* (Oxford, 1983), chapter 1.

6 See Henry Bernstein, "Underdevelopment and the law of value: a critique of Kay," *Journal of Political Economy*, vol. 6 (1976), p. 57.

7 Carlos F. Díaz Alejandro, "Argentina, Australia and Brazil before 1929" in D.C.M. Platt and Guido di Tella (eds.), *Argentina, Australia and Canada. Studies in Comparative Development, 1870–1965* (Oxford, 1985), pp. 95–109; Barrie Dyster, "Argentine and Australian development compared," *Past and Present*, 84 (1979), pp. 109–10. On Sweden see A.S. Milward S.B. Saul, *The Economic Development of Continental Europe, 1780–1870* (London, 1973), chapter 8.

8 Barrington Moore, Jr., *Social Origins of Dictatorship and Democracy* (London, 1969). pp. xii–xiii.

9 Fernando Henrique Cardoso and Enzo Faletto, *Dependency and Development in Latin America* (London, Berkeley and Los Angeles, 1979), p. xvi.

10 Karl Marx, *Capital*, vol. III, chapter 20.

11 Cardoso and Faletto, *Dependency*, p. xvii.

12 James Bryce, *South America. Observations and Impressions* (London, 1912), p. 315.

13 James R. Scobie, *Buenos Aires. Plaza to Suburb, 1870–1910* (New York, 1974), p. 36.

14 A.G. Ford, "British investment and Argentine economic development, 1880–1914" in David Rock (ed.), *Argentina in the Twentieth Century* (Pittsburgh, 1975), p. 31.

15 W. Arthur Lewis, *Growth and Fluctuations, 1870–1913* (London, 1978), pp. 196, 203.

16 Chile, Oficina Central de Estadística, *Anuario estadístico de la República de Chile 1911*, pp. 94–5.

17 Guido Di Tella y Manuel Zymelman, *Las etapas del desarrollo económico argentino* (Buenos Aires, 1967), pp. 51, 60.

18 Carlos F. Díaz Alejandro, *Essays on the Economic History of the Argentine Republic* (New Haven, 1970), p. 98.

19 *Ibid.*, pp. 209, 282.

20 James R. Scobie, *Revolution on the Pampas. A Social History of Argentine Wheat, 1860–1910* (Austin, 1964), pp. 71–88.

21 *Ibid.*, p. 162.

22 Roger Gravil, "The Anglo-Argentine connection and the War of 1914–1918," JLAS, vol. 9, no. 1 (1973), p. 61.

23 *Ibid.*, p. 63. Also, Scobie, *Revolution*, pp. 89–113.

24 Gravil, "Anglo-Argentine," p. 79.

25 R. Greenhill and C. Crossley, "The River Plate beef trade" in D.C.M. Platt (ed.), *Business Imperialism 1840–1930. An Enquiry Based on the British Experience in Latin America* (Oxford, 1977), pp. 284–334.

26 V.L. Phelps, *The International Economic Position of Argentina* (Philadelphia and London, 1938), p. 246.

27 *Ibid.*, p. 108.

28 W. Woodruff, *The Impact of Western Man. A Study of Europe's Role in the World Economy 1750–1960* (London, 1966), pp. 154–5.

29 Díaz Alejandro, *Essays*, p. 30.

30 Phelps, *International Economic Position*, p. 24.

31 A.G. Ford, *The Gold Standard 1880–1914: Britain and Argentina* (Oxford, 1962), pp. 124–5, 168.

32 C.M. Lewis, *British Railways in Argentina, 1857–1914. A Case Study of Foreign Investment* (London, 1983), p. 197.

33 *Ibid.*, p. 197.

34 W.R. Wright, *British-Owned Railways in Argentina. Their Effect on the Growth of Economic Nationalism, 1854–1948* (Austin, 1974), pp. 4–5.

35 Lewis, *British Railways*, p. 219.

36 Solberg, *Immigration*, p. 45.

37 *Ibid.*, pp. 17–20. Also Leopoldo Zea, *The Latin American Mind* (Norman, Oklahoma, 1963), pp. 218–20.

38 Solberg, *Immigration*, chapter 6.

39 Richard Alan Yoast, "The development of Argentine anarchism: a socio-ideological analysis" (PhD thesis, University of Wisconsin–Madison, 1975), chapter 3.

40 *Ibid.*, pp. 213–14.

41 David Rock, *Politics in Argentina 1890–1930. The Rise and Fall of Radicalism* (Cambridge, 1975), chapter 3.

42 *Ibid.*, pp. 38–9.

43 Roberto Cortés Conde, *The First Stages of Modernization in South America* (New York, 1974), p. 151.

44 L. Brewster Smith and H.T. Collins, *The Economic Position of Argentina during the War*, US Dept. of Commerce, Miss. Series No. 88 (Washington DC, 1920) pp. 122–3.

45 Ernesto Laclau, "Modos de producción, sistemas económicos y población excedente–approximación histórica a los casos argentino y chileno," *Revista Latinoamericano de Sociología*, vol. V, no. 2, (1969), 297.

46 Bryce, *South America*, pp. 415,419.

47 Lewis, *Growth*, pp. 193, 203.

48 A.V. Villela and W. Suzigan, *Government Policy and the Economic Growth of Brazil, 1889–1945* (Rio, 1977), p. 361.

49 Nathaniel Leff, *Underdevelopment and Development in Brazil* vol. I *Economic Structure and Change, 1822–1947* (London, 1982), p. 83.

50 *Ibid.*, p. 22.

51 Díaz Alejandro, "Argentina," p. 98.

52 Stanley Stein, *Vassouras: A Brazilian Coffee County, 1850–1900* (Cambridge, Mass., 1957), *passim*.

53 Barbara Weinstein, *The Amazon Rubber Boom, 1850–1920* (Stanford, 1983), *passim*.

54 Robert Greenhill, "The Brazilian Coffee Trade", in Platt (ed.), *Business Imperialism*, p. 214.

55 Leff, *Underdevelopment*, vol. I, p. 88.

56 Greenhill, "Brazilian coffee," p. 207.

57 See below, p. 87.

58 Greenhill, "Brazilian coffee," p. 229.

59 Thomas H. Holloway, *The Brazilian Coffee Valorization of 1906. Regional Politics and Economic Dependence* (Madison, 1975), pp. 56–75.

60 Steven C. Topik, "Economic nationalism and the state in an underdeveloped country: Brazil 1889–1930" (unpublished PhD thesis, University of Texas, 1978), p. 152.

61 Marcelo P. Abreu, "A dívida pública do Brasil, 1824–1931," *Estudos Econômicos*, vol. 15, no. 2 (1985) p. 168.

62 Bill Albert, *South America and the World Economy from Independence to 1930* (London, 1983), p. 39.

63 Ana Célia Castro, *As empresas estrangeiras no Brasil 1860–1913* (Rio, 1979), pp. 80–3, 116–22; Abreu, "Dívida," p. 168.

64 Castro, *Empresas*, pp. 80, 116.

65 This section based on J.S. Duncan, *Public and Private Operation of Railways in Brazil* (New York, 1932), chapters 3 & 4.

66 Thomas H. Holloway, *Immigrants on the Land. Coffee and Society in São Paulo* (Chapel Hill, 1980), p. 63.

67 Skidmore, *Black into White*, chapter 4.

68 Robert F. Foerster, *The Italian Emigration of Our Times* (Cambridge, Mass., 1919), pp. 285–6.

69 Holloway, *Immigrants*, chapter 3.

70 São Paulo, *Boletim do Departamento Estadual do Trabalho*, no. 38 & 39 t. 1 & 2, 1921, pp. 84–5.

71 Brazil, Instituto Brasileiro de Geografía e Estatística, *O Brasil em números* (Rio, 1960), p. 8.

72 Holloway, *Immigrants*, p. 63.

73 Michael Hall, "Immigration and the early São Paulo working class," *Jahrbüch für Geschichte von Staat, Wirtschaft und Gesellschaft Lateinamerikas*, 12 (1975) pp. 393–4.

74 Warren Dean, *The Industrialization of São Paulo, 1880–1945* (Austin, 1969), chapter 4.

75 See below, pp. 236, 245, 261.

76 Topik, "Nationalism," chapter 8.

77 Skidmore, *Black into White*, chapter 3.

78 *Ibid.*, p. 170.

79 José Maria Bello, *A History of Modern Brazil, 1889–1964* (Stanford, 1966), pp. 234–5.

80 Bryce, *South America*, pp. 217–18.

81 See below, chapter 6.

82 Solberg, *Immigration*, pp. 162–8. See below, pp. 317–18.

83 M.J. Mamalakis, *The Growth and Structure of the Chilean Economy: From Independence to Allende* (New Haven, 1976), p. 29.

84 Albert, *South America*, p. 38.

85 See below, p. 273.

86 Gabriel Palma, "External disequilibrium and internal industrialization: Chile, 1914–1935" in C. Abel and C.M. Lewis (eds.), *Latin America Economic Imperialism and the State: The Political Economy of the External Connection from Independence to the Present* (London, 1985), p. 319.

87 Chile, Oficina Central de Estadística, *Sinopsis estadística de la República de Chile* (Santiago, 1924), p. 148.

88 *Ibid.*, pp. 64, 148.

89 W.F.V. Scott, *Report on the Industrial and Economic Situation in Chile, September 1924* (London, 1925), p. 95.

90 C. Cariola and O. Sunkel, "Nitrate expansion and socio-economic transformation in Chile: 1880–1930," Institute of Development Studies, University of Sussex, Discussion Paper no. 129 (1978), *passim*.

91 J. Fred Rippy, *British Investments in Latin America 1822–1949* (Minneapolis, 1959), p. 68; Charles McQueen, *Chilean Public Finance* (Washington DC, 1924), pp. 34–6, 42–3.

92 R. Greenhill, "The nitrate and iodine trades, 1880–1912" in D.C.M. Platt (ed.), *Business Imperialism*, p. 259.

93 McQueen, *Chilean Public Finance*, p. 106.

94 Markos Mamalakis, "The role of government in the resource transfer and resource allocation processes: the Chilean nitrate sector, 1880–1930" in Gustav Ranis (ed.), *Government and Economic Development* (New Haven, 1971), p. 195.

95 Palma, "External disequilibrium," pp. 319–20.

96 See below, chapter 5.

97 Palma, "External disequilibrium," p. 319.

98 Arnold J. Bauer, *Chilean Rural Society from the Spanish Conquest to 1930* (Cambridge, 1975), p. 229.

99 M.J. Cavarozzi and J. Petras, "Chile" in R.H. Chilcote and J.C. Edelstein (eds.), *Latin America: The Struggle with Dependency and Beyond* (Cambridge, Mass., 1974), p. 495.

100 Bryce, *South America*, p. 223.

101 See below, p. 276.

102 Bryce, *South America*, pp. 52–3.

103 Alejandro Garland, *Perú en 1906* (Lima, 1907), p. 80, cited in Manuel Burga and Alberto Flores Galindo, *Apogeo y crisis de la República Aristocrática* (Lima, 1980), pp. 15–16.

104 Emilio Romero, *Historia económica del Perú*, vol. II (Lima, nd), p. 157.

105 Burga and Flores Galindo, *Apogeo*, pp. 14–15.

106 José María Arguedas, *Perú vivo* (Lima, 1966), p. 12, quoted in *ibid.*, p. 12.

107 Unless otherwise noted details on Peruvian exports from, Rosemary Thorp and Geoffrey Bertram, *Peru 1890–1977. Growth and Policy in an Open Economy* (London, 1978), chapters 3, 4 and 5.

108 See for example, Peter Klarén, "Social and economic consequences of modernization in the Peruvian sugar industry, 1879–1930" in K. Duncan and I. Rutledge (eds.), *Land and Labour in Latin America* (Cambridge, 1977) p. 229.

109 Thorp and Bertram, *Peru*, chapter 4; Albert, *An Essay*, pp. 33a–64a; W.S. Bell, "An Essay on the Peruvian Cotton Industry, 1825–1920," University of Liverpool, Centre for Latin American Studies, Working Paper, no. 6 (1985), *passim*.

110 Rory Miller, "Small business in the Peruvian oil industry: Lobitos Oilfields Limited before 1934," *The Business History Review*, vol. LVI, no. 3 (1982), *passim*.

111 Rippy, *British Investments*, p. 68; Max Winkler, *Investments of United States Capital in Latin America* (Boston, 1928. reprint 1971, New York and London), p. 275.

112 Rory Miller, "The Grace contract, the Peruvian corporation, and Peruvian history," *Ibero-Amerikanisches Archiv*, nf Jg 9 H. 3/4, (1983), *passim*.

113 Thorp and Bertram, *Peru*, chapter 3.

114 *Ibid.*, pp. 143–4.

115 Burga and Flores Galindo, *Apogeo*, pp. 88–103; Julio Cotler, *Clases, estado y nación en el Perú* (Lima, 1978), chapter 3.

116 Rory Miller, "The Coastal elite and Peruvian politics, 1895–1919" JLAS, vol. 14, part 1 (1982), *passim*; Stephen M. Gorman, "The state, elite, and export in nineteenth-century Peru. Toward an alternative reinterpretation of political change," *Journal of Interamerican Studies and World Affairs*, vol. 21, no. 3 (August 1979), pp. 395–418.

117 Jesús Chavarría, "La desaparición del Perú colonial (1870–1919)," *Aportes* (Paris) no. 23 (January 1973), pp. 121–53; Vincent C. Peloso, "Cotton planters, the state and rural labor policy: ideological origins of the Peruvian *República Aristocrática*, 1895–1908," *The Americas*, vol. XL, no. 2 (October 1983), pp. 209–28.

118 Peter Blanchard, "A populist precursor: Guillermo Billinghurst," JLAS, vol. 9, no. 2 (1977), pp. 251–73.

119 Burga and Flores Galindo, *Apogeo*, p. 157; Denis Sulmont S., *Historia del movimiento obrero peruano (1890–1977)* (Lima, 1977), pp. 32–3.
120 See below, chapter 6.
121 Burga and Flores Galindo, *Apogeo*, pp. 114–19.
122 Jesús Chavarría, *José Carlos Mariátequi and the Rise of Modern Peru* (Albuquerque, 1979), pp. 1–2.

2 The early impact of the war

1 Ford, *Britain and Argentina*, p. 178.
2 *Ibid.*, p. 174. Also see Phelps, *International Economic Position*, pp. 22–6.
3 Buenos Aires, 30 March 1914 (RG59 514–835.51/107).
4 Winston Fritsch, "Aspectos da política econômica no Brasil, 1906–1914," in P. Neuhaus (ed.), *Economia brasileira. Uma visão histórica* (Rio, 1980), pp. 291–6.
5 Rio, 12 August 1913 (RG59 514–832.551/61).
6 L.S. Rowe, *Early Effects of the War upon the Finance, Commerce, and Industry of Peru* (New York, 1920), pp. 3–7.
7 *Ibid.*, p. 14; Peter Blanchard, *The Origins of the Peruvian Labor Movement, 1883–1919* (Pittsburgh, 1982), chapter 6.
8 *Ibid.*, p. 14.
9 *Boletín de la Sociedad de Fomento Fabril*, January 1914.
10 *The Economist*, 11 July 1914, pp. 60–1.
11 W.H. Lough, *Financial Developments in South American Countries*, Dept. of Commerce, BFDC, Special Agent Series no. 103 (Washington DC, 1915), p. 29.
12 *Sinopsis estadística 1924*, pp. 64, 115, 147–8.
13 Lough, *Financial Developments*, p. 29.
14 *Ibid.*, p. 182.
15 *The West Coast Leader*, 14 August 1914.
16 *The Economist*, 19 September 1914.
17 SCR, no. 40b, 11 August 1915, p. 6.
18 SCR, no. 38b, 17 April 1915, p. 18.
19 SCR, no. 40d, 16 November 1915, p. 7.
20 Rowe, *Peru*, pp. 47–8; Rowe, *The Early Effects of the European War on the Finance, Commerce and Industry of Chile* (New York, 1918), pp. 72–5.
21 Rowe, *Peru*, p. 47.
22 Smith and Collins, *Argentina*, p. 83.
23 *Boletín de la Sociedad Nacional Agricultura*, 15 September 1914.
24 Smith and Collins, *Argentina*, p. 83; "Maritime transportation of Chile" in *Proceedings of the Second Pan-American Financial Conference* (Washington DC, 1921), pp. 16–17.
25 W.A. Brown, Jr., *The International Gold Standard Reinterpreted 1914–1934* (New York, 1940), vol I, book I, "The breakdown 1914–1918."

26 Hartley Withers, *War and Lombard Street* (New York, 1915), p. 56.
27 Lough, *Financial Developments*, pp. 11–12, 23–5, 30–1, 35–7.
28 F.W. Fetter, *Monetary Inflation in Chile* (Princeton, 1932), pp. 137–8.
29 David Joslin, *A Century of Banking in Latin America* (London, 1963), p. 215.
30 SCR, no. 40b, 11 August 1915, p. 6.
31 Pernambuco, 10 September 1914 (RG59 519–24, 832.5/76).
32 Rio, 22 September 1914 (RG59 519–24, 832.51/74).
33 *La Revista Comercial* (Valparaíso), 8 August 1914.
34 *El Comercio* (Lima), 7 August 1914; Cayaltí Correspondence, Cartas Kendal, Lima–London, 27 August 1914.
35 *Boletín de la Sociedad Agrícola del Sur* (Concepción), August 1914.
36 *O Brasil em números*, p. 146.
37 Villela and Suzigan, *Government Policy*, pp. 255, 361.
38 *The South American Journal*, 6 January 1915, p. 23.
39 Lough, *Financial Developments*, pp. 24–5.
40 Villela and Suzigan, *Government Policy*, p. 255.
41 B.I. Kaufman, "United States Trade and Latin America: the Wilson years," *Journal of American History*, vol. 58, no. 2 (1971), p. 353.
42 Rio, 3 August 1914 (RG59 519–24, 832.51/71); "The Argentine market," Buenos Aires, 21 August 1914 (RG84, 310–610, 1914 part 5).
43 SCR, no. 40a, 12 May 1915, p. 3.
44 "Concerning the coffee production in Brazil," Rio, 26 July 1915 (RG59 519–41 832.61333/165).
45 Antonio Delfim Netto, "Foundations for the analysis of Brazilian coffee problems" in C.M. Peláez (ed.), *Essays on Coffee and Economic Development* (Rio, 1973), p. 95.
46 SCR, no. 40a, 12 May 1915, 3; *O Brasil em números*, p. 88.
47 "Enclosure" prices from Nitrate Propaganda Association of Iquique, Iquique, 22 October 1914 (RG84, 610).
48 Rowe, *Chile*, p. 51.
49 *The Economist*, 16 January 1915, p. 95.
50 "Financial condition of Nitrate of soda industry," Iquique, 22 October 1914 (RG84 610).
51 Michael Monteón, *Chile in the Nitrate Era. The Evolution of Economic Dependence, 1880–1930* (Madison, 1982), p. 112.
52 *The Economist*, 20 February 1915, pp. 370–2.
53 *Boletín de la Sociedad Nacional de Minería*, 18 August 1914.
54 *Sinopsis estadística 1924*, pp. 147–8.
55 Albert, *An Essay*, pp. 112a–27a.
56 *The West Coast Leader*, 10 April 1915.
57 Albert, *An Essay*, pp. 150a–2a.
58 *El Comercio*, 19 August 1914.
59 "Argentine exports and imports and financial condition July to December

1914 compared with same period 1913," L.J. Keena, Buenos Aires, 18 March 1915 (RG84, 610).

60 *The Economist*, 21 November 1914, p. 921.

61 *The Economist*, 9 January 1915.

62 Smith and Collins, *Argentina*, pp. 13–32, 88.

63 SCR, no. 40a, 12 May 1915, pp. 5–6.

64 *Ibid.*, p. 12; Chile, Oficina Central de Estadística, *Estadística Comercial de la República de Chile* (1913, 1914, 1915); "Argentine Exports" (RG84, 610), p. 10; Peru, *Extracto Estadístico del Perú 1918*.

65 See below, chapter 4.

66 Smith and Collins, *Argentina*, pp. 122–3; Villela and Suzigan, *Government Policy*, pp. 346–9; Peru, *Extracto estadístico 1918*, 113.

67 Charles McQueen, *Chilean Public Finance* (Washington DC, 1924), p. 12.

68 *Sinopsis estadística 1924*, p. 64.

69 *The South American Journal*, 6 January 1916, p. 26.

70 H.E. Peters, *The Foreign Debt of the Argentine Republic* (Baltimore, 1934), chapter 3.

71 Joseph S. Tulchin, "The Argentine economy during the First World War," *Review of the River Plate*, Part II, 30 June 1970, 965–7.

72 Rowe, *Peru*, p. 15.

73 Charles McQueen, *Peruvian Public Finance*, Dept. of Commerce, BFDC, Trade Promotion Series no. 30 (Washington DC, 1926), p. 24.

74 Rowe, *Chile*, p. 75.

75 "Commercial conditions in Iquique," 11 August 1914 (RG84 610).

76 Rowe, *Chile*, pp. 65–6, 76–9, 82–4; *El Despertar de Trabajadores*, 15 September 1914; A.L. Stickell, "Migration and mining in Northern Chile in the nitrate era, 1880–1930" (PhD thesis, Indiana University, 1979), pp. 114–18.

77 *Ibid.*, p. 136.

78 *The South Pacific Mail*, 1 October 1914.

79 Rowe, *Chile*, pp. 79–82.

80 *The South Pacific Mail*, 20 August 1914.

81 Peter Blanchard, "The Peruvian working class movement, 1883–1919" (unpublished PhD thesis, University of London, 1975) p. 402.

82 Blanchard, *Origins*, p. 103.

83 "Situation at Rosario," 3 and 7 August 1914 (RG84/610).

84 Buenos Aires, 5 August 1914 (RG59/835.50 Roll 21).

85 *The Economist*, 12 September 1914, p. 466.

86 "The Argentine Market," 21 August 1914 (RG84/610).

87 Pernambuco, 15 August 1914, 10 September 1914 (RG59 Rolls 4 and 24).

88 Boris Fausto, *Trabalho urbano e conflicto social 1890–1920* (Rio and São Paulo, 1976), p. 158; J.F.W. Dulles, *Anarchists and Communists in Brazil, 1900–1935* (Austin, 1973), p. 30.

89 *The South American Journal*, 4 November 1914, 3 April 1915; *El Diario Ilustrado*, 19 October 1914; Peter De Shazo, *Urban Workers and the*

Labor Unions in Chile, 1902–1927 (Madison, 1983), pp. 144–5.

90 Yoast, "Anarchism," p. 213.
91 Sheldon Maram, "Anarchists, immigrants and the Brazilian labor movement" (unpublished PhD thesis, University of California at Santa Barbara, 1972), pp. 166–7.
92 Blanchard, *Origins*, p. 102.
93 De Shazo, *Urban Workers*, p. 129.
94 *Ibid.*, pp. 139–40.
95 Rowe, *Peru*, p. 30.
96 Skidmore, *Black into White*, p. 152.

3 The recovery of trade during the War

1 Gerd Hardach, *The First World War, 1914–1918* (London, 1977), pp. 77–8.
2 William H. Beveridge, *British Food Control* (London, 1928), pp. 120–6.
3 *Ibid.*, pp. 13, 22.
4 Hardach, *First World War*, chapters 2 and 3.
5 See below, pp. 116–17.
6 *The South American Journal*, 30 March 1918, p. 194.
7 See below, chapter 6.
8 Mira Wilkins, *The Emergence of Multinational Enterprise: American Business Abroad from the Colonial Era to 1914* (Cambridge, Mass., 1970), pp. 178–90; Joseph S. Tulchin, *The Aftermath of War: World War I and US Policy toward Latin America* (New York, 1971), *passim*.
9 Robert Neil Seidel, *Progressive Pan-Americanism: Development and United States Policy Toward South America, 1906–1931*, Cornell University, Latin American Studies Program Dissertation Series, no. 45, (1973), p. 67.
10 Kaufman, "Wilson years," p. 352.
11 John H. Williams, "Latin American foreign exchange and international balances during the War," *Quarterly Journal of Economics*, vol. 33 (1918–19) facing p. 426.
12 Díaz Alejandro, *Essays*, p. 52.
13 Joseph Tulchin, "The Argentine economy", part 1, p. 901.
14 *Ibid.*, p. 901.
15 "Important economic changes in Argentina during the War," Buenos Aires, 13 June 1914 (RG84 600).
16 J.A. Salter, *Allied Shipping Control* (London, 1921), p. 103.
17 *The Review of the River Plate*, 11 May 1917, 1 April 1919.
18 "Annual report on commerce and industry," Rosario, 7 April 1917 (RG84 600).
19 Smith and Collins, *Argentina*, pp. 23–7.
20 Gravil, "Anglo-Argentine," *passim*.
21 Unless otherwise noted, this section is based on *ibid*.

22 *Ibid.*, p. 68.

23 "Annual report on commerce and industries for 1916," Buenos Aires, 26 November 1917, pp. 49–50 (RG84 600).

24 *La Prensa*, 7 April 1917, quoted in Simon G. Hanson, *Argentine Meat and the British Market. Chapters in the History of the Argentine Meat Industry* (Stanford, 1938), p. 200fn.

25 *Ibid.*, p. 55.

26 Beveridge, *Food*, p. 81.

27 Gravil, "Anglo-Argentine," p. 73; *The Economist*, 12 May 1917, p. 816.

28 See for example, Rock, *Politics in Argentina*, pp. 111, 115–18.

29 For full US position RG59 835.6131/3–60 Roll 32; Also see, "Argentine Republic. Purchase of Argentine crops." "Negs. & Rels. with US & Allies" (RG 182, War Trade Board, Executive Country Files, 1917–19).

30 Gravil, "Anglo-Argentine," p. 75.

31 *Ibid.*, p. 74.

32 *The South American Journal*, 16 February 1918, pp. 103–4.

33 Stimson to Secretary of State, Buenos Aires, 29 December 1917 (RG59 835.6131/41 Roll 32).

34 *Ibid.*

35 Gravil, "Anglo-Argentine," p. 75; Beverage, *Food*, p. 87.

36 Robbens to Sec. of State, Buenos Aires, 3 July 1918 (RG59 835.6131/69, Roll 32); French High Commission to Auchincloss, Department of State, Washington, 18 June 1918 (RG59 835.6131/68); for further details on Allied attempts to impede independent sales see RG59 835.6131/60–71 Roll 32.

37 US Consul to Sec. of State, Rosario, 18 June 1918 (RG59 835.6131/70 Roll 32).

38 Unless noted, all information on the meat trade taken from Hanson, *Argentine Meat*, chapter 7.

39 Smith and Collins, *Argentina*, p. 99.

40 SCR, no. 38a, 27 February 1919.

41 Gravil, "Anglo-Argentine," pp. 80–3.

42 Di Tella and Zymelman, *Las etapas*, pp. 308, 340; Hanson, *Argentine Meat*, pp. 207–8.

43 Argentina, Cámara de Diputados de la Nación, *Informe de la Comisión Investigadora de los Trusts* (Buenos Aires, 1919), pp. 202–3.

44 Peter H. Smith, *Politics and Beef in Argentina. Patterns of Conflict and Change* (New York and London, 1969), p. 70.

45 *Ibid.*, pp. 76–8; *Informe*, pp. 220–5.

46 SCR, no. 38b, 22 July 1914.

47 Gravil, "Anglo-Argentine," p. 60.

48 A.E. Bunge, *Los problemas económicos del presente* (Buenos Aires, 1920), pp. 203, 261.

49 A.E. Bunge, *El costo de la vida y el poder de compra de la moneda* (Buenos Aires, 1924), p. 14.

50 Gravil, "Anglo-Argentine," p. 79.

51 Bunge, *El costo*, p. 14.

52 Tulchin, "The Argentine economy," part II, 30 June 1971, pp. 966–7.

53 *Ibid.*, p. 967; see below, pp. 149–54.

54 Hanson, *Argentine Meat*, pp. 211–16.

55 Calculated from Di Tella and Zymelman, *Las etapas*, pp. 293, 313, 346.

56 Díaz Alejandro, *Essays*, p. 144.

57 Argentina, Dir. Gen. de Estadística de la Nación, *Análisis del comercio exterior argentino en los años 1910 a 1922* (Buenos Aires, 1923), p. 96.

58 Díaz Alejandro, *Essays*, pp. 152–5.

59 SCR, no. 38a, 13 July 1916.

60 Smith and Collins, *Argentina*, p. 78.

61 Joseph Tulchin, "The Argentine economy," part III, p. 44.

62 See chapter 5.

63 United States, Dept. of Commerce, BFDC, "Argentina's mounting trade balance," *Circular of Latin American Division*, no. 29, 26 January 1918.

64 Unless noted the section on coal based on "The coal situation in the Argentine Republic," nd (War Trade Board, RG182, Box 904).

65 Carl Solberg, *Oil and Nationalism in Argentina: A History* (Stanford, 1979), chapter 2.

66 *Ibid.*, p. 27.

67 Smith and Collins, *Argentina*, pp. 102–3.

68 Gravil, "Anglo-Argentine," pp. 88–9.

69 Williams, "Argentine foreign exchange and trade since the Armistice," *Review of Economic Statistics*, vol. 3, 1921. pp. 448–65.

70 *Ibid.*, pp. 448–9.

71 Carlos Manuel Peláez, "World War I and the economy of Brazil: some evidence from monetary statistics," *Journal of Interdisciplinary History* vol. VII, no. 4, (1977), p. 686.

72 See below, p. 193.

73 Brazil, Ministry of Industry, Agriculture and Commerce, *Economical Notes on Brazil*, 2nd edn. (Rio, 1916), 4th edn. (Rio, 1921).

74 Brazil, Ministério da Fazenda, Directoria de Estatística Comercial, *Comércio exterior do Brasil (Resumo por Mercadorias) Jan. a Dez. de 1913 a 1914* (Rio, 1915); *Comércio exterior do Brasil Jan. a Dez. 1915–1919* (Rio, 1920).

75 WBR, 28 August 1917, p. 178.

76 *Ibid.*, 14 August 1917, pp. 140–1.

77 V.D. Wickizer, *The World Coffee Economy* (Stanford, 1943), pp. 240–1.

78 WBR, 18 January 1916, p. 37.

79 WBR, 13 February 1917, p. 118.

80 See below, p. 88.

81 Unless otherwise noted this section based on Arthur Redfield, *Brazil: A Study of Economic Conditions since 1913*, Department of Commerce, BFDC, Miss. Series no. 86 (Washington DC, 1920), pp. 27–9.

82 See above, p. 2.
83 WBR, 25 May 1915, pp. 235–6.
84 WBR, 16 October 1915, pp. 559–60. Also see, Affonso de E. Taunay, *História do café no Brasil* (Rio, 1941), vol. 11, pp. 339–412.
85 C.M. Peláez and W. Suzigan, *História monetária do Brasil: análise da política, comportamento e instituições monetárias* (Rio, 1976), pp. 208–9; Netto, "Foundations," pp. 95–7.
86 WBR, 8 January 1918, p. 31.
87 *Ibid.*, 5 March 1918, p. 207.
88 This section based on various documents in FO368/1706 and/1707.
89 FO to Peel (Brazil), 5 December 1916, (FO371/2900).
90 WBR, 11 December 1917, pp. 492–3. For an excellent account of the shipping controversy see Winston Fritsch, "Il Brasile durante la Grande Guerra: problemi strutturali e politiche economiche," *Rivista di storia economica*, ns, 2 (1985), 64–73.
91 "Report on conditions in Rio," 30 November 1916 (FO371/2900/5613).
92 Various documents including minutes of interdepartmental meetings FO371/3167–/64280,65282,106107 and 120191.
93 Sir Francis Elliot, President Foreign Trade Department, Meeting of Interdepartmental Committee, 10 June 1918 (FO371/3167 XC/A/3523).
94 Dean, *Industrialization*, p. 100.
95 WBR, 28 May 1918, pp. 499–503.
96 Boris Fausto, "Expansão de café e política cafeeira" in Boris Fausto (ed.), *História geral da civilização brasileira, III O Brasil Republicano, estrutura de poder e economia (1889–1930)* (São Paulo, 1975), p.226.
97 WBR, 3 August 1915, p. 378.
98 All information on Dumont from yearly reports published in WBR. See Table 3.13 for references.
99 WBR, 28 August 1917, pp. 178–80; 22 August 1918, pp. 1013–14.
100 Weinstein, *Rubber*, pp. 219–33.
101 *Ibid.*, p. 224.
102 WBR, 7 August 1915, p. 412.
103 *Ibid.*, 28 August 1917, p. 175.
104 *Ibid.*, 29 January 1918, p. 98.
105 *Ibid.*, 16 July 1918, p. 683.
106 *Ibid.*, 27 August 1918, p. 828.
107 Weinstein, *Rubber*, pp. 232–9.
108 *Ibid.*, pp. 252–3.
109 *Economical Notes*, 2nd edn. and 4th edn.
110 *Ibid.*
111 SCR, no. 40b, 11 August 1915; no. 40c, 30 August 1916; no. 40a, 25 September 1917; no. 40c, 23 May 1919; no. 43b, 24 November 1920.
112 Peter L. Eisenberg, *The Sugar Industry in Pernambuco. Modernization without Change, 1840–1910* (Berkeley, 1974), *passim*.
113 SCR, no. 43b, 20 November, 1920.
114 *Economical Notes*, 2nd and 4th edns.

115 SCR, no. 43b, 24 November 1920.

116 José C. Gnaccarini, "A economia do açúcar. Processo de trabalho e processo de acumulação," in Fausto (ed.), *História Geral...*, p. 329.

117 Redfield, *Brazil*, pp. 34–5; SCR, no. 43b, 24 May 1920, pp. 11–12. Also see WBR, 28 January 1918, pp. 89–90; 20 August 1918, pp. 790–1.

118 Redfield, *Brazil*, pp. 61–3.

119 *Ibid.*, p. 61; SCR, no. 43a, 24 May 1920.

120 Brazil, *Comercio Exterior do Brasil, Jan–Dez. 1915–1919* p. 132.

121 SCR, no. 40a, 6 April 1916; no. 40a, 25 September 1917; no. 40b, 4 March 1919.

122 Peláez, "World War I," p. 687.

123 See above, p. 48.

124 See below, chapter 6.

125 "Brazilian trade and finance," selected statistics, May 1918 (FO368/1889).

126 Redfield, *Brazil*, pp. 20–5.

127 Villela and Suzigan, *Government Policy*, pp. 105–6.

128 See below, chapter 6.

129 Brazil, Ministério da Viação e Obras Públicas, *Relatório do Ministério da Viação e Obras Publicas* (Rio, 1922), p. 9.

130 WBR, 19 March 1918, p. 242.

131 "The fuel problem of Brazil," 25 October 1918 (WTB RG 182, Box 906). Also Redfield, *Brazil*, pp. 37–9.

132 Victor V. Valla, *A penetração norte-americana na economia brasileira, 1898–1928* (Rio, 1978), chapter IV.

133 See below, pp. 189–194.

134 Valla, *Penetração*, p. 70.

135 See below, pp. 197–8, 315.

136 SCR, no. 41a, 16 June 1916, p. 1.

137 *Ibid.*, pp. 1–2.

138 See above, p. 59.

139 Williams, "Foreign Exchange," pp. 443–4.

140 See below, pp. 98–9, 101–2.

141 McQueen, *Chilean Public Finance*, p. 66; See below, pp. 159–60.

142 Strong to Grey, 29 October 1914 (FO 371/2297). For a detailed treatment of the nitrate trade see Juan Ricardo Couyoumdjian, "Anglo-Chilean economic relations during the First World War and its aftermath 1914–1920," unpublished PhD thesis, University of Londan, 1975, chapter 6; US War Trade Board, "A study of the Chilean nitrate industry," pp. 77–85 (RG182, Records of Executive Office, Box 15); J.R. Partington and L.H. Parker, *The Nitrogen Industry* (London, 1922), pp. 65–71.

143 Williams, "Foreign exchange," p. 439.

144 *Ibid.*, p. 441.

145 The following account of costs and dividends from Michael Monteón, *Nitrate Era*, pp. 116–17.

146 Partington and Parker, *Nitrogen*, p. 25.

147 Couyoumdjian, "Economic Relations," p. 160.

148 *Circulares de la Asociación Salitrera de Propaganda* (Valparaíso/Iquique, December 1915), p. 18; Anglo-South American Bank, *Business Statements*, 11 October 1915.

149 *El Diario Ilustrado*, 11 May 1916.

150 Monteón, *Nitrate Age*, pp. 121–2.

151 British Consul, Antofagasta–Balfour, 30 June 1917 (FO 368/1709).

152 *Ibid.*, Strong (Santiago)–Balfour, 11 September 1917.

153 *Ibid.*, 30 June 1917.

154 Monteón, *Nitrate Age*, p. 118.

155 Herbert Gibbs to Chairman Nitrate of Soda Executive, 26 March 1918, Department of State, Records Relating to Nitrates in Chile (Microcopy 487/33).

156 Couyoumdjian, "Economic Relations," p. 173; Strong to Balfour, 1 July 1918 (FO 371/3170).

157 The following section is based on Monteón, *Nitrate Age*, pp. 120–4.

158 See below, p. 158.

159 R.F. Mikesell, *The World Copper Industry* (London, 1979), p. 6; C.W. Reynolds, "Development problems in an export economy. The case of Chile and copper" in M. Mamalakis and C.W. Reynolds, *Essays on the Chilean Economy* (New Haven, 1965), pp. 213–14.

160 Joanne Fox Przeworski, *The Decline of the Copper Industry in Chile and the Entrance of North American Capital* (New York, 1980), pp. 292–6.

161 *Ibid.*, p. 258.

162 F.F. Hunter Jr., "Copper" in G.A. Roush (ed.), *The Mineral Industry—its Statistics, Technology and Trade during 1914*, vol. xxiii, pp. 190–1.

163 Walter Harvey Weed, "Copper" in G.A. Roush (ed.), *Mineral Industry 1918*, vol. xxvii, p. 176. Also see Pope Yeatman, "Mine of Chile Exploration Co., Chuquicamata, Chile" in *The Engineering and Mining Journal*, vol. 101, no. 17 (12 February 1916), pp. 307–14.

164 Weed, "Copper," *Mineral Industry 1915*, vol. xxv, p. 195. Also see, James E. Harding, "Andes Copper Mining Co.'s development at Potrerillos, Chile" in *The Engineering and Mining Journal*, vol. 105, no. 3 (19 January 1918), pp. 137–9.

165 *The West Coast Leader*, 10 June 1915, quoted in *US Commerce Reports*, no. 166, 17 July 1915, p. 277.

166 Weed, "Copper," *Mineral Industry 1916*, vol. xxvi, p. 193.

167 Weed, "Copper," *Mineral Industry 1917*, vol. xxvii, pp. 142–4.

168 Weed, "Copper," *Mineral Industry 1918*, vol. xxvii, p. 143.

169 *The Engineering and Mining Journal*, vol. 102, no. 7 (12 August 1916), p. 290.

170 *Sinopsis Estadística 1924*.

171 Sociedad Nacional Agraria, *Asamblea de agricultores celebrada en*

Santiago de Chile en los dias 22, 23, 24 de setiembre de 1919 (Santiago, 1920), pp. 65–7.

172 Julio Heise González, *Historia de Chile 1861–1925. El período parlamentario*, vol. I (Santiago, 1974), p. 431.

173 See below, chapter 5.

174 "The fuel problem in South America," US Dept. of Commerce, BFDC, *Latin American Circular to District Officers*, no. 15, 19 October 1917 (War Trade Board, RG 182 Box 909).

175 "The commerce of Chile with special reference to trade interdependence between Chile and the entente Allies," 1918? (War Trade Board RG182 Box 909).

176 *The South Pacific Mail*, 1 January 1916.

177 Mamalakis, "The role of government," pp. 200–5.

178 See below, p. 173 and "Peruvian exchange during the War," *Latin American Circular* no. 63, Latin American Division, BFDC (Washington DC, 10 January 1918?), reprinted in *The West Coast Leader*, 3 and 10 July 1920.

179 See below, p. 171.

180 Bertram and Thorp, *Peru*, pp. 39–40, 49.

181 See above, p. 47.

182 Howard J. Gray, *War Time Control of Industry. The Experience of England* (New York, 1918), 169–70.

183 *The Economist*, 19 September 1914, p. 488; 20 February 1915, p. 343.

184 Great Britain, *British Parliamentary Papers, First (Interim) Report with Statement Showing the Operations of the Royal Commission on Sugar Supply from the Date of Appointment to Beginning of December 1916* (cd 8728, 1917–1918, xviii), pp. 3–4.

185 Albert, *An Essay*, pp. 119a–20a.

186 Cayaltí mss., Kendall Correspondence, London–Lima, 16 February 1916.

187 Joshua Bernhardt, *Government Control of the Sugar Industry in the United States. An Account of the Work of the United States Food Administration and the United States Equilization Board* (New York, 1920), pp. 9, 15.

188 Details of this episode from US Dept. of State, *Records Relating to WWI and its Termination* (Microcopy 367/265).

189 *Ibid.*, "Memo of conversation with Mr. Lay regarding big enemy businesses in South America," 24 January 1918 (763.721/2 c.26/9).

190 *The West Coast Leader*, 14 May 1914; *The Economist*, 5 December 1914, pp. 991–2.

191 Albert, *An Essay*, pp. 67a–71a.

192 Unless otherwise noted, all profit data from *Ibid.*, p. 126a.

193 Heraclio Bonilla y Alejandro Rabanal, "La Hacienda San Nicolás (Supe) y la Primera Guerra Mundial," *Economia* (Lima), vol. I no. 3, (1979), p. 32.

194 Cayaltí mss., Cartas Reservadas, Lima–Cayaltí, 16 February 1918.

195 See below, p. 297.

196 Albert, *An Essay*, p. 141a.

197 *Ibid.*, pp. 139a–40a.

198 Thorp and Bertram, *Peru*, p. 49.

199 Albert, *An Essay*, pp. 140a–56a; Bell, *Cotton*, *passim*; Thorp and Bertram, *Peru*, pp. 51–62.

200 *Commerce Reports*, 12 September 1916, pp. 8–9.

201 Rowe, *Peru*, p. 33.

202 *Commerce Reports*, 12 September 1916, pp. 8–9.

203 *Commerce Reports*, 27 July 1915, p. 10; Cayaltí mss., Palto Correspondence, Lima–Palto, 4 October 1914.

204 *Ibid.*, Lima–Palto, 29 May 1915, Cartas Administrativas, Lima-Cayaltí, 26 February 1915.

205 Bell, *Cotton*, pp. 61–2.

206 Cayaltí mss., Cartas Reservadas, Lima–Cayaltí, 6 September 1917.

207 Albert, *An Essay*, pp. 152a–5a.

208 Thorp and Bertram, *Peru*, pp. 132–40.

209 *The West Coast Leader*, 14 July 1917; *El Comercio*, 21 September 1916; *La Industria* (Trujillo), 24 January 1920; "The War and Peruvian foodstuffs," *Commerce Reports*, no. 249, 23 October 1918.

210 SNA mss., Letter from A. Velarde (Barranca) to Don S. Graña, 22 December 1914.

211 Cayaltí mss., Cartas Reservadas, Lima–Cayaltí, 14 July 1914.

212 Thorp and Bertram, *Peru*, pp. 61–2.

213 Bill Albert, "Notas sobre la modernización y el cambio estructural en la industria azucarera peruana, 1880–1914," *Análisis*, no. 6, Lima (1979), pp. 88.

214 William S. Bollinger, "The rise of United States influence in the Peruvian economy, 1869–1921" (unpublished MA thesis, University of California at Los Angeles, 1972), pp. 174–203; Thorp and Bertram, *Peru*, pp. 72–95.

215 Lester W. Strauss, "Peru in 1913," *The Engineering and Mining Journal*, 10 January 1914, pp. 145–6; "The Cerro de Pasco Mines, Peru," *The Engineering and Mining Journal*, 24 February 1917, pp. 351–3.

216 *The Mineral Industry* 1914, vol. xxiii, pp. 199–200; SCR, no. 46a, 27 July 1915, pp. 11–12.

217 Blanchard, *Origins*, p. 139.

218 SCR, no. 46a, 27 July 1915, pp. 11–12; Strauss, "Peru," pp. 145–6.

219 Thorp and Bertram, *Peru*, pp. 87–8.

220 See below, pp. 168–9.

221 SCR, no. 46a, 12 September 1916, pp. 14–15.

222 Bollinger, "US influence," p. 218.

223 *Ibid.*, pp. 218–33; Thorp and Bertram, *Peru*, pp. 83, 85.

224 *Ibid.*, pp. 87–95.

225 *Ibid.*, pp. 95–111; Geoffrey Bertram, "Development problems in an export economy: a study of domestic capitalists, foreign firms and

government in Peru, 1919–1930" (unpublished DPhil thesis, Oxford, 1974), chapter 6.

226 Bollinger, "US influence," chapter 3.

227 Bill Albert, "Sugar and Anglo-Peruvian trade negotiations in the 1930s," JLAS, vol. 14, part 1 (1982), pp. 122–4.

228 See below, p. 297.

229 See below, pp. 301–2.

4 Seeking financial solutions

1 An important exception being the recent work by Alfonso Walter Quiroz, "Financial institutions in Peruvian export economy and society, 1884–1930" (unpublished PhD thesis, Columbia, 1986).

2 Triffin, *Evolution*, pp. 8–9.

3 Ford, *Britain and Argentina*, pp. 46–7.

4 Quiroz, "Financial institutions," p. 329.

5 Flávio A.M. De Saes and Tamás Szmrecsányi, "O capital estrangeiro no Brasil 1880–1930," *Estudos Econômicos*, vol. 15, no. 2 (1985), p. 197.

6 See below; p. 168; Winston Fritsch, "Aspects of Brazilian economic policy under the First Republic (1889–1930)" (unpublished PhD thesis, Cambridge, 1983), pp. 247–52.

7 Topik, "Nationalism," p. 154; Figure on Chile from P.J. Conoboy, "Money and politics in Chile, 1878–1925" (unpublished PhD thesis, University of Southampton, 1976), p. 333.

8 Joslin, *Banking*, pp. 110–11; W.H. Lough, *Banking Opportunities in South America*, US Dept. of Commerce, BFDC, Special Agent Series no. 106 (Washington DC, 1915), pp. 1–42.

9 Charles Jones, "The state and business practice in Argentina 1862–1914" in C. Abel and C. Lewis (eds.), *Latin America: Economic Imperialism and the State* (London, 1985), p. 194.

10 See, for example, Richard Graham, *Britain and the Onset of Modernization in Brazil 1850–1914* (Cambridge, 1968), pp. 134–6.

11 Charles Jones, "Commercial banks and mortgage companies" in D.C.M. Platt (ed.), *Business Imperialism*, pp. 17–19.

12 Fritsch, "Aspects," pp. 111–12.

13 Jones, "Commercial Banks," p. 52.

14 Hyman Minsky, "A theory of systemic fragility" in E.I. Altman and A.N. Sametz, *Financial Crises. Institutions and Markets in a Fragile Environment* (New York, 1977), pp. 38–52.

15 Quiroz, "Financial Institutions," pp. 185–6.

16 Ronald I. McKinnon, *Money and Capital in Economic Development* (Washington DC, 1973), p. 8.

17 Brown, *Gold Standard*, p. 50.

18 *Ibid.*, p. 96.

19 *Ibid.*, p. 97.

20 See above, pp. 66–7.

21 Williams, "Foreign exchange," p. 449.

22 *Comercio Exterior 1913–1914*, p. 176; *Comercio Exterior 1915–1919*, p. 38.

23 Paulo Neuhaus, *História monetária do Brasil, 1900–45* (Rio, 1975), p. 50.

24 J.L. Love, *São Paulo in the Brazilian Federation, 1889–1937* (Stanford 1980), pp. 244–6; WBR, 24 August 1915, p. 5.

25 WBR, 9 March 1915, p. 95.

26 WBR, 4 January 1916, p. 704.

27 WBR, 28 May 1918, p. 492.

28 Villela and Suzigan, *Government Policy*, pp. 348–9.

29 Abreu, "Dívida" p. 170.

30 *O Brasil em números*, p. 146.

31 Albert, *South America*, p. 39.

32 For details on these negotiations see various letters in RG59/832.51/63–72, 519 Roll 24.

33 *The Economist*, 7 October 1916, p. 600.

34 WBR, 28 May 1918, p. 491; Letter from Rio, 22 October 1914 (RG59/832.51/81, 519 Roll 24).

35 For example, see letters in RG59/832.51/90, 98, 122, 129, 130, 519 Roll 24); Fritsch, "Grande Guerra", pp. 62–3.

36 WBR, 13 July 1915, p. 336.

37 Calculated from Frederic M. Halsey, *Investments in Latin America and the British West Indies*, Dept. of Commerce, BFDC, Special Agent Series no. 169 (Washington DC, 1918), pp. 124–39.

38 *South American Journal*, 6 January 1916, p. 26.

39 Tele. Rio, 22 November 1916 (RG59 832.51/133, 519 Roll 24).

40 Castro, *Empresas*, pp. 80–3, 116–22.

41 Abreu, "Dívida," p. 168.

42 *South American Journal*, 6 January 1916, p. 24, 10 January 1917, p. 21.

43 Redfield, *Brazil*, pp. 61–3, 67, 75.

44 Elysio de Carvalho, "Opportunities in Brazil for American capital," *The Pan-American Magazine*, November 1918, p. 20.

45 *O Brasil em números*, p. 147.

46 WBR, 16 February 1915, p. 61. The data on the total amount issued taken from Presidential Message to Congress, 18 May 1918, reprinted in WBR, 28 May 1918, p. 489.

47 WBR, 16 February 1915, p. 62.

48 WBR, 13 July 1915, p. 336, 18 April 1916, p. 238.

49 Fritsch, "Grande Guerra," p. 70.

50 Letters: Rio, 7 February 1917, 19 March 1917, 23 March 1915, 23 July 1917 (RG59/832.51/145,151,155,163).

51 WBR, 28 May 1918, p. 489.

52 US, Dept. of Commerce BFDC, *Banking and Credit in Argentina, Chile and Peru*, Special Agent Series no. 90 (Washington DC, 1914), pp. 36–7.

53 Fritsch, "Grande Guerra," pp. 48–9.
54 WBR, 28 May 1918, p. 489.
55 WBR, 21 August 1917, p. 153; see above, p. 81.
56 WBR, 10 December 1918, p. 1170.
57 Fritsch, "Aspects," chapter 2.
58 Steven Topik, "The state's contribution to the development of Brazil's internal economy, 1850–1930," HAHR, vol. 65, no. 2 (1985), p. 207fn.
59 Redfield, *Brazil*, p. 70; Williams, "Foreign exchange," p. 463.
60 WBR, 20 February 1917, p. 136.
61 WBR, 17 July 1917, p. 53.
62 Villela and Suzigan, *Government Policy*, p. 256.
63 *Relatório do Banco do Brasil 1918*, (Rio, 1919), pp. 12–21.
64 WBR, 24 April 1917, p. 307.
65 Fritsch, "Aspects," pp. 250–3.
66 Fritsch, "Grande Guerra," pp. 52–3.
67 Claudio L.S. Haddad, *Crescimento do produto real no Brasil, 1900–1947* (Rio, 1978), p. 15.
68 Fritsch, "Grande Guerra," pp. 54–5.
69 WBR, 28 May 1918, pp. 489–90.
70 *Relatório do Banco do Brasil 1916*, pp. 16–17; *Relatório 1918*, p. 42.
71 Topik, "Nationalism," pp. 152–3.
72 *Ibid.*, pp. 258–9.
73 Williams, "Foreign exchange," p. 430.
74 See above, pp. 65–7.
75 Smith and Collins, *Argentina*, p. 114.
76 Tulchin, "The Argentine Economy," part II, pp. 966–7.
77 Jane Van Der Karr, *La Primera Guerra Mundial y la política económica Argentina* (Buenos Aires, 1974), p. 101. The remainder of this section is based on this study, especially chapters 1–5, and pp. 209–27.
78 Smith and Collins, *Argentina*, p. 122; Di Tella and Zymelman, *Las etapas*, pp. 312–13.
79 Argentina, Ministerio de Hacienda, *Ley de presupuesto general de la República Argentina para el ejercicio de 1918* (Buenos Aires, 1919). All reference to budgeted expenditure has been taken from these publications covering the years 1915, 1917, 1918 and 1920.
80 Frederic M. Halsey and G. Butler Sherwell, *Investments in Latin America. I. Argentina*, Dept. of Commerce, BFDC, Trade Information Bulletin no. 362 (Washington DC, 1925), p. 8.
81 Karen L. Remmer, *Party Competition in Argentina and Chile. Political Recruitment and Public Policy, 1890–1930* (Lincoln and London, 1984), pp. 155–6.
82 Phelps, *International Economic Position*, pp. 243–55.
83 Albert, *South America*, p. 48.
84 Colin Lewis, "British railway companies and the Argentine Government" in Platt (ed.), *Business Imperialism*, p. 415.

85 Unless otherwise noted this section drawn from Peters, *Foreign Debt*, pp. 79–99.

86 *The South American Journal*, 6 January 1915, p. 24.

87 Smith and Collins, *Argentina*, p. 121. For details on municipal and provincial debt see Halsey, *Investments*, pp. 33–7.

88 C.A. Tornquist, "Balance of payments of the Argentine republic for economic year 1916–1917," *The Review of the River Plate*, 29 March 1918, p. 764.

89 *The Economist*, 15 September 1917, p. 392.

90 Argentina, Ministerio de Hacienda, *Memoria del Departamento de Hacienda Correspondiente al año 1917* (Buenos Aires, 1918), p. xxxiv.

91 From advertised rates by Banco de la Nación and London and River Plate Bank Ltd in *The Review of the River Plate*, various numbers 1912–21.

92 *The South American Journal*, 12 June 1915, p. 482, quoted in Tulchin, "Argentine Economy," Part II, p. 966.

93 See above, p. 138.

94 *The Economist*, 30 September 1916, pp. 567–8.

95 "Annual report on commerce and industries for 1916," Buenos Aires, 26 November 1917, pp. 10–11; "Important economic changes in Argentina during the War" (RG84/600).

96 Phelps, *International Economic Position*, facing p. 238.

97 Williams, "Argentine foreign exchange," p. 49. Also see Tornquist, *Economic Development*, pp. 235–42.

98 SCR, 38a, 13 July 1916, p. 17; "Financial crisis in Argentina," Rosario, 1 March 1918, War Trade Board (RG182, Box 904).

99 Tulchin, "Argentine economy," part III, 44.

100 Charles Jones, "The fiscal motive for monetary and banking legislation in Argentina, Australia and Canada before 1914," Platt and Di Tella (eds.), *Argentina, Australia*, pp. 123–38.

101 Albert, *South America*, p. 39.

102 For Brazil see above; Argentine figures calculated from Tornquist, *Business Conditions in Argentina*, p. 287.

103 Henry Kirsch, *Industrial Development in a Traditional Society, the Conflict of Entrepreneurship and Modernization in Chile* (Gainesville, 1977), pp. 141–2; L. Domeratsky, *Customs Tariff of Chile*, Dept. of Commerce, BFDC, Tariff Series no. 36, Washington DC, October 1917.

104 Rowe, *Chile*, pp. 52–3; McQueen, *Chilean*, pp. 13–16.

105 Remmer, *Party Competition*, pp. 46–8.

106 *Ibid.*, p. 154. For an excellent analysis of this issue see P.J. Conoboy, "Money," *passim*. Also see below, pp. 276–81.

107 Fetter, *Inflation*, p. 193.

108 Figures from, *Anuario estadístico 1918*, vol. vi, p. 32.

109 McQueen, *Chilean*, p. 39.

110 Ricardo Anguita, *Leyes promulgadas en Chile. Suplemento 1913–1918*,

vol. v (Santiago–Valparaíso, 1918), p. 458; Conoboy, "Money," pp. 277–8.

111 *Commerce Reports*, no. 143, 19 June 1916, p. 1057.

112 *Commerce Reports*, no. 203, 29 August 1916, p. 786; Conoboy, "Money," p. 277.

113 Halsey, *Investment*, p. 221; *Anuario estadístico 1918*, p. 60.

114 Conoboy, "Money," *passim*; Fetter, *Inflation*, *passim*; McQueen, *Chilean*, chapter 3.

115 G. Subercaseaux, *Monetary and Banking Policy of Chile* (Oxford, 1922), pp. 156–7. The following section is based on this work, pp. 156–9; Fetter, *Inflation*, pp. 137–9; Rowe, *Chile*, pp. 58–60, 70–1; Conoboy, "Money," pp. 270–7.

116 *Commerce Reports*, no. 222, 22 September 1915, p. 1405.

117 Fetter, *Inflation*, pp. 149, 155.

118 Rates from McQueen, *Chilean*, p. 66.

119 Fetter, *Inflation*, pp. 125–36; Subercaseaux, *Monetary*, pp. 144–56.

120 This section based on Conoboy, "Money," pp. 280–3; Subercaseaux, *Monetary*, pp. 162–5; Fetter, *Inflation*, pp. 143–5.

121 Fetter, *Inflation*, pp. 170–82.

122 *The South Pacific Mail*, 13 August 1914.

123 Anglo-South American Bank Ltd, Correspondence between Santiago and London, Private Letters, 11 August 1914 (University College, London).

124 Rowe, *Chile*, pp. 61–2.

125 Solberg, *Immigration*, pp. 159–65.

126 SCR, no. 41a, 6 June 1916, p. 3; *Commerce Reports*, no. 11, 13 January 1917, p. 167.

127 See below, p. 231.

128 Kirsch, *Modernization*, pp. 81–7.

129 Conoboy, "Money," p. 331.

130 Fetter, *Inflation*, p. 141.

131 Halsey, *Investment*, pp. 322–3.

132 Albert, *South America*, p. 39.

133 *Extracto estadístico 1928*, pp. 24–7.

134 McQueen, *Peruvian*, p. 24; Rowe, *Peru*, p. 14.

135 SCR, no. 46a, 12 September 1916, p. 20.

136 Rowe, *Peru*, pp. 14–15.

137 Details on changes in taxation from US Department of Commerce, BFDC, *Foreign Tariff Notes*, no. 19, 1915, pp. 42–4; Rowe, *Peru*, pp. 18–22; SCR, no. 46a, 12 September 1916, pp. 20–3.

138 Hernando de Lavalle, *La Gran Guerra y el organismo economico nacional* (Lima, 1919), p. 74.

139 Rowe, *Peru*, p. 22.

140 *El Comercio*, 28 August 1914, 1 September 1914; *West Coast Leader*, 5 August 1915.

141 *La Agricultura*, no. 25, June 1917.
142 Cayaltí Corres., Kendall Letters, Lima–London, 1 September 1915.
143 Rory Miller, "Coastal elite", pp. 109–10.
144 Albert, *An Essay*, pp. 95a–99a.
145 McQueen, *Peruvian Public Finance*, p. 14.
146 *The South American Journal*, 7 October 1916, pp. 282–3; Thorp and Bertram, *Peru*, pp. 109, 374–5.
147 Information on wartime borrowing from: McQueen, *Peruvian*, pp. 81–2; Rowe *Peru*, pp. 20–1, 26–7; Halsey, *Investments*, pp. 322–3.
148 Rowe, *Peru*, p. 27.
149 Unless otherwise noted, this section is based on McQueen, *Peruvian*, pp. 100–7; *Commerce Reports*, no. 232, 4 October 1917, pp. 58–61.
150 Quiroz, "Financial institutions," pp. 430–1.
151 *Ibid.*, pp. 353, 359–60.
152 Thorp and Bertram, *Peru*, pp. 49–50.
153 Quiroz, "Financial institutions," p. 352.
154 *Ibid.*, pp. 48–9, 132fn.
155 Halsey, *Investments*, pp. 324–5.
156 Quiroz, "Financial institutions," p. 5.
157 *Extracto estadístico, 1925*, pp. 66–81.
158 Thorp and Bertram, *Peru*, p. 47.
159 Halsey, *Investments*, p. 322.
160 Thorp and Bertram, *Peru*, p. 338.
161 *Ibid.*, pp. 79–100.
162 See above, pp. 112–15.
163 Quiroz, "Financial institutions," p. 362.

5 The war and the growth of manufacturing industry

1 André Gunder Frank, *Capitalism and Underdevelopment in Latin America* (New York and London, 1969), pp. 11–12.
2 Miller, "Manufacturing," p. 714.
3 Kay, *Development*, p. 126.
4 Roberto C. Simonsen, *Evolução industrial do Brasil e outros estudos* (São Paulo, 1973), p. 16.
5 Warren Dean, "A industrialização durante a República Velha" in Boris Fausto (ed.), *História Geral*, vol. 8, pp. 251–3.
6 Flávio Rabelo Versiani, *Industrial Investment in an "Export" Economy: The Brazilian Experience before 1914*, Institute of Latin American Studies, Working Paper no. 2 (London, 1979), *passim*.
7 Stanley Stein, *The Brazilian Cotton Manufacture. Textile Enterprise in an Underdeveloped Area, 1850–1950* (Cambridge, Mass., 1957), chapters 1–6.
8 Albert Fishlow, "Origins and consequences of import substitution in Brazil" in Luís E. de Marco (ed.), *International Economics and*

Development. Essays in Honor of Raul Prebisch (New York and London, 1972), pp. 315–17.

9 Versiani, *Industrial Investment*, pp. 20–4.
10 Leff, *Underdevelopment*, pp. 174–6.
11 Wilson Cano, *Raízes da concentração industrial em São Paulo* (Rio and São Paulo, 1977), pp. 17–18.
12 Dean, *Industrialization*, pp. 3, 85.
13 Cano, *Raízes*, pp. 42–86.
14 Versiani, *Industrial Investment*, p. 25.
15 Leff, *Underdevelopment*, p. 168.
16 Centro Industrial do Brasil, *O Brasil, suas riquezas naturaes, suas indústrias*, vol. 3 (Rio, 1909), pp. 255–60.
17 *Ibid.*, p. 265.
18 Dean, "A industrialização," pp. 258–9.
19 Cano, *Raízes*, pp. 153, 162.
20 Centro Industrial, "Mapas estatísticos da indústria fabril" in *O Brasil*, p. 150.
21 *British Parliamentary Papers 1899*, p. xcvi, "Reports received from Mr. T. Worthington... upon conditions and prospects of British trade in various South American countries," 5th Report, Brazil, part I, pp. 25–6, part II, 21.
22 Centro Industrial, *O Brasil*, p. 261.
23 Redfield, *Brazil*, p. 56.
24 Brazil, Ministério de Agricultura Industria e Comércio, Directoria Geral de Estatística, *Recenseamento do Brazil*, vol. IV (Rio, 1920), p. ixix.
25 Simonsen, *Evolução industrial*, pp. 26–7.
26 Dean, *Industrialization*, pp. 93–5.
27 *Ibid.*, p. 104.
28 Fishlow, "Origins," pp. 320–6.
29 Villela and Suzigan, *Government Policy*, pp. 106–9. Also see A.V. Villela, "Surto industrial durante a Guerra de 1914–18" in Mircea Buescu (ed.), *Ensaios econômicos: homenagem a Octávio Gouvea de Bulhões* (Rio, nd), pp. 536–49.
30 C.H. Peláez and W. Suzigan, *História Monetária, do Brasil: Análise da política, compartamento e instituições monetárias* (Rio, 1976), pp. 95–9.
31 Also see Wilson Suzigan, "Uma nota sobre 'Origens e conseqüências da substituição de importações no Brasil' de Albert Fishlow," Werner Baer and A.V. Villela, "Alguns comentários a 'Origens e conseqüências da substituição de importações no Brasil' de Albert Fishlow;" Albert Fishlow, "Algumas observações adicionais sobre a discussão," all in *Estudos Econômicos*, vol. 3 no. 1 (1973), pp. 121–34, 148–52.
32 Carlos Manuel Peláez, *História econômica do Brasil. Um elo entre a teoria e realidade econômica* (São Paulo, 1979), pp. 130–2.
33 F.R. Versiani and M.T. Versiani, "A industrialização brasileira antes de

1930: uma contribuição," *Estudos Econômicos*, vol. 5 no. 1 (1975), pp. 40–3.

34 *Ibid.*, p. 62.

35 Cano, *Raízes*, pp. 154–74.

36 "O desenvolvimento industrial do Estado" in São Paulo, Secretaria da Agricultura, Comercio y Obras Públicas do Estado de São Paulo, *Boletim da Directoria de Industria e Comercio*, 9th series, nos. 3–4 (March-April 1918), pp. 137–49.

37 W.S. Callaghan, "Obstacles to industrialization: the iron and steel industry in Brazil during the Old Republic" (unpublished PhD thesis, University of Texas, 1981), pp. 110–11.

38 Fishlow, *Origins*, pp. 322–5.

39 Leff, *Underdevelopment*, pp. 171–4.

40 *Ibid.*, p. 186.

41 *Ibid.*, pp. 224–38 and *passim*.

42 N. Leff, *Underdevelopment and Development in Brazil: Reassessing the Obstacles to Economic Development*, vol. II (London, 1982), p. 90.

43 See below, p. 315.

44 Nícia Vilela Luz, *A luta pela industrialização do Brasil: (1808–1930)* (São Paulo, 1961), *passim*.

45 *Ibid.*, pp. 67, 70.

46 Topik, "Nationalism," p. 281. Also see Joan L. Bak, "Some antecedents of corporatism: state economic intervention and rural organization in Brazil. The case of Rio Grande do Sul, 1890–1937" (unpublished PhD thesis, Yale, 1977) pp. 83–4.

47 See below, p. 315.

48 Kirsch, *Modernization*, pp. 1–2.

49 José Gabriel Palma, "Growth and structure of Chilean manufacturing industry from 1890 to 1914: origins and development of a process of industrialization in an export economy" (unpublished DPhil thesis, Oxford, 1979), chapters 1 and 2; Luis M. Ortega, "Change and crises in Chile's economy and society, 1865–1879" (unpublished PhD thesis, University of London, 1979), chapter 3.

50 Kirsch,*Modernization*, chapter 1.

51 Oscar Muñoz, *Crecimiento industrial de Chile 1914–1965*, 2nd edn. (Santiago, 1971), p. 22; Palma, "Growth and structure," pp. 276–9; Kirsch, *Modernization*, pp. 133–41.

52 Kirsch, *Modernization*, p. 24.

53 *Ibid.*, p. 11.

54 J. Pfeiffer, "Notes on the heavy equipment industry in Chile, 1880–1910," HAHR, vol. 32 (1952), pp. 143–4.

55 Kirsch, *Modernization*, pp. 32–3.

56 *Ibid.*, pp. 28–45.

57 Palma, "Growth and structure," pp. 2, 343.

58 Kirsch, *Modernization*, pp. 172–3.

59 *Ibid.*, p. 173.

60 *Ibid.*, p. 40.

61 M.A. Ballasteros and Tom E. Davis, "The growth in output and employment in basic sectors of the Chilean economy, 1908–1957," *Economic Development and Cultural Change*, vol. XI (1963), p. 163.

62 Muñoz, *Crecimiento*, p. 35.

63 Marcello Carmaganini, *Sviluppo industriale e sottoviluppo economico. Il caso chileano (1860–1920)* (Torino, 1971), p. 169.

64 Palma, "Growth and structure," pp. 35, 326; Kirsch, *Modernization*, pp. 171–4.

65 Muñoz, *Crecimiento*, pp. 40–1.

66 Oscar Muñoz, *Estado e industrialización en el ciclo de expansión del salitre*, Estudios CEIPLAN no. 6 (January 1977), pp. 26–8.

67 Palma, "Growth and structure," pp. 329–30.

68 *Ibid.*, pp. 331–2.

69 Kirsch, *Modernization*. p. 172.

70 Palma, "Growth and structure," p. 326.

71 Kirsch, *Modernization*, p. 173.

72 "El año industrial de 1913," BSFF, vol. xxxi, no. 1 (January 1914), p. 20.

73 "Estadística de las industrias," BSFF, vol. xxxvii, no. 10 (October 1920), pp. 577–8.

74 Kirsch, *Modernization*, p. 47.

75 Roberto Mario, "Producción nacional impulsada por la Guerra," BSFF, vol. xxxiii, no. 1 (January 1916), pp. 10–17; no. 3 (March 1916), pp. 155–61.

76 Kirsch, *Modernization*, pp. 45–8.

77 *Ibid.*, pp. 47–8.

78 Kirsch, *Modernization*, p. 15; Muñoz, *Crecimiento*, pp. 43–7.

79 Palma, "Growth and structure," pp. 329–39.

80 Palma, "Growth and structure," appendices 47–60.

81 Kirsch, *Modernization*, p. 52.

82 Palma, "Growth and structure," pp. 339–47.

83 Kirsch, *Modernization*, p. 51.

84 Adolfo Dorfman, *Historia de la industria argentina* (Buenos Aires, 1970), p. 128.

85 Donna Guy, "Carlos Pellegrini and the politics of early Argentine industrialization, 1873–1906," JLAS, vol. XI, no. 1 (1979) pp. 127–8.

86 *Ibid.*, p. 129; Dorfman, *Industria*, pp. 128–9.

87 On the tariff see; Lucio Geller, "El crecimiento industrial argentino hasta 1914 y la teoría del bien primario exportable" in Marcos Giménez Zapíola (ed.), *El régimen oligárquico. Materiales para el estudio de la realidad argentina (hasta 1930)* (Buenos Aires, 1975), pp. 188–92; Díaz Alejandro, *Essays*, chapter 5; Dorfman, *Industria*, chapter 5.

88 US, Federal Trade Commission, *Report on Trade and Tariffs in Brazil, Uruguay, Argentina, Chile, Bolivia and Peru* (Washington DC, 1916), pp. 62–72, 141–3, 181–5. Also see Frank R. Rutter, *Tariff Systems of*

South American Countries, Dept. of Commerce, BFDC, Tariff Series no. 34 (Washington DC, 1916), pp. 12–13.

89 All data calculated from Argentina, *Segundo Censo de la República Argentina (1895)*, vol. iii (Buenos Aires, 1898), pp. 20–71, xc-cxxxix.

90 Guy, "Pelligrini," p. 130.

91 "Reports from T. Worthington," 3rd Report , the Argentine Republic, Appendix 5, pp. 33–44.

92 Díaz Alejandro, *Essays*, pp. 6–10, 428.

93 Argentina, *Tercer Censo National 1914*, vol. vii (Buenos Aires, 1917), p. 34.

94 Smith and Collins, *Argentina*, p. 67.

95 Dorfman, *Industria*, chapter 11.

96 *Ibid.*, p. 334.

97 Di Tella and Zymelman, *Las etapas*, pp. 308–12.

98 H.O. Chalkley, *Report on the Economic and Industrial Situation of the Argentine Republic for the Year* 1919, Dept. of Overseas Trade (London, 1920), pp. 11–13.

99 See, for example, Smith and Collins, *Argentina*. pp. 67–9.

100 Dorfman, *Industria*, pp. 229–30.

101 Tornquist, *Economic Conditions*, p. 45.

102 Dorfman, *Industria*, p. 335.

103 Smith and Collins, *Argentina*, p. 69

104 Tornquist, *Economic Development*, p. 73.

105 Unless otherwise noted the details on the shoe industry taken from, Donna Guy, "Dependency, the credit market and Argentine industrialization, 1860–1940," *Business History Review*, vol. 58 (Winter 1984), pp. 550–3.

106 *Tercer Censo*, p. 28.

107 Herman G. Brock, *Boots, Shoes, Leather and Supplies in Argentina Uruguay, and Paraguay*, Dept of Commerce, BFDC, Special Agent Series no. 177 (Washington DC, 1919), p. 44.

108 Argentina, Dirección General de Estadística de la Nación, *El comercio exterior de la República Argentina*, various years.

109 Dorfman, *Industria*, pp. 335–42.

110 Díaz Alejandro, *Essays*, p. 450fn.

111 United Nations, CEPAL, *Análisis y proyecciones del desarrollo económico. El desarrollo económico de la Argentina*, vol 5, part 2 (Mexico, 1959), p. 258.

112 A. Bunge, *Las industrias argentinas durante la Guerra. Investigación preliminar* (mimeo) (Buenos Aires, 1919). Donna Guy kindly provided me with a copy of this.

113 No reference to it was found in a complete bibliography of his work, A. Bunge, *Una Nueva Argentina* (Buenos Aires, 1940), pp. 487–513.

114 See below, p. 248.

115 Dorfman, *Industria*, pp. 326–7.

116 Argentina, Dirección General de Estadística de la Nación, *El comercio exterior argentina*, Boletín no. 176, 1917.

117 Díaz Alejandro, *Essays*, p. 282.

118 See above, pp. 143–4.

119 Solberg, *Oil and Nationalism*, chapters 2 and 3.

120 Brock, *Boots, Shoes*, p. 45. Partly quoted in Guy, "Dependency," p. 560.

121 Dorfman, *Industria*, pp. 330–4.

122 Donna Guy, "Threads of progress. Argentine cotton textile production 1860–1950" (Unpublished draft mss.)

123 Díaz Alejandro, *Essays*, pp. 9–11; Ezequiel Gallo, "Agrarian expansion and industrial development in Argentina, 1880–1930" in R. Carr (ed.), *Latin American Affairs* (Oxford, 1971), pp. 45–61.

124 Gravil, "Anglo-Argentine," pp. 88–9.

125 Geller, " El crecimiento," pp. 158–9.

126 Gallo, "Agrarian expansion," p. 56.

127 Solberg, *Oil and Nationalism*, pp. 29–30.

128 Enrique Ruiz Guiñazú, *Las fuerzas perdidas en la economía nacional* (Buenos Aires, 1917), pp. 51–2. Partially quoted in Solberg, *Oil and Nationalism*, p. 29.

129 Wright, *Railways*, pp. 115–23. For further discussion of the various strands of nationalism, see below, pp. 315–17.

130 Jorge Basadre, *Historia de la República del Perú*, vol. x (Lima, 1968), pp. 301–2.

131 Albert, *South America*, p. 38.

132 For Chile see below, p. 281. Argentine and Peruvian figures from, FAO, *The World Sugar Economy in Figures 1880–1959* (Rome, 1960), pp. 112–13.

133 Thorp and Bertram, *Peru*, pp. 112–18.

134 Calculated from *Tercer Censo*, pp. 27–31.

135 Unless otherwise noted the following is based on Thorp and Bertram, *Peru*, chapter 3 and pp. 118–26.

136 Alejandro Garland, *Reseña industrial del Perú en 1905* (Lima, 1905), cited in Thorp and Bertram, *Peru*, p. 35.

137 *Ibid.*, pp. 121–3, 347–51.

138 Alberto Salomón, *Peru. Potentialties of Economic Development*, Lima, ? (1919), pp. 90–1.

139 de Lavalle, *La Gran Guerra* pp. 33–6.

140 Thorp and Bertram, *Peru*, p. 128.

141 *Ibid.*, p. 127.

142 See above, pp. 116–17. Also Bollinger, "US influence" p. 145; de Lavalle, *La Gran Guerra*, p. 42.

143 Thorp and Bertram, *Peru*, p. 126.

144 Frank Stirton Weaver, *Class, State and Industrial Structure. The Historical Process of South American Industrial Growth* (Westport, Conn., 1980), p. 105.

145 Kirsch, *Modernization*, p. 157.

146 For example, Eugene W. Ridings, "Class sector unity in an export economy: the case of nineteenth century Brazil," HAHR, vol. 58 no. 3

(1978), pp. 432–50; Thorp and Bertram, *Peru*, pp. 31–2; Laclau, "Modos de producción," p. 297.

6 The War and the Workers

1 For a general treatment of labor in Latin America during this period see, Hobart A. Spalding Jr., *Organized Labor in Latin America. Historical Case Studies of Urban Workers in Dependent Societies* (London, New York, San Francisco, 1977), chapter 1; Michael M. Hall and Hobart A. Spalding, Jr., "The urban working class and early Latin American labour movements, 1880–1930" in Leslie Bethell, (ed.), *The Cambridge History of Latin America*, vol. 4 (Cambridge, 1986), pp. 325–66; Pablo González Casanova, *Historia del movimiento obrero en America Latina*, vols. 1, 3, & 4 (Mexico, 1984).

2 James O. Morris, *Elites, Intellectuals and Consensus. A Study of the Social Question and the Industrial Relations Systems in Chile* (Ithaca, 1966), p. 113.

3 Alejandro Witker, "El movimiento obrero chileno" in Gonzáles Casanova (ed.), *Historia*, vol. 4, pp. 88–9; See below, p. 276.

4 Spalding, *Organized Labor*, pp. 50–1.

5 *Ibid.*, p. ix.

6 See below, pp. 254, 269, 315–16.

7 E.P. Thompson, *The Making of the English Working Class* (London, 1968), pp. 9–10.

8 All demographic data from Tornquist, *Economic Conditions*, chapter 2.

9 Solberg, *Immigration*, pp. 33–6.

10 Roberto Cortés Conde, *El progreso argentino, 1880–1914* (Buenos Aires, 1979), pp. 196–9.

11 Argentina, *Tercer Censo Nacional*, vol. iv, pp. 384–9.

12 *Ibid.*, pp. 199–201.

13 Hobart Spalding, *La clase trabajadora argentine. (Documentos para su historia–1890/1912)* (Buenos Aires, 1970), p. 51.

14 Ronaldo Munck, "The formation and development of the working class in Argentina, 1857–1919", in B Munslow and H. Finch (eds.), *Proletarianisation in the Third World. Studies in the Creation of a Labour Force under Dependent Capitalism* (London, 1984), p. 263.

15 Julio Godio, *Historia del movimiento obrero argentino. Migrantes asalariados y lucha de clases, 1880–1910* (Buenos Aires, 1973), pp. 78–80, pp. 128–9.

16 Iaacov Oved, *El anarquismo y el movimiento obrero en Argentina* (Mexico, 1978), pp. 163–73, pp. 214–24, pp. 303–9, pp. 356–63.

17 Munck, "Formation," p. 263.

18 Spalding, *Clase trabajadora*, p. 79.

19 *Ibid.*, pp. 80–1, Oved, *Anarquismo*, pp. 421–3.

20 Rock, *Politics in Argentina*, p. 90. For details of the 9th Congress, see Sebastian Marotta, *El movimiento sindical argentino, Su genesis y*

desarrollo, vol. II, 1907–20 (Buenos Aires, 1961), pp. 177–98.

21 Based on Rock, *Politics in Argentina*, pp. 70–6; Spalding, *Clase trabajadora*, pp. 65–76; Jorge N. Solomonoff, *Ideologías del movimiento obrero y conflicto social* (Buenos Aires, 1971), pp. 172–85.

22 The details on anarchism and syndicalism drawn from: Rock, *Politics in Argentina*, pp. 77–90; Solomonoff, *Ideologías*, pp. 185–208; Yoast, "Anarchism," *passim*; Oved, *Anarquismo, passim*.

23 Ruth Thompson, "The limitations of ideology in the early Argentine labour movement: anarchism in the trade unions, 1890–1920," JLAS, vol. 16 (1985), pp. 81–99.

24 Spalding, *Clase trabajadora*, pp. 84–5, 449–54.

25 Solberg, *Immigration*, pp. 110–11.

26 *Ibid.*, pp. 113–15.

27 José Elias Niklison, "Las organizaciones obreras de Buenos Aires," chapter IV, "La federación obrera maritima" in *Boletín del Departamento Nacional del Trabajo*, no. 40, February 1919, pp. 29–30; Marotta, *Movimiento*, pp. 136–40.

28 Rock, *Politics in Argentina*, pp. 83, 91.

29 Munck, "Formation," p. 262.

30 See above, p. 16.

31 Solberg, *Immigration*, pp. 124–6.

32 *Ibid.*, pp. 125–6.

33 Carl Solberg, "Descontento rural y política agraria en la Argentina, 1912–1930" in Zapíola (ed.), *El Régimen oligárquico*, pp. 251–4; Aníbal Arcondo, "El conflicto agrario argentino de 1912. Ensayo de interpretación," *Desarrollo Económico*, vol. 29, no. 79 (October-December, 1980), pp. 351–81.

34 A.E. Bunge, *El Costo*, p. 4.

35 See above, pp. 50–1.

36 "Situation at Rosario," US Consul, Rosario, 7 August 1914 (RG84, 1984 part 5, file 610).

37 Rock, *Politics in Argentina*, p. 125fn.

38 See above, p. 146.

39 "The Argentine market," US Consul General, Buenos Aires, 21 August 1914 (RG84, 1914, part 5, file 610).

40 See above, pp. 64–5.

41 Bunge, *El Costo*, p. 14.

42 Rock, *Politics in Argentina*, pp. 203–9.

43 Marotta, *Movimiento*, p. 200.

44 Yoast, "Anarchism," pp. 213–14.

45 Rock, *Politics in Argentina*, pp. 129–31; Marotta, *Movimiento*, pp. 202–4; *Boletín del Departamento Nacional del Trabajo*, no. 37, March 1918.

46 Marotta, *Movimiento*, pp. 206–8; *Boletín del Departamento Nacional de Trabajo*, no. 37, March 1918, pp. 61–72.

47 *Ibid.*, no. 42, 1919, p. 69.

48 *Ibid.*, pp. 70, 247.

49 Rock, *Politics in Argentina*, pp. 131–4.

50 *Ibid.*, pp. 152–4; Smith, *Politics and Beef*, pp. 72–3. For a detailed analysis of this strike see Charles Bergquist, *Labor in Latin America. Comparative Essays on Chile, Argentina, Venezuela, and Colombia* (Stanford, 1986), pp. 126–31.

51 Marotta, *Movimiento*, pp. 222–4.

52 *Ibid.*, pp. 222–7.

53 Details on the railway strikes drawn from Paul A. Goodwin, Jr., "British-owned railways and the Unión Civica Radical: A study in the political uses of foreign capital" (unpublished PhD thesis, University of Massachusetts, 1971), chapters 3 and 4; Rock, *Politics in Argentina*, pp. 134–52.

54 *Review of the River Plate*, 24 August 1917, p. 445, quoted in Goodwin, "British-owned railways," p. 91.

55 Rock, *Politics in Argentina*, p. 150.

56 Julio Godio, *La Semana Trágica de enero de 1919* (Buenos Aires, 1972), p. 15; Clodomiro Zavalía *Defensa social de la nación* (Buenos Aires, 1919), p. 55.

57 There are a great many accounts of *La Semana Trágica*. The account here is drawn from the following: Rock, *Politics in Argentina*, pp. 157–79; Julio Godio, *La Semana, passim*; Marotta, *Movimiento*, pp. 241–8; John Raymond Hébert, "The Tragic Week of January, 1919 in Buenos Aires: background, events, aftermath" (unpublished PhD thesis, Georgetown University, 1972), *passim*.

58 Katherine S. Dreier, *Five Months in the Argentine from a Woman's Point of View. 1918–1919* (New York, 1920), pp. 171–4.

59 Rock, *Politics in Argentina*, pp. 184–98.

60 Godio, *La Semana*, p. 102.

61 *Ibid.*, pp. 128–43; Rock, *Politics in Argentina*, pp. 128–9.

62 Sandra F. McGee, "The social origins of counterrevolution in Argentina 1900–1932" (unpublished PhD thesis, University of Florida, 1979), chapter 1.

63 Sandra F. McGee, "The visible and invisible Liga Patriótica Argentina, 1919–1928: gender roles and the right wing," HAHR, vol.64 no. 2 (1984), p. 239.

64 Rock, *Politics in Argentina*, pp. 182–98, 209–17.

65 *Ibid.*, p. 168.

66 Unless otherwise noted, all reference to 1920 Census from, *Recenseamento do Brasil 1920*, Vol. IV, parts 1 and 5.

67 *Brasil em Números*.

68 Boris Fausto, *Trabalho urbano*, pp. 29–33.

69 Maram, "Anarchists," pp. 7–8.

70 Fausto, *Trabalho urbano*, p. 21.

71 Hall, "Immigration," pp. 393–407.

72 Sheldon Maram, "Labor and the Left in Brazil, 1890–1920: a movement aborted," HAHR, vol. 57, no. 2 (1977), p. 264.

73 Unless otherwise noted information for this section from *ibid.*, pp. 269–72; Fausto, *Trabalho urbano*. On weakness of labor in Rio as compared with São Paulo see, Eileen Keremitsis, "The early industrial worker in Rio de Janeiro 1870–1920" (unpublished PhD thesis, Columbia University, 1982), *passim*.

74 *Ibid.*, p. 107.

75 Maram, "Labor and the Left," p. 271.

76 Maram, "Anarchists," pp. 127–8; Fausto, *Trabalho urbano*, pp. 41–8.

77 Fausto, *Trabalho urbano*, pp. 102–4.

78 Paulo Sérgio Pinheiro, "O proletariado industrial na Primeira República" in Fausto (ed.), *História Geral* vol. III, no. 11, pp. 167–70.

79 Dulles, *Anarchists and Communists*, pp. 24–6.

80 On Brazilian anarchism see Maram, "Anarchists," *passim*; Fausto, *Trabalho urbano*, pp. 62–97; Eric A. Gordon, "Anarchism is Brazil: Theory and Practice, 1890–1920" (unpublished PhD thesis, Tulane University, 1978), *passim*.

81 Gordon, "Anarchism," pp. 18–19.

82 Details on the strikes from Maram, "Anarchists," pp. 159–67; Fausto, *Trabalho urbano*, pp. 133–53; Dulles, *Anarchists and Communists*, pp. 17–26.

83 Maram, "Labor and the Left," pp. 255–6.

84 See above, pp. 246–7.

85 Fausto, *Trabalho urbano*, p. 158.

86 Dulles, *Anarchists and Communists*, pp. 37–8.

87 Maram, "Anarchists," pp. 167–8.

88 Dean, *Industrialization*, pp. 94–5.

89 Leff, *Underdevelopment*, vol. I, pp. 120–1.

90 See for example, WBR, 3 September 1918, pp. 839–40.

91 *Ibid.*, 20 August 1918, p. 790.

92 Dean, *Industrialization*, pp. 95–6.

93 Villela and Suzigan, *Government Policy*, pp. 105–6; Cano, *Raízes*, pp. 168–9.

94 Cano, *Raízes*, p. 63.

95 Miguel Bodea, *A greve geral de 1917 e as origens do trabalhismo gaúcho* (Porto Alegre, nd), pp. 36–46.

96 Tele. Rio to Washington, 5 November 1917 (RG59 832/50/4/ Roll 23).

97 Rio to Wash., 28 June 1918, 21 August 1918, and 19 September 1918 (RG59 832/50/6–8 Roll 23).

98 WBR, 10 September 1918, pp. 867–8.

99 *Ibid.*, 3 September 1918, p. 839.

100 WBR, 29 October 1918, p. 1032.

101 Peel to Curzon, Petrópolis, 13 January 1919 (FO 371/3653).

102 Fausto, _Trabalho urbano_, p. 169.

103 Unless otherwise noted, the accounts of the strikes between 1917 and 1920 drawn from Fausto, _Trabalho urbano_, pp. 157–248; Maram, "Anarchists," pp. 52–79, 167–200; Dulles, _Communists and Anarchists_, pp. 44–140.

104 Edgard Carone, _A Republica Velha. (Instituições e classes sociais_ (São Paulo, 1970), pp. 228–30.

105 Details on strikes in Porto Alegre from Bodea, _Greve geral, passim._

106 Keremitsis, "Early industrial worker," _passim_; Fausto, _Trabalho urbano_, pp. 11–40.

107 Carlos Stephen Bakota, "Crisis and the middle classes: the ascendancy of Brazilian nationalism 1914–1922" (unpublished PhD thesis, UCLA, 1973), pp. 91–3.

108 Moniz Bandeira, Clovis Melo, A.T. Andrade, _O ano vermelho. A revolução russa e seus reflexos no Brasil_ (Rio, 1967), pp. 72–88, _passim._

109 _Ibid._, p. 115.

110 Fausto, _Trabalho urbano_, pp. 170–3.

111 Carone, _Republica Velha_, pp. 232–5.

112 Bakota, "Crisis," p. 86.

113 Maram, "Anarchists," p. 193.

114 Ilan Rachum, "Nationalism and revolution in Brazil, 1922–1930: a study of intellectual, military and political protesters and of the assault on the Old Republic" (unpublished PhD thesis, Colombia University, 1970), chapters 3 and 4.

115 Maram, "Anarchists," p. 59.

116 De Shazo, _Urban Workers_, pp. xxvii-xxx.

117 M. Monteón, "The enganche in the Chilean nitrate sector, 1880–1930," _Latin American Perspectives_ (22), vol. VI, no. 3 (1979), p. 70.

118 Kirsch, _Modernization_, pp. 8–10.

119 Solberg, _Immigration_, p. 36. Unless otherwise noted this section is based on Solberg's study.

120 Chile, Dirección General de Estadística, _Censo de población de la República de Chile levantado el 15 de diciembre de 1920_ (Santiago, 1925), pp. 405–8.

121 M.A. Fernández, "British nitrate companies and the emergence of Chile's proletariat, 1880–1914" in Munslow and Finch (eds.), _Proletarianisation in the Third World_ (London, Sydney and Dover, N.H., 1984), p. 67; Bergquist, _Labor_, chapter 2.

122 De Shazo, _Urban Workers_, p. xxv.

123 M. Poblete and B.G. Burnett, _The Rise of the Latin American Labor Movement_ (New York, 1960), p. 58.

124 De Shazo, _Urban Workers_, pp. 130–2.

125 Witker, "Movimiento," pp. 86–7.

126 Alan Angell, *Politics and the Labour Movement in Chile* (London, 1972), pp. 20–1.

127 De Shazo, *Urban Workers*, pp. xxvii-xxviii.

128 Solberg, *Immigration*, pp. 103–7.

129 De Shazo, *Urban Workers*, pp. 132–3.

130 Witker, "Movimiento," pp. 84–5.

131 Brian Loveman, *Chile. The Legacy of Hispanic Capitalism* (New York, 1979), pp. 206–7.

132 De Shazo, *Urban Workers*, p. 277.

133 De Shazo, "The Valparaíso maritime strike of 1903 and the development of a revolutionary labour movement in Chile," JLAS, vol. II, no. 1, (1979).

134 Thomas C. Wright, "Origins of the politics of inflation in Chile, 1888–1918," HAHR, vol. 53, no. 2 (1973), pp. 252–5.

135 Loveman, *Chile*, p. 227.

136 De Shazo, *Urban Workers*, pp. 137–8.

137 R.J. Alexander, *Organized Labor in Latin America* (New York, 1965), p. 85.

138 De Shazo, *Urban Workers*, pp. 141–2.

139 Morris, *Elites*, chapter 4.

140 *Ibid.*, pp. 87–93; Fetter, *Inflation*, p. 122; Wright, "Origins," *passim*.

141 De Shazo, *Urban Workers*, p. 126.

142 *The South Pacific Mail*, 1 July 1920.

143 De Shazo, *Urban Workers*, p. 45.

144 *Ibid.*, p. 34.

145 *Ibid.*, p. 136.

146 *Ibid.*, p. 134.

147 *The South American Journal*, 14 November 1914, 3 April 1915.

148 *The South Pacific Mail*, 4 January 1917.

149 De Shazo, *Urban Workers*, p. 66.

150 *Sinopsis estadística, 1923*, pp. 83–6.

151 US, BFDC, Latin American Division, "Crop conditions in Chile," 22 March 1918; BFDC, Latin American Division, "The War and Chilean foodstuffs," Latin American Circular no. 48, 7 March 1918 (RG182 War Trade Board File "Chile Commercial").

152 *Ibid.*, De Shazo, *Urban Workers*, p. 163.

153 *Ibid.*, p. 174.

154 *Acción Obrera*, 1 March 1916.

155 Details of strike from, *The South Pacific Mail*, 24 February 1916; *Acción Obrera*, 1 March and 15 March 1916; *El Diario Illustrado*, 18 February, 3 March and 13 March 1916.

156 Angell, *Politics*, 33.

157 *El Socialista*, 3 August 1917.

158 *La Nación*, 30 July, 1 August and 17 August 1917; *El Socialista*, 27 July, 3 August 1917.

159 *La Nación*, 13 August 1918.

160 *Ibid.*, 17 August 1918.

161 Unless otherwise noted details on union formation from De Shazo, *Urban Workers*, pp. 147–58.

162 *South Pacific Mail*, 16 January 1919.

163 De Shazo, *Urban Workers*, p. 157.

164 *Ibid.*, pp. 159–64.

165 *Ibid.*, pp. 179–85.

166 Morris, *Elites*, chapter 5.

167 Robert J. Alexander, *Arturo Alessandri: A Biography* (Ann Arbor, 1977), pp. 179–84. Julio Heise González, *Historia de Chile*, pp. 176–87.

168 See below, pp. 301–2.

169 J. Petras, *Política y fuerzas sociales en el desarrollo chileno* (Buenos Aires, 1971), pp. 112–13; A. Edwards, *La fronda aristocrática* (Santiago, 1976), chapter 36.

170 Alexander, *Arturo Alessandri*, p. 18.

171 Lucía Sala de Touron and Jorge E. Landinelli, "50 años del movimiento obrero uruguayo" in González Casanóva, *Historia*, vol. 4, pp. 253–7.

172 Details on population and number of workers from Blanchard, *Origins* pp. 11–12.

173 Albert, *An Essay*, pp. 89a–104a; Alberto Flores Galindo, *Los mineros de Cerro de Pasco 1900–1930*, 2nd edn. (Lima, 1983), pp. 21–9.

174 Michael J. González, *Plantation Agriculture and Social Control in Northern Peru, 1875–1933* (Austin, 1985), p. 134.

175 "The Cerro de Pasco mines, Peru," *The Engineering and Mining Journal*, 24 February 1917, pp. 351–2.

176 Unless otherwise noted information on mutual societies and early political activity from Blanchard, *Origins*, chapters 2 and 3.

177 Blanchard, *Origins*, p. 54. On Peruvian anarchism see, *ibid.*, chapter 4; Piedad Pareja, *Anarquismo y sindicalismo en el Perú* (Lima, 1978).

178 Chavarría, *Mariátegui*, chapter 2.

179 Details on strikes from, Blanchard, *Origins*, chapter 5.

180 *Ibid.*, pp. 138–9, 142–3.

181 Albert, *An Essay*, pp. 106a–9a; González, *Social Control*, pp. 174–5.

182 *The West Coast Leader*, 15 May 1912.

183 Unless otherwise noted, the account of the Billinghurst episode based on Blanchard, "A populist," *passim*; Basadre, *Historia*, vol. 12, chapters clv–clvii.

184 On the Aspíllaga family see Dennis L. Gilbert, *La oligarquía peruana: historia de tres familias* (Lima, 1982), chapter 3.

185 Peruvian Corporation, *Representatives' Annual Reports*. For year ending 30 June 1914 (University College, London), p. 7.

186 *The West Coast Leader*, 31 May 1919.

187 Blanchard, *Origins*, p. 130.

188 Albert, *An Essay*, p. 1.

189 *El Comercio*, 9 August, 10 August, 2 September, and 4 September 1914.
190 Blanchard, *Origins*, p. 115.
191 See above, pp. 50, 113.
192 *El Despertar de los Trabajadores*, 18 August 1914.
193 Blanchard, *Origins*, chapter 7.
194 See above, pp. 49–51, and Albert, *An Essay*, pp. 156a–60a.
195 Basadre, *Historia*, vol. 12, p. 357; Rowe, *Peru*, p. 27.
196 Basadre, *Historia*, vol. 12, pp. 453–7.
197 Blanchard, *Origins*, p. 106.
198 Manuel Burga and Wilson Reategui, *Lanas y capital mercantil en el sur. La Casa Ricketts, 1895–1935* (Lima, 1981), pp. 37–8.
199 Albert, *An Essay*, p. 158a.
200 *Ibid.*, pp. 129a, 158a.
201 Blanchard, *Origins*, pp. 115–16.
202 Zitor, *Historia de las principales huelgas y paros obreros habidos en el Peru, 1896–1946* (Lima, 1976), pp. 44–7.
203 Blanchard, *Origins*, pp. 116–18.
204 Blanchard, *Origins*, chapter 7.
205 *Ibid.*, pp. 140–1.
206 Unless otherwise noted, details on rural unrest from Albert, *An Essay*, pp. 178a–92a.
207 Cayaltí mss., Cartas Reservadas, Lima–Cayaltí, 18 August 1916.
208 *La Prensa*, 6 September 1916.
209 There are a great number of accounts of the labour unrest of 1919. The most useful of these include: Blanchard, *Origins*, chapter 9; Ricardo Martínez de la Torre, *Apuntes para una interpretación marxista de historia social del Perú* (Lima, 1928, Reprint 1978), pp. 23–52; César Lévano, *La verdadera historia de la jornada de las Ocho Horas* (Lima, 1967); Rolando Pereda Torres, *Haya de la Torre y las Ocho Horas* (Lima, 1984); Raúl Fernández Llerena, *La jornada de las 8 Horas, la primera huelga general* (Arequipa, 1983); Flores Galindo, *Los mineros*, pp. 44–53.
210 Details on Leguía from Cotler, *Clases*, pp. 181–4; Basadre, *Historia*, vol. 13, chapter clxviii; Caravedo Molinari, *Clases*, *passim*.
211 Peter Klarén, *Modernization, Dislocation and Aprismo: Origins of the Peruvian Aprista Party, 1870–1921* (Austin, 1973), p. 44.
212 Steve Stein, *Populism in Peru. The Emergence of the Masses and the Politics of Social Control* (Madison, 1980) pp. 76–7.
213 Blanchard, *Origins*, pp. 168–9.
214 Pareja, *Anarquismo*, chapter 4.
215 Stein, *Populism*, *passim*.
216 César Germana, "La Polemica Haya de la Torre–Mariátegui," *Análisis*, nos. 2 and 3 (1977), p. 143.
217 Spalding, *Organized Labor*, chapter 1.
218 Kay, *Development*, p. 116.
219 See below, pp. 310–11.

7 After the war

1 *Proceedings of the First Pan-American Conference* (Washington DC, 1915), p. 165.
2 Seidel, *Pan-Americanism*, especially chapter 3. Also see Emily S. Rosenberg, "War World I and growth of United States preponderance in Latin America" (unpublished PhD thesis, State University of New York at Stonybrook, 1972).
3 Winkler, *United States Capital*, pp. 68–73; Valla, *Penetração*, chapter 5.
4 Derek H. Aldcroft, *From Versailles to Wall Street, 1919–1929* (Berkeley, 1977), chapter 9.
5 Sheldon B. Liss, *Marxist Thought in Latin America* (London, 1984), p. 34.
6 Juan Carlos Portantiero, *Estudiantes y política en America Latina 1918–1938. El proceso de la reforma universitaria* (Mexico, 1978), *passim*.
7 Fernando de Azevedo, *Brazilian Culture* (New York, 1950), p. 465n.
8 Pereda Torres, *Haya, passim*.
9 Portantiero, *Estudiantes*, p. 60.
10 McGee, "Counterrevolution," *passim*; Bakota, "Crisis," chapter 6.
11 Loveman, *Chile*, p. 237.
12 De Shazo, *Urban Workers*, pp. 183–5.
13 Topik, "Nationalism," pp. 257–9.
14 Rachum, "Nationalism," chapters 4 and 5.
15 Remmer, *Party Competition*, especially chapter 5.
16 Basadre, *Historia*, vol. xiii, pp. 41–6.
17 Caravedo Molinari, *Clases*, chapter 4, Burga and Flores Galindo, *Apogeo*, pp. 130–48.
18 Heise González, *Historia*, vo. I, p. 433.
19 Martin S. Stabb, *In Quest of Identity. Patterns in the Spanish American Essay of Ideas, 1890–1960* (Chapel Hill, 1967), chapter 3. Also see E. Bradford Burns, *The Poverty of Progress. Latin America in the Nineteenth Century* (Berkeley, Los Angeles and London, 1980), chapter 4.
20 Gerald Martin, "The literature, music and art of Latin America, 1870–1930" in Bethell, *Cambridge History*, vol. IV, p. 476.
21 Stabb, *Essay of Ideas*, p. 59.
22 José Carlos Mariátegui, "La emoción de nuestro tiempo," *Amauta*, no. 31 (1930), pp. 4–5 (first published in 1925).
23 See for example, Jeffery D. Needell, "Rio de Janeiro at the turn of the century. Modernization and the Parisian ideal," *Journal of Interamerican Studies and World Affairs*, vol. 25, no. 1 (1983), pp. 83–103; Darrell E. Levi, *A família Prado* (São Paulo, 1977), chapter 4; Skidmore, *Black into White*, chapter 3.
24 Skidmore, *Black into White*, p. 92.
25 Rachum, "Nationalism," chapter 1; Bakota, "Middle classes," pp. 41–65; Skidmore, *Black into White*, pp. 106–23; Needell, "Rio de Janeiro," pp. 95–7.

26 Skidmore, *Black into White*, p. 15.
27 Rachum, "Nationalism," p. 72.
28 Bakota, "Middle classes," chapter 6.
29 Rachum, "Nationalism," p. 213.
30 Topik, "Nationalism," p. 281.
31 Skidmore, *Black into White*, p. 172.
32 Solberg, *Immigration*, chapter 6.
33 Carlos Payá and Eduardo Cárdenas, *El primer nacionalismo argentino en Manuel Gálvez y Ricardo Rojas* (Buenos Aires, 1978), *passim*; Earl T. Glauert, "Ricardo Rojas and the emergence of Argentine nationalism (1903–1933)" (unpublished PhD thesis, University of Pennsylvania, 1962), *passim*.
34 Solberg, *Immigration*, p. 141.
35 *Ibid.*, p. 154.
36 Jesús Méndez, "Argentine intellectuals in the 20th century, 1900–1943" (unpublished PhD thesis, University of Texas, 1980), pp. 109–10.
37 Portantiero, *Estudiantes*, pp. 29, 367.
38 *Ibid.*, p. 29.
39 McGee, "Counterrevolution," chapters 3 and 4; Rock, *Politics in Argentina*, pp. 180–3.
40 Solberg, *Immigration*, p. 168.
41 Wright, *Railways*, chapter 5.
42 *Ibid.*, pp. 111, 114, 123.
43 Solberg, *Oil and Nationalism*, pp. 34–7.
44 *Ibid.*, p. 29.
45 Solberg, *Immigration*, pp. 159–68.
46 Fredrik R. Pike, *Chile and the United States, 1880–1962. The Emergence of Chile's Social Crisis and the Challenge of United States Diplomacy* (Notre Dame, 1963), pp. 162–3.
47 Monteón, *Nitrate Era*, p. 133.
48 Daniel Martner, "Prólogo" to Moisés Poblete Troncoso, *El problema de la producción agrícola y la política agraria nacional* (Santiago, 1919), pp. xxiii-iv.
49 Solberg, *Immigration*, p. 133.
50 Jesús Chavarría, "The intellectuals and the crisis of modern Peruvian nationalism: 1870–1919," HAHR, vol. 50, no. 2 (1970), *passim*.
51 *Ibid.*, pp. 260–6.
52 Chavarría, *Mariategui*, p. 84.
53 Portantiero, *Estudiantes*, pp. 28–9.
54 Burns, *Poverty*, p. 151.
55 Rosemary Thorp (ed.), *Latin America in the 1930s. The Role of the Periphery in the World Crisis* (Oxford, 1984), *passim*.

Bibliography

General

Albert, Bill. *South America and the World Economy from Independence to 1930*, London, 1983.

Albert, Bill and Henderson, Paul. "Latin America and the Great War: a preliminary survey of developments in Chile, Peru, Argentina and Brazil," *World Development*, vol. 9, no. 8 (1981).

Aldcroft, Derek H. *From Versailles to Wall Street, 1919–1929*, Berkeley, 1977.

Alexander, R.J. *Organized Labor in Latin America*, New York, 1965.

Anglo-South American Bank. Private Letters and Statements, University College Library, London.

Bergquist, Charles. *Labor in Latin America. Comparative Essays on Chile, Argentina, Venezuela, and Colombia*, Stanford, 1986.

Bernhardt, J. *Government Control of the Sugar Industry in the United States. An Account of the Work of the United States Food Administration and the United States Equilization Board*, New York, 1920.

Bernstein, Henry. "Underdevelopment and the law of value: a critique of Kay," *Journal of Political Economy*, vol. 6 (1976).

Beveridge, Sir. Wm. H. *British Food Control*, London, 1928.

Brown, W.A. Jr. *The International Gold Standard Reinterpreted, 1914–1934*, vol. I, New York, 1940.

Bryce, James. *South America. Observations and Impressions*, London, 1912.

Burns, E. Bradford. *The Poverty of Progress. Latin America in the Nineteenth Century*, Berkeley, Los Angeles and London, 1980.

Cardoso, Fernando Henrique and Faletto, Enzo. *Dependency and Development in Latin America*, London Berkeley and Los Angeles, 1979.

Cortés Conde, Roberto. *The First Stages of Modernization in South America*, New York, 1974.

Deerr, Noel. *The History of Sugar*, vol. 2, London, 1950.

Díaz Alejandro, Carlos F. "Argentina, Australia and Brazil before 1929," D.C.M. Platt and Guido di Tella (eds.), *Argentina, Australia and Canada. Studies in Comparative Development, 1870–1965*, Oxford, 1985.

The Economist (London).

The Engineering and Mining Journal.

Foerster, Robert F. *The Italian Emigration of Our Times*, Cambridge, Mass., 1919.

Frank, André Gunder. *Latin America: Underdevelopment or Revolution*, New York, 1969.
Capitalism and Underdevelopment in Latin America, New York and London, 1969.

Friedman, Douglas. *The State and Underdevelopment in Spanish America. The Political Roots of Dependency in Peru and Argentina*, Boulder and London, 1984.

Genovese, E. and Fox-Genovese, E. *Fruits of Merchant Capital. Slavery and Bourgeois Property in the Rise and Expansion of Capitalism*, Oxford, 1983.

González Casanova, Pablo. *Historia del movimiento obrero en America Latina*, vols. 1, 3 and 4, Mexico, 1984.

Gray, Howard J. *War Time Control of Industry. The Experience of England*, New York, 1918.

Great Britain. *British Parliamentary Papers, First (Interim) Report with Statement Showing the Operations of the Royal Commission on Sugar Supply from the date of Appointment to Beginning of December 1916*, cd 8728, 1917–18, xviii.
Foreign Office Documents, FO 368 and FO 371, Public Record Office.
War Trade Department, *Bulletin of Trade Information and Confidential Reports* (weekly), FO 902, Public Record Office.

Hall, Michael M. and Spalding, Hobart A. Jr. "The urban working class and early Latin American labour movements, 1880–1930" in Leslie Bethell (ed.), *The Cambridge History of Latin America*, vol. 4, Cambridge, 1986.

Halsey, F.M. *Investments in Latin America and the British West Indies*, Department of Commerce, Bureau of Foreign and Domestic Commerce, Special Agent Series no. 169, Washington DC, 1918.

Hardach, Gerd. *The First World War, 1914–1918*, London, 1977.

Jones, Charles. "Commercial banks and mortgage companies" in D.C.M. Platt (ed.), *Business Imperialism, 1840–1930. An Enquiry Based on the British Experience in Latin America*, Oxford, 1977.

Joslin, David. *A Century of Banking in Latin America*, London, 1963.

Kaufman, Burton I. "United States trade and Latin America: the Wilson years," *Journal of American History*, vol. 58, no. 2, 1971.

Kay, G. *Development and Underdevelopment. A. Marxist Analysis*, London, 1975.

Laclau, Ernesto. "Modos de producción, sistemas económicos y problación excedente – aproximación histórica a los casos argentino y chileno," *Revista Latinoamericana de Sociología*, vol. v, no. 2, 1969.

Lewis, W. Arthur. *Growth and Fluctuations, 1870–1913*, London, 1978.

Liss, Sheldon B. *Marxist Thought in Latin America*, London, 1984.

Lough, W.H. *Banking Opportunities in South America*, Department of Commerce, Bureau of Foreign and Domestic Commerce, Special Agent Series no. 106, Washington, DC, 1915.

  Financial Developments in South American Countries, Department of Commerce, Bureau of Foreign and Domestic Commerce, Special Agent Series no. 103, Washington DC, 1915.

Mariátegui, José Carlos. "La emoción de nuestro tiempo," *Amauta* (Lima) no. 31 (1930).

Martin, Gerald. "The literature, music and art of Latin America, 1870–1930" in Leslie Bethell (ed.), *The Cambridge History of Latin America*, vol. 4, Cambridge, 1986.

Marx, Karl. *Capital*, vol. III.

McKinnon, Ronald I. *Money and Capital in Economic Development*, Washington DC, 1973.

Mikesell, R.F. *The World Copper Industry*, London, 1979.

Miller, Rory. "Latin American manufacturing and the First World War: an exploratory essay," *World Development*, vol. 9, no. 8 (1981), 707–16.

Milward, A.S. and Saul, S.B. *The Economic Development of Continental Europe, 1780–1870*, London, 1973.

The Mineral Industry: Its Statistics, Technology and Trade during.... (ed.) G.A. Roush.

Minsky, Hyman. "A theory of systemic fragility" in E.I. Altman and A.N. Sametz, *Financial Crises. Institutions and Markets in a Fragile Environment*, New York, 1977.

Moore, Barrington Jr. *Social Origins of Dictatorship and Democracy*, London, 1969.

Pan-American Union, *Proceedings of the First Pan-American Conference*, Washington, DC, 1915.

  Proceedings of the Second Pan-American Financial Conference, Washington DC, 1921.

Poblete, M. and Burnett, B.G. *The Rise of the Latin American Labor Movement*, New York, 1960.

Portantiero, Juan Carlos. *Estudiantes y política en America Latina 1918–1938. El proceso de la reforma universitaria*, Mexico, 1978.

Remmer, Karen L. *Party Competition in Argentina and Chile. Political Recruitment and Public Policy, 1890–1930*, Lincoln and London, 1984.

Rippy, J. Fred. *British Investments in Latin America, 1822–1948*, Minneapolis, 1959.

Rosenberg, Emily S. "World War I and the growth of United States preponderance in Latin America," unpublished PhD thesis, State University of New York at Stonybrook, 1972.

Rutter, Frank R. *Tariff Systems of South American Countries*, Department of Commerce, Bureau of Foreign and Domestic Commerce, Tariff Series no. 34, Washington DC, 1916.

Sala de Touron, L. and Landinelli, J.E. "50 años de movimiento obrero uruguayo" in P. González Casanova, *Historia...*, vol. 4.

Salter, J.A. *Allied Shipping Control*, London, 1921.

Seidel, Robert Neal. *Progressive Pan-Americanism: Development and United States Policy Toward South America, 1906–1931*, Cornell University, Latin American Studies Program Dissertation Series, no. 45, Ithaca, 1973.

Solberg, Carl. *Immigration and Nationalism. Argentina and Chile 1890–1914*, Austin, 1970.

Spalding, Hobart A. Jr. *Organized Labor in Latin America. Historical Case Studies of Urban Workers in Dependent Societies*, London, New York, San Francisco, 1977.

The South American Journal (London).

Stabb, Martin S. *In Quest of Identity. Patterns in the Spanish American Essay of Ideas 1890–1960*, Chapel Hill, 1967.

Thompson, E.P. *The Making of the English Working Class*, London, 1968.

Thorp, Rosemary (ed.), *Latin America in the 1930s. The Role of Periphery in the World Crisis*, Oxford, 1984.

Triffin Robert. *The Evolution of the International Money System: Historical Reappraisal and Future Perspectives*, Princeton, 1964.

Tulchin, J.S. *The Aftermath of War: World War I and US Policy toward Latin America*, New York, 1971.

United Nations, ECLA. *Economic Survey of Latin America 1949*, New York, 1951.

FAO. *The World Sugar Economy in Figures, 1880–1959*, Rome, 1960.

United States, Department of Commerce, Bureau of Foreign and Domestic Commerce. *Banking and Credit in Argentina, Chile, and Peru*, Special Agent Series no. 90, Washington DC, 1914.

Commerce Reports.

Foreign Tariff Notes.

Supplements to the Commerce Reports.

United States, Federal Trade Commission. *Report on Trade and Tariffs in Brazil, Uruguay, Argentina, Chile, Bolivia and Peru*, Washington DC, 1916.

United States. *Records of the Foreign Service Posts of the Department of State*, Record Group 84, National Archives.

Records of War Trade Board, Record Group 182, National Archives.

Weaver, Frederick Stirton. *Class, State and Industrial Structure. The Historical Process of South American Industrial Growth*, Westport, Conn., 1960.

Wilkins, Mira. *The Emergence of Multinational Enterprise: American Business Abroad from the Colonial Era to 1914*, Cambridge, Mass., 1970.

Williams, John H. "Latin American foreign exchange and international balances during the War," *Quarterly Journal of Economics*, vol. 33 (1918–1919).

Winkler, Max. *Investments of United States Capital in Latin America*, Boston, 1928. Reprint 1971, New York and London, 1928.

Withers, Hartley. *War and Lombard Street*, New York, 1915.

Woodruff, W. *The Impact of Western Man. A Study of Europe's Role in the World Economy 1750–1960*, London, 1966.

Zea, Leopoldo. *The Latin American Mind*, Norman, Oklahoma, 1963.

Argentina

Arcondo, A. "El conflicto agrario argentino de 1912. Ensayo de interpretación," *Desarrollo Económico*, vol. 20 no. 79 (October-December 1980).

Argentina, Cámara de Diputados de la Nación. *Informe de la Comisión Investigadora de los Trusts*, Buenos Aires, 1919.

Argentina, Departmento Nacional de Trabajo. *Boletín del Departmento Nacional del Trabajo*

Argentina, Dirección General de Estadística de la Nación. *Análisis del comercio exterior argentino en los años 1910 a 1922*, Buenos Aires, 1923.

El comercio exterior de la República Argentina, Boletín nos. 168, 176, 180, 184.

Veinte años de stadística bancaria de la República Argentina 1908–1927, Buenos Aires, 1928.

El Comercio Exterior de la República Argentina, various years.

Argentina, Ministerio de Hacienda. *Memoria del Departmento de Hacienda al año…1917–1920*, Buenos Aires.

Ley de Presupuesto General de la República Argentina para el ejercicio de…1915–1920, Buenos Aires.

Argentina. *Segundo Censo de la República Argentina*, vol. III, Buenos Aires, 1898.

Tercer Censo Nacional 1914 vol. IV (Población), vol. VII (Censo de las Industrias), Buenos Aires, 1917.

Brock, H.G. *Boots, Shoes, Leather and Supplies in Argentina, Uruguay and Paraguay*, Department of Commerce, Bureau of Foreign and Domestic Commerce, Special Agent Series no. 177, Washington DC, 1919.

Bunge, A.E. *El costo de la vida y el poder de compra de la moneda*, Buenos Aires, 1924.

Las industrias argentinas durante la Guerra. Investigación preliminar (mimeo), Buenos Aires, 1919.

Una nueva Argentina, Buenos Aires, 1940.

Los problemas económicos del presente, Buenos Aires, 1920.

Chalkley, H.O. *Report on the Economic and Industrial Situation of the Argentine Republic for the Year 1919*, Department of Overseas Trade, London, 1920.

Cortés Conde, Roberto. *El progreso argentino, 1880–1914*, Buenos Aires, 1979.

Díaz Alejandro, Carlos F. *Essays on the Economic History of the Argentine Republic*, New Haven, 1970.

Di Tella, Guido and Zymelman, Manuel. *Las etapas del desarrollo económico argentino*, Buenos Aires, 1967.

Dorfman, Adolfo. *Historia de la industria argentina*, Buenos Aires, 1970.

Dreier, Katherine S. *Five Months in the Argentine from a Woman's Point of View 1918–1919*, New York, 1920.

Dyster, B. "Argentine and Australian development compared," *Past and Present*, no. 84 (1979).

Ford, A.G. *The Gold Standard 1880–1914: Britain and Argentina*, Oxford, 1962.

Ford, A.G. "British investment and Argentine economic development, 1880–1914," in D. Rock (ed.), *Argentina in the Twentieth Century*, Pittsburgh, 1975.

Gallo, Ezequiel. "Agrarian expansion and industrial development in Argentina, 1880–1930" in R. Carr (ed.), *Latin American Affairs*, Oxford, 1971.

Geller, Lucio. "El crecimiento industrial argentino hasta 1914 y la teoría del bien primario exportable" in M. Giménez Zapíola (ed.), *El régimen oligárquico. Materiales para el estudio de la realidad argentina (hasta 1930)*, Buenos Aires, 1975.

Glauert, Earl T. "Richard Rojas and the emergence of Argentine Nationalism (1903–1933)," unpublished PhD thesis, University of Pennsylvania, 1962.

Godio, Julio. *Historia del movimiento obrero argentino, migrantes asalariados y lucha de clases, 1880–1910*, Buenos Aires, 1973.

La Semana trágica de enero de 1919, Buenos Aires, 1972.

Goodwin, Paul A., Jr. "British-owned railroads and the Unión Civica Radical. A study in the political uses of foreign capital," unpublished PhD thesis, University of Massachusetts, 1971.

Gravil, Roger. "The Anglo-Argentine connection and the War of 1914–1918," *Journal of Latin American Studies*, vol. 1 (1973).

Great Britain. "Reports received from Mr. T. Worthington... upon conditions and prospects of British trade in various South American countries," 3rd Report, the Argentine Republic, Appendix 5, *British Parliamentary Papers 1899*, p. xcvi.

Greenhill, R. and Crossley, C. "The River Plate beef trade" in D.C.M. Platt (ed.), *Business Imperialism 1840–1930. An Enquiry Based on the British Experience in Latin America*, Oxford, 1977, pp. 284–334.

Guy, Donna. "Carlos Pellegrini and the politics of early Argentine industrialization, 1873–1906," *Journal of Latin American Studies*, vol. II, no. 1, (1974).

"Dependency, the credit market and Argentine industrialization, 1860–1940," *Business History Review*, vol. 58 (Winter 1984).

"Threads of progress. Argentine cotton textile production 1860–1950," unpublished draft manuscript.

Halsey, F.M. and Sherwell, G.B. *Investments in Latin America. I. Argentina*, Department of Commerce, Bureau of Foreign and Domestic Commerce, Trade Information Bulletin no. 362, Washington, DC, 1925.

Hanson, Simon G. *Argentine Meat and the British Market. Chapters in the History of the Argentine Meat Industry*, Stanford, 1938.

Hébert, John Raymon. "The Tragic Week of January, 1919 in Buenos Aires. Background, Events, Aftermath," unpublished PhD thesis, Georgetown University, 1972.

Jones, Charles. "The fiscal motive for monetary and banking legislation in Argentina, Australia and Canada before 1914" in D.C.M. Platt and Guido Di Tella (eds.), *Argentina, Australia and Canada. Studies in Comparative Development 1870–1965*, Oxford, 1985, pp. 95–109.

"The state and business practice in Argentina, 1862–1914" in C. Abel and C. Lewis (eds.), *Latin America: Economic Imperialism and the State*, London, 1985.

Lewis, Colin. "British railway companies and the Argentine government" in D.C.M. Platt (ed.), *Business Imperialism 1840–1930. An Enquiry Based on the British Experience in Latin America*, Oxford, 1977.

British Railways in Argentina, 1857–1914. A Case Study of Foreign Investment, London, 1983.

Marotta, Sebastian. *El movimiento sindical argentino. Su génesis y desarrollo*, vol. II, Período 1907–20, Buenos Aires, 1961.

McGee, Sandra F. "The social origins of counterrevolution in Argentina, 1900–1932," unpublished PhD thesis, University of Florida, 1979.

"The visible and invisible Liga Patriótica Argentina, 1919–28: gender roles and the right wing," *Hispanic American Historical Review*. vol. 64, no. 2 (1984).

Méndez, Jesús. "Argentine intellectuals in the 20th Century, 1900–1943," unpublished PhD thesis, University of Texas, Austin, 1980.

Munck, Ronaldo. "The formation and development of the working class in Argentina, 1857–1919" in B. Munslow and H. Finch (eds.) *Proletarianisation in the Third World. Studies in the Creation of a Labour Force under Dependent Capitalism*, London, 1984.

Niklison, José Elias. "Las organizaciones obreras de Buenos Aires," *Boletín del Departamento Nacional de Trabajo*, no. 40, February 1919.

Oved, Iaacov. *El anarquismo y el movimiento obrero en Argentina*, Mexico, 1978.

Payá, Carlos M. y Cárdenas, Eduardo J.C. *El primer nacionalismo argentino en Manuel Gálvez y Ricardo Rojas*, Buenos Aires, 1978.

Peters, Harold Edwin. *The Foreign Debt of the Argentine Republic*, Baltimore, 1934.

Phelps, Vernon Lovell. *The International Economic Position of Argentina*, Philadelphia and London, 1938.

Revista de Economia Argentina (Buenos Aires).

Rock, David. *Politics in Argentina 1890–1930. The Rise and Fall of Radicalism*, Cambridge, 1975.

Ruiz Guiñazú, Enrique. *Las fuerzas perdidas en la economía nacional*, Buenos Aires, 1917.

Scobie, James R. *Revolution on the Pampas. A Social History of Argentine Wheat. 1860–1910*, Austin, 1964.

Scobie, James R. *Buenos Aires. Plaza to Suburb, 1870–1910*, New York, 1974.

Sharkey, Eugene G. "Unión Industrial Argentina, 1887–1920: problems of industrial development," unpublished PhD thesis, Rutgers University, 1977.

Smith, L. Brewster and Collins, Henry. *The Economic Position of Argentina during the War*, US Department of Commerce, Bureau of Foreign and Domestic Commerce, Miss. Series no. 88, Washington DC, 1920.

Smith, Peter H. *Politics and Beef in Argentina. Patterns of Change and Conflict*, New York and London, 1969.

Solberg, Carl E. "Descontento rural y política agraria en la Argentina, 1912–1930" in M. Giménez Zapíola (ed.), *El régimen oligárquico. Materiales para el estudio de la realidad argentina (hasta 1930)*, Buenos Aires, 1975.

Oil and Nationalism in Argentina: A History, Stanford, 1979.

Solomonoff, Jorge N. *Ideologías del movimiento obrero y conflicto social. De la organización nacional hasta la Primera Guerra Mundial*, Buenos Aires, 1971.

Spalding, Hobart. *La clase trabajadora argentina. (Documentos para su historia–1890/1912)*, Buenos Aires, 1970.

Thompson, Ruth, "The limitations of ideology in the early Argentine labour movement: anarchism in the trade unions, 1890–1920," *Journal of Latin American Studies*, vol. 16 (1985).

Tornquist, Ernesto y Co., *The Economic Development of the Argentine Republic in the Last Fifty Years*, Buenos Aires, 1919.

Business Conditions in Argentina, various issues.

Tulchin, Joseph S. "The Argentine economy during the First World War," part I, part II, part III, *The Review of the River Plate*, 19 June 1970, 30 June 1970, 10 July 1970.

United Nations, CEPAL, *Análisis y proyecciones del desarrollo económico. El desarrollo económico de la Argentina*, vol. 5, part 2, Mexico, 1959.

United States, Department of Commerce, Bureau of Foreign and Domestic Commerce. "Argentina's mounting trade balance," *Circular of Latin American Division*. no. 9, 26 January 1918.

United States. *Records of the Department of State Relating to Internal Affairs of Argentina. 1910–1929*, Record Group 59. Microcopies no. 514, National Archives.

Van Der Karr, Jane. *La Primera Guerra Mundial y la política económica argentina*, Buenos Aires, 1974.

Williams, John H. "Argentine foreign exchange and trade since the Armistice," *Review of Economic Statistics*, vol. 3 (1921).

Argentine International Trade under Inconvertible Paper Money 1880–1900, Cambridge Mass., 1920.

Wright, Winthrop R. *British-Owned Railways in Argentina. Their Effect on the Growth of Economic Nationalism, 1854–1948*, Austin, 1974.

Yoast, Richard Alan. "The development of Argentine anarchism: a socio-ideological analysis," PhD thesis, University of Wisconsin–Madison, 1975.

Zavalía, Clodomiro. *Defensa social de la nación*, Buenos Aires, 1919.

Brazil

Abreu, Marcelo P. "A dívida pública externa do Brasil, 1824–1931," *Estudos Econômicos*, vol. 15, no. 2 (1985).

Azevedo, Fernando de. *Brazilian Culture*, New York, 1950.

Baer, W. and Villela, A. "Alguns comentários a 'Origens e conseqüências da substituição de importações no Brasil' de Albert Fishlow" *Estudos Econômicos*, vol. 3, no. 1 (April 1973).

Bak, Joan L. "Some antecedents of corporatism: state economic intervention and rural organization in Brazil. The case of Rio Grande do Sul, 1890–1937," unpublished PhD thesis, Yale, 1977.

Bakota, Carlos S. "Crisis and the middle classes: the ascendancy of Brazilian nationalism 1914–1922," unpublished PhD thesis, UCLA, 1973.

Banco do Brasil. *Relatório do Banco do Brasil 1918*, Rio, 1919.

Bandeira, Moniz, Melo, Clovis and Andrade, A.T. *O ano vermelho. A revolução russa e seus reflexos no Brasil*, Rio, 1967.

Bello, José Maria. *A History of Modern Brazil, 1889–1964*, Stanford, 1966.

Bodea, Miguel. *A greve geral de 1917 e as origens do trabalhismo gaúcho*, Porte Alegre, nd.

Brazil, Ministério da Agricultura, Indústria e Comércio, Directoria Geral de Estatística. *Recenseamento do Brasil*, vol. IV, parts 1 and 5, vol. V, part 1, Rio, 1920.

Brazil Instituto Brasileiro de Geografia e Estatística. *Anuário estatístico do Brasil*, ano V 1939–40, Rio, 1945.

Anuário estatístico do Brasil, ano VII, 1946, Rio, 1947.

O Brasil em numeros, Rio, 1960.

Brazil, Ministério da Fazenda, Directoria de Estatística Comercial. *Comércio exterior do Brasil (Resumo por mercadorias, Jan-Dez. 1913 & 1914)*, Rio, 1915.

Comércio exterior do Brasil Jan.-Dez. 1910–1913, 2 vols., Rio, 1913.

Comércio exterior do Brasil, Jan.-Dez. 1915–1919, Rio, 1920.

Brazil, Ministério da Viação e Obras Públicas. *Relatório do Ministério de Viação e Obras Públicas 1921*, Rio, 1922.

Brazil, Ministry of Industry, Agriculture and Commerce. *Economical Notes on Brazil*, 2nd edn, Rio, 1916, 4th edn, Rio, 1921.

Callaghan, William Stuart. "Obstacles to industrialization: the iron and steel industry in Brazil during the old Republic," unpublished PhD thesis, University of Texas, 1981.

Cano, Wilson. *Raízes da concentração industrial em São Paulo*, Rio and São Paulo, 1977.

Carone, Edgard. *A Republica Velha. (Instituições e classes sociais)*, São Paulo, 1970.

Carvalho, Elysio de. "Opportunities in Brazil for American capital," *The Pan-American Magazine*, November 1918.

Castro, Ana Célia. *As empresas estrangeiras no Brasil 1860–1913*, Rio, 1979.

Centro Industrial do Brasil. *O Brasil, suas riquezas naturaes, suas indústrias*, vol. III, Rio, 1909.

Dean, Warren. *The Industrialization of São Paulo 1880–1945*, Austin, 1969.

Dean, Warren, "A industrialização durante a República Velha" in Boris Fausto (ed.), *História geral da civilização brasileira. O Brasil republicano tomo III. vol. 1 A estrutura de poder e economia (1889–1930)*, São Paulo, 1975.

Dulles, J.F.W. *Anarchists and Communists in Brazil, 1900–1935*, Austin, 1973.

Duncan, Julian Smith. *Public and Private Operation of Railways in Brazil*, New York, 1932.

Eisenberg, Peter L. *The Sugar Industry in Pernambuco. Modernization without Change, 1840–1910*, Berkeley, 1974.

Fausto, Boris. "Expansão de café e política cafeeira," in Boris Fausto (ed.), *História geral da civilização brasileria, III, O Brasil republicano, A estrutura de poder, e economia (1889–1930)*, São Paulo, 1975.

Trabalho urbano e conflicto social, Rio and São Paulo, 1976.

Fishlow, Albert. "Algumas observações adicionais sobre a discussão," *Estudos Econômicos*, vol. 3, no. 1 (1973).

"Origins and consequences of import substitution in Brazil" in Luís Eugenio de Marco (ed.), *International Economics and Development. Essays in Honor of Raul Prebisch*, New York and London, 1972.

Fritsch, Winston. "Aspectos da política econômica no Brasil, 1906–1914," in Paulo Neuhaus (ed.), *Economia brasileira. Uma visão histórica*, Rio, 1980.

"Aspects of Brazilian economic policy under the First Republic (1889–1930)," unpublished PhD thesis, Cambridge, 1983.

"Brazil and the Great War, 1914–1918," Texto para discussão, no. 62, Department of Economics, Pontífica Universidade Católica do Rio de Janeiro, January, 1984.

"Il Brasile durante la Grande Guerra: problemi strutturali e politiche economiche," *Rivista di Storia Economica*, vol. 2, no. 1 (1985).

Gnaccarini, José C. "A economia açúcar. Processo de trabalho e processo de acumulação" in Boris Fausto (ed.), *História geral da civilização brasileira III. O Brasil republicano. A estrutura de poder e economia (1889–1930).*

Gordon, Eric. A. "Anarchism in Brazil: theory and practice, 1890–1920," unpublished PhD thesis, Tulane University, 1978.

Great Britain. "Reports received from Mr. T. Worthington... upon conditions and prospects of British trade in various South American Countries," 5th Report, Brazil, part I, *British Parliamentary Papers 1899*, p. xcvi.

Greenhill, Robert. "The Brazilian coffee trade" in D.C.M. Platt (ed.), *Business Imperialism 1840–1930. An Enquiry Based on the British Experience in Latin America*, Oxford, 1977.

Haddad, Claudio L.S. *Crescimento do Produto Real no Brasil, 1900–1947*, Rio, 1978.

Hall, Michael M. "Immigration and the early São Paulo working class" in *Jahrbüch für Geschichte von Staat, Wirtschaft und Gesellschaft Lateinamerikas*, vol. 12 (1975).

Holloway, Thomas H. *The Brazilian Coffee Valorization of 1906. Regional Politics and Economic Dependence*, Madison, 1975.

Immigrants on the Land. Coffee and Society in São Paulo, Chapel Hill, 1980.

Keremitsis, Eileen. "The early industrial worker in Rio de Janeiro 1870–1930," unpublished PhD thesis, Colombia University, 1982.

Lahmeyer Lobo, E.M. et al, "Evolução dos preços e do padrão da vida no Rio de Janeiro, 1820–1930–resultados preliminares," *Revista Brazileira de Economia*, vol. 25, no. 4 (October-December 1971).

Leff, N. *Underdevelopment and Development in Brazil. vol. I. Economic Structure and Change, 1822–1947*, London, 1982.

Underdevelopment and Development in Brazil. vol. II. Reassessing the Obstacles to Economic Development, London, 1982.

Levi, Darrell E. *A família Prado*, São Paulo, 1977.

Love, J.L. *São Paulo in the Brazilian Federation, 1889–1937*, Stanford, 1980.

Luz, Nícia Vilela, *A luta pela industrialização do Brasil (1808–1930)*, São Paulo, 1961.

Maram, Sheldon L. "Anarchists, immigrants, and the Brazilian labor movement," unpublished PhD thesis, University of California at Santa Barbara, 1972.

"Labour and the Left in Brazil, 1890–1920; a movement aborted," *Hispanic American Historical Review*, vol. 57, no. 2, 1977.

Netto, Antonio Delfim. "Foundations for the analysis of Brazilian coffee problems" in C.M. Peláez (ed.) *Essays on Coffee and Economic Development*, Rio, 1973.

Needell, Jeffery D. "Rio de Janeiro at the turn of the century. Modernization and the Parisian ideal," *Journal of Interamerican Studies and World Affairs*, vol. 25, no. 1 (1983).

Neuhaus, Paulo. *História monetária do Brasil, 1900–45*, Rio, 1975.

Peláez, Carlos Manuel. *História econômica do Brasil. Um elo entre a teoria e a realidade econômica*, São Paulo, 1979.

"World War I and the economy of Brazil: some evidence from the monetary statistics," *Journal of Interdisciplinary History*, vol. VII, no. 4 (spring, 1977).

Peláez, C.M. and Suzigan, W. *História monetária do Brasil: análise da política, comportamento e instituições monetárias*, Rio, 1976.

Pinheiro, Paulo Sérgio. "O proletariado industrial na Primeira República" in Boris Fausto (ed.), *História geral da civilização brasileira*, vol. III, O Brasil Republicano, no. II, Sociedade e Instituições (1889–1930), Rio and São Paulo, 1977.

Rachum, Ilan. "Nationalism and revolution in Brazil, 1922–1930: a study of intellectual, military and political protesters and of the assault on the Old Republic," unpublished PhD thesis, Colombia University, 1970.

Redfield, A. *Brazil: A Study of Economic Conditions 1913*, Department of Commerce, Bureau of Foreign and Domestic Commerce, Miss. Series no. 86, Washington DC, 1920.

Ridings, Eugene W. "Class sector unity in an export economy: the case of nineteenth-century Brazil," *Hispanic American Historical Review*, vol. 58, no. 3 (1978).

São Paulo, Secretaria da Agriculutra, Comércio y Obras Públicas do Estado do São Paulo. *Boletim da Directoria de Indústria a Comércio*, various numbers.

Boletim do Departamento Estadual do Trabalho, various numbers.

Saes, Flávio A.M. de and Szmrecsányi Tamás, "O capital estrangeiro no Brasil, 1880–1930," *Estudos econômicos*, vol. 15, no. 2 (1985).

Simonsen, Roberto C. *Evolução industrial do Brasil e outros estudos*, São Paulo, 1973.

Skidmore, Thomas E. *Black into White. Race and Nationality in Brazilian Thought*, New York, 1974.

Stein, Stanley. *Brazilian Cotton Manufacture. Textile Enterprise in an Underdeveloped Area. 1850–1950*, Cambridge, Mass., 1957.

Vassouras: A Brazilian Coffee County, 1850–1900, Cambridge, Mass., 1957.

Suzigan, Wilson. "Uma nota Sobre 'Origens e conseqüências da substituição de importações no Brasil' de Albert Fishlow," *Estudos econômicos*, vol. 3, no. 1, April 1973, pp. 121–8.

Taunay, Alfonso do E. *História do café no Brasil*, vol. XI, Rio, 1941.

Topik, Steven C. "Economic nationalism and the state in an underdeveloped country: Brazil 1889–1930," unpublished PhD thesis, University of Texas, 1978.

"The state's contribution to the development of Brazil's internal economy, 1850–1930," *Hispanic American Historical Review*, vol. 65, no. 2 (1985).

United States, *Records of the Department of State Relating to Internal Affairs of Brazil 1910–1929*, Record Group 59, Microcopies no. 519, National Archives.

Valla, Victor V. *A penetração norte-americana na economia brasileira, 1898–1928*, Rio, 1978.

Versiani, Flávio Rabelo. *Industrial Investment in an "Export" Economy: The Brazilian Experience before 1914.* Institute of Latin American Studies Working Paper No. 2, London, 1979.

Versiani, Flávio R. and Maria T. "A industrialização brasileira antes de 1930: uma contribuição," *Estudos econômicos,* vol. 5, no. 1 (1975).

Villela, A.V. "Surto industrial durante a Guerra de 1914–8" in Mircea Buescu (ed.) *Ensaios econômicos: Homenagem a Octávio Gouvea de Bulhões,* Rio, nd.

Villela, A.V. and Suzigan, W. *Government Policy and the Economic Growth of Brazil, 1889–1945,* Rio, 1977.

Weinstein, Barbara. *The Amazon Rubber Boom, 1850–1920,* Stanford, 1983.

Wileman's Brazilian Review.

Chile

Acción Obrera.

Alexander, Robert J. *Arturo Alessandri: A Biography,* 2 vols. Ann Arbor, 1977.

Angell, A. *Politics and the Labour Movement in Chile,* London, 1972.

Anguita, Ricardo. *Leyes promulgadas en Chile. Suplemento 1913–1918,* vol. v, Santiago–Valparaíso, 1918.

Asociación Salitrera de Propaganda, *Circulares de la Asociación Salitrera de Propaganda,* Valparaíso and Iquique, December 1915.

Ballasteros, M.A. and Davis, T.E. "The growth in output and employment in basic sectors of the Chilean economy, 1908–1957," *Economic Development and Cultural Change,* vol. xi (1963).

Bauer, Arnold J. *Chilean Rural Society from the Spanish Conquest to 1930,* Cambridge, 1975.

Cariola, C. and Sunkel, O. "Nitrate expansion and socio-economic transformation in Chile: 1880–1930," Institute of Development Studies, University of Sussex, Discussion Paper no. 129, 1978.

Carmaganini, Marcello. *Sviluppo industriale e sottoviluppo economico, Il caso chileano (1860–1920),* Turin, 1971.

Cavarozzi, M.J. and Petras, J. "Chile" in R.H. Chilcote and J.C. Edelstein (eds.), *Latin America: The Struggle with Dependency and Beyond,* Cambridge, Mass., 1974.

Chile, Dirección General de Estadística. *Censo de población de la República de Chile levantado el 15 de diciembre de 1920,* Santiago, 1925.

Chile, Oficina Central de Estadística. *Anuario estadístico de la República de Chile,* Santiago, various years.

Estadística comercial de la República de Chile, Santiago, various years.

Sinopsis estadística de la República de Chile, Santiago, various years.

Conoboy, P.J. "Money and politics in Chile, 1878–1925" (unpublished PhD thesis, University of Southampton, 1976).

Couyoumdjian, Juan Ricardo. "Anglo-Chilean economic relations during the First World War and its aftermath 1914–1920", unpublished PhD thesis, University of London, 1975.

De Shazo, Peter Charles. *Urban Workers and the Labor Unions in Chile, 1902–1927*, Madison, 1983.

"The Valparaíso maritime strike of 1903 and the development of the revolutionary labor movement in Chile," *Journal of Latin American Studies*, vol. 11, no. 1 (1979).

El Despertar de los Trabajadores (Iquique).

El Diario Ilustrado.

Domeratsky, L. *Customs Tariff of Chile*, Department of Commerce, Bureau of Foreign and Domestic Commerce, Tariff Series no. 36, Washington DC, 1917.

Edwards, A. *La fronda aristocrática*, Santiago, 1976.

Fernández, Manuel A. "British nitrate companies and the emergence of Chile's proletariat 1880–1914" in B. Munslow and H. Finch (eds.), *Proletarianisation in the Third World. Studies in the Creation of a Labour Force under Dependent Capitalism*, London, Sydney and Dover, N.H., 1984.

"The development of the Chilean economy and its British connections 1895–1914," unpublished PhD thesis, University of Glasgow, 1978.

Fetter, F.W. *Monetary Inflation in Chile*, Princeton, 1932.

Fox Przeworski, J. *The Decline of the Copper Industry in Chile and the Entrance of North American Capital*, New York, 1980.

Greenhill, Robert. "The nitrate and iodine trades, 1880–1912" in D.C.M. Platt (ed.), *Business Imperialism 1840–1930. An Enquiry Based on the British Experience in Latin America*, Oxford, 1979.

Harding, James E. "Andes Copper Mining Co.'s development at Potrerillos, Chile," *The Engineering and Mining Journal*, vol. 105, no. 3, 19 January (1918).

Heise González, Julio. *Historia de Chile 1861–1925. El período parlamentario*, vol. I, Santiago, 1974, vol. II, Santiago, 1982.

Kirsch, Henry W. *Industrial Development in a Traditional Society. The Conflict of Entrepreneurship and Modernization in Chile*, Gainesville, 1977.

Lamb, Mark R. "Copper smelting at Naltagun in Central Chile," *Engineering and Mining Journal*, October 28 (1916).

Loveman, Brian. *Chile. The Legacy of Hispanic Capitalism*, New York, 1979.

Mamalakis, Markos J. *The Growth and Structure of the Chilean Economy: From Independence to Allende*, New Haven, 1976.

"The role of government in the resource transfer and resource allocation processes: the Chilean nitrate sector, 1880–1930" in Gustav Ranis (ed.), *Government and Economic Development*, New Haven, 1971.

Mario, Roberto. "Producción nacional impulsada por la Guerra," *Boletín de la Sociedad de Fomento Fabril*, vol, xxxiii, no. 1 (January 1916).

Martner Daniel. "Prólogo," to Moisés Poblete Troncoso, *El problema de la producción agrícola y la política agraria nacional*, Santiago, 1919.

McQueen, Charles A. *Chilean Public Finance*, Department of Commerce, Bureau of Foreign and Domestic Commerce, Special Agent Series no. 224, Washington DC, 1924.

Miller, Benjamin L. & Singlewald, Joseph T. Jr. "Exploitation of Chilean mines," *Engineering and Mining Journal* (12 August 1916).

Monteón Michael. *Chile in the Nitrate Era. The Evolution of Economic Dependence, 1880–1930*, Madison, 1982.

"The enganche in the Chilean nitrate sector, 1880–1930," *Latin American Perspectives* (22), vol. vi, no. 3 (1979).

Morris, James O. *Elites, Intellectuals and Consensus. A Study of the Social Question and the Industrial Relations System in Chile*, Ithaca, 1966.

Muñoz, Oscar. *Crecimiento industria de Chile 1914–1965*, Santiago, 1971.

Estado e industrialización en el ciclo de expansión del salitre, Estudios CIEPLAN, no. 6, Santiago, January 1977.

La Nación.

Ortega, Luis M. "Change and Crises in Chilean economy and society, 1865–1879," unpublished PhD thesis, University of London, 1979.

Palma, José Gabriel. "Growth and structure of Chilean manufacturing industry from 1830 to 1914: origins and development of a process of industrialization in an export economy," unpublished D Phil thesis, Oxford, 1979.

"External disequilibrium and internal industrialization in Chile, 1914–1935" in C. Abel and C. Lewis (eds.), *Latin America Economic Imperialism and the State: The Political Economy of the External Connection from Independence to the Present*, London, 1985.

Partington, J.R. and Parker, L.H. *The Nitrogen Industry*, London, 1922.

Petras, J. *Política y fuerzas sociales en el desarrollo chileno*, Buenos Aires, 1917.

Pfeiffer, J. "Notes on the heavy equipment industry in Chile, 1880–1910," *Hispanic American Historical Review*, vol. 32 (1952).

Pike, F.R. *Chile and the United States, 1880–1962. The Emergence of Chile's Social Crisis and the Challenge of United States Diplomacy*, Notre Dame, 1963.

La Revista Comercial (Valparaíso).

Reynolds, C.W. "Development problems in an export economy. The case of Chile and copper" in M. Mamalakis and C.W. Reynolds, *Essays on the Chilean Economy*, New Haven, 1965.

Remmer, Karen. L. "The timing, pace, and sequence of political change in Chile, 1891–1925," *Hispanic American Historical Review*, vol. 57, no. (1977).

Rowe, L.S. *The Early Effects of the European War on the Finance, Commerce, and Industry of Chile*, New York, 1918.

Scott, W.F.V. *Report on the Industrial and Economic Situation in Chile, September, 1924*, London, 1925.

El Socialista.

Sociedad Agrícola del Sur. *Boletín de la Sociedad Agrícola del Sur,* (Concepción).

Sociedad de Fomento Fabril. *Boletín de la Sociedad de Fomento Fabril.*

Sociedad Nacional Agraria. *Asamblea de agricultores celebrada en Santiago de Chile en los días 22, 23, 24 de setiembre de 1919,* Santiago, 1920.

Sociedad Nacional Minería. *Boletín de la Sociedad Nacional Minería.*

The South Pacific Mail.

Stickell, Arthur L. Jr. "Migration and mining in Northern Chile in the nitrate era, 1880–1930," unpublished PhD thesis, Indiana University, 1979.

Subercaseaux, Guillermo. *Monetary and Banking Policy of Chile,* Oxford, 1922.

United States, Department of Commerce, Bureau of Foreign and Domestic Commerce. "The War and Chilean foodstuffs," *Latin American Circular* no. 48, March, 1918.

United States. *Records Relating to Nitrates in Chile,* Microcopy 487/33, National Archives.

Witker, Alejandro. "El movimiento obrero chileno" in P. González Casanova (ed.), *Historia...,* vol. 4.

Wright, Thomas C. "Origins of the politics of inflation in Chile, 1888–1918." *Hispanic American Historical Review,* vol. 53, no. 2 (1973).

"The Sociedad Nacional de Agricultura in Chilean Politics, 1869–1938," unpublished PhD thesis, University of California, Berkeley, 1971.

Yeatman, Pope. "Copper production in Chile," *Engineering and Mining Journal* (8 January 1916).

"Mine of Chile Exploration Co., Chuquicamata, Chile," *Engineering and Mining Journal,* February 12, 1916.

Peru

La Agricultura.

Albert, Bill. *An Essay on the Peruvian Sugar Industry 1880–1920 and the Letters of Ronald Gordon, Administrator of the British Sugar Company in Cañete, 1914–1920,* Norwich, 1976.

"Notas sobre la modernización y el cambio estructural en la industria azucarera peruana, 1880–1914," *Análisis* no. 6 (Lima) (1979).

"Sugar and Anglo-Peruvian trade negotiations in the 1930s," *Journal of Latin American Studies,* vol. 14, part 1 (1982).

Arguedas, José María. *Perú vivo,* Lima, 1966.

Arrús, Oscar F. *El costo de la vida en Lima y causas de su carestía,* Lima, 1925.

Basadre, Jorge. *Historia de la República del Perú,* 16 vols., Lima, 1970.

Bell, W.S. "An essay on the Peruvian cotton industry, 1825–1920," University of Liverpool, Centre for Latin American Studies, Working Paper no. 6, (1985).

Bertram, Geoffrey. "Development problems in an export economy: a study of domestic capitalists, foreign firms and government in Peru 1919–1930," unpublished D. Phil thesis, Oxford, 1974.

Blanchard, Peter. *The Origins of the Peruvian Labor Movement, 1883–1919*, Pittsburgh, 1982.

"A populist precursor: Guillermo Billinghurst," *Journal of Latin American Studies*, vol. 9, no. 2 (1977).

"The Peruvian working class movement, 1883–1919," unpublished PhD thesis, University of London, 1975.

Bollinger, W.S. "The rise of United States influence in the Peruvian economy, 1869–1921," unpublished MA thesis, UCLA, 1972.

Bonilla, Heraclio and Rabanal, Alejandro. "La Hacienda San Nicolás (Supe) y la Primera Guerra Mundial," *Economia* (Lima), vol. ii, no. 3, 1979.

Burga, Manuel and Flores Galindo, Alberto. *Apogeo y crisis de la República Aristocrática*, Lima, 1980.

Burga, Manuel and Reategui, Wilson. *Lanas y capital mercantil en el sur. La Casa Rickets, 1895–1935*, Lima, 1981.

Caravado Molinari, B. *Clases, lucha política y gobierno en el Perú (1919–1933)*, Lima, 1977.

Cayaltí Manuscripts, Archivo del Fuero Agraria, Lima.

Chavarría, Jesús. "La desaparición del Perú colonial (1870–1919)," *Aportes*, (Paris) no. 23 (January 1973).

"The intellectuals and the crisis of modern Peruvian nationalism: 1870–1919," *Hispanic American Historical Review*, vol. 50, no. 2 (1970).

José Carlos Mariátegui and the Rise of Modern Peru, Albuquerque, 1979.

El Comercio.

Cotler, Julio. *Clases, estado y nación en el Perú*, Lima, 1978.

Fernández Llerena, Raúl. *La jornada de las 8 Horas. La primera huelga general*, Arequipa, 1983.

Flores Galindo, Alberto. *Los mineros de Cerro de Pasco, 1900–1930*, 2nd edn, Lima, 1983.

Garland, Alejandro. *Perú en 1906*, Lima, 1907.

Germana, César. "La polémica Haya de la Torre–Maríategui," *Análisis* (Lima), nos. 2 and 3, (1977).

Gilbert, Dennis L. *La oligarquía peruana: historia de tres familias*, Lima, 1982.

Gonzalez, Michael J. *Plantation Agriculture and Social Control in Northern Peru, 1875–1933*, Austin, 1985.

Gorman, Stephen M. "The state, elite and export in nineteenth-century Peru. Toward an alternative reinterpretation of political change," *Journal of Interamerican Studies and World Affairs*, vol. 21, no. 3 (1979), 395–418.

Hunt, Shane. *Price and Quantum Estimates of Peruvian Exports, 1830–1962*, Princeton, 1973.

La Industria (Trujillo).

Jiménez, C.P. "Estadística Industrial del Perú en 1918," *Boletín del Cuerpo de*

Ingenieros de Minas, no. 105, Lima (1922).

Klarén, Peter. *Modernization, Dislocation and Aprismo: Origins of the Peruvian Aprista Party, 1870–1921*, Austin, 1973.

"Social and economic consequences of the modernization of the Peruvian sugar industry, 1879–1930" in K. Duncan and I. Rutledge (eds.), *Land and Labour in Latin America*, Cambridge, 1977.

Lavalle, Hernando de. *La Gran Guerra y el organismo económico nacional*, Lima, 1919.

Lévano, César. *La verdadera historia de la Jornada de las Ocho Horas*.

Mariátegui, José Carlos. *Seven Interpretive Essays on Peruvian Reality*, Austin, 1974.

Martinez de la Torre, Ricardo. *Apuntes para una interpretación marxista de historia social del Perú*, Lima, 1928. Reprint 1978.

McQueen, Charles. *Peruvian Public Finance*, Department of Commerce, Bureau of Foreign and Domestic Commerce, Trade Promotion Series no. 30, Washington DC, 1926.

Miller, Rory. "The Grace contract, the Peruvian corporation and Peruvian history," *Ibero-Amerikanisches Archiv*, nf Jg 9 H. 3/4 (1983).

"Small business in the Peruvian oil industry: Lobitos Oilfields Limited before 1934," *The Business History Review*, vol. LVI, no. 3 (1982).

"The coastal elite and Peruvian politics, 1895–1919," *Journal of Latin American Studies*, vol. 14, part 1 (1982).

Pareja, Piedad. *Anarquismo y sindicalismo en el Perú*, Lima, 1978.

Peloso, Vincent. "Cotton planters, the state and rural labor policy: ideological origins of the Peruvian *Republica Aristocratica*, 1895–1908," *The Americas*, vol. XL, no. 2 (1983).

Pereda Torres, Rolando. *Haya de la Torre y las Ocho Horas*, Lima, 1984.

Peru, Ministerio de Fomento, Dirección de Agricultura y Ganadería. *Estadística de la industria algodonera en el Perú*, various years.
Estadística de la industria azucarera en el Perú, various years.

Peru, Ministerio de Fomento, Dirección de Estadística. *Extracto estadístico del Perú*, Lima, various years.

Peruvian Corporation. *Representatives' Annual Reports*, University College Library, London.
La Prensa.

Quiroz, Alfonso Walter. "Financial institutions in Peruvian export economy and society, 1884–1930," unpublished PhD thesis, Columbia University, 1986.

Romero, Emilio. *Historia económica del Perú*, vol. II, Lima, nd.

Rowe, L.S. *Early Effects of the War upon the Finance, Commerce and Industry of Peru*, New York, 1920.

Salómon, Alberto. *Peru. Potentialities of Economic Development*, Lima (?), 1919.

Sociedad Nacional Agraria, Manuscript Collection, Archivo del Fuero Agraria, Lima.

Singlewald, Joseph T. Jr. & Miller, Benjamin LeRoy. "The mining industry of Peru," *Engineering and Mining Journal*, vol. 101, no. 20, May 13, 1916.

"The Morococha and Casapalca Districts in Peru," *Engineering and Mining Journal*, vol. 102, no. 21 (18 November, 1916).

Stein, Steve. *Populism in Peru. The Emergence of the Masses and the Politics of Social Control*, Madison, 1980.

Strauss, Lester W. "Peru in 1913," *The Engineering and Mining Journal* (10 January 1914).

Sulmont, Denis. *Historia del movimiento obrero peruano (1890–1977)*, Lima, 1977.

Thorp, Rosemary and Bertram, Geoffrey. *Peru 1890–1977. Growth and Policy in an Open Economy*, London, 1978.

United States, Department of State. *Records Relating to WWI and its Termination*, Microcopy 367/265, National Archives.

The West Coast Leader.

Zitor, *Historia de las principales huelgas y paros obreros habidos en el Perú, 1896–1946*, Lima, 1976.

Index

CAMBRIDGE LATIN AMERICAN STUDIES